Christmas

COLLECTION

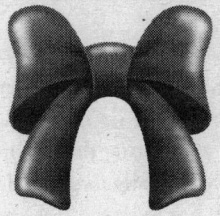

Three new full-length stories from
three favourite Mills & Boon® authors

MILLS & BOON®

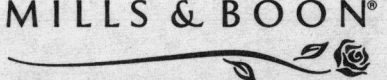

Carole Mortimer—Presents™ author—says: 'I was born in England, the youngest of three children—I have two older brothers. I started writing in 1978, and now have written over ninety books for Mills and Boon®.

'I have four sons—Matthew, Joshua, Timothy and Peter—and a bearded collie dog called Merlyn. I'm in a very happy relationship with Peter Senior; we're best friends as well as lovers, which is probably the best recipe for a successful relationship. We live on the Isle of Man.'

Betty Neels—Enchanted™ author—spent her childhood and youth in Devonshire before training as a nurse and midwife. She was an army nursing sister during the war, married a Dutchman, and subsequently lived in Holland for fourteen years. She lives with her husband in Dorset, and has a daughter and grandson. Her hobbies are reading, animals, old buildings and writing. Betty started to write on retirement from nursing, incited by a lady in a library bemoaning the lack of romantic novels.

Betty has now written more than 120 novels—her stories are loved by readers everywhere.

Mrs Neels is always delighted to receive fan letters. You can write to her at Harlequin Mills and Boon Limited, 18-24 Paradise Road, Richmond, Surrey TW9 1SR

Jo Leigh—Temptation® author—is a native Californian currently living in Texas. Storytelling has always been a part of her life, whether as a producer in Hollywood, a screenwriter or a novelist. *One Wicked Night* is Jo's first Temptation, though she has several more in the works. Look for her next title, a Mail Order Men story, coming next summer. Enjoy!

The *Christmas* COLLECTION

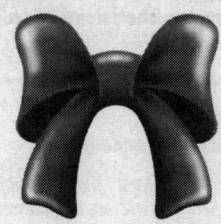

CAROLE MORTIMER

BETTY NEELS

JO LEIGH

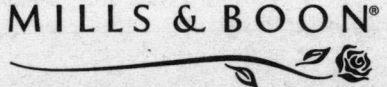

MILLS & BOON®

*MILLS & BOON and MILLS & BOON with the Rose Device
are registered trademarks of the publisher.
Harlequin Mills & Boon Limited,
Eton House, 18-24 Paradise Road,
Richmond, Surrey, TW9 1SR*

THE CHRISTMAS COLLECTION
© by Harlequin Enterprises II B.V., 1998

*First published in Great Britain 1998
by Harlequin Mills & Boon Limited,
Eton House, 18-24 Paradise Road, Richmond, Surrey TW9 1SR*

MARRIED BY CHRISTMAS © Carole Mortimer 1998
A WINTER LOVE STORY © Betty Neels 1998
ONE WICKED NIGHT © Jolie Kramer 1998

ISBN 0 263 81509 9
101-9809

*Printed and bound in Great Britain
by Caledonian Book Manufacturing Ltd, Glasgow*

MARRIED BY CHRISTMAS

BY

CAROLE MORTIMER

CHAPTER ONE

'WHO *is* that gorgeous-looking man over there?' Sally gushed eagerly at Lilli's side.

Until that moment, Lilli had been staring sightlessly at a barman across the room as he quickly and efficiently served drinks to the multitude of people attending what had so far been a pretty boring party.

Or maybe it wasn't the party that was boring; maybe it was just Lilli who felt slightly out of sync with the rest of the people here: if the babble of noise was anything to go by they were having such a good time.

She hadn't attended a party like this in such a long while, and so much had happened in the preceding months. Once upon a time, she acknowledged, she would have thought this was a great party too, would have been at the centre of whatever was going on, but tonight—well, tonight she felt like a total outsider, rather as the only sober person in a room full of inebriates must feel. Except she had already consumed several glasses of champagne herself, so that wasn't the reason she felt so out of touch with this crowd with which she had once spent so much time.

As for gorgeous men, the house was full of them— gorgeous and rich. When Geraldine Simms threw a party, this a pre-Christmas one, only the rich and beautiful were invited to attend, in their hundreds. Geraldine's house, in a fashionable part of London, was as huge and prepossessing as its neighbours, and tonight it was bursting at the seams with bejewelled women and handsome men.

Lilli dragged her gaze away from the efficient barman, obviously hired for the evening. It was time she looked away anyway—the man had obviously noticed her attention several minutes ago, and, from the speculative look in his eyes, believed he had made a conquest! He couldn't have been further from the truth; the last thing Lilli was interested in was a fling with any man, let alone someone as transient as a hired barman!

'What gorgeous man?' she asked Sally without interest. Sally was the one who had persuaded her to come in the first place, on the basis that a Geraldine Simms party, an event that only happened twice a year, was a party not to be missed.

'Over by the door— Oh, damn it, he's disappeared again!' Sally frowned her irritation. She was a petite blonde, with a beauty that could stop a man in his tracks, the black dress she almost wore doing little to forestall this.

Lilli had met her several years ago, during the usual round of parties, and, because neither of them had any interest in becoming permanently entangled with any of the handsome men they encountered, they often found themselves spending the evening together laughing at some of the antics of the other women around them as they cast out their nets and secured some unsuspecting man for the evening. Rather a cruel occupation, really, but it had got Lilli and Sally through many a tedious occasion.

'He must be gorgeous if you've taken an interest,' Lilli said dryly, attracting more than her own fair share of admiring glances as she stood tall and slender next to Sally, her hair long and straight to her waist, as black as a raven's wing, eyes cool and green in a gaminely beautiful face, the strapless above-knee-length red dress that she wore clinging to the perfection of her body. Her legs were long and shapely, still tanned from the summer months, the red high-heeled shoes she wore only adding to her height—and to the impression of unobtainable aloofness that she had practised to perfection over the years.

'Oh, he is,' Sally assured her, still searching the crowd for the object of her interest. 'He makes all the other men here look like callow, narcissistic youths. He— Oh, damn,' she swore impatiently. 'Oh, well,' she sighed, turning back to Lilli with a rueful grimace. 'That was fun while it lasted!' She sipped her champagne.

Lilli's eyes widened. 'You've given up already?' She sounded surprised because she was. On the few occasions she had known Sally to take an interest in a man, she hadn't given up until she had got him! And, as far as Lilli was aware, her friend had always succeeded...

'Had to.' Sally grimaced her disappointment, taking another sip of her champagne. 'Unobtainable.'

'You mean he's married,' Lilli said knowingly.

Sally arched her brows. 'I'm sorry to say that hasn't always been a deterrent in the past.' She shook her head. 'No, he belongs to Gerry,' she explained disappointedly. 'As far as I'm aware, no woman has ever taken one of our hostess's men and lived to tell the tale. And I'm too young to die!'

Lilli laughed huskily at her friend's woebegone expression. Sally was exaggerating, of course, although Geraldine's succession of lovers was legendary. In fact, Lilli doubted there were too many men in this room the beautiful Geraldine Simms hadn't been involved with at some time or other during the last few years. But at least she seemed to stay good friends with them, which had to say something about the bubbling effervescence of their hostess!

Sally glanced across the room again. 'But he is *so* gorgeous…' she said longingly.

Lilli gave a shake of her head. 'Okay, I give up; where is he?' She turned to look for the man who was so attractive that Sally seemed to be about to throw caution to the wind and challenge Gerry for him, on the other woman's home ground, no less!

'Over there.' Sally nodded to the far side of the elegantly furnished room. 'Standing next to Gerry near the window.'

Sally continued to give an exact description of the gorgeous man but Lilli was no longer listening to her, having already located the intimately engrossed couple, feeling the blood drain from her cheeks as she easily spotted the man standing so arrogantly self-assured at Geraldine's side.

No!

Not him. Not here. Not with *her*!

Oh, God…! How could he? How dared he?

'Isn't he just—? I say, Lilli, you've gone very pale all of a sudden.' Sally looked at her concernedly.

Pale? She was surprised she hadn't gone grey, shocked she was still standing on legs that seemed to be shaking so badly her knees were knocking together, surprised she wasn't screaming, *accusing*. What was *he* doing here? And so obviously with Geraldine Simms, a woman with the reputation of a man-eater.

'Are you feeling okay?' Sally touched her arm worriedly.

She wasn't feeling at all, seemed to have gone completely numb. It wasn't an emotion she was unfamiliar with, but she had never thought he would be the one to deal her such a blow.

Oh, God, she had to get out of here, away from the noise, away from *them*!

'I'm fine, Sally,' she told her friend stiltedly, the smile she forced not quite managing to curve her lips. 'I—I think I've had enough for one night. It's my first time out for months,' she babbled. 'I'm obviously out of practice. I—I'll call you.' She put her champagne glass down on the nearest available table. 'We'll have lunch.'

Sally looked totally bewildered by Lilli's sudden urgency to be gone. 'But it's only eleven-thirty!'

And the party would go on until almost morning. In the past Lilli would probably have been among the last to leave. But not tonight. She had to get out of here now. She had to!

'I'll call you, Sally,' she promised distantly, turning to stumble across the room, muttering her apologies as she bumped into people on the way, blind to where she was going, just needing to escape.

She had a jacket somewhere, she remembered. It was in a room at the back of the house. And she didn't want to leave without it, didn't want to have to come back to this house again to collect it. She didn't want to ever have to see Geraldine Simms again. Not ever!

Where had they stored the coats? Every room she looked in appeared to be empty. One of them turned out not to be as empty as it at first appeared, a young couple in there taking advantage of the sofa to make love. But there were no coats.

She would just abandon her damn coat in a minute, would send someone over tomorrow for it, would just have to hope that it was still here.

She thrust open another door, deciding that if this

room proved as fruitless as the others she would quietly leave and find herself a taxi.

'Oh!' She gasped as she realised she had walked into what must be the main kitchen of the house. It wasn't empty. Not that there were any chefs rushing around preparing the food for the numerous guests. No, all the food, put out so deliciously on plates in the dining-room, had been provided by caterers.

A man sat at a long oak table in the middle of the room, his dark evening suit and snowy white shirt, with red bow-tie, tagging him as part of the elegant gathering in the main part of the house. Yet he sat alone in the kitchen, strong hands nursing what looked to be a glass of red wine, the open bottle on the table beside him, the only light in the room a single spotlight over the Aga.

But Lilli could see the man well enough, his dark, overlong hair with distinguished strands of grey at the temples, grey, enigmatic eyes in a face that might have been carved from granite, all sharp angles and hard-hewn features. From the way his long legs stretched out beneath the table, he was a very tall man, well over six feet, if Lilli had to guess. She would put his age in the late thirties.

She also knew, from that very first glance, that she had never seen him before!

She really was very much out of touch with the party scene! Once upon a time she would have known all the other guests at any occasion she went to, which was ultimately the reason they had become so boring to attend. But tonight there were at least two men present that she hadn't encountered at one of these parties before—one she didn't know at all, the other she most certainly did!

Her mouth tightened at her thoughts. 'I'm sorry to

have disturbed you,' she told the man distractedly, turning to leave.

'Not at all,' the man drawled in a weary voice. 'It's quite pleasant to meet another refugee from that free-for-all out there!'

Lilli turned slowly back to him, dark brows raised. 'You aren't enjoying the party?'

His mouth quirked into a humourless smile, and he took a swallow of the wine before answering. 'Not particularly,' he dismissed disgustedly. 'If I had known—!' He picked up the bottle and refilled his glass, turning back to Lilli and raising the bottle in her direction. 'Can I offer you some wine? It's from Gerry's private stock,' he explained temptingly. 'Much preferable to that champagne being served out there.' He waved the bottle in the direction of the front of the house.

Gerry... Only Geraldine's really close friends shortened her name in that way. He also knew where Geraldine kept her cellar of wine.

Lilli looked at the man with new interest. He obviously was—or had been—a close friend of Geraldine Simms. And, while Geraldine might remain on good terms with her ex-lovers, she certainly didn't give them up to another woman easily...

Lilli entered the kitchen fully, aware of the man's gaze on her as she moved across the dimly lit room, able to tell by the cool assessment in those pale grey eyes that he liked what he saw. 'I would love some wine,' she accepted as she sat down at the table, not opposite him but next to him, pushing a long swathe of her dark hair over her shoulder as she did so, turning to look at him, green eyes dark, a smile curving lips coloured the same red as her dress. 'Thank you,' she added huskily.

'Good.' He nodded his satisfaction with her answer, standing up to get a second glass.

Now it was Lilli's turn to watch him. She had been right about his height; he must be at least six feet four, the cut of his suit doing nothing to hide the powerfully muscled body beneath. It also did nothing to mask his obvious contempt for these elegant trappings of civilised company!

She had no doubt that Sally would also have described him as gorgeous!

Her smile faded somewhat as she vividly brought to mind that image of the other man Sally had called gorgeous tonight; her last vision had been of Geraldine Simms draped decoratively across him as the two of them talked softly together.

'Thank you,' she told the man as he sat down beside her to pour her wine, picking up the glass when it was filled to swallow a grateful gulp. She could instantly feel the warmth of the wine inside her, merging with the glasses of champagne she had already consumed.

'Patrick Devlin.' The man held out his hand.

'Lilli.' She shook his hand, liking its cool strength, his name meaning absolutely nothing to her.

He raised dark brows, still retaining his light hold on her hand. 'Just Lilli?'

Her gaze met his, seeing a wealth of experience in those grey depths. Some of that experience had been with Geraldine Simms, she felt sure. 'Just Lilli,' she nodded, sensing his interest in her. And she intended to keep that interest...

'Well, Just Lilli...' He slowly released her hand, although his gaze still easily held hers. 'As we're both bored with this party, what do you suggest we do with ourselves for the rest of the evening?' He quirked mocking lips.

She laughed softly, well versed in the art of seduction herself. 'What do you suggest we do?' she encouraged softly.

He turned back to sit with his elbows resting on the table, sipping his wine. 'Well...we could count how many patterned tiles there are on the wall over there.' He nodded to the wall opposite.

Lilli didn't so much as glance at them. 'I have no interest in counting tiles, patterned or otherwise,' she returned dryly, drinking some of her own wine. He was right—this wine was much nicer than champagne. It was taking away the numbness she had felt earlier, too.

'No? Oh, well.' He shrugged at the playful shake of her head, refilling her glass. 'We could swap life stories?'

'Definitely not!' There was an edge of bitterness to her laugh this time.

He pursed his lips thoughtfully. 'You're probably right,' he said. 'We could bake a cake? We're certainly in the right place for it!' He looked about them.

'Can you cook?' Lilli prompted; he didn't look as if he knew one end of a cooker—or Aga!—from the other!

He grinned at her, showing very white and even teeth—and unlike most of the men here tonight, she would swear that he'd had none of them capped. 'No one has yet complained about my toast,' he drawled. 'And I've been told I pour a mean glass of orange juice!'

She nodded as he gave her the answer she had expected. 'And a mean glass of wine.' She raised her glass as if in a salute to him.

He poured the last of the wine into her glass. 'I'll open another bottle.' He stood up, moving confidently about the kitchen, walking to the cupboard at the back of the room, emerging triumphantly seconds later with a second bottle of the same wine.

Which he then proceeded to open deftly, refilling his own glass before sitting down next to Lilli once again. 'Your turn. To make some suggestions,' he elaborated huskily at her questioning look.

His words themselves were suggestive, but at this particular moment Lilli didn't care. She was actually enjoying herself, and after the shock she had received earlier this evening that was something in itself.

'Let me see…' She made a show of giving it some thought, happily playing along with the game. 'Do you play chess?'

'Tolerably,' he replied.

'Hmm. Draughts?'

'A champion,' he assured her confidently. 'That's the one with the black and white discs—'

'Not draughts, either,' Lilli laughed, green eyes glowing, her cheeks warm, whether from the effect of the wine and champagne, or their verbal flirtation, she wasn't really sure.

And she didn't care, either. This man was a special friend of Geraldine Simms', she was sure of it, and at this moment she had one hundred per cent of his attention. Wonderful!

'Snakes and ladders?' she suggested lightly.

'Yes…' he answered slowly. 'Although my sister always said I cheated when we played as children; I used to go up the snakes and down the ladders!'

Lilli laughed again. Either the man really was funny, or else the wine was taking effect; either way, this was the most fun she had had in a long time. 'I used to do that too,' she confided, lightly touching his arm, instantly feeling the steely strength beneath his jacket. 'And there's no way we can play if we both cheat!'

'True,' he agreed, suddenly very close, his face mere inches away from hers now. 'You know, Just Lilli, there's one game I have an idea we're both good at—and at which neither of us cheats!' His voice was mesmerisingly low now, his aftershave faintly elusive, but at the same time completely masculine. 'What do you say to the two of us—?'

'Patrick!' A feminine voice, slightly raised with impatience, interrupted him. 'Why aren't you at the party?'

He held Lilli's eyes for several seconds longer, a promise in his own, lightly squeezing her hand as it still rested on his arm, before turning to face the source of that feminine impatience. 'Because I prefer to be here,' he answered firmly. 'And, luckily for me, so does Lilli.'

'Lilli...?' The woman sounded startled now.

So much so that Lilli finally turned to look at her too. Geraldine Simms! She looked far from pleased to see the two of them sitting so close together, Patrick's hand still resting slightly possessively on Lilli's.

Lilli looked coldly at the other woman. 'Geraldine,' she greeted her hardly.

'I didn't realise you were here,' Geraldine said faintly.

She could easily have guessed that! 'Sally Walker telephoned me earlier and persuaded me to come with her.' Lilli finished abruptly, 'Wonderful party,' her sarcasm barely veiled.

'So wonderful Lilli and I were just about to leave.' Patrick stood up, lightly pulling Lilli to her feet beside him, his arm moving about the slenderness of her waist now. 'Weren't we,' he prompted.

As far as Lilli was aware—no, but it did seem like an excellent idea.

She turned her head slightly to give Geraldine a triumphant look. 'Yes, we were just about to leave,' she agreed brightly.

'But—' Geraldine looked flustered, not at all her usually confident self. 'Patrick, you can't leave!' She looked at him beseechingly, not at all certain of herself—or him.

His arm tightened about Lilli's waist. 'Watch me,' he stated determinedly.

'But—' Geraldine wrung her hands together. 'Patrick, I threw this party partly for you—'

'I hate parties, you know that.' There was a hard edge to his voice that hadn't been there when he'd flirted with Lilli. 'I'll come back tomorrow when all of this is over. In the meantime, I intend booking into a hotel for the night. Unless Lilli has any other ideas?' he added, looking at her with raised brows.

'Just Lilli' had realised, from the conversation between these two, that the original plan must have been for Patrick to spend the night here. And, considering Geraldine's intimacy with the man she had been draped over in the other room, that was no mean feat in itself; what did this woman do, line them up in relays? Whatever, Patrick had obviously decided he would rather spend the night with her, though the house she shared in Mayfair with her father was not the place for her to take him; she felt hurt and betrayed, but not *that* hurt and betrayed!

'A hotel sounds fine,' she accepted with bravado, green eyes challenging as she looked across the room at Geraldine.

The other woman's stare relaxed slightly as she met that challenge. 'Lilli, don't do something you'll regret,' she cautioned gently.

Geraldine knew she had seen the two of *them* together,

knew why she was doing this! All the better; there was no satisfaction in revenge if the person targeted was unaware of it...!

Lilli turned slightly into Patrick's body, resting her head against the hardness of his chest. 'I'm sure Patrick will make sure I don't regret a thing,' she said huskily.

'Lilli—'

'Gerry, just butt out, will you?' Patrick told her impatiently. 'Go and find your ageing lover and leave Lilli and me to get on with our lives. I'm not a monster intent on seducing an innocent, and you aren't the girl's mother, for goodness' sake,' he added disgustedly.

Lilli looked at the other woman with pure venom in her eyes; she had never disliked anyone as much as she did Geraldine Simms at that moment. 'Yes, Geraldine,' she said flatly. 'Please go back to your lover; I'm sure he must be wondering where you are.'

'We'll go out the back way,' Patrick suggested lightly. 'Unless you want to fight your way out through the chaos?'

'No, the back way is fine.' Her coat didn't matter any more; no doubt it would be returned to her in time!

'Patrick!' Geraldine had crossed the room to stop them at the door, a restraining hand on Patrick's arm now. 'I realise you're angry with me right now, but please don't—'

'I'm not angry with you, Gerry,' he cut in contemptuously. 'No one has any ties on you; they never had!' His face was cold as he looked down at her.

'This isn't important just now,' the beautiful redhead dismissed impatiently. 'Anyone but Lilli, Patrick,' she groaned.

So the woman did have a conscience, after all! Unless, of course, she just didn't want Lilli, in particular, walking off with one of her men…? In the circumstances, that was probably closer to the truth.

'Please don't worry on my account, Geraldine.' Lilli deliberately used the other woman's full name. The two of them had never been particularly close in the past, although Lilli did usually call her Gerry; but after this evening she hoped they would never meet again. 'I know exactly what I'm doing,' she affirmed.

Geraldine looked at Lilli searchingly for several long seconds. 'I don't think you do.' She shook her head slowly. 'And I'm absolutely positive you don't, Patrick,' she added firmly. 'Lilli is—'

'Could we leave now, Patrick?' Lilli turned to him, open flirtation in the dark green of her eyes. 'Before I decide snakes and ladders is preferable!'

He looked at her admiringly. 'We're leaving, Gerry,' he told the other woman decisively. 'Now.'

'But—'

'Now, Gerry,' he insisted, opening the back door for Lilli to precede him. 'Enjoy your party,' he called over his shoulder, his arm once more about Lilli's waist as they stepped out into the cold December evening.

The blast of icy cold air was like a slap on the face, and Lilli could feel her head swimming from the amount of champagne and wine she had drunk during the evening. In fact, she suddenly felt decidedly light-headed.

'Steady.' Patrick's arm tightened about her waist as he held her beside him. 'My car is just over here. Don't you have a coat?' He frowned as she shivered from the cold while he unlocked the doors of his sleek black sports car.

She suddenly couldn't remember whether she had a coat or not. In fact, she was having trouble putting two thoughts together inside her head!

She gave a laugh as he opened the car door for her to get in, showing a long expanse of shapely leg as she dropped down into the low passenger seat. 'I'm sure you'll help me to get warm once we reach the hotel,' she told him seductively.

His mouth quirked. 'I'll do my best, Just Lilli,' he assured her, the promise in his voice unmistakable.

Lilli leant her head back against the seat as he closed her door to move around the car and get in behind the wheel. What was she doing here…? Oh, yes, she was getting away from Geraldine and him!

'Any preference on hotels?' Patrick glanced at her as he turned on the ignition.

Hotels? Why were they going to a hotel…? Oh, yes…this man was going to make love to her.

She shook her head, instantly wishing she hadn't as it began to spin once again. 'You choose,' she said weakly.

She wasn't actually going to be sick, was she?

God, she hoped not. Although she had no idea where they were going as Patrick turned the car out onto the road. And at that moment she didn't care either. Nothing mattered at the moment. Not her. Not him. Not Geraldine Simms!

'All right?' Patrick reached out to squeeze her hand reassuringly.

She didn't think she would ever be 'all right' again. She had felt as if her world had shattered three months ago; tonight it felt as if it had ended completely.

'Fine,' she answered as if from a long way away. 'Just take me somewhere private and make love to me.'

'Oh, I intend to, Just Lilli. I intend to.'

Lilli sat back with her eyes closed, wishing at that moment for total oblivion, not just a few hours in Patrick Devlin's arms…

CHAPTER TWO

'YOUR jacket.' The garment was thrown over the back of a dining-room chair.

Lilli didn't move, didn't even raise her head. She wasn't sure that she could!

She had been sitting here at the dining-table for the last hour, just drinking strong, unsweetened black coffee; the smell of food on the serving plates sitting on the side board had made her feel nauseous, so she had asked for them to be taken away. There was no one else here to eat it, anyway. At least, there hadn't been...

'Did you hear what I said?'

'I heard you!' She winced as the sound of her own voice made the thumping in her head even louder. 'I heard you,' she repeated softly, her voice almost a whisper now. But it still sounded too loud for her sensitive ears!

'Well?'

He wasn't going to leave it at that. She should have known that he wouldn't. But all she really wanted to do, now that her head had at least stopped spinning, was to crawl into bed and sleep for twenty-four hours.

Fat chance!

'Lilli!' The impatience deepened in his voice.

At last she raised her head from where it had been resting in her hands as she stared down into her coffee cup, pushing back the dark thickness of her hair to look up at him with studied determination.

'My God, Lilli!' her father gasped disbelievingly. 'You look terrible!'

'Thank you!' Her smile was merely a caricature of one, even her facial muscles seeming to hurt.

She knew exactly how she looked, had recoiled from her own reflection in the mirror earlier this morning. Her eyes were a dull green, bruises from lack of sleep visible beneath them, her face chalk-white. Her tangled hair she had managed to smooth into some sort of order with her fingers, but the overall impression, she knew, was not good. It wasn't helped by the fact that she still had on the revealing red dress she had worn to the party the night before. A fact Grimes, the family butler, had definitely noted when she'd arrived back here by taxi an hour ago!

But if her father thought she looked bad now he should have seen her a couple of hours ago, when she'd first woken up; then she hadn't even been wearing the red dress! And the rich baritone voice of Patrick Devlin had been coming from the bathroom as he'd sung while he took a shower...!

Her father dropped down heavily into the chair opposite her. 'What were you thinking of, Lilli?' He looked at her searchingly. 'Or were you just not thinking at all?' he added with regret.

He knew; she could tell by the expression in his eyes that he did. Of course he knew; Geraldine would have told him!

Because her father had been the man at Geraldine Simms' side last night, the gorgeous man that Sally had referred to so interestedly, the man Geraldine had been draped over so intimately, her 'ageing lover', as Patrick had called him.

'Were *you*?' Lilli challenged insultingly. 'Yes, I saw

you last night,' she scorned as a guarded look came over her father's handsome face. 'With Geraldine Simms,' she continued accusingly, so angry she didn't care about the pounding in her head at that moment. 'But I suppose *you* call her Gerry.' Her top lip curled back contemptuously. 'All her *intimate* friends do!'

He drew in a harshly controlling breath. 'And is that why you did what you did?' he asked flatly. 'Went off with a man you had only just met? A man you obviously spent the night with,' he added as he looked pointedly at her dress.

'And what about you?' Lilli accused emotionally. 'I don't need to ask where *you* spent the night. Or with whom!' She was furiously angry, but at the same time tears of pain glistened in her eyes.

Her father reached out to touch her hand, but she drew back as if she had been burnt. 'You don't understand, Lilli,' he told her in a hurt voice. 'You—'

'Oh, I understand only too well.' She stood up so suddenly, her chair fell over behind her with a loud clatter, but neither of them took any notice of it as their green eyes locked. 'You spent last night in the bed of a woman everyone knows to be a man-eating flirt, a woman who has been involved with numerous men since her brief marriage—and equally quick divorce!—five years ago. And with my mother, your wife, barely cold in her grave!' She glared across the table at him, her breathing shallow and erratic in her agitation, her hands clenched into fists at her sides.

For that was what hurt the most about all this. After a long illness, her mother had died three months ago— and now her father was intimately involved with one of the biggest flirts in London!

It was an insult to her mother's memory. It was—it

was— God, the pain last night of seeing her father with another woman—with that woman in particular!—had been almost more than she could bear.

Her father looked as if she had physically hit him, his face as pale as her own, the likeness between them even more noticeable during those seconds. Lilli had always been so proud of her father, had adored him as a child, admired him as an adult, had always loved the fact that she looked so much like him, her hair as dark as his.

Now she wished she looked like anyone else but him—because at this particular moment she hated him!

'You're right, Father; I don't understand,' she told him coldly as she rose and walked away from him. 'But then, I don't think I particularly want to.'

'Lilli, did you spend the night with Patrick Devlin?'

She stopped at the door, her back still towards him. Then, swallowing hard, she turned to face him, her head held back defiantly. 'Yes, I did,' she told him starkly.

He frowned. 'You went to bed with him?'

Lilli stared at her parent woodenly. She had woken up in a hotel bedroom this morning, wearing only her lace panties, with Patrick Devlin singing in the adjoining bathroom as he took a shower, the other side of the double bed showing signs of someone having slept there, the pillow indented, the sheet tangled; so it was probably a fair assumption that she had been to bed with him!

But the real truth of the matter was she didn't actually remember, couldn't recall anything of the night before from the moment she had closed her eyes in the car— and even some of the events before that were a bit hazy!

Her mouth tightened stubbornly. 'What if I did? I'm over twenty-one.' Just! 'And a free agent.' Definitely that, since the end of her engagement. She had barely been out of the house during the last six months—which was the reason the champagne and wine she'd drunk last night had hit her so strongly, she was sure. At least, that was what she had told herself this morning when she'd finally managed to open her eyes and face the day. 'Who was I hurting?' she added challengingly.

Her father gave a weary sigh, shaking his head. 'Well, I believe the intention was to hurt me. But the person you've hurt the most is yourself. Lilli, do you have any idea who Patrick Devlin is?'

Why should she? As her father had already said, she had only met the man last night. And her nonsensical conversation with Patrick in the kitchen had told her nothing about him, except that he had a sense of humour. But then, she had told him nothing about herself either, was 'Just Lilli' as far as he was concerned. She never expected to see or hear from him again!

'I only wanted to go to bed with him, not hear his life story!' she scorned dismissively.

Her father drew a harsh breath. 'Perhaps if you had done the latter, and not the former, this conversation wouldn't be taking place. In fact, I'm sure it wouldn't,' he rasped abruptly. 'You really don't have any idea who he is?'

'Why do you keep harping on about the man?' She snapped her impatience. 'He isn't important—'

'Oh, but he is,' her father cut in softly.

'Not to me.' She gave a firm shake of her head, wincing as she did so.

She just wanted to forget about Patrick Devlin. Last night she had behaved completely out of character, mostly because, as her father had guessed, she wanted to hit out at him. But also at Geraldine Simms. Well, she had done that—more than done that if her father's reaction was anything to go by!—and now she just wanted to forget it had ever happened. She couldn't even remember half of last night's events, so it shouldn't be that hard to do!

'Oh, yes, Lilli, he is important to you too.' Her father nodded grimly. 'Patrick Devlin is the Chairman of Paradise Bank.'

She thought back to the man she had met last night in Geraldine Simms' kitchen—she couldn't count this morning; she had left the hotel before he'd stopped singing and emerged from the bathroom! She remembered a tall, handsome man, with slightly overlong dark hair, and laughter in his deep grey eyes. He hadn't looked anything like a banker.

She shrugged. 'So? Is he married, with a dozen children; is that the problem?' Although if he were he must have a very understanding wife, to have gone off to a party on his own and then have felt no compunction about staying out all night. No...somehow she didn't think he was married.

Her father gave a sigh at the mockery in her tone. 'Okay, let's leave that part alone for a while. Do you know what else he is, Lilli?'

'A Liberal Democrat,' she taunted.

'Oh, very funny!' Her father, a staunch Conservative voter, wasn't in the least amused at her continued levity.

'Look, Father, I don't—'

'And will you stop calling me "Father" in that judgemental tone?' he bit out tautly.

'I'm sorry, but you just don't seem like "Daddy" to me at the moment,' she told him in a pained voice, unable to look at him at that moment, too.

Her father had always been there for her in the past, she had always been 'Daddy's little girl', and now he suddenly seemed like a stranger...

'I'm really sorry you feel that way, Lilli.' He spoke gently. 'It wasn't meant to be this way.'

'I'm not even going to ask what you mean by that remark,' she said scathingly, turning towards the door once again.

'I haven't finished yet, Lilli—'

'But I have!' She swung round, eyes flashing deeply green. 'To be honest, I'm not sure I can listen to any more of this without being sick!' This time she did turn and walk out the door, her head held high.

'He's Geraldine's brother,' her father called after her. 'Patrick Devlin is Geraldine's older brother!'

She faltered only slightly, and then she just kept on walking, her legs moving automatically, that numbness she had known the night before thankfully creeping over her once again.

'Where are you going?' Her father now stood at the bottom of the stairs she had half ascended.

'To bed,' she told him flatly. 'To sleep.' For a million years, if she was lucky!

'This mess will still be here when you wake up, Lilli,' her father told her fiercely. '*I'll* still be here!'

She didn't answer him, didn't even glance at him, continuing up to her bedroom, closing the door firmly behind her, deliberately keeping her mind blank as she threw off the clothes she had worn last night, not even bothering to put on a nightgown before climbing in between the sheets of her bed, pulling the covers up over the top of her head, willing herself to go to sleep.

And when she woke up maybe she would find the last twelve hours had been a nightmare…!

Geraldine Simms' brother!

She didn't know what time it was, how long she had

slept, only that she had woken suddenly, sitting up in the bed, her eyes wide as that terrible truth pounded in her brain.

Patrick Devlin wasn't a past or present lover of Geraldine Simms, but her *brother*!

No wonder he had been so familiar with the house, with where the wine was kept. And he hadn't been going to spend the night there with Geraldine, but was obviously her guest at her house during his visit to London.

Lilli had thought she was being so clever, that she was walking away with a prize taken from under Geraldine's nose. But all the time Patrick was the woman's brother! No wonder Geraldine had tried to stop the two of them leaving together; considering her own involvement with Lilli's father, any relationship between Lilli and her brother was a complication she could well do without!

Lilli had been to bed with the enemy…!

But she wasn't involved with Patrick Devlin, had no 'relationship' with him; one night in bed together did not a relationship make!

One night in bed…

And she didn't even remember it, she inwardly groaned. But Patrick had been singing quite happily to himself in the shower this morning, so he obviously did!

With the exception of her ex-fiancé, she had spent the majority of the last four years ignoring the obvious advances of the 'beautiful men' she met at parties, not even aware of the less obvious ones. But in a single night she had wiped all of that out by going to bed with the one man she should have stayed well away from.

Her father was right—this was a mess!

She fell back against the pillows, her eyes closed. A

million years of sleep couldn't undo what she had done
last night.

Her only consolation—and it was a very slight one!—
was that she was sure Patrick had been involved in a
conversation with his sister this morning very similar to
the one she'd had with her father. She wouldn't be 'Just
Lilli' to Patrick any more, but Elizabeth Bennett, daughter of Richard Bennett, of Bennett International Hotels,
the current man in Geraldine's life. No doubt her identity
as the daughter of his sister's 'ageing lover' had come
as much of a shock to him as it had to her to realise he
was Geraldine's brother.

Lilli opened her eyes, her expression thoughtful now.
Patrick hadn't seemed any more pleased than she was at
his sister's choice of lover, which meant he wouldn't be
too eager ever to meet the lover's daughter again, either.
Which meant she could forget the whole sorry business.

End of mess.

Of course it was.

Now if she could just make her father see sense over
this ridiculous involvement with Geraldine Simms—

She turned towards the door as a knock sounded on
it. She hadn't left instructions that she wasn't to be disturbed, but even so she was irritated at the intrusion.
'Yes?' she prompted impatiently, getting out of bed to
pull on her robe.

'There's someone downstairs waiting to see you, Miss
Lilli, and—'

The young maid broke off in surprise as Lilli
wrenched open the door. 'There's someone to see you,'
the maid repeated awkwardly.

'What time is it?' Lilli frowned, totally disoriented
after her daytime sleep.

'Three-thirty,' Emily provided, a girl not much

younger than Lilli herself. 'Would you like me to serve tea to you and your visitor?'

She wasn't in the mood to receive visitors, let alone sit and have tea with them. 'I don't think so, thank you,' she replied distractedly. 'Who is it?' She frowned.

'A Mr Devlin,' Emily told her chattily. 'I asked him to wait in the small sitting-room——'

'Devlin!' Lilli repeated forcefully, causing the young maid to look alarmed all over again. 'Did you say a Mr Devlin, Emily?' Her thoughts raced.

Patrick was here? So much for her thinking he wouldn't ever want to see her again either once he realised who she was!

'Yes.' The young girl's face was alight with infatuation—all the evidence Lilli needed that indeed it was the handsome Patrick Devlin downstairs.

Thinking back to the way he had looked last night—tall, and so elegantly handsome—she found it easy to see how a woman's breath could be taken away just to look at him. And she had just spent the night with him!

Lilli drew in a sharp breath. 'Please tell him I'll be down in a few minutes.' Once she was dressed. His last memory of her must be of her wearing only cream lace panties; she intended the memory he took away of her today to be quite different!

It took more than the few minutes she had said to don a black sweater, fitted black trousers, apply a light make-up to hide the pallor of her face, and to braid her long hair into a loose plait down her spine. But at least when she looked in the mirror at her reflection she was satisfied with the result—cool and elegant.

Nevertheless, she took a deep breath before entering the room where Patrick Devlin waited for her. She had no idea what he was doing here—didn't a woman walk-

ing out on him without even a goodbye, after spending
the night with him, tell him that she didn't want to see
him again—ever? Obviously not, if his presence here
was anything to go by…

He was standing in front of the window looking out
at the winter garden when she entered, slowly turning to
look at her as he became aware of her presence.

Lilli's breath caught in her throat. God, he was handsome!

She hadn't really registered that last night, but in the
clear light of day he was incredibly attractive, ruggedly
so, his hair so dark a brown it almost appeared black,
with those distinguished wings of silver at his temples.
His skin was lightly tanned, features so finely hewn they
might have been carved from stone, his eyes a light,
enigmatic grey.

He was dressed very similarly to her, except he wore
a fine checked jacket over his black jumper. Which
meant he had been back to Geraldine's house this morning—if only to change his clothes!

He moved forward in long, easy movements, looking
her critically up and down. 'Well, well, well,' he finally
drawled. 'If it isn't Just Lilli—alias Elizabeth Bennett.'
His voice hardened over the latter.

'Mr Devlin.' She nodded coolly in acknowledgement,
none of her inner turmoil—she hoped!—in evidence.

She had chosen to go with this man the evening before
for two reasons: to hurt her father, and hit out at
Geraldine Simms. And at this moment Patrick Devlin
seemed very much aware of that!

His mouth twisted mockingly. 'Mr. Devlin…? Really,
Lilli, it's a little late for formality between us, isn't it?'
he taunted.

She moved pointedly away from him; his derisive

manner was deliberately insulting. 'Why are you here?' She looked at him across the room with cool green eyes.

Dark brows rose at her tone. 'Well, I could say you left your bra behind and I've come to return it, but as you weren't wearing a bra last night...!'

'That's enough!' she snapped, two bright spots of embarrassed colour in her cheeks now.

'More than enough, I would say,' he agreed, his eyes glittering icily. 'Lilli, exactly what did you hope to achieve by going to bed with me?'

To hit out at her father, to hurt Geraldine Simms. Nothing more. But certainly nothing less. At the time she hadn't realised the man she had chosen to help her was actually the other woman's brother. She accepted it complicated things a little. Especially as he had come here today...

She deliberately gave a careless shrug. 'A good time.' It was half a question—because she couldn't remember whether or not they'd had a good time together!

He gave an acknowledging nod at her reply. 'And did you? Have a good time,' he persisted dryly at her puzzled expression.

She frowned. 'Didn't you?' she instantly returned. Two could play at this game!

His mouth quirked. 'Marks out of ten? Or do you have some other method of rating your lovers—?'

'There's no need to be insulting!' Lilli told him sharply.

'There's every need, damn you!' Patrick advanced towards her, his hand on her arm, fingers warm against her skin.

'Don't touch me!' she told him angrily, pulling away, and only succeeding in hurting herself. 'Let me go,' she ordered with every ounce of Bennett arrogance she possessed. This was her home, damn it, and he couldn't just come in here—uninvited!—and insult and manhandle her!

He thrust her away from him. 'I ought to break that beautiful neck of yours!' he ground out fiercely, eyes narrowed. 'You looked older last night... Exactly how old are you?' he bit out, his gaze sweeping over her scathingly.

She looked startled. 'What does my age have to do with anything?'

'Just answer the question, Lilli,' he rasped. 'And while you're at it explain to me exactly how the haughty Elizabeth Bennett ended up with a name like Lilli!'

Her own cheeks were flushed with anger now. 'Neither of those things is any of your business!'

'I'm making them so,' he told her levelly.

This man might be as good-looking as the devil, but he had the arrogance to match! Why hadn't she realised any of this the previous evening when she had met him? Because she hadn't been thinking straight, she acknowledged heavily, had been blinded by the fury she felt towards her father and the woman he was obviously involved with. This man's sister... She still had trouble connecting the two—they looked absolutely nothing alike!

'Well?' he prompted at her continued silence.

She glared at him resentfully, wanting him to leave but knowing he had no intention of doing so until he was good and ready—and he wasn't either of those things yet! 'I'm twenty-one,' she told him tautly.

'And?' He looked at her hardly.

'And three months,' she supplied challengingly, knowing it wasn't what he had been asking. But she had no intention of telling him that she had acquired the name Lilli because the baby brother she had adored, the baby brother who had died when he was only two years old, hadn't been able to manage the name Elizabeth. Just as she had no intention of telling him that she knew to the day exactly how old she was, because her mother, the mother she had also adored, had died on her twenty-first birthday... It was also the day her fiancée, her father's assistant, had walked out of her life...

He grimaced ruefully at her evasion. 'A mere child,' he ground out disgustedly. 'The sacrificial lamb!' He shook his head. 'I hate to tell you this, Lilli, but your efforts—enjoyable as they were!—were completely wasted.' His gaze hardened. 'If my own sister's pleadings failed to move me, you can be assured that a night of pleasure in your arms would have had even less effect!'

Lilli looked at him with haughty disdain. 'I don't have the least idea what you're talking about,' she snapped.

'No?' he queried sceptically.

'No,' she echoed tartly. 'I don't even know what you're doing here today. We were at a party, we decided to spend the night together—and that should have been the end of it. You came here, I didn't come to you,' she reminded him coldly.

'Actually, Lilli,' he drawled softly, 'I came to see your father, not you.'

Her head went back in astonishment. 'My father...?' she repeated in a puzzled voice.

Patrick nodded abruptly. 'Unfortunately, I was informed he isn't in,' he said grimly.

'So you asked to see me instead?' she realised incredulously.

'Correct,' he affirmed, with a slight inclination of his head. 'Sorry to disappoint you, Lilli,' he added.

She swallowed hard, quickly reassessing the situation. 'And just why did you want to see my father?'

Patrick looked at her with narrowed eyes. 'I'm sure you already know the answer to that question.'

'Because he's having a relationship with your sister?' Lilli scorned. 'It must keep you very busy if you pay personal calls on all her lovers in this way!'

Anger flared briefly in the grey depths of his eyes, and then they became glacially enigmatic, that gaze sweeping over her with deliberate assessment. 'I'm sure you keep your father just as busy,' he drawled.

After her comment about Geraldine, she had probably deserved that remark. Unfortunately, both this man and his sister brought out the worst in her; she wasn't usually a bitchy person. But then, this whole situation was unusual!

'Perhaps he's paying a similar call on you at this very moment?' Lilli returned.

'I very much doubt it.' Patrick gave a smile. 'It hasn't been my impression, so far in our acquaintance, that your father has ever deliberately gone out of his way to meet me!'

Her eyes widened. 'The two of you have met?' If they had, her father hadn't mentioned that particular fact earlier!

'Several times,' Patrick confirmed enigmatically.

Exactly how long had her father been involved with Geraldine? Lilli had assumed it was a very recent thing, but if the two men had met 'several times'...

'Perhaps you could pass on a message to him that we will be meeting again, too. Very soon,' Patrick added grimly, walking to the door.

Lilli watched him frowningly. 'You're leaving...?' She hadn't meant her voice to sound wistful at all—and yet somehow it did. In the fifteen minutes Patrick had been here he had made insulting comments to her, enigmatic remarks about her father—but he hadn't really said anything. She wasn't really sure what she had expected him to say... But the two of them had spent the night together, and—

He turned at the door, dark brows raised questioningly. 'Do we have anything else to say to each other?' he questioned in a bored voice.

No, of course they didn't. They had had nothing to say to each other from the beginning. It was just that—

'Ten, Lilli,' he drawled softly. 'You were a ten,' he explained dryly as she gave him a puzzled look.

He laughed huskily as his meaning became clear and her cheeks suffused with heated colour.

She hadn't wanted to know—hadn't asked—

'I'll let myself out, Lilli,' he volunteered, and did so, the door closing softly behind him.

Which was just as well—because Lilli had been rooted to the spot after that last statement.

Ten...

And she didn't remember a single moment of it...

CHAPTER THREE

'I WANT to know exactly what is going on, Daddy,' Lilli told him firmly, having waited in the sitting-room for two hours before he came home, fortified by the tray of tea things Emily had brought in to her. After Patrick Devlin's departure, Lilli had felt in need of something, and whisky, at that hour of the day, had been out of the question. Although the man was enough to drive anyone to drink!

She had heard her father enter the house, accosting him in the hallway as he walked towards the wide staircase.

He turned at the sound of her voice, his expression grim. 'I was left in no doubt by you earlier that you didn't want to hear anything more about Geraldine.'

'I still don't,' Lilli told him impatiently. 'Her brother, however, is a different matter!'

'Patrick?' her father replied.

Her mouth twisted. 'Unless she has another brother—yes!'

Her father stiffened, striding forcefully across the hallway to join her as she went into the sitting-room, closing the door firmly behind him. 'What about him?' he said warily.

She gave an impatient sigh. 'That's what I just asked you!'

'You spent the night with him, Lilli,' her father reminded her. 'I would have thought you would know all

36

there is to know about the man! We none of us have defences in bed. Or so I'm told...'

She bit back the reply she would have liked to make; that sort of conversation would take them absolutely nowhere, as it had this morning. 'I'm not talking about the man's prowess—or otherwise!—in the bedroom,' she snapped. 'He said the two of you know each other.'

'Did he?' her father returned with studied indifference.

'Daddy!' She glared at her father's back as he stood looking out of the window now—very much as Patrick had done earlier. He was trying to give the impression that the subject of the other man bored him, and yet, somehow, she knew that it didn't...

He sighed. 'I'm sorry. I just didn't realise the two of you had spent part of your night together discussing me—'

'We didn't,' Lilli cut in. 'He was here earlier.'

Her father froze, slowly turning to face her. 'Devlin came here?'

She wasn't wrong; she was sure she wasn't; she had never seen this emotion in her father before, but he actually looked slightly fearful. And it had something to do with Patrick Devlin...

'Yes, he was here,' she confirmed steadily. 'And he said some things—'

'He had no right, damn him!' her father told her fiercely, his hands clenched into fists at his sides.

'I'm your daughter—'

'And this is a business matter,' he barked tensely. 'If I had wanted to tell you about it then I would have done so.'

'Tell me now?' Lilli encouraged softly. Her father had mentioned this morning that Patrick Devlin was the

chairman of Paradise Bank—could that have something
to do with this 'business matter'? Although, as far as she
was aware, her family had always banked with
Cleveley…

'I told you, Patrick Devlin *is* Paradise Bank,' her father grated.

And she was none the wiser for his repeating the fact!
'Yes?'

'Don't you ever read the newspapers, Lilli?' her father
said tersely. 'Or are you more like your mother than
I realised, and only interested in what Bennett
International Hotels can give you in terms of money and
lifestyle?'

The accusation hung between them, everything suddenly seeming very quiet; even the air was still.

Lilli stared at her father, barely breathing, a tight pain
in her chest.

Her father stared back at her, obviously mortified at
what he had just said, his face very pale.

They never talked about her mother, or baby Robbie;
they had, by tacit agreement, never talked about the loss
of either.

Lilli drew in a deep breath. 'I know Mummy had her
faults—'

'I'm sorry, Lilli—'

They had both begun talking at the same time, both
coming to an abrupt halt, once again staring at each
other, awkwardly this time. The last three months had
been difficult; Lilli's grief at her mother's death was
something she hadn't been able to share with anyone.
Not even her father.

She had known that her father had his own pain to
deal with. The years during which her mother's illness
had deteriorated had been even more difficult for him

than they had for Lilli, her mother's moods fluctuating between self-pity and anger. It had been hard to cope with, Lilli freely acknowledged. But she had had no idea how bitter her father had become...

'I shouldn't have said that.' Her father ran a weary hand through dark hair liberally peppered with grey. 'I'm sorry, Lilli.'

She wasn't sure whether he was apologising for the remarks about her mother, or for the fact that he felt the way he did...

'No, you shouldn't,' she agreed quietly. 'But a lot of things have been said and done in the last twenty-four hours that shouldn't have been.' She included her own behaviour with Patrick Devlin in that! 'Perhaps it would be better if we just forgot about them?' She certainly wanted to forget last night!

'I wish we could, Lilli.' Her father sat down heavily in one of the armchairs, shaking his head. 'But I don't think Devlin will let either of us do that.' He leant his head back against the chair, his eyes closed. 'What did he have to say when he came here earlier?' He opened his eyes to look at her frowningly.

Besides marking her as a ten...?

'Not a lot, Daddy.' She crossed the room to kneel on the carpet at his feet. 'Although he did say to tell you the two of you would be meeting again. Soon. Tell me what's going on, Daddy?' She looked up at him appealingly.

He reached out to smooth gently the loose tendrils of dark hair away from her cheeks. 'You're so young, Lilli.' He sounded pained. 'So very young,' he groaned. 'You give the outward impression of being so cool and self-possessed, and yet...'

'It's just an impression,' she acknowledged ruefully.

'How well you know me, Daddy.' She gave a wistful smile.

'I should do,' he said with gentle affection. 'I love you very much, Lilli. No matter what happens, I hope you never forget that.' He gave a heavy sigh.

Lilli once again felt that chill of foreboding down her spine. What was going to happen? And what did Patrick Devlin have to do with it? Because she didn't doubt that he was at the root of her father's problem.

Her father straightened determinedly in his chair, that air of defeat instantly dispelled. 'Devlin and I are involved in some business that isn't going quite the way he wishes it would,' he explained briskly.

Lilli frowned, realising that, with this blunt statement, her father had decided not to tell her anything. 'He called me a sacrificial lamb,' she persisted.

'Did he, indeed?' her father rapped out harshly. 'What the hell does he think I am?' he cried angrily, rising forcefully to his feet. 'Devlin is right, Lilli—it's past time the two of us met again. Damn Gerry and her diplomatic approach—'

'About Geraldine Simms—'

'She's not for discussion, Lilli,' her father cut in defensively, those few minutes of father-daughter closeness definitely over.

Obviously Geraldine Simms was too important in his life to be discussed with her! It made Lilli question exactly how long this relationship with the other woman had been going on. Since her mother's death—or before that? The thought of her father having an affair with a woman like Geraldine Simms while her mother was still alive made Lilli feel ill. He couldn't have—could he...?

Lilli stood up too, eyes flashing deeply emerald. 'In

that case,' she rebutted angrily, 'neither is the night I spent with her brother!'

'Lilli!' Her father stopped her as she was about to storm out of the room.

She turned slowly. 'Yes?' she said curtly.

'Stay away from Devlin,' he advised heavily. 'He's trouble.'

He might be, and until a short time ago she had been only too happy with the idea of never setting eyes on him again. But not any more. Patrick Devlin was the other half of this puzzle, and if her father wouldn't tell her what was going on perhaps Patrick would!

She met her father's gaze unblinkingly. 'Stay away from Geraldine Simms,' she mocked. 'She's trouble.'

Her father steadily met her rebellious gaze for several long seconds, and then he wearily shook his head. 'This is so much deeper than you can possibly realise. You're playing with fire where Devlin is concerned. He's a barracuda in a city suit,' he added bitterly.

'Sounds like a fascinating combination,' Lilli replied.

'More like deadly,' her father rasped, scowling darkly. 'Lilli, I'm ordering you to stay away from him!'

Her eyes widened in shock. This was much more serious than she had even imagined; she couldn't remember the last time her father had ordered her to do anything. If he ever had. But the fact that he did it now only made her all the more determined.

The real problem with that was she had no idea—yet!—how to even make contact with Patrick Devlin again, without it seeming as if she was doing exactly that. Because she had a feeling he would react exactly as her father was doing if she went to him and asked for answers to her questions: refuse to give any!

Well, she might be young, as both men had already

stated quite clearly today, but she was the daughter of one man, and had spent the previous night in the arms of the other—she certainly wasn't a child, and she wasn't about to be treated like one. By either of them!

'Save that tone of voice for your employees, Father,' she told him coldly. 'Of which I—thankfully!—am not one!' She closed the door decisively behind her as she left the room.

It was only once she was safely outside in the hallway that she allowed some of her defiance to leave her. But she had meant every word she'd said in there, she would get to the bottom of this mystery. And she knew the very person to help her do that...

'Sally!' she said warmly a few minutes later when the other woman answered her call after the tenth ring. She had begun to think Sally must be out. And that didn't fit in with her plans at all. 'It's Lilli.'

'Wow, that was quick,' Sally returned lightly. 'I didn't expect to hear from you again for weeks.'

Lilli forced a bright laugh. 'I said I would call you,' she reminded her.

'It's a little late in the day for lunch,' Sally said dryly. 'Although to be honest,' she added confidingly, 'I've only just got out of bed. That was some party last night!'

Lilli wouldn't know. 'Any luck with that gorgeous man?' she said playfully—knowing full well there hadn't been; her father had spent the night with Geraldine Simms.

'None at all.' Sally sounded disappointed. 'But then, with Gerry on the hunt, I never expected it. She monopolised the man all night, and then—'

'Are you free for dinner this evening?' Lilli cut in sharply—she knew what came 'then'!

'Well...I was due to go to the Jameses' party this

evening, but it will just be like every other party I've been to this month. Christmas-time is a bitch, isn't it? Everyone and his cousin throws a party—and invites exactly the same people to every one! In all honesty, I'm all partied out. And there's another ten days to go yet!' Sally groaned with feeling.

'Does that mean you're free for dinner?' Lilli prompted.

'Name the place!' The grin could be heard in Sally's voice.

Lilli did, choosing one of her own favourite restaurants, knowing the other woman would like it too. She also promised that it was her treat; Sally knew 'everyone and his cousin', and anything there was to know about them. Lilli didn't doubt she would know about Patrick Devlin too...

She wasn't disappointed in her choice of informant!

'Patrick!' Even the way Sally said his name spoke volumes. 'Now there *is* a gorgeous man. Tall, dark, handsome— He's Gerry's brother, you know—'

'I do know,' Lilli confirmed—she knew now!

'He's also intelligent, rich—oh yes, very rich.' Sally laughed softly.

'And single.' It was almost a question—because Lilli wasn't absolutely sure of his marital status. She had been to bed with the man, and she didn't even know whether he was married!

'He is now,' Sally nodded, nibbling on one of the prawns she had chosen to start her meal. 'Sanchia wasn't the faithful kind, and so he went through rather a messy divorce about five years ago. Sanchia took him for millions. Personally, I would rather have kept the man, but

Sanchia settled for the cash and moved back to France, where she originally came from.'

Sanchia... Patrick had been married to a woman called Sanchia. A woman who had been unfaithful to him. She couldn't have known him very well if she had thought he would put up with that; Lilli had only known him twenty-four hours, but, even so, she knew he was a man who kept what he had. Exclusively.

But at least he wasn't married now, which was a relief to hear after last night. Although there was still so much Lilli wanted to know about him...

'What does he do?' Lilli frowned; chairman of a bank didn't tell her anything.

'I just told you.' Sally laughed. 'He makes millions.'

'And then gives them away to ex-wives,' Lilli scorned; that didn't sound very intelligent to her!

'One ex-wife,' Sally corrected her. 'And he didn't give it away. It was probably worth it to him to get that embarrassment out of his life. Sanchia liked men, and made no secret of the fact...'

'She sounds a lot like his sister,' Lilli said bitterly. How could her father have been so stupid as to have got mixed up with such a family?

'Gerry's okay,' Sally said grudgingly. 'Although Patrick is even better,' she added suggestively.

Lilli gave her a guarded look. 'Sally, you haven't— You and he haven't—'

'I should be so lucky!' Sally laughed again ruefully. 'But Patrick doesn't. Not any more. Not since Sanchia,' she amended wistfully.

Lilli hoped she succeeded in hiding the shock she felt at this last statement. Because Patrick most certainly did! At least, he had last night. With her...

Sally gave her a considering look. 'You do realise I'm

going to have a few questions of my own at the end of this conversation?' she teased. 'And the first one is going to be, just when and where did you get to meet Patrick? As far as I'm aware, he's lived in New York for the last five years, and he's very rarely seen over here.'

Lilli kept her expression deliberately bland. 'Hey, I'm the one buying you dinner, remember,' she reminded her. She liked Sally very much, found her great fun to go out with, but she was also aware that her friend was the biggest gossip in London—that was the reason she had been the perfect choice for this conversation in the first place! 'Besides, just what makes you think I have met him?' She opened widely innocent eyes.

Sally gave a throaty chuckle, attracting the attention of several of the men at adjoining tables. Not that she seemed in the least concerned by this male interest; she was still looking thoughtfully at Lilli. 'Only a woman who had actually met Patrick would show this much interest in him; he's a presence to be reckoned with!'

Well, from all accounts—his account!—Lilli had met that challenge all too capably. 'I'm more interested in the business side of his life than his personal one.' Now that she had assured herself he wasn't married or seriously involved with anyone!

Sally shrugged. 'I've just told you he's based in New York. Chairman of Paradise Bank. Rich as Croesus. What else is there to know?'

His business connection to her father! 'English business interests?' she prompted skilfully.

'Oh, that one's easy,' the other woman returned. 'It was all in the newspapers a couple of months ago.' She smiled warmly at the waiter as he brought their main course.

Lilli barely stopped herself grinding her teeth together

in frustration. What had been in the newspapers months ago? 'I was a little out of touch with things at the time,' she reminded Sally once they were alone again.

'I'm sorry, of course you were.' Sally at once looked contrite. 'Paradise Bank took over Cleveley Bank.'

Cleveley Bank… Her father's bank. But that still didn't make a lot of sense to Lilli. Bennett International Hotels had shown a profit since before she was born, so it couldn't possibly have anything to do with them.

'Personally, I thought it was wonderful news.' Sally grinned across at Lilli as she gave her a puzzled glance. 'It means Patrick will probably start spending more time in England. More chance for us eager women to make a play at being the second Mrs Patrick Devlin,' she explained. 'I could quite easily give up this round of parties and the bachelor-girl life if I had Patrick coming home to me every evening!'

'It wasn't enough for the first Mrs Devlin,' Lilli said sharply as she realised she was actually jealous of Sally's undoubted interest in Patrick. Ridiculous! The man was arrogant, insulting, dangerous. And she had spent last night in his arms…

'Sanchia was stupid,' Sally rejoined unhesitatingly. 'She thought Patrick was so besotted with her that he would forgive her little indiscretions with other men.' Sally shook her head disgustedly. 'What Patrick owns, he owns exclusively.'

Exactly what Lilli had thought earlier! 'Not even Patrick Devlin can own people,' she said quickly.

'You have met him!' Sally said speculatively.

She could feel the guilty colour in her cheeks. 'Perhaps,' she acknowledged grudgingly. Obviously Patrick hadn't spent any time at the party last night, otherwise Sally would have seen him there too…

'But you're not telling, hmm?' Sally said knowingly. 'Oh, don't worry, Lilli.' She lightly touched Lilli's arm. 'I wouldn't be telling anyone about it either if I had Patrick tucked away in my pocket. But you will invite me to the wedding, won't you?'

Lilli drew back in shocked revulsion at the very suggestion. 'I think you've misunderstood my interest, Sally—'

'Not in the least.' The other woman gave her a conspiratorial wink. 'And if you have him, Lilli, hang onto him. There are dozens of women out there—including me!—who would snap him up given the chance!'

'But—'

'I won't tell a soul, Lilli,' Sally assured her softly. 'It will be our little secret.'

Perhaps her choice of informant hadn't been such a wise one, after all. Lilli had forgotten, in her need to know more about Patrick Devlin, just how much Sally loved what she considered a tasty piece of gossip—and how she loved sharing it with other people, despite what she might have just said to the contrary! The news of Lilli's interest in Patrick Devlin would be all over London by tomorrow if she didn't think of some way to avert it!

Her only hope seemed to be to give the other woman such a good time she wouldn't remember where they had spent the evening, let alone what they had talked about at the beginning of it—least of all Patrick Devlin.

A bottle of champagne later and Lilli wasn't sure what they had talked about either! Sally's suggestion that they go on to a club seemed an excellent idea. The restaurant staff seemed quite happy to see their last customers leave too, ordering a taxi to take them on to the club.

'I know I'm going to regret this some time tomorrow

when I finally wake up,' Sally giggled as they got out
of the taxi outside the club. 'But what the hell!'

Lilli's sentiments exactly. It seemed like years, not
just months, since she had been out and enjoyed herself
like this. Last night certainly didn't count!

She was enjoying herself, couldn't remember when
she had had so much fun, dancing, chatting with friends
she hadn't seen for such a long time, once again the life
and soul of the party, as she always used to be.

'Well, if it isn't Just Lilli, come out to play once
again,' drawled an all-too-familiar voice close behind
her. 'It's our dance, I believe,' Patrick Devlin added
forcefully—and before Lilli could so much as utter a
protest she found herself on the dance floor with him.

And it wasn't one of the fast numbers she had danced
to earlier, the evening was now mellowing out into early
morning, and so was the music. Lilli found herself firmly
moulded against Patrick's chest and thighs, his arms
about her waist not ungentle, but unyielding nonetheless.

And Lilli knew, because she tried to move, pulling
back to look up at him with furious green eyes. 'Let me
go,' she ordered between gritted teeth.

God knew what Sally was going to make of this after
their earlier conversation! Not that Lilli could be in the
least responsible for this meeting; she hadn't even realised he was at the club, certainly hadn't seen him
amongst the crowd of people here. But he had obviously
seen her!

For all that she was tall herself, the high heels on her
shoes making her even more so, she still had to tilt her
head to look up into his face. 'I said—'

'I heard you,' he returned unconcernedly, continuing
to move slowly in rhythm to the music, his warm breath
stirring the loose tendrils of hair at her temples.

She glared up at him. 'I thought you didn't like parties,' she said accusingly. He had no right being here, spoiling her evening once again.

He glanced down at her. 'This isn't a party,' he dismissed easily. 'But you're right—I don't particularly like noisy clubs like this one. I came here to conclude a business deal.'

Business! She should have known he had a calculated reason for being here. 'Like last night,' she said waspishly.

His mouth tightened. 'Last night I expected a quiet dinner party with my sister, with perhaps a dozen or so other guests. Not including your father,' he bit out tersely. 'Or that madhouse I walked into—and as quickly walked out of again! To the kitchen, as it happens. Which was where I met you.'

Lilli stiffened in his arms. 'Earlier today you seemed to have the impression that *I* had deliberately found *you*,' she reminded him.

He shrugged unconcernedly. 'Earlier today I was talking to the haughty Elizabeth Bennett. Tonight you're Just Lilli again.' He looked down at her admiringly. 'I like your hair loose like this.' He ran one of his hands through her long, silky black tresses. 'And as for this dress…!' His eyes darkened in colour as he looked down at the figure-hugging black dress.

All Lilli could think of at that moment was that they were attracting too much attention. Obviously Patrick was well known by quite a lot of the people here, and the speculation in the room about the two of them was tangible. Especially as Sally was in the midst of one particular crowd, chatting away feverishly, Lilli sure their 'little secret' was no longer any such thing!

'I wouldn't worry about them if I were you,' Patrick

followed her gaze—and, it seemed, her dismayed thoughts. 'Gossip, true or false, is what keeps most of them going. It's probably because they lead such boring lives themselves,' he added scornfully.

She knew he was right; it was one of the aspects of being part of a 'crowd' that she hadn't liked. But, even so, she wasn't sure she particularly liked being the subject—along with Patrick Devlin—of that gossip, either.

Patrick made no effort to leave the dance floor as one song ended and another began, continuing to guide her smoothly around. 'Forget about them, Lilli,' he suggested as she still frowned.

She would have liked to, but unfortunately she had a feeling that by tomorrow half of London would believe she was involved in an affair with Patrick Devlin. And the other half wouldn't give a damn whom she was involved with—because they had never heard of her or Patrick!

'Lilli and Elizabeth Bennett are one and the same person.' She coldly answered his earlier remark.

'No, they aren't. Just Lilli is warm and giving, fun to be with. Elizabeth Bennett is as cold as ice.' He looked down at her with mocking grey eyes. 'I'm curious; which one were you with your ex-fiancé?'

How did he—? Not a single person she had met this evening had so much as mentioned Andy, let alone their broken engagement. Surely Patrick hadn't done the same as her—spent part of the day finding out more about her...?

If so, *why* had he?

'Don't bother to answer that, Lilli; I think I can guess.' Patrick grinned. 'If you had been Just Lilli with him then he would probably still be around—despite his other interests.'

Lilli deeply resented his even talking about her broken engagement. She had been deeply distressed by her mother's death, and then for Andy to walk out on her too…! It had seemed like a nightmare at the time.

She had just started to feel she was coming out of it when she had been plunged into another one—with the name of Patrick Devlin!

'Just Lilli is a pretty potent woman, you know.' Patrick's arms tightened about her as he moulded her even closer against his body, showing her all too forcibly just how 'potent' he found her! 'In fact, I haven't been able to get her out of my mind all day.'

She swallowed hard, not immune herself to the intimacy of the situation, her nipples firm and tingling, her thighs aching warmly. 'And Elizabeth Bennett?' she prompted huskily.

'A spoilt little rich girl who needs her bottom spanked,' he replied unhesitatingly.

Lilli gasped. How dared he—? Just who did he think he was, suddenly appearing in her life, and then proceeding to arrogantly—?

'And if I had been her fiancé that's exactly what I would have done,' he continued unconcernedly.

They were still dancing slowly to the music, the room still as noisy and crowded, and yet at the moment they could have been the only two people in the room, their gazes locked in silent battle, grey eyes calmly challenging, green eyes spitting fire.

Finally Lilli was the one to break that deadlock as she pulled away from him, ending the dance abruptly, the two of them simply standing on the dance floor now. 'I would never have agreed to marry you in the first place,' she told him insultingly.

Patrick shrugged, totally unmoved by her anger. 'But you will, Lilli,' he said softly. 'I guarantee that you will.'

'I—you— Never!' She spluttered her indignation. 'You're mad!' She shook her head incredulously.

'But not, thank God, about you,' he said calmly. 'I've been there, and done that. And I've realised that loving the person you marry is a recipe for disaster. I've found qualities in you that are infinitely more preferable.'

'Such as?' she challenged. She still couldn't believe they were having this conversation!

'Loyalty, for one. A true sense of family.' He shrugged. 'And, of course, I find you very desirable.' This last was added, it seemed, as an afterthought.

Loyalty? A sense of family! Desire! They weren't reasons for marrying someone—

She was *not* going to marry Patrick Devlin!

He was mad. Completely. Utterly insane!

His mouth quirked with amusement as he saw those emotions flashing across her expressive face. 'A month, Lilli,' he told her softly. 'You will be my wife within the month.'

Lilli looked up at him frowningly; his gaze was enigmatic now. He sounded so sure of himself, so calmly certain...

She was not going to marry him.

She was not!

CHAPTER FOUR

'HE WHAT?' her father gasped as he once again sat across the breakfast table from her.

Lilli sighed, still slightly shell-shocked about last night herself. She had walked away from Patrick, and the club, after his ridiculous claim, still had trouble even now believing he could possibly have said what he did. But the bouquet of red roses, delivered early this morning, told her that Patrick had indeed stated last night that he intended marrying her.

Her father had been intrigued by the delivery of the roses when he'd joined her for breakfast, especially since there was no accompanying card with the flowers to say who they were from. But Lilli had no doubts who had sent them; only someone as arrogant as Patrick Devlin could have red roses delivered before the shops were even open!

'Your business associate, Mr Devlin, has decided he wants to marry me,' she repeated wearily, pushing her scrambled eggs distractedly about her plate. She couldn't possibly eat anything after the delivery of the roses!

Her father had lost interest in his bacon and eggs too now. 'What the hell did you do to him the other night?'

Lilli could feel the blush in her cheeks. She couldn't remember being with Patrick Devlin the night before last; she only wished she could. Well...part of her wished she could. The other part of her just wished it had never happened at all. Because Patrick wasn't going to let her forget it, that was for sure!

'I don't think his marriage proposal has anything to do with that,' she dismissed hurriedly.

Or did it? After all, he *had* said she was a ten...

Her father looked at her through narrowed lids. 'What does it have to do with, then?'

Lilli met his gaze steadily. 'You tell me?' She arched questioning brows.

'I have no idea.' Her father stood up, obviously having trouble coming to terms with this strange turn of events. *He* was having trouble coming to terms with it? *She* found it totally incredible.

'Why ever does he want to marry you?' Her father scowled darkly.

'Having already "had" me?' Lilli returned dryly.

'I didn't mean that at all!' Her father looked flustered. Dressed in a dark suit and formal tie and shirt, he was on his way to his office. Although he seemed in no hurry to get there... 'The two of you barely know— The two of you only met two days ago,' he hastily corrected as Lilli's expression clearly questioned his initial choice of words.

'Oh, don't imagine this proposal is based on love,' Lilli assured him. '"Loyalty" and "desire" were the words Patrick used.'

'Loyalty and—! Do you have "loyalty" and "desire" for him?' her father said incredulously.

She didn't even know the man!

Patrick Devlin was obviously a successful businessman, so she supposed he was to be admired for that, but whether or not he was an honest one was another matter. If her father's state of anxiety at being involved in business with him was anything to go by, then he probably wasn't.

As for desire... She supposed she must have wanted him the other night...

If she were honest, she had felt a stirring of that attraction towards him last night as well—

'The whole thing is ridiculous!' She stood up abruptly too. 'The man has obviously tried marrying for love, and it was not a success, so now he seems to have decided to marry for totally different reasons.' Loyalty and desire...

Her father shook his head. 'Why does he want to marry at all?'

'It's time I provided the Devlin name with a couple of heirs,' drawled that all-too-familiar voice. The two of them turned to confront Patrick Devlin, a flustered Emily standing in the doorway behind him.

'I did ask Mr Devlin to wait, but—'

'Who knows?' Patrick continued softly. 'After the other night, perhaps Lilli is already pregnant with my child.'

Lilli gasped, her father went pale—and poor Emily looked as if she was about to faint!

Which wasn't surprising, in the circumstances. How dared Patrick Devlin just walk in here as if he owned the place? And make such outrageous remarks too!

Lilli turned dismissively to the young maid. 'That will be all, thank you, Emily.' She had no intention of giving the young girl any more information for gossip among the household staff.

'Perhaps you could bring us all a fresh pot of coffee?' Patrick Devlin smiled disarmingly at Emily before she could make good her escape. 'I'm sure we could all do with some,' he added dryly as he sat down—uninvited—at the dining-table.

Emily hesitated in the doorway, looking uncertainly

at Lilli. Patrick Devlin might be behaving as if he owned the place, but Emily, at least, knew that he didn't!

'A pot of coffee will be fine, Emily,' Lilli said, waiting for the maid to leave and close the door behind her before turning to Patrick Devlin. 'What are you doing here?' she demanded, this man, with his arrogant behaviour, didn't deserve customary politeness!

He met her question unconcernedly. 'Waiting for fresh coffee to arrive,' he replied easily. 'Good morning, Richard. Has Lilli told you our good news?'

'If you're referring to that ridiculous marriage proposal,' her father blustered, 'then—'

'It isn't ridiculous, Richard,' Patrick cut in steadily. 'Ah, I see the roses arrived,' he said with satisfaction. 'I hope you like red roses?' He smiled across at Lilli.

There probably wasn't a woman alive who didn't, especially if you happened to be the lucky woman who received them. But in this case it depended who the sender was!

'You can't marry Lilli,' her father told the other man fiercely.

'Why not?' Patrick returned lightly. 'She isn't married already, is she?'

'No, of course not,' her father denied impatiently. 'But you—'

'I'm not married, either,' Patrick told him firmly. 'In which case, I can see no obstacle to our marrying each other.'

'But you don't know each other—'

'I know Lilli is beautiful. Popular—if last night is anything to go by. Well educated. And, as your daughter, an accomplished hostess. There's no doubting she's young, and she certainly seems healthy enough—'

'To provide you with those Devlin heirs you mentioned?' Lilli broke in disgustedly. 'You sound as if you're discussing buying a horse, or—or arranging a business contract, not considering taking a wife!'

'Marriage is a business, Lilli,' Patrick told her evenly, eyes coldly unmoving. 'And anyone who approaches it from any other angle is just asking for trouble. Not that it will be all business, of course,' he continued smoothly. 'I'm well aware of the fact that women like a little romance attached to things. I'm quite willing to play my role in that department too. If you think it necessary.' His derisive expression was indicative of his own feelings on the subject.

'Hence the sending of the roses,' Lilli guessed scornfully.

'Hence the roses.' He nodded in acknowledgement. 'Ah, coffee.' He turned to Emily as she came in carrying the steaming pot. 'Thank you.' He nodded to her, looking back at Lilli and her father once they were alone again. 'Shall I pour? Although you look as if you're on your way to your office, Richard, so perhaps you don't want another cup of coffee?' He quirked dark brows.

This man's arrogance was like nothing Lilli had ever encountered before; he had already taken over the staff, and now he appeared to be telling her father what to do too!

'Sit down and have some coffee, Daddy.' Lilli looked at Patrick pointedly as she resumed her own seat at the table—on the opposite side to him. 'I'm sure Patrick won't be staying very long.' She looked challengingly at the younger man.

'Oh, I'm in no hurry to leave,' Patrick replied, completely unperturbed by the fact that he obviously wasn't welcome here. 'I have nothing to do today until my business appointment with you this afternoon, Richard.' He

looked across at the older man. 'You did ask my secretary for a three o'clock appointment, didn't you?' he
queried pleasantly, pouring the three cups of coffee as
he spoke.

Her father sat down abruptly. 'I did,' he confirmed
gruffly.

'Good.' Patrick grinned his satisfaction. 'That means
I'll have time to take Lilli to lunch first.'

'I—'

'You have to eat, Lilli.' Patrick gently forestalled her
refusal.

'Not with you, I don't,' she told him heatedly; he
wasn't being polite, so why should she be?

'What do you think, Richard?' He looked at Lilli's
father. 'Don't you think Lilli would enjoy having lunch
with me?'

Richard Bennett looked frustrated once again. 'I—'

'As my father won't be the one having lunch with
you, his opinion on the subject is irrelevant!' Lilli
snapped frostily.

Patrick raised dark brows at her vehemence. 'There
speaks Miss Bennett,' he drawled, his expression innocent.

Too damned innocent! Lilli remembered all too well
what his opinion of Elizabeth Bennett was!

'Mm, this is good coffee,' Patrick said appreciatively
as he sipped the hot brew. 'I think I must have drunk
too much champagne last night,' he opined ruefully.

Lilli glared at him. 'Is that your excuse for your outrageous announcement last night?' she said contemptuously.

'Do I take it you're referring to my marriage proposal?' He frowned.

'Of course.'

'Sorry for the confusion, but I don't consider it an "outrageous announcement",' he returned. 'Especially as I've made it again this morning. Several times,' he added in a bored voice.

'And I have dismissed it as ludicrous—several times!' Lilli told him with feeling.

'You know, Richard…' Patrick looked calmly across the table. 'You really should have taken Lilli in hand years ago—you've made the job of becoming her husband all the more difficult by not doing so!'

Lilli was so enraged by this last casually condemning remark about her independent nature that for a moment she couldn't even speak.

And her father laughed!

Considering he hadn't done so for some time, it was good to hear—but not at her expense! There was nothing in the least funny about this situation.

Her father looked a little shamefaced, sobering slowly. 'I'm sorry, Lilli.' He touched her hand in apology. 'It was just that—well—'

'He knows I'm right,' Patrick put in. 'Although I'm probably the first person brave enough to actually say as much.'

She had realised the first night she met him that he was very direct, but she hadn't known it was to the point of rudeness. What on earth had she been thinking of two nights ago, becoming involved with such a man? The trouble was, she hadn't been thinking at all, had just wanted to hit out and hurt, the way she had been hurt when she saw her father with Geraldine Simms.

How that had rebounded on her! Spending the night with Patrick had changed nothing—except that the man now seemed to think he was going to marry her! Oh, she had hurt her father, but he was still seeing Geraldine, and now she, it seemed, was stuck with the infuriating Patrick Devlin!

'Although I can quite easily see how it happened, Richard.' Patrick continued his conversation with her father. 'Lilli is the sort of woman you want to spoil.'

'Thank you.' Laughter still gleamed in her father's eyes. 'She was incredibly endearing as a little girl.'

'I can imagine.' Patrick nodded, turning back to Lilli. 'Make sure you stop me from spoiling our daughters, Lilli, because they're sure to look like you, and—'

'Daughters!' She gasped at the plural. 'How many children do you want?'

'You see, I knew you would come round.' Patrick grinned at her approvingly. 'I would like you to be mother to two sons and two daughters.'

Four children. 'You said "a couple of heirs" earlier,' she reminded him.

He shrugged. 'Four sounds a much better number. Besides, I'm sure you'll look even more beautiful when you're pregnant than you do now, so I'll—'

Her father stood up noisily, effectively cutting off the indignant reply he could see Lilli had been about to make. 'I'll leave the two of you to continue discussing this,' he said. 'And the outcome, as I've told you before—' he turned to Patrick with narrowed eyes '—will have no bearing whatsoever on our—business arrangement.'

'Agreed,' the other man conceded easily. 'Although, as your son-in-law, I could be more helpful to you...'

'I don't think so,' Lilli's father replied slowly, giving Lilli a considering look. 'As my son-in-law, you're likely to end up with a knife sticking in your back on your wedding night!'

Patrick's mouth twisted humorously. 'All the more

reason for you to encourage the marriage, I would have thought,' he drawled.

'Ah, but then I would have to explain to Gerry how I let this happen to the older brother she so obviously adores. And, as I know to my cost,' Richard dramatically added, 'an angry and upset Gerry is a force to be reckoned with!'

'But you have no personal objections to this marriage?' Patrick prompted.

'None at all—because it will never happen,' Lilli's father returned easily. 'I know my Lilli.' He kissed her lightly on the forehead in parting. 'I'll see you later, Devlin,' he said hardly before leaving the room.

Patrick turned back to Lilli with calm grey eyes. '*Does* he know you?' he asked. 'Did he really believe you could go off and spend the night with a man you had only just met?'

She could too easily recall the pained expression on her father's face yesterday morning. No, her father hadn't believed her capable of that. But then, neither had she!

Her head went back in haughty dismissal. 'No one has to spend a lifetime paying for the mistake of one night of stupidity any more.'

'Don't they?' Patrick said softly, standing up to move round the table to stand at her side. 'The other night wasn't stupid, Lilli,' he told her huskily as he pulled her easily to her feet to stand in front of him. 'I wouldn't still have it on my mind if it had been. You were warm and responsive, gave yourself—'

'Stop it!' she cut in desperately, not wanting to hear about what she couldn't even remember. Or did she...

Even as he spoke she had images flitting in and out of her head, of the two of them in bed together, of their bodies entwined, of Patrick's lips and hands on her body, of her own pleasure in those caresses—

No! She didn't want to remember. It had been a mistake, and not one for which she intended paying for the rest of her life.

'But you were, Lilli,' Patrick told her, suddenly very close. 'And you did.'

He was too close! She could smell his aftershave, see black specks amongst the grey in his irises, feel the warmth of his breath on her cheek, knew—

His mouth, as it claimed hers, was warm and gently caressing, his arms enfolding her against the hardness of his body, moulding her to each sinewed curve, deepening the kiss, desire and wanting suddenly taking over.

Lilli felt the same need, her body responding instinctively to the caress of his hands down her spine, shivers of delight coursing through her body, her mouth opening to the intimacy of his kiss, a feeling of hard possession sweeping over her.

It was the force of that feeling that made her at last struggle to be free of his arms. Yes, she responded to him. Yes, she could feel the heat in her body for him, for the need of him. But she didn't want to be possessed, by him or any other man. Especially not by Patrick Devlin!

Patrick felt her struggles and at once released her, his eyes dark with his own emotions as he looked at her. 'It would work between us, Lilli,' he whispered. 'What further proof do you want?'

Heated colour warmed her cheeks. 'Physically we—'

'Match completely,' he completed for her.

Lilli looked at him. 'We have a certain response to each other,' she allowed. 'But when you came here yesterday afternoon you believed I had spent the night with you for devious reasons of my own—reasons I'm still not fully sure of. Although I do know they involve my father, in some way.' She frowned. 'Last night when we met, your attitude towards me had changed yet again. For some reason you announced you wanted to marry me!' She shook her head, not acknowledging for the moment the fact that she had needed to see him again, anyway. His arrogant announcement about marrying her had made null and void any intention she might have had of asking him for the truth about his business dealings with her father. She would rather never know the truth about that than have to be nice to this man! 'You're inconsistent, as well as—'

'Not in the least, Lilli,' he interrupted smoothly, his eyes coolly grey once more. 'The things you just spoke of are the very reasons why I've realised you will make me an excellent wife.'

She became very still. 'I don't see how...'

'I'm under no illusions where you're concerned, Lilli,' he explained. 'I even respect the fact that you tried to help your father—'

'By—as you think—going to bed with you!' Her eyes glittered deeply green at the accusation.

He shrugged. 'By whatever means were at your disposal,' he countered. 'It shows loyalty to your father. And loyalty, if not love, is something to be admired in a wife. My wife,' he added softly.

That word again! She was not going to be his wife, no matter what warped logic he might have used to come to that decision. 'That's no guarantee I would be loyal to you,' she pointed out spiritedly. 'Why should I be? You're arrogant, domineering—'

'So are you,' he mocked in reply.

'And you seem to have some sort of hold over my

father that no one will explain to me!' The last was said almost questioningly.

Patrick's mouth tightened. 'I agree with your father: business is business. Haven't I just explained that these two things are completely separate?'

'You don't "explain" things, Patrick,' she sighed. 'You simply make statements, and expect them to happen!'

He grinned. 'I think that's the first time you've called me Patrick. Plenty of other things, to my face, and otherwise, I suspect.' His grin widened to a smile. 'But never Patrick before.'

'It's your name. But you can be assured I'll never call you husband!' she said vehemently.

He seemed unconcerned. 'Never say never, Lilli. Stranger things have happened. I always said I would never marry again, but you see how wrong I was,' he reasoned patiently.

This man was so exasperating; she was going to scream in a minute! No wonder her father was having problems conducting business with him; he didn't listen to what anyone else had to say. About anything!

She gave an impatient shake of her head. 'Wasn't your first experience at marriage bad enough?' she challenged—and then wished she hadn't as his face darkened ominously. It was obviously still a sensitive subject... And it was also the reason he had no intention of marrying for love... She couldn't help wondering what the beautiful Sanchia had been like as a person, to have created such bitterness in a man as self-assured as Patrick...

'And what do you know of my first marriage?' he said softly—too softly. 'You would have been thirteen when

I married, and sixteen when I divorced—in neither case old enough to be part of that scene.'

Lilli raised her eyebrows. 'You obviously continue to have gossip value, because people are still talking about it!'

'Indeed?' Patrick's voice became frostier. 'And what are these "people" saying about my marriage?'

She looked at him warily; obviously, despite his comment last night about the social gossips, he didn't like the thought that his own life might have been under discussion. 'Only that it didn't work out,' she answered evasively.

He met her gaze compellingly. 'And?'

'What else is there to say?' she said quickly, feeling decidedly uncomfortable now. She wished she had never mentioned his marriage! But she wouldn't have done so if he hadn't come out with that ridiculous statement about marrying her... 'A failed marriage, for whatever reason, is surely a good enough reason not to repeat the experience?'

Patrick gave an assenting nod of his head. 'As is a failed engagement,' he rejoined pointedly.

Lilli felt the heat of resentment in her cheeks. 'Now that isn't open for discussion,' she said sharply.

'Why not?' he taunted. 'The man was a fool. Given the same choices he was, I would have opted for the money *and* you. Although, for my own sake, I'm glad that he didn't.'

Lilli stared at him in frozen fascination. What was he talking about? She and Andy had been engaged for six months when he decided he no longer wanted to marry her, and that in the circumstances he couldn't continue to work for her father, either. It had been a terrible blow at the time, happening, as it did, at the same time as her mother's death. But she had got on with her life, hadn't even seen Andy since the day he broke their engagement. In fact, she had no idea where he was now. And she wasn't interested, either.

Although the comments Patrick had just made about him were rather curious...

'Would you?' she said. 'But then, you're rich in your own right.'

'True,' Patrick conceded dryly. 'Now isn't that a better prospect in a husband than a man who's only interested in embezzling money from your father so that he can go off with his male lover?'

Lilli's stare became even more fixed. He *was* talking about Andy. She knew he was.

Could what he said possibly be true? Had Andy stolen money from her father? Before leaving with *another man*...?

Andy had joined the company as her father's assistant two years ago, a tall blond Adonis, with a charm to match—a charm Lilli, having become disenchanted with the 'let's go to bed' attitude of the men in her social set, had found very refreshing.

She had enjoyed his company too, often finding excuses to visit her father at his office, on the off chance she might bump into Andy there. More often than not, she had, although it had been a few months before he'd so much as invited her to join him for lunch. Over that lunch Lilli had found he was not only incredibly handsome, but also very intelligent, enjoying the verbal challenge of him as well as the physical one.

Looking back, she supposed she had done most of the chasing, but she'd realised it must be awkward for him as she was the boss's daughter. She had followed up that initial lunch with an invitation of her own, so that she might return the hospitality, suggesting the two of them go out to dinner this time. Again Andy had been fun, a witty conversationalist, and again he had behaved like the perfect gentleman when it came time for them to part.

Lilli had been persistent in her interest in him, and after that they'd had dinner together often. That her father approved of the relationship she hadn't doubted; in fact, he'd seemed deeply relieved she was spending so much time with his assistant and less time with her group of friends who seemed to do nothing but party.

Lilli had been thrilled when Andy had asked her to marry him, and if she had been a little disappointed in his continued lack of ardour after their engagement she had accepted that it was out of respect for her, and could ultimately only bode well for their future marriage.

But now Patrick seemed to be saying something else completely, was implying that Andy's lack of physical interest in her hadn't stemmed from respect for her at all, but from the fact that his sexual inclinations lay elsewhere!

He also seemed to be saying that Andy's engagement to her had enabled him to steal from her father's company...

Admittedly, as her father's future son-in-law, Andy had been given more responsibility in the company, and as Lilli's mother's illness had deteriorated Andy had been left more and more in charge of things while her father spent time at home.

Had Andy used that trust in him to take the opportunity to steal from Bennett Hotels?

As she looked at Patrick, the certainty in his gaze, that contemptuous twist to his lips, she knew that was exactly what Andy had done. He had used her to cheat her father...!

The blackness was only on the outer edge of her consciousness at first, and then it seemed to fill her whole being. Darkness. No light. Her legs buckled beneath her as she crumpled to the carpeted floor.

CHAPTER FIVE

LILLIE couldn't focus properly when she opened her eyes, but she did know enough to realise she was no longer on the floor of the dining-room, that someone—and that someone had to be Patrick Devlin!—had carried her through to the adjoining sitting-room and had laid her on the sofa there.

'My God, woman,' he rasped from nearby. 'Don't ever give me a scare like that again!'

He sounded angry—but then, he sounded like that a lot of the time!

What had she—? Why—?

Their conversation suddenly came flooding back in a sickening rush. Andy. Her father. The money...!

She moved to sit up, only to find herself pushed firmly back down once more.

'You aren't moving until I'm sure you aren't going to fall down again!' Patrick ordered as he bent over her, scowling darkly.

His expression alone was enough to make her want to shut her eyes and black out the world again, but even as she wished for that to happen she knew that the terrible truth would still be there when she was conscious again.

'Who else knows?' Her voice was barely audible. 'About Andy, I mean. The money. And—and the other man.' Her fiancé hadn't just walked out on her, which she had thought was bad enough—he had actually gone with another man!

Had the friends she'd spent the last two evenings with

known about that? Had they all been laughing, or pitying her, behind her back? Had they all known that Andy's only reason for being with her at all was so that he had easier access to the Bennett funds? She didn't want to face any of them ever again if that were the case!

'I believe your father has managed to keep all of it in the family.' Patrick's mouth twisted wryly as he moved away from her. 'Besides, I'm more interested in the fact that you obviously didn't know. Not until I just told you. Did you?'

She drew in a shaky breath, sitting up, feeling at too much of a disadvantage lying supine on the sofa. She was at too much of a disadvantage with this man already! 'Obviously not,' she managed coolly. 'Who told you about—about Andy?'

'Gerry,' he said quietly. 'Yesterday. In an effort to warn me off you.'

'Which obviously didn't work,' Lilli returned, their conversation giving her the time she needed to collect her thoughts together—and God knew they had fragmented after Patrick's earlier revelation.

'Obviously not.' Patrick grinned. 'You didn't seem exactly heartbroken to me about the loss of your fiancé—even before you knew the truth about him!'

Too much had happened at that time for her to dwell on Andy's sudden disappearance from her life. Since her mother's death she had got through every day as it arrived; there had been no time to cry for her broken engagement. And now that she knew the truth she felt more like punching Andy on the nose than crying for him! How dared he used her in that way? How dared he abuse her father's trust in him?

She stood up, smoothing her pencil-slim black skirt down over her thighs, straightening her emerald-green cashmere sweater, before moving to stand before the mirror over the fireplace, tidying the wispy tendrils of her hair back into the neat plait that hung down her spine.

She could sense Patrick watching her as she smoothed her hair, could have seen his reflection in the mirror if she had chosen to turn her head slightly—but she didn't.

He and his sister were not 'family', even if her father was involved in an affair with Geraldine, even if Patrick did keep insisting he was going to marry her—and she hated the fact that her father seemed to have confided all of this to his mistress. She hated Geraldine Simms more than she had before because her father had confided in the other woman about Andy's betrayal and yet he hadn't told her!

Because now Patrick Devlin knew about it too...

'I'm afraid I'm busy for lunch today, Patrick.' She turned back to him casually.

His mouth quirked as he looked at her, his gaze mocking. 'And every other day, hmm?' he said knowingly.

Lilli calmly met his eyes. 'It is Christmas,' she shrugged.

But despite the numerous invitations she had received during the last few weeks she hadn't accepted any of them. She hadn't refused them either, had been too listless to bother with them. In view of what she had learned about Andy, she had no intention of accepting them now either. But Patrick Devlin didn't need to know that.

'I'm aware of what time of year it is,' Patrick replied. 'But I didn't think you were.' He looked around at the lack of any Christmas decorations in the room.

Neither she nor her father had felt like putting up a tree or their usual decorations this year. It would be their first Christmas without her mother, and so far neither of them had the heart for seasonal celebrations.

Although now that her father was involved with Geraldine Simms he might feel differently about that; the other woman's home had certainly been highly festooned with decorations at the party two days ago!

Lilli's mouth tightened, her eyes glacially green as she looked across at Patrick. 'We're still in mourning for my mother,' she stated flatly. Although she somehow didn't think her father was any more!

'Caroline.' Patrick nodded in acknowledgement of Lilli's mother. 'I met her several times. Before her illness curtailed her social life. She was a very beautiful woman. You look a lot like her,' he added softly.

Pain flickered in the depths of Lilli's eyes. Somehow it had never occurred to her that this man could have known her mother. Although, as he'd said, until her illness had incapacitated her a year before her death, her mother had been a familiar part of the social scene. Even her illness hadn't robbed her of her incredible beauty, the two of them often able to fool people into believing they were sisters rather than mother and daughter.

'I really do have to get on now, Patrick.' She gave a pointed look at her slender gold wristwatch.

To her chagrin he grinned across at her. 'Miss Bennett has spoken,' he taunted.

Angry colour darkened her cheeks at his continued insistence that she was two people. 'At least she's polite!' she snapped.

'To the point of coldness,' he acknowledged dryly. 'Why aren't you curious to know more about your ex-fiancée, Lilli?' His eyes were narrowed thoughtfully.

Because so much made sense now—Andy's initial reluctance to ask her out, his lack of ardour during their engagement. She didn't want to dwell on those things, felt humiliated enough already!

'My father will tell me anything I need to know,' she dismissed quickly.

Patrick gave a disgusted snort. 'He doesn't seem to have told you very much so far!'

She glared at him. 'My father is very protective of me.' She was positive that was the reason her father hadn't told her about Andy. She had been devastated by her mother's death, and to have learnt of Andy's complete betrayal at the same time would have been unbearable. In fact, the more she thought about it, the more she was sure Andy had chosen his timing for that very reason...! She had felt hurt before, but what she thought of Andy now wasn't even repeatable!

'To the point of stupidity, I now realise,' Patrick countered harshly. 'You simply have no idea.'

She swallowed hard at his accusing tone. She was beginning to realise, and she only loved her father all the more for trying to spare her further pain. Although it seemed to have caused him complications he could well have done without, including, she was sure, being at loggerheads with this man.

'The love of a parent for a child is all-forgiving,' she defended chokily, aware as she said so that it was time this 'child' stopped being cocooned and began to be of some help to her father. He had carried this heavy burden on his own for too long.

Possibly it was the reason he had become involved so quickly with someone so unsuitable as Geraldine Simms...?

In recent years, with her mother so ill, her father had begun to confide in Lilli instead when it came to business matters, but she realised that for the last few months

she had been too engrossed in her own pain to give him
the attention he had so obviously needed. Which was
why he had turned to someone outside the family for
comfort.

'And the love of a child for the parent?' Patrick
prompted softly.

Lilli gave him a sharp look. This man was too astute;
he had guessed she was thinking of her father's involvement with his sister!

'Yes,' she answered unhesitating. She didn't like her
father's involvement with Geraldine Simms, but after
what she had just learnt of her father's recent worries
she was no longer going to give him a hard time over
it. She would just have to be around to help pick up the
pieces when Geraldine tired of playing with him!

Patrick was still watching her closely. 'Do you like
children, Lilli?'

She met his gaze defensively. 'Yes—did you think I
wouldn't?' She and Andy had discussed the idea of having—

She and Andy...! How ridiculous the idea of them
having children seemed now!

Patrick shrugged. 'You didn't seem too keen earlier
when I mentioned having four—'

'I like children, would dearly like some of my own,'
Lilli interrupted firmly. 'I just don't intend for them to
be yours!'

He looked totally unconcerned by her vehemence.
'But think of the social coup you will have made by
getting me to the altar,' he mocked. 'I've made no secret
of my contempt for the institution of marriage!'

As Sally had clearly told her last night. Certainly,
walking off with the much coveted prize of Patrick
Devlin as a husband would more than compensate for

the humiliation of having had a fiancé who had left her for another man! But once all the excitement had died down she was the one who would be married to this man, and was a lifetime of his torment really worth that? At this moment in time, she didn't think so!

'Thank you for the offer—but no,' she said crisply.

He looked at her with assessing eyes. 'It won't be open for ever, you know,' he said.

She gave a wry smile. 'I never thought that it would.' She was still dazed he had asked her at all!

His mouth twisted mockingly. 'But the answer is still no?'

'Most definitely,' she agreed forcefully.

'For now,' he said.

Lilli looked at him suspiciously. She was still reeling from the shock of Andy's betrayal, couldn't even think straight yet. But she did know she didn't want to marry this man.

'I really do have things to do, Patrick,' she told him again firmly, wishing he would just leave now so that she could think.

He studied her for several seconds, and then he gave a brief nod. 'I have no doubts our paths will cross again,' he murmured huskily.

She didn't know how he could be so sure. They hadn't met at all in the previous five years. Admittedly, Patrick seemed to have lived in America for most of that time, but he had no doubt been in London on several occasions during those years, if only to see his sister, and Lilli had managed to avoid ever meeting him. The only connection she could see between them now was the business he had with her father, and her father's relationship with his sister.

'Maybe,' she returned enigmatically.

He grinned again. 'But not if you can manage to avoid it!' he guessed.

'We've managed never to meet socially before, so perhaps it would be better if we left it that way,' she told him coolly.

'For whom?' he drawled. 'Having met you, Lilli, I'm in no hurry to lose you again.'

Was he never going to leave? She did have things to do—and going to see her father was top of that list. She intended speaking to him before his meeting with Patrick later this afternoon...

'And please don't say I've never had you to lose,' Patrick went on mockingly. 'You may have chosen to have a convenient memory lapse about the other night, but, believe me, I remember all of it!' he assured her.

She clearly, to her intense mortification, remembered waking up to the sound of him singing happily in the shower yesterday morning; he certainly hadn't sounded like a man dissatisfied with his night! But she hadn't 'chosen' to forget anything; she just didn't, apart from that brief memory flash earlier, remember what had happened between them that first night.

'I'm sure you do,' she dismissed briskly. 'But at the same time I doubt you ask every woman you go to bed with to marry you!'

He raised dark brows. 'In the last five years since my divorce?' he said thoughtfully. 'I think so—yes...' He nodded.

Lilli stared at him. Oh, Sally had said he didn't get involved, but— But Patrick couldn't really be saying she was the first woman he had been to bed with since his divorce. Could he...?

Patrick smiled at her stunned expression. 'It isn't exactly a secret, Lilli. Sanchia taught me never to trust anyone. Especially a woman,' he added hardly. 'And I never have,' he ground out harshly.

She drew in a sharp breath. 'I'm a woman,' she told him shakily.

'Undoubtedly so,' he agreed, touching her lightly on one creamy cheek. 'But I don't have to trust you to marry you. As I've already said, our marriage would be a business arrangement.'

She moved abruptly back from that caressing hand. 'No doubt with a suitable pre-nuptial agreement,' she derided scornfully.

He met her gaze steadily. 'That sort of agreement is only relevant if you intend divorcing each other at some later date. I have no wish to go through another divorce. The next time I marry it will be for life.'

She couldn't break her gaze away from his! She wanted to. Desperately wanted to. But she felt as if she was drowning in the depths of those dark grey eyes. And she knew he meant every word he said...!

She tilted her head back, flicking her plait back over her shoulder. 'No love, no divorce; is that the way it works?' she challenged, wishing she sounded a little more forceful. But she was seriously shaken by the determination of his gaze.

'Exactly.'

Lilli shook her head. 'I find that very sad, Patrick.' She frowned. 'Marriage should be for love.'

'Always?'

'Always,' she echoed firmly.

His mouth twisted. 'You can still say that, after the experience you've just gone through? With your parents' marriage as another shining example of marital bliss?' He shook his head. 'There's scepticism, and then there's stupidity, Lilli, and I'm very much afraid that you—'

'That is enough!' she cried, eyes as hard as emeralds now. 'Leave my parents out of this discussion. You know nothing about them or their marriage. All you know is that my father is now involved with your sister. But it won't last.' Her lips pursed disdainfully. 'Your sister's affairs never do.'

'And your father's affairs?' he taunted.

'My father doesn't have affairs!' Her cheeks were hot with indignation, her hands clenched angrily at her sides. 'Your sister has just caught him on the rebound from my mother's death. He wouldn't have looked at her twice while my mother was alive!' she added heatedly.

Patrick looked at her pityingly. 'Is everything this black and white for you, Lilli? No shades of grey at all?'

'My father brought me up never to accept less than the best,' she told him with passion. 'And so far I never have…!'

Patrick looked at her wordlessly for several long seconds, and then he slowly shook his head. 'And I hope—sincerely hope, Lilli—that you never do,' he murmured. 'And I mean that, Lilli. I really do.'

Somehow she believed him. 'Thank you,' she accepted.

His mouth quirked. 'Now go away?'

She gave a rueful smile. 'Yes.'

He laughed softly. 'I've enjoyed knowing you, Lilli. It's certainly never been boring. See me to the door?' he prompted throatily.

She had intended doing that anyway; as he had already said, she had been brought up to be a good hostess, and telling a guest to find his own way out, no matter who he was, was not polite! Besides, after trying to get him to leave for the last twenty minutes, she wanted to make sure he had actually gone!

'Certainly,' she agreed.

Patrick chuckled as the two of them walked down the hallway to the door, grinning as Lilli turned to him questioningly. 'You're very refreshing, Lilli; as far as I'm aware, you're the first woman who couldn't wait for me to go!' he explained self-derisively.

Not such a perfect hostess, after all! 'I—'

'Have things to do,' he finished for her. 'So you've already said.'

'Several times,' she reminded him playfully, relieved they had at last reached the door.

Patrick turned to her. 'Don't say goodbye, Lilli,' he murmured as she would have spoken. 'You may wish it were, but we both know it isn't.'

She knew no such thing! There was absolutely no reason—

There was no time for further thought as Patrick bent down and kissed her!

And it wasn't a light kiss either, as he pulled her easily into his arms and moulded her body against his.

Lilli felt as if she was drowning, couldn't breathe, was aware of nothing but the possession of this man. And it was complete possession, of the mind, body, and senses.

She could only look up at him with dazed green eyes as he released her as suddenly as he had kissed her.

'No matter what you think to the contrary, neither of us can say goodbye to that, Lilli,' he told her gruffly in parting, the door closing softly behind him as he finally left.

Lilli didn't move, could hear the thunder of her own blood as it rushed around her body. She had been out with men before Andy, quite a few of them, but none of them, including Andy, had evoked the response that Patrick did. It was incredible. Unbelievable.

Dangerous…! How could she respond to a man she didn't even like very much? For there was no denying the force of electricity that filled the air whenever they were together.

Well, despite what Patrick might have claimed to the contrary, she intended them not to be together again.

'Lilli…?' Her father stood up uncertainly from behind his desk, his eyes searching as he moved to kiss her lightly on the cheek in greeting. 'I didn't expect to see you again until this evening.' He looked at her a little warily, Lilli thought.

Which wasn't surprising, considering what she had learnt from Patrick earlier. Her father had carried that knowledge around with him for months now, and, on closer inspection, he looked grey with worry. Until today Lilli had put his gauntness down to the loss of her mother, but she now realised it was so much more than that. But she had no intention of letting him worry alone any longer.

She had been lucky when she'd arrived at his office a few minutes ago, his secretary able to happily inform her he was alone, and could see her immediately. Her father didn't look quite so pleased to see her!

Lilli looked at him with wide, unblinking eyes. 'Exactly how much money did Andy take?' she said evenly. 'And what are you doing about it?'

Her father staggered, as if she had actually hit him, sitting back down in the leather chair behind his desk, his face white now, eyes as green as her own gleaming brightly.

Her own legs felt slightly shaky, she had to admit, knowing from her father's reaction to those two simple questions that Patrick had told her the truth about Andy's disappearance. And, having told her the truth about the money, he no doubt had also told her the truth about whom Andy had gone away with...!

'Oh, Daddy!' She moved around the desk to hug him. 'You should have told me,' she said emotionally.

'No prizes for guessing exactly who did,' he muttered bitterly.

She moved back slightly to look down at him, her own eyes glittering with unshed tears. 'It's irrelevant who did the telling, Daddy. And to give Patrick his due,' she added grudgingly, 'he didn't realise I didn't already know.'

Her father's smile came out as more of a grimace. 'Did he survive the telling unbruised?'

Her mouth twisted at the memory of their conversation. 'Physically, yes. Verbally—probably not.' She shrugged. 'But I'm really not interested in Patrick Devlin's feelings just now; he isn't important.'

'I'm afraid he is, Lilli,' her father sighed. 'Very much so, in fact.'

She moved to sit on the edge of his desk. 'Tell me,' she invited.

It wasn't very pretty in the telling, and for the main part her father avoided meeting her gaze. It was more or less as Lilli had worked out in her own mind; Andy had used her father's preoccupation with his wife's illness to embezzle money from the company.

'How much?' she prompted softly.

'A lot—'

'How much Daddy?' she said forcefully.

He swallowed hard. 'Several million—'

'Several million!' Lilli repeated incredulously. 'Oh, my God...!' she groaned—this was so much worse than she had thought. Her eyes widened. 'That's why Patrick is involved in this, isn't it?' she realised weakly.

Her father scowled darkly. 'He had no right telling you that part,' he rasped harshly.

'He didn't,' she assured him shakily. 'I'm not completely stupid, Daddy; I can add two and two together and come up with the correct answer of four. Andy stole money from you, Patrick is a banker, you are now having difficult business discussions with Patrick; it isn't hard to work out that the two things are connected!'

'I wish to God they weren't!' Her father stood up abruptly, his expression grim. 'The money that Andy took was made through transactions at Cleveley Bank. It had been put in a separate account, ready to pay a loan we took out just over a year ago when we expanded into Australia. The loan was due for repayment two months ago. But when I accessed the account before that I found all the funds had been redirected out of the country,' he recalled heavily, even the memory of it, Lilli could see, bringing him out in a cold sweat.

'Into an account in Andy's name,' she easily guessed.

'Yes,' her father acknowledged dully.

'And Patrick now owns Cleveley Bank,' she said flatly. 'That's why the two of you have been locked in some sort of negotiation.'

Her father nodded. 'And Devlin won't give an inch.'

'But surely if you're prosecuting Andy Patrick can't just—'

'I'm not prosecuting Andy, Lilli,' her father told her.

'What?' she cried. 'But why on earth not? If you bring a case against Andy surely the bank can't— It's because of me, isn't it?' she suddenly realised, becoming very still. 'You haven't charged Andy because you don't want to involve me in this,' she groaned, realising this was what Patrick had meant earlier about the extent of her father's protectiveness of her. Well she knew now, and she had no intention of letting this situation continue. 'Daddy, I know all about Andy, about the money, about—about the other man.' She gave a pained grimace as he looked at her worriedly. 'And when you have your meeting with Patrick this afternoon I want you to tell him you are in the process of bringing a case against Andy. There's no way he can continue to hound you in this way if you're involved in a court case to try and retrieve the money.' Even as she spoke she wasn't sure of the truth of that statement.

She wasn't really sure how her father would stand legally even if he were prosecuting Andy over the theft of the money. And from what she had gathered from Patrick's comments the night she had met him—comments she now understood completely!—his sister's pleadings on behalf of her lover hadn't moved him, so perhaps this was going to make no difference to him either. After all, her father was the one who owed the money, and it probably wasn't the business of the bank if that money had been embezzled...

Her father sighed again wearily. 'Lilli, if I bring charges against Andy, then the whole story will come out.'

'I'm aware of that.'

'And you will end up looking totally ridiculous,' he continued gravely.

Her mouth twisted wryly. 'It won't be the first time!'

'I mean seriously humiliated, Lilli.' Her father shook his head. 'Andy's sexual inclinations are of no interest to anyone at this moment, but they will make headlines when put together with his engagement to you and his embezzling money from me. You would end up a laughing-stock, Lilli, and I won't have that,' he stated determinedly.

'At any price?' she prompted softly.

His mouth tightened stubbornly. 'At any price.'

Her expression softened lovingly, her smile a little shaky. 'I appreciate what you're saying Daddy. And I thank you for your loving protectiveness. But there's really no need,' she added brightly. 'You see, I won't end up a laughing-stock at all. Because I intend marrying Patrick Devlin!'

The answer to the problem was suddenly so simple. As Patrick had said, he was a good catch as a husband—and no one could possibly laugh at her, or pity her over her engagement to Andy, when she had managed to captivate such an eligible man as Patrick Devlin.

There was also the additional fact that, although Geraldine's pleadings on her lover's behalf might have fallen on stony ground, Patrick could hardly appear callous enough to the business world as to actually hound his own father-in-law.

Her marriage to Patrick was the answer to all their problems...

CHAPTER SIX

'LILLI!' Geraldine Simms looked totally stunned as her maid showed Lilli into her sitting-room. She stood, very beautiful in slim-fitting black trousers and an even more fitted black jumper, her hair a tumble of deep red onto her shoulders and down her spine, her expression of surprise turning to one of wariness. 'What can I do for you?' she asked slowly.

Lilli steadily returned the other woman's stare, seeing Geraldine as men must see her—as her own father must see her! She was a self-assured woman of thirty-two, and there was no doubting Geraldine's beauty—almost as tall as Lilli, with that gorgeous abundance of red hair, eyes of deep blue, her face perfectly sculptured.

No wonder her father was smitten!

Lilli mouth tightened as she thought of Geraldine's relationship with her father. 'You can tell me where I might find Patrick,' she said abruptly. Contacting the man seemed to be her problem at the moment, and as her father had refused to tell her where Patrick's office was Lilli had had no choice but to come to Geraldine.

In fact, her father was proving altogether difficult at the moment where Patrick was concerned. Richard Bennett had been horrified by her announcement that she intended marrying Patrick, and had flatly refused to have any part of it when Lilli had proved stubbornly decided on the matter, to the point where he wouldn't even tell her where he was meeting with Patrick this afternoon. So, much as Lilli had wanted to avoid the other woman,

Geraldine had seemed the obvious source—was sure to know, as he was a guest in her home, where her brother was.

'Patrick?' Geraldine looked even more startled. 'Why do you want to see Patrick?'

Lilli stiffened. She hadn't relished the idea of coming here at all, wished there were some other way of contacting Patrick; she certainly didn't intend to engage in a dialogue with Geraldine! 'I believe that's between Patrick and myself,' she returned coolly. The pluses of accepting Patrick's proposal far outweighed the minuses, but at the top of the minuses was definitely the fact that this woman was his sister!

Geraldine shook her head. 'Lilli—'

'I believe Lilli said it was private between the two of us, Gerry,' Patrick interjected as he strolled into the room, wearing a dark blue business suit and white shirt now, obviously dressed for the office. 'Did you decide to accept my lunch invitation, after all?' He turned enquiringly to Lilli.

'Yes,' she agreed thankfully. She hadn't actually expected him to be here, had no intention of accepting his marriage proposal in front of his sister. She had never been so pleased to see him!

'Fine.' He took a firm hold of Lilli's arm. 'See you later, Gerry,' he added dismissively, turning Lilli firmly toward the door.

'But—'

'Later, Gerry,' Patrick repeated hardly.

Lilli released her arm from Patrick's grip as soon as they were outside, silent as he unlocked his car before opening the door for her to get inside. She was silent, because at this moment she couldn't think of anything to say. Now that she was actually face to face with

Patrick again, the enormity of what she was about to do was quite mind-boggling. How could she agree to be this man's wife, bear his children? But, by the same token, how could she not?

'Save it until we get to the restaurant.' Patrick reached out and briefly clasped her clenched hands as they lay in her lap, his eyes never wavering from the road ahead. 'I booked a table for one o'clock.'

She turned to him sharply. 'You booked...? You knew I would have lunch with you all the time?' Anger sharpened her voice.

'I—hoped that you would change your mind,' he answered carefully.

He had known she would have lunch with him after all. What else did he know...?'

Lilli gave him an assessing look before turning her head to stare rigidly out of the front windscreen. She felt as a mouse must do when being tormented by a cat— and she didn't like the feeling any more than the mouse did! This man always seemed to be one step ahead of her, and in a few short minutes she was going to agree to be his wife. What on earth was her life going to be like, married to him?

Even the restaurant he had chosen had been picked with privacy in mind, each table secluded in its own booth, the service quietly discreet as they were shown to one, Patrick obviously known here as he was greeted with obsequious politeness; Lilli, as his guest, was treated with that same solicitousness.

'Is it too early to order champagne?' Patrick asked her lightly as the waiter hovered for their drinks order.

Lilli's chin rose defiantly, she might be down, but she wasn't defeated! 'As long as it's pink,' she told him haughtily. 'I never drink any other sort of champagne.'

Patrick's mouth twisted wryly. 'I'll try to remember that.' He turned to the waiter. 'A bottle of your best pink champagne,' he ordered.

'I don't think I've ever been here before.' Lilli gave a bored look round the room once they were alone again, noting how it was impossible, from the angle at which the booths were placed, to see any of the other people dining at the adjoining tables. 'It looks like the ideal place for a man to bring his mistress without fear of them being seen together,' she added scathingly.

Patrick smiled at her description. 'I wouldn't know,' he drawled, also looking casually about them. 'But you could be right.' He turned back to her. 'The food is excellent.' He indicated she should look at the menus they had been given.

Lilli looked at him for several long seconds, until she could withstand the laughter in his eyes no longer. 'The food,' she finally conceded, looking down at her menu.

'And the company,' Patrick added softly. 'Just Lilli,' he murmured huskily.

And she had been trying so hard to be Elizabeth Bennett. Damn him!

Her mouth tightened. 'Let's just get this over—'

'The champagne, Lilli,' he cut in softly, drawing her attention to the waiter waiting to pour their bubbling wine.

She drew in a ragged breath, sitting back in her seat while the champagne was poured into their glasses. She really did just want to get this over with now, and these constant interruptions weren't helping her at all.

Patrick raised his glass in a toast as soon as their glasses were full. 'To us, Lilli,' he stated firmly. 'Or am I being a little premature?' he prompted as she made no move to pick up her own glass.

'How long have you known?' she said heavily. 'That I would marry you,' she explained as he raised questioning brows.

He shrugged. 'I told you last night as we danced, but I suppose I actually realised the merits of it after I had left you yesterday afternoon—'

'I mean, how long have you known I would marry you?' she cut in impatiently, glaring at him frustratedly.

'Oh, that.' He sipped his champagne before glancing down at his menu.

'Yes—that,' she bit out tautly. 'You really are the most arrogant, infuriating—'

'I love it when you talk to me like that.' He grinned. 'No one else does, you know. Except Gerry, and— I realise you don't even like the mention of her name.' He frowned and she flinched. 'But she is my sister, and as such will become your sister-in-law once we're married.'

Lilli met his remark coldly. 'Even so, I don't see that I have to have anything to do with her.'

'Lilli—'

'I mean it, Patrick,' she told him. 'I accept your marriage proposal—but it won't all be on your terms!'

'I never for a moment thought it would—'

'Oh, yes, you did.' Her eyes flashed deeply green. 'But you chose me because of the person I am, and that means the whole person; no matter what you think to the contrary, Lilli and Elizabeth Bennett are not two divisible people—and neither of them wants anything to do with your sister!'

'Hmm, this is difficult,' Patrick murmured thoughtfully.

'Not as difficult as trying to pretend the two of us will

ever accept each other! She's your sister. I will be your wife. The two of us—'

'I wasn't referring to that situation,' Patrick dismissed with a wave of his hand. 'I simply don't know whether to have the salmon or the pheasant for lunch.' He pursed his lips thoughtfully as he studied the menu once again.

Lilli stared at him incredulously. Did nothing trouble this man? Did he make a joke out of everything?

'No, Lilli, I don't,' he murmured softly as if reading her mind, reaching out to clasp one of her hands with his as it lay on the table-top. 'Close your mouth, my darling, and stop upsetting yourself,' he teased. 'The problem between you and Gerry will sort itself out in its own good time. You're both adult women. And I have no intention of interfering.'

Lilli wasn't incredulous any more, she was stunned. 'Darling'. He had called her his 'darling'... And as her husband he would have a perfect right to call her any endearment he pleased. He would have the right to do a lot more than that!

She hastily removed her hand from beneath his. 'I want a long engagement—'

'No,' he cut in calmly, to all intents and purposes still studying his menu.

Colour heightened her cheeks. 'I told you this isn't going to be all on your terms,' she reminded him tautly.

He gave a brief nod. 'And I agreed it wouldn't,' he said. 'But a long engagement is out of the question. With a special licence we can be married before Christmas.'

Lilli gasped. 'Before—! You can't be serious,' she protested, sitting forward. 'It's only nine days away; I can't possibly be ready to marry you between now and then!'

'Of course you can,' he assured her smoothly. 'Now

I suggest we order our meal,' he added pleasantly as the waiter approached their table. 'I have a meeting at three o'clock,' he reminded her.

His meeting was with her father. They really didn't have the time before that meeting to sort this out properly. She couldn't decide on the rest of her life in an hour and a half!

'I haven't even had a chance to read the menu yet,' she told him dully; she had looked at it, but she hadn't actually read it.

'Another few minutes,' he told the waiter pleasantly.

Lilli shook her head. 'I'm really not hungry.'

Grey eyes looked compellingly into hers. 'You have to eat, Lilli.'

She swallowed hard. 'I really don't think I can—'

'Avocado salad and the salmon,' Patrick told the waiter decisively. 'For both of us.' He turned back to Lilli once they were alone again. 'I'll agree to any other terms you care to suggest, Lilli,' he offered. 'But the timing of our marriage is not for negotiation.' His mouth tightened. 'I have no intention of your father settling his problem with Andrew Brewster—and you breaking our engagement so fast you end up bruising yourself in your speed to get my ring off your finger!' His eyes glittered coldly as he looked at her between narrowed lids.

'A 'barracuda in a city suit' was how her father had described this man—and how right he was. Breaking off the engagement was exactly what she had been hoping to do! She really didn't want to be married to this man, had hoped—oh, God, she had hoped her father would be able to solve his financial problems without her actually having to go through with marriage to Patrick Devlin.

She should have known Patrick would see straight through any ideas like that!

Her head went back proudly, her eyes glittering brightly. 'I suppose you've decided what I'm to wear for this wedding, too?'

'White, of course, Lilli.' He sipped his champagne, surveying her over the rim of his glass. 'Or are you telling me you don't have the right to wear that colour?' he challenged tauntingly.

'You can ask that, after the other night?' she scoffed.

'Our night together?'

'Of course our night together! Or doesn't it count if the bridegroom was the lover?'

Patrick looked at her thoughtfully for several long seconds. 'I think I should make one thing plain, Lilli,' he finally said. 'My first marriage, after the initial honeymoon period, was a battleground. It's not an experience I care to repeat!'

'Then why choose to marry someone you don't love and who doesn't even pretend to love you?' Lilli asked sceptically.

'Respect, Lilli. I have respect for you, for the love and loyalty you've shown towards your father—'

'A love that gives you the leverage to pressurise me into marrying you!' she accused heatedly.

His facial muscles tightened. 'I believe we both said we would keep my business with your father out of this?'

'You don't honestly think I would give marrying you a second thought if it weren't for that, do you?' She shook her head scathingly.

'It wasn't mentioned in the proposal. And I don't believe it was mentioned in the acceptance?' He raised dark brows pointedly.

'It may not have been mentioned, but—'

'Let's leave it that way, hmm?' His voice was dangerously soft now.

Lilli surveyed him mutinously, silenced by the coldness in his voice. But he couldn't seriously expect her to act as if she were in love with him? That would be asking the impossible!

She drew in a ragged breath. 'Patrick—'

'Our food, Lilli.' He sat back as the avocado was placed in front of them.

This was ridiculous. They couldn't possibly discuss something as important as the rest of their lives over lunch, with the constant interruptions that entailed. How on earth did he think—?

'Try the avocado, Lilli,' Patrick encouraged gently. 'I think we might both feel a little more—comfortable, once we've eaten something.'

She very much doubted this man knew what it was like to feel uncomfortable. But he was probably right about the food settling her ragged nerves; she hadn't eaten anything at all today. The only problem with that was that her stomach was churning so much she wasn't sure she would keep the food inside her if she ate it!

'Try it, Lilli.' Patrick held a forkful of his own avocado temptingly in front of her mouth.

She gave him a startled glance, slightly alarmed by his close proximity. But the determined look in his eyes told her he wasn't about to move away until she took the avocado from the fork he held out.

'This is ridiculous,' she muttered as she moved slightly forward to take the food into her mouth. 'Anyone would think we were a couple really in love,' she added irritably before moving back from him, picking up her own fork to eat her meal.

'Better?' He nodded his satisfaction with her compliance.

She had to admit, inwardly, that the food was indeed excellent, and it wasn't choking her as she had thought it might—but Patrick treating her as a recalcitrant child was! 'Don't treat me like a six-year-old, Patrick—'

'Then don't act like one,' he came back swiftly. 'I certainly don't want a temperamental child for a wife! Think, Lilli,' he continued hardly. 'Your father—does he know you've come to accept my proposal...?'

She swallowed. 'Yes.'

'And?'

'And what?' She frowned her tension.

Patrick's mouth twisted mockingly. 'And he's ecstatic at your choice of husband?' he taunted.

She gave a snort. 'Don't be ridiculous—'

'Exactly,' Patrick acknowledged dryly. 'As Gerry is going to be overjoyed at my choice of wife!'

Lilli stiffened. 'I'm really not interested in how your sister feels about me.'

'And your father's approval is of little importance to me, either,' he returned. 'But, if I'm correct in my assumption concerning your reasons for accepting my proposal, after all, then it's primarily to help your father, but also because once your father prosecutes Brewster the man's private life is bound to become public knowledge. But you will obviously have caught a much bigger fish on your marital hook, and so have no fear of becoming the object of the scorn or gossip that could ensue. Stop me if I'm wrong—'

'You know you aren't!' she snapped resentfully; did this man know everything? 'But exactly where is all this leading to?' she prompted impatiently.

'This is leading to the fact...' he deliberately held

another morsel of avocado temptingly in front of her, leaning intimately forward as he did so '…that our engagement, and subsequent marriage, will be more believable to everyone, including your father and my sister, if it seems that we are genuinely in love with each other.'

Lilli stared at him as if he had gone insane—because at that moment it seemed he actually might be! No one could possibly believe the two of them really loved each other, least of all her father.

'Without that belief, Lilli,' Patrick continued, 'everyone will know the whole thing is a sham—and you will end up looking more foolish than if this whole thing had become public months ago!'

He was right… Once again he was right! Why hadn't she thought of that? Because she hadn't been thinking at all, only feeling, and this marriage to Patrick had seemed to solve everything.

She swallowed hard. 'What do you suggest?'

His mouth quirked. 'That you eat this avocado; it's in danger of falling off my fork!'

She was in danger of being at the centre of the biggest social farce to become public in years!

She ate the avocado, knowing as she did so exactly what she was committing herself to. The avocado, for all Patrick was making light of it, represented something so much more than a morsel of food. It took all of her will-power to chew it and actually swallow it down.

Patrick touched her cheek gently. 'I'm willing to give this a try if you are, Lilli.'

What choice did she have? She wanted her father to do something about the money that had been taken from his company, and for that to happen the whole thing had to become public. And it would only work if she and Patrick had a believable relationship.

She drew in a ragged breath. 'I'm not sure I can,' she told him honestly.

'I'll try and make it easy for you.' He leant forward and brushed his lips against hers. 'There, that wasn't so difficult, was it?'

He was so close, his breath was lightly ruffling the hair at her temples. So close she could see the dark flecks of colour in his grey eyes. So close she could smell the elusiveness of his aftershave. So close she couldn't stop the slight trembling of her knees, the tight feeling in her chest, the disruption of her breathing.

'Not so difficult,' she admitted gruffly.

'And do you agree it will be better than people thinking we hardly know each other?' he teased.

That was the last thing she wanted! 'I agree.'

'The wedding will be next week—I thought a three out of three in the agreeing department was expecting a bit much!' He grinned as she looked panicked at the suggestion. 'It will fit in with the idea of a whirlwind romance,' he explained. 'Everyone loves a romance, Lilli—especially if it appears a love-match!'

Her stomach had given a sickening lurch at the very thought of being married to this man in only a matter of days. She swallowed hard. 'That sounds—reasonable.' What difference did it make? Patrick intended them to be married, had no intention of her dragging out their engagement in the hope she might never need to tie the knot. So she might as well get on with it!

He sat back so that their plates could be taken away—and allowed Lilli to breathe again!

This man was going to be her husband. They would live together. Patrick would come to know her body more intimately than she knew it herself. He—

She was panicking again! Take each step as it comes!

she told herself. If she looked at the whole thing she would become hysterical. Yes, that was it; she just had to take each day, each step, as it arrived. She would be fine. After all—

'Make sure you have a white dress for the wedding, Lilli.' Patrick interrupted her thoughts. 'I'm aware you've been desperately trying to forget the night we spent together, but—'

'Please,' she hastily cut in. 'That night was completely out of character. I have never done anything like that before, and—'

'And you haven't done anything like that now, either, Lilli,' Patrick dismissed mockingly.

'How can you possibly say that?' She shook her head in self-disgust. 'I—'

'You were very beautiful that night, Lilli, very alluring, and I have to admit that, for the first time in years, I was physically interested. And I would probably have been only too happy to enjoy all the pleasure you were so obviously promising. Unfortunately—' he shook his head dramatically '—the champagne and wine took their toll on you, and you fell asleep on the bed in the hotel while I was in the bathroom.'

Lilli stared at him, not sure she was hearing him correctly.

He laughed softly at her stunned expression. 'I can see you're having trouble believing me. But I can assure you it's the truth.'

'But I—I was undressed,' she protested disbelievingly. She could clearly remember her embarrassment the next morning when she'd woken up to find she was only wearing her lace panties!

He nodded. 'You most certainly were. And you have a very beautiful body. But the only reason I know that, the reason you were undressed, is because I couldn't let you spoil that beautiful gown you were wearing. You looked lovely in it, and I'd like to see you in it again one day. You were asleep, so I simply took the dress off you and settled you more comfortably beneath the bed-clothes.'

'And you—where did you sleep?' She was still reeling from the shock of realising she hadn't made love with this man at all.

But that memory flashback she had had...? She couldn't have dreamt being in his arms, being kissed by him, caressed by him—could she?

Patrick smiled. 'There was only the one double bed in the bedroom, Lilli, and I have to admit I'm not that much of a gentleman; I slept beside you, of course. And very cuddly you were too. In fact, you became quite charmingly friendly at about four o'clock in the morning,' he added wistfully. 'But there was no way I could make love to a woman who was too much asleep still to know where she was, let alone who she was with—'

'Stop it!' she cut in sharply. 'What you're saying is incredible.' She shook her head dazedly. 'How do I know you're telling the truth?' She frowned her uncertainty.

He gestured carelessly. 'What reason do I have to lie? It wouldn't do my reputation any good at all if it became public knowledge that I'd spent the whole night in bed with you and didn't even attempt to make love to you! Although, in retrospect, I can't say I'm disappointed by the fact. Unless I'm very much mistaken,' he continued at her questioning look, 'you have more right than most to wear white on your wedding day. And our wedding night will be the first time you've ever made love with any man. I feel very privileged that I'm going to be that man,' he added huskily.

This was incredible. Unbelievable...! But, as Patrick had so rightly pointed out, what reason could he possibly have for lying about it?

But until just now he had let her continue to think— Knew what she had believed had happened between them, and he hadn't disabused her of that belief.

She really had thought she had made love with this man two nights ago, had had no reason to think otherwise. And Patrick had perpetuated that belief with his remarks after that night, had known how she hated the idea of having gone to bed with him in that reckless way. He had continued to let her believe it...

Because it suited him to. Because he had enjoyed watching her discomfort over an incident she would rather forget had happened.

And she had just agreed to marry this man, to live with him, to bear his children. All four of them!

She had, she now realised, made a pact with the devil himself!

CHAPTER SEVEN

'I BELIEVE we have guests coming to dinner this evening?' Lilli's father addressed her stiffly when he came in from his office a little after six; Lilli was in the day-room pretending to be interested in a magazine.

Pretending, because she couldn't really concentrate on anything at the moment!

How she had got through the rest of the lunch with Patrick, she had no idea. She vaguely remembered him talking about trivial things through the rest of their meal, seeming unconcerned with her monosyllabic answers, putting her in a taxi at two forty-five, so that he could go to his meeting with her father. His parting comment, she now remembered, had been something about them dining together this evening, so that her father could get used to the idea of him as a son-in-law.

But, however long his meeting with her father had taken, Patrick had somehow also found the time to call a prestigious newspaper and have notice of their forth-coming marriage put in the classifieds!

Lilli knew all about this because a reporter from the newspaper had telephoned her here just over an hour ago wanting further information on their whirlwind romance. Lilli's answer to this had been, 'No comment.' But not ten minutes later Sally had also telephoned to find out if it was true; it seemed a friend of a friend also worked on the newspaper, and, knowing Sally was a friend of Lilli's, had telephoned her for information. Which Sally couldn't give, thank goodness—because she didn't know any of the details of Lilli's relationship with Patrick!

There was no doubt that Patrick was going to give her no chance for second thoughts, was making this marriage a foregone conclusion by publicly announcing it.

Not that Lilli could have had second thoughts even if she had wanted to. But, Patrick being Patrick, he had made sure that she couldn't, not without causing even more publicity for herself.

She looked up at her father with dull green eyes, noting how strained he looked, matching her own dark mood of despair. 'Guest,' she corrected flatly.

'Guests,' her father insisted as he came further into the room, moving to the tray of drinks on the side table, pouring himself a liberal amount of whisky, swallowing half of the liquid down in one needy gulp. 'Patrick is bringing Gerry with him,' he told Lilli abruptly before swallowing the remaining contents of the glass he held.

This information brought Lilli out of her mood of despondency, her eyes now sparkling angrily. 'He is not bringing that woman to this house,' she stated furiously. 'I told him earlier exactly how I felt about his sister. He knows that I—'

'Lilli, Gerry isn't only Patrick's sister, she's the woman in my life,' her father cut in carefully. 'And while you might have strong feelings about that—in fact, I'm sure you do!—I would rather not hear them.'

'But—'

'I mean it, Lilli,' he told her in a voice that brooked no further argument. 'Now, as my banker, Patrick has advised that I go ahead with bringing a case against Andy for embezzlement,' he continued without a pause. 'He also told me the two of you are to be married before Christmas!'

Lilli's anger against Geraldine Simms left her so suddenly she felt like a deflated balloon. 'If that's what Patrick says, then it must be true,' she told him dryly.

'Lilli—'

'It's what I want, Daddy.' She stood up forcefully, moving restlessly about the room, tidying objects that didn't really need tidying.

'Do you also want to go and live in New York?' he asked.

'New York...?' Lilli stopped her restless movements, staring at her father. 'Did you say New York?'

Her father nodded. 'It's where Patrick is based. His business in England is almost concluded,' he added bitterly. 'He'll be returning to New York in the New Year. And, as his wife, you will go with him.'

She had to admit, she hadn't given much thought to where they would live after their wedding; she was still having trouble coming to terms with the idea of marrying Patrick at all! But New York...! She had completely forgotten he was based in America...

'Lilli, you haven't really thought this thing through at all,' her father sighed as he saw her confused expression. 'You don't even know anyone in New York.'

Except Patrick...

'You'll be all alone over there,' her father continued quietly.

Except for Patrick...

'There will be no one there to love and take care of you,' her father added in a wavering voice.

Except Patrick...!

This was turning out to be worse than she had realised. Her father was right; she hadn't really thought it through at all, had just been looking for a solution to their immediate problems. The long term was something she hadn't really considered.

'Did Patrick tell you we would be going to New York?' she enquired.

'No, it was Gerry who thought of it—I called in to see her on my way home from the office,' he explained defensively as Lilli looked troubled.

Which explained why he was home later than usual. Geraldine had really got her claws into him, hadn't she?

'She's as worried as I am about your marriage to Patrick,' her father told her harshly.

Lilli stiffened. 'Well, thank her for her concern, but I'm quite capable of making my own decisions—and living with the consequences of them, even a move to New York.' She walked angrily to the door, wrenching it open. 'I think you underestimate my ability to adapt to living in New York. I'm sure I'll have a wonderful time. Now, if you'll excuse me, I have to go and change for dinner.' She closed the door firmly behind her.

How dared her father discuss her with that woman? How dared he?

'You look very beautiful,' Patrick told her huskily.

He had arrived at the house with his sister only minutes ago, the four of them in the sitting-room, Lilli's father busy with the dispensing of drinks, the beautiful Gerry already at his side. There was no doubt the other woman *was* beautiful, or that Lilli's father obviously thought so too—he seemed to have come quite boyishly alive in her company. Lilli hated even seeing the two of them together!

'Thank you.' She distantly accepted the compliment, very aware of the other couple in the room.

'As usual,' Patrick added softly.

Lilli turned to look at him, a contemptuous movement to her lips. 'You don't have to keep this up when it's just the two of us, Patrick!'

'But it isn't just the two of us.' He looked pointedly across the room at her father and his sister.

She drew in a ragged breath. 'My father would see straight through any effort on my part to pretend I'm in love with you.'

'Then I would advise you to try a little harder,' Patrick told her hardly. 'Unless you want to cause him even more grief! Andy Brewster was *your* fiancé, Lilli,' he callously reminded her.

As if to confirm Patrick's words, her father glanced worriedly across at the two of them, Lilli forcing a reassuring smile before turning back to Patrick. 'You don't play fair,' she told him in a muted voice.

'I don't ''play'' at all, Lilli,' he corrected her harshly. 'You should have realised that by now!'

Her eyes flashed her resentment. 'Is that the reason you've already sent the announcement of our marriage to that newspaper?'

Patrick didn't seem at all surprised at her accusation. 'I'm not even going to ask how you know about that; the London gossip grapevine must be one of the busiest in the world! But talking of our marriage...I have a present for you,' he tacked on gently.

She didn't want presents from him; she wished she didn't want anything at all from him!

'Don't look so alarmed, Lilli.' He pretended to chide her. 'This is perfectly in keeping with our new relationship. Ah, Richard, perfectly on cue with the champagne,' he greeted the other man as he held out the two glasses of bubbly pink liquid. 'I was just about to give Lilli her engagement ring.'

An engagement ring! There had been no mention of an engagement, only the wedding. She couldn't—

'We can change it if you don't like it, Lilli,' Patrick assured her as he took the small blue ring-box from his jacket pocket, flicking open the lid to show her the contents.

If she didn't like it! How could any woman not like such a ring? It was beautiful, the hugest emerald Lilli had ever seen surrounded by twelve flawless small diamonds.

Lilli had never seen a ring like it before, let alone been offered such a beautiful piece of jewellery; the ring Andy had given her on their engagement, a ring she had discarded to the back of a drawer when their engagement had ended, had been a diamond solitaire, delicate, unobtrusive. Patrick was intent on making a statement with this magnificent emerald and diamond ring. Of ownership. 'Oh, Patrick,' Gerry breathed in an awestruck voice. 'It's absolutely beautiful!'

He replied ruefully, 'I believe that should be Lilli's line.'

Maybe it would be—if she could actually speak. But all she could do was stare at the ring. It was too much. Just too much. It must have cost a small fortune!

She had been brought up within a well-off family, could never remember being denied anything she had ever wanted, but this ring, and what it must have cost, had suddenly brought home to her exactly how wealthy Patrick was. Such wealth was, in its own way, quite frightening. And she was about to marry into it!

'You don't like it,' Patrick said, his gaze narrowed on the sudden paleness of her face.

She moistened dry lips. 'It isn't that...'

'Richard, you mentioned showing me the Turner you have in the dining-room?' Geraldine prompted.

Lilli looked sharply at the other woman, her mouth tightening at the obvious ease of the relationship between this handsome woman and her own father. 'There's no need to leave Patrick and I alone, Geraldine,' she announced. 'We aren't about to have an argument.'

She had to admit, for a few minutes she had been thrown totally by the ring Patrick had bought for her, but that one glance at how close Geraldine was standing to her father was enough to shake her out of that. Yes, the ring was beautiful. Yes, it had cost a small fortune. But then, Patrick Devlin wouldn't expect his future wife to wear anything but the best. The very best. The ring wasn't actually for her, it was for Patrick Devlin's fiancée—who just happened to be her. Once she had all that sorted out in her mind, there was no problem.

'Of course I like it, Patrick,' she assured him lightly. 'Any woman would,' she added with cool dismissal.

His eyes glittered dangerously. 'I'm not interested in "any woman's" opinion, Lilli,' he rasped. 'I wanted *you* to like it. I should obviously have let you choose it yourself.' He snapped the ring-box shut. 'We'll go out tomorrow and look at some others—'

'You chose this ring, Patrick.' She grasped his wrist to stop him putting the blue velvet box back in his pocket.

He looked down at the paleness of her slender fingers against his much darker skin, before slowly bringing his gaze back to her face.

Lilli withstood his probing assessment of her unflinchingly—although she couldn't say she wasn't relieved when he finally smiled. She couldn't have held his gaze for much longer, would have had to look away. 'The ring, Patrick,' she reminded him chokily.

'Only if you're sure it's what you want.' His smile had gone again now; that harshness was back in his face.

'I'm sure.' There was a challenge in her voice, and she slowly released his wrist, leaving the next move to him.

'Well, I'm not sure I am,' her father asserted. 'This whole thing is ridiculous—'

'The ring is absolutely gorgeous, Daddy.' Lilli smoothly stopped what she was sure was going to be her father's tirade.

'Lilli, you have no idea what you're doing,' he told her exasperatedly. 'You don't have to do—'

'Daddy!' She silenced him. 'Let's drink our champagne. After all, this is supposed to be a celebration.'

'I see nothing to celebrate!' Her father slammed down the glasses he had been holding for them. 'In fact—'

'Richard, I really would like to see that Turner.' Geraldine was the one to interrupt this time, taking a determined hold of his arm.

For long moments it looked as if Lilli's father would refuse, and then he acquiesced with an abrupt nod of his head, his back rigid as he and Geraldine left the room.

'I gather he doesn't approve of your choice of husband?' Patrick drawled softly as he watched the other man depart.

Lilli looked at him with flashing green eyes. 'Did you honestly expect him to?'

Patrick shrugged. 'I think he could be a little more understanding of what you're doing—'

'Understanding!' she echoed scathingly. 'I think he's too angry and upset at the moment to understand anything!'

'I did warn you he would need convincing this marriage was something you really want.'

'And just how am I supposed to do that?' she scorned. 'You can't be trusted, Patrick. You totally deceived me about that night we spent together—'

'That really rankles, doesn't it?' he mocked.

'Of course it rankles!' She had thought of little else since parting from him this afternoon. 'You—'

'Would you rather we had spent the whole night making mad, passionate love to each other?' he taunted.

'Of course not!' Her cheeks went hot with embarrassment just at the thought of it.

'Of course not,' he mimicked softly, suddenly very close. 'Lilli, your first time should be gentle and sensitive. Special. Not a night you don't even remember!'

She swallowed hard, moved, in spite of herself, by the seduction in his voice. 'You still lied to me—'

'When I said you were a ten?' he supplied.

Her blushed deepened. 'About the whole thing! You—'

'I never lied, Lilli,' he assured her. 'I never lie. Remember that,' he added. 'Because I expect the same honesty from the people I deal with.'

Especially wives! God, Sanchia had to have been incredibly brave—or incredibly stupid!—to have deceived this man.

'You're beautiful, Lilli.' He touched her cheek gently, his fingers trailing lightly down her throat to the milky softness of her slightly exposed breasts in the close-fitting black dress she wore. 'You respond to my lightest touch,' he murmured in satisfaction as she trembled. 'I know we're going to be physically compatible.'

Her skin felt on fire where his fingers had caressed. 'A ten...' she murmured weakly.

'Perfect,' he corrected her firmly. 'I only made that remark that day because I was damned angry with you and what I thought you had done. I don't give scores on sexual performance, Lilli. I'm sure I made it plain to you there haven't been any women since I parted from Sanchia five years ago?'

'You said as much, yes...'

'If I said it, then it's the truth,' he bit out harshly.

'Patrick Devlin doesn't lie!'

'You know, Lilli,' he said with pleasant mildness, 'I'm getting a little tired of having to deal with your temper—'

'I never knew I had one until I met you!' she returned heatedly.

'You mean no one ever said no to you until me,' he derided.

He was mocking her again now. And that just made her more angry than ever!

She looked at him defiantly. 'I don't want to live in New York after we're married,' she stated—and then wondered where on earth it had come from. She hadn't meant to say that in anger at all, had intended discussing it with him calmly and reasonably. The problem with that was, she never felt calm and reasonable when she was with him!

'I don't think it's right to discuss that now, Lilli,' he dismissed predictably. 'Stop fighting me over everything, woman,' he ordered as he pulled her into his arms. 'And then maybe we can both start enjoying this!'

Enjoy being with this man? Enjoy being held by him? Enjoy being kissed by him!

Because he was kissing her. Again. And, as on those other occasions when he had kissed her, her body suddenly felt like liquid fire, her legs turning to jelly, so that she clung to his shoulders as the kiss deepened, Patrick's lips moving erotically against hers, his tongue moving lightly over the sensitivity of her inner lip. Lilli moaned low in her throat as he did so.

.'Good God...!'

It was her father's shocked outburst that intruded into the complete intimacy of the moment, and it was with some reluctance that Lilli dragged her mouth away from Patrick's, turning slowly to look dazedly in her father's direction.

'Don't look so shocked, Richard.' Patrick was the one to break the awkward silence. 'I realise you have some strange ideas about the reason Lilli and I are to be married, but as you've just witnessed—only too fully!—one of those reasons is that we are very attracted to each other. Haven't you ever heard of "love at first night"?'

Lilli ignored the pun, recovering her senses a lot slower than Patrick had. But with their return came the realisation that Patrick must have heard the other couple's impending return—and this show of passion had been all for their benefit, so that Geraldine and her father would believe the two of them were seriously in love!

If her father's nonplussed expression was anything to go by, it had succeeded! Why shouldn't it have done? Lilli was able to visualise all too easily—to her acute discomfort!—exactly the scene of intimacy her father and Geraldine had just walked in on. She had obviously been a more than willing recipient of Patrick's kisses and caresses!

'It happens this way sometimes, Richard,' Patrick continued, his arm like a steel band about Lilli's waist as he secured her to his side. 'Now that the two of you are back, we can put on Lilli's ring and drink the champagne.'

Lilli watched in a dreamlike state as Patrick slid the ring onto her finger, all the time having the feeling that, once it was on, her fate was sealed.

Who was she trying to fool? Her fate had been sealed from the moment she first met Patrick Devlin.

And as she watched the ring being put on her finger, weighed down by the emerald and diamonds, she knew it was now too late to turn back.

Too late for all of them...

CHAPTER EIGHT

'HOLD still, Lilli, or we'll never get these flowers straight in your hair,' Sally chided lightly.

Lilli stared at her own reflection in the mirror. Hardly the picture of the ecstatic bride on her wedding day!

Oh, the trappings were all there—the white dress, her hair in long curls down her spine, the veil waiting on the back of the chair to be put over the flowers Sally was now entwining in her dark curls.

Sally, the friend she had chosen as her attendant. Sally, who had been absolutely astonished to discover the 'gorgeous man', from the night of Gerry Simms' party, was in fact Lilli's father.

If Lilli had been in the mood for humour, she would have found Sally's incredulity funny. It was definitely the first time she had seen her friend lost for words!

'There.' Sally stood back now to admire her handiwork. 'You look absolutely beautiful, Lilli. Breathtaking!'

She did. The white satin dress and long veil made her look like something from a fairy tale.

Except she wasn't marrying Prince Charming.

She was marrying Patrick Devlin.

Her heart still sank just at the thought of being his wife. It had not been an easy week; Patrick had been at the house constantly as hurried arrangements were made for their wedding. Lilli had given in over everything— the timing of the wedding, the white dress, the private reception later today for family and a few close friends, even the choosing of identical wedding rings.

The one thing she hadn't agreed to—though her father was her choice of witness and Gerry was Patrick's—was Gerry helping her get ready for the wedding. Her mother should have been the one here with her, and as her father's mistress Gerry Simms did not fit the bill! Hence Sally's presence instead.

Thirty more minutes and Lilli and Patrick would be husband and wife. She would be Mrs Patrick Devlin.

As far as Sally—and most of London, it seemed!—was concerned, she should be the happiest woman in the world at this moment.

Happy! She was far from being that. She was going to be married to Patrick, his to do with whatever and whenever he wished. Tonight, they would make love.

God, how she wished she could claim the shiver that ran down her spine at the mere thought of it was caused by revulsion, but she knew in her heart of hearts that it wasn't. The thought of making love with Patrick, of the two of them naked in bed together, entwined in each other's arms, certainly made her quiver—but with anticipation!

Because something else had been happening during the last few days, with Patrick constantly teasing her, bullying her a little, kissing her—oh, yes, the kissing hadn't stopped. In fact, he seemed to take delight in kissing her and touching her whenever the opportunity arose for him to do so. And there seemed to be all too many of those!

To her dismay, Lilli found she was falling in love with him… She had made a pact with the devil—and, to her horror, had found she was falling in love with him!

'What is it, Lilli?' Sally seemed concerned.

From a very long way away, it seemed, Lilli looked up at her dazedly.

'You've gone as white as those tea-roses in your hair,' Sally explained anxiously. 'Lilli, I— Please don't think I'm intruding,' she continued hurriedly, lightly touching Lilli's arm, 'but are you sure you aren't rushing this? I mean, you and Patrick haven't known each other that long, and— Well, he was so very much in love with Sanchia.' She shook her head, looking very good herself in a sleek red suit, blonde hair loose about her slender shoulders. 'I wouldn't want you to be hurt again,' she added worriedly. 'Andy was such a swine to walk out on you the way he did, and I—'

'I don't want to talk about Andy,' Lilli interjected; without Andy's involvement in her family, today wouldn't be happening at all! 'And I appreciate your concern, Sally,' she went on with a softening of her voice, genuinely fond of the other woman, despite the penchant she had for gossiping. 'But I can assure you I do know what I'm doing.'

How could she not know? Patrick had made it more than obvious that, while they would have a full marriage, and hopefully several children, love would never come into it.

That was what bothered her about this marriage. She was falling in love with a man who had told her quite bluntly he would never feel the same way about her. Courtesy of Sanchia. Well, he might have loved her very much, but the collapse of that marriage, in the way that it had, meant he would never love again. Legacy of Sanchia.

Lilli hated Patrick's first wife, and she had never even met her!

And how was she going to survive in a marriage without love, loving her husband, but never being loved by him in return?

Somehow this was worse than the completely loveless marriage she had initially anticipated.

So very much worse!

So, yes, she knew what she was doing, but she had no choice in the matter; the wedding was mere minutes away now instead of days—days that had flown by all too swiftly!—and, more importantly, her father's lawyers had already started work on bringing a case against Andy. In fact, he might already be aware of it!

Sally sat down, leaning forward conspiratorially. 'Well, Patrick is an absolutely—'

'Gorgeous man,' Lilli finished for her, smiling teasingly. 'I never realised before, Sally, the fascination you have for gorgeous men!' She stood up to pick up her veil, placing the circle of flowers on top of her shining hair, studying her reflection in the mirror. The 'sacrificial lamb' was well and truly ready for the altar!

'You're referring to your father, of course.' Sally ruefully accepted her teasing. 'I still can't believe he's the man from the party. When I arrived here the other day to find the two of you together in the sitting-room, I must admit that my first thought was you were being unfaithful to Patrick even before the wedding!' She gave a grimace. 'Do you think he's serious about Gerry? Or do I actually stand a chance where he's concerned?' She looked questioningly at Lilli.

'He isn't serious about Gerry,' Lilli replied defensively, her eyes flashing deeply green at the mere suggestion of it.

'So would you mind if I—?'

'Be my guest,' she invited, although the fact that her own father suddenly seemed very sought after, by beautiful young women, was still a rather strange concept for her to accept. Admittedly, he was only in his mid-forties, but she had somehow never thought of him in that light before. 'But for the record, Sally,' she went on, 'I don't intend ever to be unfaithful to Patrick—before or after the wedding!'

'Fine,' Sally accepted, grimacing at Lilli's vehemence.

'Sally…' Lilli remonstrated firmly.

Her friend held her hands up defensively. 'I believe you—okay?'

Lilli laughed. 'Time will tell. In the meantime, I think we have a wedding to go to!'

'Oh, gosh, yes.' Sally stood up hurriedly. 'It may be traditional for the bride to be late, but in this case I'm not so sure the groom wouldn't come looking for you! I'll get off now, and see you at the registry office.' She gave Lilli a reassuring hug before leaving.

Amazingly Lilli's conversation with Sally had lifted her feelings somewhat, and she was smiling as she descended the wide staircase, her smile widening warmly as she saw her father standing at the bottom waiting for her, looking especially handsome today in his grey morning suit.

'Daddy, you look magnificent,' she praised glowingly as she reached him.

'*I* look—!' There were tears in his eyes as he looked down at her. 'Lilli, you look beautiful. So like your mother did at this age. I wish she could have been here to see you—'

'Not now, Daddy,' she dismissed briskly; talking about her mother was the one thing she couldn't cope with today, of all days. It was going to be difficult enough to get through anyway, without thoughts of her mother. Besides, she very much doubted this marriage was what her mother would have wished for her. It wouldn't do to dwell on that thought... 'Patrick will be becoming impatient,' she said brightly.

'Talking of Patrick...' Her father frowned, turning to the table that stood in the centre of the reception area, picking up a flat blue velvet box. 'He sent this for you earlier.' Her father snapped open the lid of the box, the two of them gasping as he revealed the most amazing necklace Lilli had ever seen. The emerald and diamond droplet in the centre of the delicate gold chain was an exact match for the engagement ring Lilli had transferred to her right hand for the marriage ceremony...

Her hand trembled slightly as she picked up the card that lay in the circle of gold, recognising the large scrawling handwriting as Patrick's before she even read the words written there. His cryptic sense of humour was all too apparent in the message.

Something new, Lilli—and if your eyes had been blue instead of green it could have been something blue too! Please wear it for me today.

Yours, Patrick.

'Lilli...!' her father breathed dazedly, still staring at the perfection of the necklace.

She swallowed hard, carefully replacing the card in the box before releasing the necklace and holding it out to her father. 'Would you help me put it on, Daddy?' She turned around, carefully lifting up her hair so that he could secure the catch. 'We'll have to hurry, Daddy,' she encouraged as he made no effort to do so. 'The car is waiting outside.'

'I still can't believe—Lilli, you're my little girl, and—'

'Please, Daddy.' Her own voice quivered with emotion. 'Put the necklace on and let's just go!' Before she totally destroyed the work of the last hour and began to cry.

He did so with slightly shaking fingers, careful not to ruffle her hair. 'Absolutely incredible,' her father said huskily as he stepped back to look at her.

Lilli gave a tight smile, not bothering to glance in the hall mirror as they walked out to the car. 'Only the best for Patrick. He would hardly give his future wife anything less.'

'I was referring to you, not the necklace,' her father gently rebuked. 'But then, you are the best; those jewels only enhance what is already perfection.'

She laughed. 'I think you may be slightly biased, Daddy!'

'I think Patrick Devlin is a very lucky man,' he stated. 'Take a deep breath before we go outside, Lilli,' he warned as he held her arm. 'I think half the world's press is gathered outside to snap a photograph of Patrick Devlin's bride!'

Which certainly wasn't an understatement!

A barrage of flashing cameras and intrusive microphones were pointed at the two of them as soon as they stepped outside into what was a crisply cold but bright, sunny December day. Questions were flung at them thick and fast, questions Lilli chose to ignore as she and her father hurried to the waiting car. The press had been hounding her continuously since the announcement of the wedding had appeared in the newspaper, and the wedding day itself had been sure to engender this excess of interest.

It was all so ridiculous to Lilli. Didn't these people have a war or something to write about and fill their newspapers with? This interest in what was, after all, just another society wedding, albeit with one of the principal players possibly being one of the richest men in England, seemed rather obscene to Lilli, and—

She was half in the car and half out of it when, her face paling, she caught sight of a familiar face amongst the crowd.

Andy...

She shook her head in denial of her imaginings. It couldn't have been Andy. Not here; this was the last place he would ever be seen. The only place she *wanted* to see him was in a courtroom, in the dock!

'Lilli...? Her father was waiting to get into the car beside her. 'What is it?' He saw her ashen cheeks.

'Nothing.' She turned to give him a glowing smile, the cameras clicking anew at what she supposed must look like the blushing bride on her way to her wedding. 'We'll be late if we don't go now,' she encouraged.

Her father looked as if he was about to add something to that, but at her determined expression he seemed to change his mind.

She had made her decision last week; there would be no last-minute nerves, no change of plan. That glimpse of someone she had thought looked a little like Andy had shaken her a little, but that was all...

'If I don't have the chance to tell you so again, you look absolutely beautiful,' Patrick whispered to her as they awaited the arrival of their guests to the private reception her father had organised at the Bennett Hotel.

Lilli barely glanced at him. She was almost afraid to. Half an hour ago she had married this man, was now his wife—and she had never been so scared of anything in her life before! In fact, she couldn't ever remember feeling scared before at all.

But Patrick had seemed like a remote stranger when they'd met at the registry office, making Lilli all too aware that that was exactly what he was!

Brides who had known their groom for years, and were secure in mutually expressed love, still had wedding-day nerves over the rightness of what they were doing; how much deeper, in the circumstances, was her own trepidation?

Just looking at the man who was now her husband was part of her panic. How on earth had she ever thought she could spend the rest of her life with this man? He was as good-looking as the devil, cool as ice, didn't love her, and had assured her he never would. God, this was—

'Gerry, when our guests arrive, greet them for us and assure them we will be with them shortly.' Patrick spoke quietly to his sister even as he grasped Lilli's arm.

Lilli's father frowned at him; the four of them had been the first to arrive at the reception room. 'Where are the two of you going?'

Patrick's hand was firm on Lilli's elbow as he led her away. 'Upstairs to our suite so that I can kiss my bride in private,' he told the other man grimly.

'But—'

'Let them go, Richard,' Gerry advised, her hand resting gently on his arm.

Lilli was shaking so badly now she could barely walk, the thought of actually being alone with Patrick sending her into a complete panic. This was real. Far, far too real, as the warmth of Patrick's guiding hand on her arm told her all too forcefully. It had seemed such a simple decision to make—the only decision she could make in the circumstances!—but the reality of it was all too much. She wanted to scream. Run away. To shout—

'Not here,' Patrick said suddenly, moving swiftly to swing her up into his arms.

Much to the interest of all the other hotel guests who stood watching them, he strode purposefully through the lobby to the lifts, several indulgent smiles directed their way as people observed their hurried departure. It didn't need two guesses to know what these people were thinking. But they were wrong! So very wrong...

Patrick, literally kicked open the door to the suite he had arranged for them to stay in tonight, setting Lilli down once they were safely inside. She looked up at him with widely apprehensive eyes.

'*Now* you can scream,' he encouraged indulgently.

Her breath left her with a shaky sigh. 'It was that obvious?'

'Only to me,' he assured her. 'I'm only surprised this didn't happen earlier. You've been too controlled this last week—'

'But I am controlled.' She swung impatiently away from him, angry with herself because she didn't seem able to stop shaking. 'I'm just being very stupid now,' she confessed self-disgustedly.

'You're being a twenty-one-year-old young lady who just made probably the biggest decision of her entire life.' Patrick's hands gently squeezed her shoulders as he turned her to face him. 'But I promise you I'll treat you well. That I'll try to curb this urge I have to dominate. I will honour and cherish you,' he added gruffly.

But he wouldn't love her; that omission was all too apparent to Lilli.

'But it isn't that, is it…?' Patrick said slowly, studying her closely. 'Tell me what it is, Lilli?'

She couldn't possibly tell him how she felt, that as she'd looked at him earlier as they'd made their wedding vows to each other she had known that she, at least, meant every word. She wasn't falling in love with him— she had already done so!

There was absolutely no doubt in her mind that she loved Patrick. It was nothing like what she had felt for Andy, was so much more intense, so— Oh, God, Andy… Had it been him she had seen earlier, or just someone that looked very like him?

Patrick shook her gently as she frowned. 'What is it, Lilli?' There was an edge of urgency to his voice now.

'I thought— You're going to think I'm imagining things now. But I—I thought I saw Andy outside the house earlier.' She frowned again up at Patrick as he released her abruptly, his expression serious now. 'I told you it was stupid—'

'Not at all,' Patrick barked. 'I have it on good authority that Brewster is back in London.'

She swallowed hard. 'He is?' She suddenly felt very sick. After what Andy had done to her father, and to her, she had no wish for him ever to come near her again. But with Patrick's confirmation that he was in London she was even more convinced that it had been Andy she'd seen outside the house…

Why? What had he been doing there? What had he hoped to achieve by being outside her father's house on her wedding day to another man?

'It's a little late for second thoughts, Lilli.' Patrick was watching her closely. 'You're my wife now.'

With all that entailed. He owned her now; it was there in every arrogant inch of his tensely held body. Minutes

ago, his gentleness and understanding drawing her close
to him, she had almost been tempted to tell him how
stupid she had been, that she was in love with him!
Thank God she hadn't. She was a Devlin possession, a
beautiful trophy to display on his arm, a wife with none
of the complications of love involved.

She nodded in cool agreement. 'Our guests will have
arrived downstairs.'

'You feel up to meeting them now?'

'Don't worry, Patrick, I won't embarrass you. My
nerves simply got the better of me for a moment. It
won't happen again.'

'No,' Patrick finally said slowly. 'I don't believe it
will.'

Regret…? Or perhaps she had just imagined that particular emotion in his voice; the last thing he wanted
was an emotional child for a wife. Her loss of control
wouldn't happen again. After all, he had just assured her
he would treat her well! He couldn't possibly realise
that, loving him as she did, there were cruel things he
could do to her…

And he must never know!

'We made a bargain, Patrick,' she told him distantly.
'And, like you, I never break my word once it's given.'

His expression hardened. 'I'm glad to hear it. Now,
as you've already pointed out, our guests will be waiting.' He indicated she should precede him out of the
suite, walking this time; the two of them were physically
apart as well as emotionally.

That moment of gentleness and understanding was
well and truly over, and for the next three hours Lilli
didn't have the time even to think, concentrating on their
guests, portraying the image that she and Patrick were a
golden couple. There was no doubting they succeeded;

family and friends smiled at them indulgently every time Lilli glanced around the large table where they all sat eating their meal. No doubt the few members of her family present thought she was very fortunate to have married someone as eligible as Patrick, especially after the 'Andy incident', as most of them referred to her previous engagement. Once the embezzlement story hit the headlines, perhaps some of them would draw their own conclusions, but for the moment everyone was obviously enjoying themselves.

Except, Lilli noticed, the late arrival standing in the doorway looking at the gathering with contemptuous blue eyes...

She didn't recognise the woman, so she could only assume she was a guest of Patrick's. A very beautiful guest, Lilli acknowledged with a stab of jealousy. Tall and blonde, with ice-blue eyes, she stood almost six feet tall, with the slender elegance of a model about to make an entrance onto the catwalk.

That icy blue gaze met Lilli's puzzled one, the woman's red pouting mouth twisting contemptuously as her hard eyes swept critically over Lilli—and obviously found her wanting—before passing on to Patrick. Now the blue eyes weren't so icy; in fact, they became positively heated, seeming to devour him at a glance!

Lilli felt herself bridle indignantly. How dared this woman—whoever she was—come here and look at her husband in that way? Patrick had told her, several times, that there had been no women in his life since his marriage ended, but the way this woman was looking at him seemed to tell a very different story!

Lilli's indignation rose. If she belonged to Patrick now, then he also belonged to her, and women from his past had no place at their wedding reception.

She turned to him sharply. 'Patrick—'

'My God...!' he exclaimed even as she spoke, the intensity of the blonde woman's stare somehow seeming to have made him aware of her presence in the doorway, his face set grimly, a nerve pulsing in his jaw. 'What the hell...?' he ground out disbelievingly.

Lilli blinked at him, unsure of his mood. She had seen him mocking, contemptuous, coldly angry, passionately aroused, even gently teasing, but she had no idea what emotion he was feeling as he took in the woman in the doorway. Every muscle in his body seemed to be tensed, and his fingers looked in danger of snapping the slender stem of the champagne glass he held.

'Patrick...?' Lilli prompted uncertainly now.

His glass landed with a thump on the table-top as he stood up abruptly, unseeing as he looked down at her. 'I'll be back in a few minutes,' he grated, turning to leave.

Lilli didn't need to be told he was going to the woman across the room, a woman he obviously knew very well if that blaze of awareness in the woman's eyes as she looked at him had been anything to go by! He couldn't do this to her, not at their wedding reception!

'Let him go, Lilli,' his sister advised quietly as Lilli would have reached out and stopped his departure. Gerry was looking across the room at the blond woman too now.

Lilli's mouth tightened resentfully, both at Gerry's intervention and Patrick's powerful strides across the room towards the beautiful woman. Her eyes flashed deeply green as she turned to the woman who was now her sister-in-law. 'You know that woman?' she asked.

'Oh, yes.' Gerry's mouth twisted contemptuously, although her gaze was soft as she looked at Lilli. 'I'm hardly likely to forget the woman who made Patrick into the hardened cynic he is today!'

Sanchia!

The beautiful woman in the doorway, the woman who had looked at Patrick so possessively, was his ex-wife? Here? Now?

Lilli turned sharply, just in time to see Sanchia smile seductively up at Patrick, before he took a firm hold of her arm and forcefully escorted her from the room.

CHAPTER NINE

'GERRY...? What the hell is she doing here?' Lilli's father hissed agitatedly.

Lilli turned to him. 'You know Patrick's ex-wife too?'

'Of course. Your mother and I were part of that crowd five years ago,' he reminded her.

Before her mother's illness became such that it was impossible for her to go anywhere...

'Where are you going, Lilli?' Her father's hand on her arm restrained her as she stood up.

Her expression was calm, a smile curving her lips—even if the green of her eyes spat fire. 'I'm going to join my bridegroom,' she told him, releasing her arm. 'Don't worry, Daddy.' Her smile was wry now at his expression of panic. 'I can assure you, I intend it to be a civilised meeting.'

Gerry grimaced. 'Sanchia isn't known for her civility!'

Lilli gave a genuinely warm smile as she bent down to answer the other woman. 'I'll let you into a secret, Gerry,' she murmured. 'Neither am I when I'm pushed into a corner!' She straightened, looking towards the door through which Patrick had left so hastily minutes earlier. 'And I've just been pushed,' she muttered as she turned to move determinedly towards that door.

Gerry touched her arm lightly as she passed her. 'Just watch out for the claws,' she warned.

Lilli nodded her thanks. 'I'll do that.'

It wasn't difficult to locate Patrick and Sanchia once

she was out in the corridor; the sound of raised voices came from a room a little further down the hallway, Patrick's icily calm, the female voice—Sanchia's—raised to the point of hysteria.

The claws Gerry had warned Lilli about were raised in the direction of Patrick's face as Lilli silently entered the room, Patrick's hands on the other woman's wrists to prevent her nails actually making contact with his cheeks.

'Dear, dear, dear,' Lilli murmured mockingly as she closed the door firmly behind her. 'Do I take it this isn't a happy reunion?'

The two people already in the room were frozen as if in a tableau. Both turned to face Lilli as she calmly stood looking at them, dark brows raised questioningly. Patrick looked far from pleased at the interruption, but Sanchia slowly lowered her hands, her icy blue eyes suddenly speculative as she looked Lilli up and down.

'The bride,' she drawled derisively.

Lilli steadily met the other woman's contemptuous glare. 'And the ex-bride,' she returned just as scathingly, knowing she had scored a direct hit as Sanchia's mouth tightened furiously. 'Patrick, our guests are waiting,' Lilli reminded him lightly.

Sanchia released her arms from Patrick's steely grip, eyes blazing. 'Unless he's changed a great deal—which I very much doubt!—Patrick doesn't respond well to orders!' The accent to her English was slightly more noticeable in this longer speech.

Green eyes met icy blue. 'Patrick hasn't changed. In any way,' Lilli added pointedly. 'Darling?' she prompted again.

He couldn't let her down now. He just couldn't! If he did, their marriage was over before it had even begun.

No matter what his feelings towards Sanchia—and Lilli
really had no idea what they were, or indeed about the
other woman's towards him; Sanchia had obviously felt
strongly enough about something, possibly Patrick, to
have turned up here today!—it was Lilli he was married
to now. And she had married him. For better or for
worse.

To her relief Patrick walked determinedly to her side,
his expression grim as his arm moved possessively about
her waist. 'As I've told you, Sanchia—' he looked at his
former wife resolutely '—there's no place for you here.'

'This—this child—' Sanchia looked at Lilli scornfully
'—could never take my place in your life! You need a
real woman, Patrick—and I was always that.'

Lilli stiffened at this mention of intimacy between the
two, although her outward expression remained calm.
She didn't particularly want to hear about Patrick's marriage to Sanchia. And Patrick, his arm still about her
waist, must have felt her reaction.

'Patrick likes them a little younger nowadays,' Lilli
told Sanchia wryly, knowing by the angry flush that appeared in the other woman's cheeks that her barb had
hit its mark. Sanchia was probably only ten years older
than her, but she obviously felt those years...

'Inexperienced, you mean,' Sanchia returned bitchily.
'Patrick bores easily too,' she warned.

Lilli smiled. 'I'm sure you would know that better
than I.' She felt the tightening of Patrick's hand on her
waist, but chose to ignore it; she knew she was playing
with fire, but at this particular moment she didn't mind
getting her fingers burnt.

Sanchia gave a snort before turning to Patrick. 'I give
this marriage a matter of months, darling,' she drawled,
picking her bag up from the table. 'And I'll still be

around when it's over. In fact, I'm thinking of moving to New York.'

'Really? I'm sure you'll enjoy the life over there.' Patrick was the one to answer her. 'Frankly—' his arm settled more comfortably about Lilli's waist '—I'm tired of it. Lilli and I will be living in London.'

That was news to Lilli! They hadn't so much as mentioned where they would live after their marriage since the night Patrick had given her the engagement ring, and she had behaved so stupidly about moving to New York. Now, it seemed, they weren't going to live there at all...

'I don't believe it,' Sanchia gasped. 'You've always loved New York.'

He gave an acknowledging nod. 'And now I love Lilli—and her family and friends are all in London.'

Two bright spots of angry colour appeared in Sanchia's cheeks. 'My family and friends were in Paris, but you refused to live there!' she accused heatedly, turning to Lilli with furious blue eyes. 'Enjoy his indulgence while you can,' she advised. 'I can assure you, it doesn't last for long!'

Considering one of this woman's indulgences had been other men, that wasn't so surprising!

Lilli met her gaze unflinchingly. 'I wouldn't hold your breath,' she said.

Sanchia gave a hard smile. 'Or you yours! Take care, Patrick.' She reached out to run a caressing hand down his cheek lightly. 'And remember, I'm still here.'

This last, Lilli knew, was said for her benefit. And while a visit from an ex-wife was enough to chill the heart of any new one—no matter what the circumstances of the divorce had been, the previous wife having an intimate knowledge of the man, of his likes and dislikes, that was totally intrusive—at that moment Lilli didn't feel in the least threatened by the other woman, had seen the look of absolute loathing in Patrick's face for Sanchia when she'd entered this room a few minutes ago. Patrick disliked his ex-wife intensely.

'Excuse us,' Patrick told Sanchia coldly. 'We have a wedding reception to attend.' His hand was firm against Lilli's back as he guided her to the door, neither of them looking back as they left. '"Patrick likes them younger nowadays"?' he repeated as soon as the two of them were out of earshot in the hallway.

Lilli glanced up at him from beneath lowered lashes, knowing by the curve to his mouth that he wasn't in the least angry at her remark. 'I believe I said "a *little* younger",' she returned, grinning up at him mischievously.

Patrick looked down at her, shaking his head incredulously. 'You weren't in the least thrown by her appearance here, were you?'

She wouldn't go quite so far as to say that, but if it was what Patrick believed...

She shrugged, the two of them standing outside the reception room now. 'Should I have been?'

'Not at all,' he returned easily. 'The part of my life that contained Sanchia is dead and buried as far as I'm concerned.' His expression was grim.

'That's what I thought.' Lilli accepted—gratefully, inside!—putting her hand in the crook of his arm. 'Let's join our guests; you still have a speech to give!'

'Oh, God, yes,' he groaned. 'I'm not quite sure what to say about my bride any more,' he added dryly.

Lilli grinned. 'Beautiful. Intelligent. Undemanding—'

'Sometimes wise beyond her years,' he put in. 'And full of surprises. I was sure you would give me hell over

Sanchia turning up here, today of all days. Full of surprises…'

She shook her head. 'You can't be held responsible
for the actions of a vindictive woman. She wanted to
cause trouble between us, unnerve you, and upset me—
I vote we don't give her the satisfaction!'

'I stopped caring years ago about anything that
Sanchia does,' Patrick revealed. 'I was more worried
about you and how you would feel about it.'

And she could see that he had been, his concern still
in the deep grey of his eyes. 'Don't be,' she told him
brightly, needing no further assurances from him concerning his ex-wife. 'And as for being full of surprises—
when did *we* decide to live in London?' She quirked
dark brows again.

He frowned in thought. 'I believe it was the night we
became engaged.'

'No.' Lilli shook her head. 'You refused to even discuss it then.'

'Because at the time I was intent on kissing you, if I
remember correctly.' He grinned as she blushed at the
memory. 'But your wish not to live in New York was
duly noted, and—'

'Acted upon.' Lilli frowned. 'I can see I'll have to be
more careful about what I say in future. Or was Sanchia
right about your indulgence?' she added teasingly.
'Won't it last?'

Patrick's arms moved smoothly about her waist. 'It
isn't a question of indulging you, Lilli. You said you
didn't want to live in New York, and, as I have no feelings either way, it seems obvious that we live here. I
want you to be happy in our marriage,' he added gruffly.
'And if living in London is going to help do that, then

this is where we'll live. I thought, with your agreement, that we could go house-hunting in the new year?'

He probably couldn't see it—and, in the circumstances, Lilli had no intention of pointing it out to him, either, because living in London suited her fine!—but the fact that he had made this decision on his own, without any consultation with her, was an act of arrogance in itself.

'Fine,' she nodded.

'Do you mind staying here in the hotel until we find a house? I somehow don't think we should move in with either your father or my sister.'

Lilli grimaced. 'Certainly not!'

Patrick grinned. 'Ditto.'

She blinked up at him. 'That's amazing, Patrick; do you realise that's three things we've agreed on in the last five minutes?'

'Three things...?' He looked serious as he thought back over their conversation.

She nodded. 'To live in London. And that your ex-wife is a bitch! She even chose to wear a white suit to come here today.' Lilli had duly noted the deliberate ploy of Sanchia to upstage the bride; the beautiful silk suit obviously had a designer label, and white was usually the colour reserved for the bride on her wedding day. She didn't doubt that Sanchia had been reminding her that she had been Patrick's bride first!

He grimaced. 'But the jacket, if I remember correctly, was edged with black. And Sanchia is more black than white!'

There was so much pain behind that stark comment. Lilli could only hope that one day he would feel comfortable enough in their relationship to talk to her about the marriage that had ended so disastrously.

For the first time that she could remember in their acquaintance Lilli was the one to reach up and initiate a kiss between them.

Patrick seemed as surprised as she was to start with, and then he kissed her back.

It hadn't been premeditated on her part; Lilli could have had no idea Sanchia would choose that particular moment to storm out of the reception room further down the hallway. But that was exactly what she did, her eyes narrowing glacially as she took in the scene of intimacy. With one last furious glare in their direction, she turned on her heel and walked away.

For good, Lilli hoped.

'Good timing,' Patrick told her dryly as he grasped her elbow to take her back to their guests.

He believed she had kissed him at that moment deliberately, so that Sanchia would see them!

And perhaps it was better if he continued to think that, Lilli decided as they moved around the huge dining-room chatting to each of their guests. Patrick had clearly stated he did not want a wife who loved him, only one that would be faithful and loyal.

Loving him as she did, those two things would be quite easy to be, and it was best to leave it at that...

'Thank goodness that's over!' Patrick pulled off his bow-tie with some relief, discarding his jacket onto a chair too, unbuttoning the top button of his shirt. 'I thought your father and Gerry were never going to leave.'

Lilli smiled at the memory of her father dithering about downstairs, drinking two glasses of champagne that he really didn't want, simply because now the time had come for him to leave Lilli alone with her husband and he was reluctant to do so.

She shook her head. 'And I thought the bride was the one that was nervous; you would have thought it was Daddy's wedding night the way he kept so obviously delaying our departure upstairs!' She smiled affectionately, sitting in one of the armchairs in the sitting-room of their suite, her veil discarded hours ago, the tea-roses still entwined in the flowing darkness of her hair.

Patrick looked across at her with dark grey eyes. 'And are you?' he said gruffly. 'Nervous,' he explained softly at her frown.

She swallowed hard. 'A little,' she acknowledged huskily.

He came down on his haunches beside her chair. 'You don't have to be, you know.' He smoothed the hair back from her cheeks. 'It's been a pretty eventful day, one way or another. And now it's very late, and we're both tired, and we have the rest of our lives together. I suggest we both take a shower and then get some sleep.' He straightened. 'There are two bathrooms in this suite; you take one and I'll take the other.'

Lilli looked at him dazedly as he picked up his jacket. He didn't want her!

'Lilli?'

She focused on him with effort. He was so tall and masculine, so devastatingly attractive. And he was her husband.

Damn it, she wanted to make love with him! This was their wedding night. And a part of her—the part that wasn't nervous!—had been anticipating the two of them making love. And now he had decided they weren't going to, after all...

He gave an impatient sigh. 'Stop looking at me as if

I've just hit you! I'm not a monster, Lilli, and I can see how tired you are. A shower and then sleep will be the best thing for you at the moment.'

The exhaustion she had felt on their way up here had suddenly vanished. Patrick didn't want to make love to her! Was this the way it was when you didn't marry for love? Or was he more affected by Sanchia's visit than he had admitted? Had seeing the other woman again made him realise he had made a mistake? What—?

'You're letting your imagination run away with you now,' he rasped suddenly, looking at her assessingly. 'Asking yourself questions that, in the clear light of day, you will recognise as nonsensical. I'm trying to be a gentleman, Lilli,' he explained. 'But if it makes you feel better I could always throw you down on the carpet right now and—'

'No!' she cut in forcefully, getting to her feet, avoiding looking at him as she did so. 'I'll go and take that shower.'

He nodded abruptly. 'I'll see you shortly.'

Lilli went through to the bedroom; her clothes had been brought here the day before and unpacked into the drawers. She took out the white silk nightgown before going through to the adjoining bathroom, thankfully closing the door behind her.

She had made a fool of herself just now, and it wasn't a feeling she was comfortable with. Patrick wasn't an eager bridegroom, in love with his new wife, desperate to make love with her. There was no urgency to consummate their marriage. They had plenty of time for that...

Patrick was already in bed when she came through from the bathroom half an hour later, the sheet resting about his waist, his chest bare, the hair there dark and curling, his skin lightly tanned. His hair was still damp from his shower, and he looked—

Lilli quickly looked away as he turned towards her, knowing the flare of desire she felt at the sight of him would be evident in her eyes. 'I'm sorry I took so long.' She moved about the room, hanging up her wedding dress and veil. 'It took me ages to get the flowers out of my hair and then pull a brush through it.' She held up a hand to her long vibrant hair. 'And then I—'

'Lilli, just leave all that and get into bed,' he interrupted wearily. 'You're wearing me out just watching you! It isn't as if it matters whether or not the dress gets creased; you won't be wearing it again.'

She thrust the dress on its hanger into the back of the wardrobe, as if it had burnt her. No, she wouldn't be wearing it again. Because she would always be married to Patrick. And look how disastrous it was turning out to be!

'Don't make me come and get you, Lilli,' Patrick urged as she still made no effort to get into the bed beside him. 'I never wear anything in bed, and I have a feeling you're the one that would end up feeling embarrassed if I were to get up right now!'

She scrambled into the bed beside him so quickly that her foot became entangled in the sheet and threatened to pull the damn thing off him anyway!

How stupidly she was behaving; she inwardly sighed once she had finally settled onto her own side of the wide double bed. Not at all like the normally composed Lilli. And as for Elizabeth Bennett...!

Patrick reached out to switch off the light, lying back in the darkness.

Lilli lay stiffly on her side of the bed, her eyes adjusting to the small amount of light shining into the room through the curtains at the window. She was never going to be able to sleep, couldn't possibly—

'If it's not too much to ask—' Patrick spoke softly beside her '—*I* would like to give my wife a cuddle before we go to sleep.'

She swallowed hard as he propped himself up on one elbow to look down at her, his individual features not discernible to her, although she could make out the shadows of his face. And he looked as if he was smiling!

'*Is* it too much to ask?' he prompted huskily.

'Of course not.' She moved in the darkness, putting her head on his shoulder as he lay back against the pillow, his arm curved around her, his hand resting possessively on her hip, the warmth of his body—his naked body!—instantly warming her too.

He gave a sigh of contentment, turning to kiss her temple lightly. 'This is worth all of the hectic circus today has been.' He relaxed against her.

Lilli still felt unsure of herself. Through the ridiculousness of his marriage proposal, her reluctant acceptance of it, the hectic activity during the week that followed, she had never doubted that Patrick desired her. In fact, he had seemed to have great difficulty keeping his hands off her! But now they were married, alone together at last, he didn't seem—

'You're letting your imagination run away with you again. Lilli, has it ever occurred to you that maybe *I'm* a little nervous?'

'You?' She turned to him, raising her head in surprise.

'Yes. Me,' he confirmed, pushing her head back down onto his shoulder. 'I told you, it's a long time since I did this. Maybe I've forgotten how to do it. Maybe I won't be able to please you.' He gave a deep sigh. 'God knows, the last time I attempted to make love to a woman, she fell asleep before we even got started! I'm talking about *you*, Lilli,' he explained as he felt her stiffen defensively in his arms. 'Five minutes earlier you had been full of sensual promise, and then—nothing.'

She buried her face in his shoulder at the memory. 'I had too much to drink. It had nothing to do with—with—'

'Well, it did absolutely nothing for my ego,' he assured her. 'Now will you accept that and just leave this for tonight?'

When he put it that way—of course she would! She had never imagined that Patrick had moments of uncertainty too. He was so damned arrogant most of the time, it was difficult to imagine him being nervous about anything. Certainly not about making love to her!

'Of course I will.' She snuggled closer to him in the darkness, her hand resting lightly on his chest. 'Mm, this is nice,' she murmured contentedly.

'Go to sleep, Lilli,' he muttered.

She slept. Not because Patrick had ordered her to, but because, as he'd said, she was truly exhausted.

Quite what woke her she had no idea, but as she slowly came awake she realised it was probably because she had subconsciously registered that she was alone in the bed, the lean length of Patrick no longer beside her.

She looked sleepily around the bedroom, realising by the fact that it was still dark in the room that it must be quite early. She finally located Patrick sitting in the chair by the window, a dark robe pulled on over his nakedness.

She moved up onto her elbows, blinking sleepily across at him. 'Patrick…?'

'Who the hell is Robbie?' he returned harshly.

CHAPTER TEN

LILLIE was dazed, not really awake yet, totally thrown by the savagely accusing question.

Patrick surged forcefully to his feet, crossing the room to sit down on the side of the bed, instantly tightening the bedclothes above her, holding her pinned to the mattress. He placed his hands on the pillow at either side of her head, glaring down at her in the semi-darkness. 'I want to know who Robbie is,' he repeated in a harsh, controlled voice.

Lilli pushed her tousled hair back from her forehead. 'I don't— What—?'

'Imagine my surprise,' Patrick ground out, 'when my bride of a few hours starts calling for another man—a man I've never heard of!—in her sleep!'

She swallowed hard, moistening her lips. She didn't remember dreaming at all, certainly not of Robbie. But Patrick said she had called out his name...? 'I did that?' She frowned her confusion.

Patrick's mouth twisted. 'It's hardly something I'm likely to have made up, is it?' he grated.

No, of course it wasn't. She just couldn't imagine why she had done such a thing...

'Lilli, I'm not going to ask you again.' He grasped her shoulders. 'Who the hell is he?'

She turned away from the livid anger in his face. '*Was* he,' she corrected him chokily. 'He's dead.'

Patrick released her abruptly, sitting back now, no

longer leaning over her so oppressively. 'You loved
him,' he stated flatly.

'Very much,' she confirmed shakily.

He stood up to pace the room. 'I don't believe this!
Now I have a damned ghost to contend with as well as
an ex-fiancé…!' He shook his head disgustedly. 'No one
has ever mentioned someone in your life called Robbie.'
He glared at her.

'There was no need for them to do so,' she said
heavily, painful memories assailing her anew. 'He's
been dead a long time.' She sighed. 'Patrick, Robbie
was—'

'I can guess,' he cut in savagely. 'He was the reason
you settled for someone like Andy Brewster. The reason
you're now married to me. He was—'

'The person that gave me the name Lilli,' she told
him, her voice very small. 'Remember you once asked
me about my name? Actually, it was Lillibet originally,'
she recalled sadly. 'But over the years it's been shortened to Lilli.'

'Lillibet?' Patrick repeated. 'It sounds like something
a child might say. What sort of—?'

'It *was* something a child might say—a very young
child,' she told him slowly, no longer looking at him,
her vision all inwards, on the past, on memories of
Robbie. 'Robbie couldn't get his tongue around the
name Elizabeth, and so his version came out as Lillibet.'
She smiled at the memory, that smile fading as quickly
as it appeared. 'He was only two when he died of men-
ingitis.' She looked at Patrick with dull eyes. 'He was
my brother.'

Patrick paled. 'He— But— I—'

Patrick at a loss for words would have been funny

under any other circumstances. But at the moment it was lost on her.

'I was eleven when he died. One day he was here, giggling and fun, and the next he had— I—I—' She fought the control she always lost when talking of her brother. 'I loved him from the day he was born. Perhaps the difference in our ages helped with that; I don't know.' She shook her head. 'But I could never accept— I didn't understand. In some ways I still don't. He was beautiful.' She looked at Patrick with tear-wet eyes. 'I loved him so much,' she added brokenly. 'I have no idea why I called for him last night. I don't remember. I just—'

'Hey, it's all right.' Patrick sank down beside her on the bed, his arms moving about her as he held her close against him. 'I had no idea, Lilli. I'm so sorry. I do vaguely remember something—God, I'm just making this worse.' He angrily berated himself. 'I shouldn't ''vaguely remember'' anything! Robbie was your brother—'

'But you didn't know him. You didn't know us.' Her voice was muffled against his chest. 'Robbie was special to me; I still can't think of him without crying. I'm sorry.' She began to cry in earnest now.

'Lilli, please don't cry,' Patrick groaned. 'I do know what it's like to lose someone you love. I was seven when my mother gave birth to Gerry. Gerry was born, and my mother died. I was left with that same bewilderment you obviously were. And my father and I were left with the onerous task of bringing up a new-born baby. For fifteen years we managed to do exactly that, and then my father died, and it was left completely to me.'

As he spoke of his mother and father, his childhood

with Gerry, his voice somehow lost its smoothness, acquiring a slightly Irish lilt to it. And Lilli could only guess, from the emotion in his voice, just how difficult it had been for him to lose his mother—and be presented with a totally helpless baby.

His statements had been starkly made, telling her about none of the trauma he and his father must have felt in surviving such sorrow. Or how difficult it must have been for him, at only twenty-two, to have the sole charge of a fifteen-year-old girl. And yet he had done it and, from the success he had made of his business life and the closeness between himself and Gerry, all too capably.

Lilli shook her head. 'I didn't know—'

'Why should you?' He lightly touched her hair. 'We have the rest of our lives to get to know about each other, both past and present.'

Lilli hoped that would include speaking about his marriage to Sanchia. As she looked up into the gentleness of his face, she thought it would...

'I didn't mean to make you cry just now,' he continued. 'I only—I just— I was jealous,' he admitted. 'I thought he was a man you had cared for.'

She looked up at him with puzzled, tear-wet eyes. If he had felt jealousy, did that mean he cared for her, after all? Even as her heart leapt at the thought, she realised it wasn't that at all; what Patrick possessed, he possessed exclusively. Didn't he despise Sanchia because she hadn't been exclusively his?

She shook her head. 'You need have no worries like that concerning me. Andy was my one and only venture into commitment—and look how disastrously that turned out!'

Patrick settled himself on the bed beside her. 'Well,

you're totally committed now,' he told her with satis-faction. 'How does it feel?'

'Not a lot different than before.'

He looked at her with teasing eyes. 'Do I detect a note of disappointment in your voice?'

Did he? Possibly. There couldn't be too many virgin brides who had built themselves up to being made love to on their wedding night—only to be told by their bride-groom that he was too tired! Although that wasn't strictly true... He had said they were both too tired. And the proof of her own tiredness was that she couldn't even remember falling asleep, although she must have done so almost immediately she shut her eyes.

But she wasn't sleepy now; in fact, she was wide awake...and suddenly very aware of Patrick as he lay beside her wearing only a robe to hide his nakedness.

Patrick gently raised her chin, smoky grey eyes look-ing straight into candid green. 'I know what you were thinking last night, Lilli,' he said gruffly. 'Oh, yes, I do,' he insisted as she would have protested. 'But the truth of the matter is, I want you too much, want us to enjoy each other too much, to have it spoilt in any way.'

She swallowed hard, the desire he spoke of evident in the burning intensity of his gaze. 'We're not tired now,' she pointed out shyly.

He laughed. 'No, we're not. And we are going to make love, Lilli.' He bent his head, his mouth claiming hers, lips moving erotically against hers, the tip of his tongue lightly caressing the inner moisture of her mouth.

Her arms curved up about his neck as she held him close to her, heart pounding, his hair feeling soft and silky beneath her fingertips, shoulders and back firmly muscled.

Lilli relaxed against the pillows, pulling Patrick with

her, his robe and her nightgown easily disposed of as flesh met flesh, Lilli's softness against Patrick's hardness, the dark hair on his chest tickling the sensitive tips of her breasts now.

And then Patrick's lips were teasing those sensitive tips, Lilli's head back as she gasped at the liquid fire that coursed through her body, groaning low in her throat as she felt the moist warmth of his tongue flicking over her hardened nipples.

His lips and hands caressed every part of her body during the timeless hours before dawn, encouraging her to touch him in return, to discover how he liked to be caressed too, to be kissed. But she seemed to know that instinctively, revelling in the response her lips and hands evoked, until his tender ministrations reached the most intimate part of her body and she could no longer think straight as heat such as she had never known before consumed her in flames.

And then Patrick was once more kissing her on the lips, his hands on her breasts as he slowly raised her to fulfilment once again. And again. And again.

And when his body finally joined with hers there was no pain, only pleasure of another kind, his slow, caressing movements deep inside her taking her to another plateau completely. A plateau Patrick joined her on, his own groans of pleasure merging with hers, before they lay damply together, their bodies merged, their breathing deep and ragged.

'I don't think you could have forgotten a thing,' Lilli finally said when she at last found the strength to talk.

Patrick laughed. 'I hope not—any more than that and I could die of a heart attack!'

She lay on top of him, moving slightly so that she could look into his face, unconcerned with her nakedness now; there wasn't an inch of her body that Patrick didn't now know intimately. 'You weren't nervous at all last night, were you?' she realised shakily.

'You needed time to get used to me.'

'Used to' him; she was totally possessed by him at this moment! 'But you weren't really nervous, were you?' she persisted.

'Lilli.' He smoothed the tangled hair back over her shoulders, revealing the pertness of her breasts. 'If you only knew the ways I've imagined making love to you!'

He still hadn't answered her question. Or perhaps he had... He had been thinking of her last night, giving her time to become accustomed to their new relationship.

'I think I just experienced them,' she recalled breathlessly.

'Oh, no, Lilli. We've barely touched the surface,' he assured her with promise.

She quivered in anticipation, only able to imagine the delights yet to come.

'But not right now,' Patrick soothed, settling her head comfortably against his shoulder. 'Now we're going to have a nap.'

She swallowed hard. 'Like this?'

'Exactly like this,' he said with satisfaction. 'I like having you as part of me. And vice versa, I hope.' He quirked dark eyebrows.

'Oh, yes,' she admitted shyly, very much aware of the way in which he was still 'part of' her! 'But it must be late.' Daylight was visible now through the curtains at the window. 'Shouldn't we—?'

'This is the morning after our wedding, Lilli,' he teased. 'No one, least of all the hotel staff, will expect to hear from us for hours yet. At which time we will order breakfast—even if it's two o'clock in the afternoon. This is a Bennett hotel; I'm sure they will accommodate us!'

Lilli was sure they would too. But whether or not she would ever, as the owner's daughter, be able to face any of the hotel staff again after her honeymoon was another matter!

But for the moment she didn't care, was content in Patrick's arms, being with him like this. And as she drifted off into sleep she had a feeling she always would be...

'What the hell—?'

Lilli woke suddenly, to the sound of Patrick's swearing, and the reason for it—a loud knocking on the outer door of their hotel suite.

She sat up groggily, just in time to see Patrick pulling on his robe and tying the belt tightly about his waist. 'I thought you said no one would disturb us today?' she giggled, pulling the sheet up to her chin as she watched him.

'I didn't think anyone would dare to!' He scowled darkly, glaring in the direction of the loud banging. 'It had better be for a good reason!'

As he strode out of the bedroom to the suite door Lilli couldn't help but feel sorry for the person who was standing on the other side of it, although she had to admit she was a little annoyed at the intrusion herself. Patrick's words, before they'd both fallen asleep, had promised so much more...

He didn't return immediately, as she had expected he would, and finally her lethargy turned to curiosity; it must be something important to keep Patrick away this long. She could hear the murmur of male voices in the sitting-room...

She pulled on her white silk robe over her nakedness, belting it securely before running a brush lightly through her hair; she might have just spent several hours of pleasure in her husband's arms, but she didn't want everyone to realise that just by looking at her!

'Daddy!' She gasped her surprise as she saw he was the man talking to Patrick. 'Good grief, Daddy, what on earth are you doing here?' She shook her head dazedly.

'Would you believe he came to make sure I hadn't strangled you on our wedding night?' Patrick drawled derisively. 'Or you hadn't stuck that knife in my back that he once suggested!'

Lilli looked at the two men, her father flushed and agitated, Patrick calm and controlled. 'Actually—no,' she answered firmly. 'So, why are you really here, Daddy?' she prompted.

'You certainly didn't raise a fool, Richard,' Patrick said appreciatively.

The older man gave him an exasperated glare before turning back to Lilli. 'Good afternoon, Lilli,' he greeted her. 'I'm sorry to interrupt—I mean, I realise I shouldn't have—' He broke off awkwardly, the way they were both dressed—or undressed!—telling its own story. 'Gerry told me I shouldn't come here...'

'You should have listened to her,' Patrick bit out tersely. 'I, for one, do not appreciate the interruption.'

Lilli had stilled at the mention of the other woman's name. Then she remembered how kind Gerry had been to her yesterday when Sanchia had appeared so inappropriately at the wedding. Although she still resented the other woman's place in her father's life, some of what Patrick had told her earlier about his sister made her realise that, as her own father was to her, Gerry was all the family Patrick had. And, as such, Lilli couldn't continue to alienate her.

'Perhaps you *should* have listened to her,' she told her father quietly.

Her father's eyes widened, but he didn't comment on the lack of the usual resentment in her voice when she spoke of the other woman. 'Maybe I should,' he agreed. 'But I thought this was important.'

Lilli returned his gaze frowningly; he must have done to risk Patrick's wrath by intruding on their honeymoon in this way. And he had obviously got more than he bargained for by finding them so obviously still in bed! 'How important?' she said slowly.

'Very,' he insisted firmly.

'I disagree,' Patrick put in hardly.

Lilli's father shot him a questioning glance. 'I think that's for Lilli to decide, don't you...?'

Patrick's head went back arrogantly. 'As it happens, no. I don't think this concerns Lilli at all. Not any more.'

She was intrigued by the mystery of her father's visit. Obviously, whatever it was about, Patrick didn't want her involved in it.

She moved to sit on one of the armchairs. 'Tell me,' she prompted her father.

He glanced uncertainly at the younger man, obviously far from reassured by Patrick's stony expression.

'Daddy!' Lilli encouraged impatiently.

He no longer met her gaze. 'Perhaps Patrick is right; this can wait until after your honeymoon—'

'We've had our honeymoon,' she assured him firmly. 'Have you forgotten we're joining you tomorrow for Christmas.' She didn't even look at Patrick now, knowing she would see disapproval in his face. But she was not a child, and she refused to be treated like one, by either man.

Her father slumped down into another of the arm-chairs. 'I'd completely forgotten it's Christmas...!' he groaned.

'Don't let Gerry hear you say that,' Patrick warned mockingly. 'She loves Christmas. I suggest you make sure you have something suitable for her by tomorrow!'

'Stop trying to change the subject, Patrick.' Again Lilli didn't so much as look at him. 'I'm not so easily deterred.'

'Does that mean you've already bought my Christmas present?' he returned tauntingly.

She had, as a matter of fact—a beautiful watch, already wrapped and ready to give him on Christmas morning. But that wasn't important just now.

'It means,' she said with slow determination, 'that I'm not going to be sidetracked. Daddy!' She was even more forceful this time.

'She gets her stubbornness from me, I'm afraid,' he told the younger man ruefully.

'It's irrelevant where she gets it from,' Patrick dismissed tersely. 'This is none of her business.'

'I'll be the judge of that,' she snapped. She had been kept in the dark too much already by these two men; it wasn't going to continue.

'You aren't Elizabeth Bennett any more, Lilli,' Patrick rasped. 'You're Mrs Lilli Devlin. And *Mr* Devlin has already decided this does not concern you!'

She stood up angrily. '*Mr* Devlin doesn't own me,' she returned furiously. 'Maybe someone should have told you: women aren't chattels any more! Now, either one of you tells me what's going on, or I'll go and ask someone who will tell me,' she added challengingly.

Patrick looked at her scathingly. 'Such as who?'

'Such as Gerry!' she announced triumphantly, know-ing by the stunned look on both the men's faces that this hadn't even occurred to them as a possibility. Lilli wasn't so sure it was either; she might feel less antago-nistic towards the other woman, but she wasn't sure she would be able to go to her about this! But hopefully neither of these two men would realise that... 'Well?' she prompted hardly when her announcement didn't pro-duce the result she wanted, looking from one man to the other, her father looking decidedly uncomfortable, Patrick stubbornly unmoved. 'Fine,' she finally snapped, walking towards the bedroom, her clear intention to go and dress before leaving. 'Gerry it is!'

'Lilli, I forbid you to go anywhere near Gerry!' Patrick thundered autocratically.

She halted in her tracks, turning slowly, looking at him with cool incredulity.

'Uh-oh,' her father muttered warily. 'You've done it now, Patrick. The last time I forbade Lilli from going near someone she ended up *marrying* you!'

Patrick's mouth quirked. 'That hardly applies in this case, does it? Besides, it's because Lilli is married to me that I—'

'Think you can tell me what to do,' she finished scath-ingly, shaking her head. 'I don't think so,' she bit out coldly. 'Daddy?' she prompted in a voice that brooked no further argument.

He sighed, giving a regretful glance in Patrick's di-rection before turning back to Lilli. 'Andy telephoned me this morning,' he stated without flourish.

She gasped in shock. Whatever she had been expect-ing, it wasn't this!

She froze momentarily. 'Andy did...?'

Her father nodded. 'He wants to see you, Lilli,' he told her softly.

She hadn't been mistaken yesterday; it had been Andy standing outside in the crowd as she went to the wedding. But why did he want to see her...?

CHAPTER ELEVEN

'YOU just aren't thinking this through at all, Lilli,' Patrick said as he sat watching her dress. 'Brewster believes that by talking to you, appealing to your softer nature, he may be able to stop your father's legal proceedings against him!'

She didn't look at him, hadn't done so since he'd followed her into the bedroom a few minutes ago. They had made love in this room, knew each other intimately, and yet she still felt slightly self-conscious at having Patrick watch her, thankfully pulling up the side zip to olive-green trousers before pulling on a matching sweater.

She was still stunned by Andy's contact with her father, couldn't imagine what had made him do such a thing. She certainly didn't agree with Patrick's last comment; she had every reason to hate Andy, and he must be well aware of that fact. Where Andy was concerned, she had no 'softer nature' to appeal to!

'And just how do you think he hopes to achieve that?' she replied, still smarting from Patrick's earlier attempt to tell her what she could and couldn't do. Marriage was a partnership—particularly this marriage!—and she was not about to be told whom she could or couldn't see.

'You were engaged to the man—'

'And he used that engagement to cheat my father,' she reminded him forcefully.

'You loved him—'

'I thought I did,' she corrected him; loving Patrick as

153

she now did, she knew damn well she had never really loved Andy at all!

'You were going to marry him—'

'And now I'm married to you.' She looked at him challengingly. 'A fact I'm unlikely to forget!'

Patrick returned her gaze. 'We made a bargain, Lilli—'

'And I won't renege on that,' she returned sharply. 'But being married to you does not make me your prisoner. I have no idea why Andy wants to talk to me,' she added as his face darkened ominously, 'but I honestly don't see that it can cause any harm.' Her father was right; telling her not to do something was a sure way of ensuring that she did!

Patrick stood up, throwing off his robe, completely unconcerned by his own nakedness as he took underwear from a drawer. 'I'm coming with you,' he informed her as he dressed.

'No!'

He halted in the action of buttoning up his shirt. 'What do you mean…no?' he said slowly.

'I mean no, Patrick,' she repeated firmly, outwardly undaunted by his fury—inwardly quaking. Patrick was again the coldly resilient man who had come to her home the day after their initial night together, a man who seemed like a stranger to her. But she wouldn't allow Patrick to see any of her inner apprehension. 'Andy asked to see me—'

'And I'm now your husband—'

'We aren't joined at the hip, Patrick!' she snapped impatiently. 'And I really don't have the time for this,' she added after glancing at her wristwatch. 'The sooner I see Andy, the sooner we'll all know what's going on.'

'I've already told you what's going on: the man believes he can use emotional pressure, or possibly black-mail—'

'Strangely, I would rather hear all this from Andy himself.' Her eyes flashed deeply green.

Patrick looked at her between narrowed lids. 'You still care for the man…!'

'Rubbish!' Her cheeks were flushed with anger at the very suggestion of it.

In truth, she had come to realise in the last week exactly how shallow her feelings for Andy had been… And it was because she loved Patrick, loved him in a totally different way, completely, intensely, in every way there was to love a man—even his anger!

Andy had been a challenge to her, she had realised, a man who didn't respond to the way she looked as other men always had—for reasons she understood only too well now! But his lack of interest had only piqued her own interest in him a year ago, and it was only since loving Patrick, when every nerve-ending, every part of her, was live to his presence, that she had realised how lukewarm her desire for Andy had been.

To have married him, she now knew, would have been a complete disaster. But she couldn't explain that to Patrick without admitting how she had come to realise that fact. And she couldn't, at this moment, admit to Patrick that he was the very reason she could now see Andy without fear of emotional pressure, of any kind, having any effect whatsoever. Loving Patrick consumed all of her emotions; there was no room for anyone else.

But it was almost as if Patrick's tenderness last night, and again this morning, might never have happened as he continued to glare at her accusingly. Lilli didn't have time to deal with his temper just now, wanted to get this meeting with Andy over and done with.

'Daddy's waiting,' she told Patrick briskly. 'We can talk when I get back—'

'I won't be here, Lilli,' Patrick said flatly.

She gave him a startled look. 'What do you mean...?'

He shrugged. 'By your own words, our honeymoon is over. In which case, I may as well go to my office for a couple of hours.'

For a moment she had thought—! Ridiculous—she and Patrick were married, for life, by his own decree. And, both being determined people, she didn't doubt they would have many disagreements in the future, but that didn't mean either of them intended giving up on their marriage. As Patrick had said earlier, they had made a bargain. For all they knew, she could already have conceived the first of those four children...

Patrick nodded abruptly. 'I'll see you later, Lilli.' He strode out of the room.

No parting kiss, not even a second glance; he just went. And it was with a heavy heart that Lilli joined her father in the suite lounge where he had sat waiting for her.

He looked up, frowning at her. 'Patrick looks—' He hesitated over his choice of description.

'Furious,' she finished for him. 'That's probably because he is.' She slipped on her jacket.

'Actually, I was going to use a much more basic word to describe how he looked,' her father returned ruefully.

She gave a warn smile. 'He doesn't want me to see Andy.'

'I think he made that more than obvious earlier.' Her father grimaced. 'And for once I have to agree with him.'

Her eyes widened accusingly. 'I wouldn't even know

Andy wanted to talk to me if you hadn't come here and told me!'

'I know,' he said wearily. 'And I think now I was probably wrong to do so.'

She laughed dismissively. 'Let's go, Daddy—before you start proving as stubborn as Patrick!' She took a firm hold of his arm and led him out of the suite, locking the door behind them; Patrick had his own key if he returned before them. 'I believe you said Andy wants me to meet him at—' She named a very exclusive hotel as they entered the lift. 'He's staying there on your money, I suppose!' she added scornfully.

Her father raised his eyebrows. 'Who knows? I'm at a complete loss as to what's going on. All he would say when he telephoned earlier was that he had to talk to you—'

'I thought you said he telephoned *you*?' she reminded him.

'I had to say that.' He grimaced. 'How do you think Patrick would have reacted to being told it was you your ex-fiancé wanted—insisted!—on talking to all the time?'

Exactly as he had reacted now—he had walked away!

But she still didn't understand; why did Andy want to talk to her? He had to know how she felt about him now, had to realise that what they had once shared had been over the moment he decided to cheat her father. And used her to do it!

She gave a heavy sigh. 'Maybe we had better not speculate any of this until we see Andy—'

'*You* see him,' her father corrected her. 'He had the damned nerve to tell me he doesn't want to speak to me. Although, to be honest, now that I'm involved in legal proceedings against him, I don't want to speak to him either. I think if I saw him, after the heartache he's caused, I would probably just hit him and think about the consequences of that action later—which wouldn't help anyone! I'll wait outside the hotel for you. But make sure he realises, exactly as I told him on the telephone this morning, that whatever he has to say to you will make no difference to the legal proceedings being brought against him.'

Now she was even more puzzled by this meeting between Andy and herself. He didn't want to see her father... She didn't know what she had been expecting—perhaps a plea from Andy, or even the blackmail that Patrick had suggested. Now she wasn't so sure...

Andy sat alone at one of the tables in the huge reception area, a pot of coffee in front of him. Lilli had time to study him before he was aware of her presence. The last three months hadn't been kind to him either; his handsome face was ravaged and tired-looking, his suit fitting him loosely, as if he had lost weight too.

Lilli hardened her heart to the way he looked; he was the cause of everyone's unhappiness, including his own, from the look of him!

She walked to the table, standing beside it looking down at him wordlessly as she waited for him to say something.

He stood up. 'At least sit down, Lilli,' he said, holding back the chair for her. 'You're looking well,' he told her as he resumed his own seat opposite her.

'What do you want, Andy?'

'I suppose it is a little late for social politeness between us,' he conceded. 'Could I just say, I never meant to hurt you, Lilli—?'

'Didn't you?' she interrupted.

He gave a sad sigh. 'No...'

'You hurt me because of what you did to my father, but on a more personal level...?' She shook her head, her eyes flashing her pain. If she had been hurt in any way by the end of their engagement then it had been her pride that had taken the blow—and, as Patrick had already assured her all too clearly, she had more than enough of that!

Andy looked at her closely for several seconds, and then he slowly nodded. 'I'm glad about that. I thought by the announcement of your marriage to Devlin that I couldn't have done you too much harm—'

'I haven't come here to discuss the harm—or otherwise!—that you did to me,' Lilli cut in. 'My father is the one— What on earth is that?' She stopped as Andy produced a small flat package from his jacket pocket, the paper brightly coloured, decorated with a silver bow and ribbon. 'I realise it's Christmas tomorrow, Andy—' her mouth twisted contemptuously as she looked at the present '—but I—'

'It isn't a Christmas present, Lilli, it's a wedding gift,' Andy told her, holding out the small present to her.

Her eyes widened, her hands tightly locked together in her lap. 'I don't want anything from you!' And she knew, without even consulting him, that Patrick wouldn't want it either!

'You'll want this.' Andy continued to hold out the gaily wrapped gift, but when she still didn't take it he put it down on the table between them, standing up. 'Please tell your father I'm sorry.'

'Where are you going?' she said incredulously as he would have walked away; she still had so much to say to him!

He gave a little smile. 'I'm not going anywhere, Lilli;

I'm staying exactly where I am. The last three months have been a nightmare—'

'You think they've been a nightmare for *you*?' she demanded disbelievingly. 'What do you think it's been like for my father? He—'

'I know,' Andy acknowledged heavily, coming down on his haunches beside her chair, reaching out to clasp both her hands in his. 'I do know, Lilli. That's why I'll understand if, after opening your present, your father still wants to prosecute me.' He shook his head sadly. 'It was all so tempting, Lilli, too much so in the circumstances.' He looked at her pleadingly. 'I was involved in a relationship that—well, I was in over my head. I thought if I had some money of my own—'

'I know about your—relationship, Andy,' she told him hardly. 'It's the reason I know you could never really have cared for me!'

He closed his eyes briefly, those eyes slightly over-bright when he raised his lids to look at her once again. 'I did—do—care for you, Lilli. You're a wonderful woman—'

'Please, Andy.' She instantly shook her head. 'Don't take me for a complete fool!'

He let out a deep breath. 'I know how it must seem to you, but I— If things had been different—'

'Don't you mean, if *you* had been different?' she countered, pulling her hands away from his.

'Yes,' he acknowledged. 'But you really are an exceptional woman, Lilli—a caring, beautiful woman. And you deserved so much better than me—'

'She got it!' interrupted a harsh voice.

Lilli and Andy turned sharply in the direction of that voice, Lilli troubled, Andy guarded, slowly straightening to face the other man. Lilli couldn't even begin to imag-

ine what Andy thought of Patrick's presence here—she
was too busy wondering about that herself!

Patrick's mouth showed his contempt as he looked at
the younger man. The two were in such stark contrast
to each other, Patrick so dark where Andy was golden,
Patrick's face masculine, Andy's, seen against such stark
masculinity, appearing much softer, his features so regular and handsome he appeared almost beautiful.

As the two men continued to stare at each other, Lilli
couldn't help wondering if Patrick had entered the hotel
in time to see Andy holding her hands...!

Whatever he had or hadn't seen, his cold anger of
earlier this afternoon certainly hadn't diminished; he still
looked furious!

'Lilli and I were married yesterday,' he informed
Andy icily, pulling Lilli to her feet so that she stood at
his side, holding her there firmly, his arm like a steel
band about her waist.

Andy nodded. 'I realise that.'

'Then you must also realise that you have intruded on
our honeymoon,' Patrick barked. 'An unwelcome intrusion.'

'I realise that too,' Andy acknowledged ruefully. 'But
I had something I had to give to Lilli.' He bent down
and picked up the gaily wrapped present before handing
it to Lilli. 'I hope the two of you will be very happy
together,' he added lightly, although he seemed to frown
as he glanced at Patrick's harshly set face, his expression
softening as he turned to Lilli. 'You're a very lucky man
to have Lilli for your wife.' Even as he spoke to Patrick
he bent forward and lightly kissed Lilli on the cheek.
'Take care, love. And be happy.' He turned and walked
away.

There was complete silence as Andy left the hotel,

Lilli still clutching the small present he had given her, Patrick silent at her side. She didn't need two guesses as to why; he was absolutely furious—at her for seeing Andy at all, but also at the fact that the man had dared to kiss her, albeit on the cheek!

'For goodness' sake, stop brooding, Patrick!' she told him spiritedly as she moved out of his grasp. 'I don't recall that I behaved this way yesterday when your ex-wife decided to turn up at our wedding!' In fact, that subject hadn't been mentioned, by either of them, since.

He looked blank, as if the memory was something he had completely forgotten about. And perhaps it was; Sanchia didn't appear to be someone he wanted to remember. But that didn't change the fact that his reaction to Andy now was completely unfair to her.

Patrick relaxed suddenly. 'Let's sit down for a while. Your father has gone home, so he isn't going to be waiting outside. I spoke to him on my way in,' he supplied at her questioning look. 'I couldn't see the point in both of us waiting for you.' The two of them sat at the table Andy had recently vacated.

Of course not. And, of course, her father would also have seen the sense of that—with a little help from Patrick...!

'Open the damned present,' Patrick instructed tersely. 'Although I still think, given the circumstances, that Brewster had a damned nerve wanting to see you at all, let alone give you a present!'

Lilli wasn't really listening to him, was staring down at the gift she had just unwrapped, the silver ribbon and bow hanging limply from her hand now.

'What is it?' Patrick prompted sharply. 'Lilli!'

She looked across at him, her eyes unfocusing, her face pale. She couldn't think, let alone speak!

'For God's sake...!' Patrick stood up to come round the table and take the package roughly out of her hand, looking quickly at the contents. 'My God...!' he finally breathed dazedly.

Lilli knew exactly what had caused his astonishment. The same thing that had caused her own... Andy's gift to her was a bank account, made out in her name. For the amount of five million pounds!

The amount he had taken from her father...?

She looked up at Patrick. 'Is that what he owed?'

His expression was grim now. 'More or less,' he grated.

She frowned. 'How much less?'

He shrugged. 'Probably the interest that should have been earned in the last three to four months. Brewster has probably needed that for his living expenses. I doubt your father will mind that, as long as he gets the capital returned to him.'

Lilli was still totally fazed, couldn't believe what had just happened. 'Why do you think Andy did it? Gave it back, I mean.' It was almost like a dream, and if it weren't for that bank account—for five million!—Lilli would have had trouble believing Andy had been here at all.

Patrick threw the bank book and account statement down onto the table, sitting in the chair opposite hers once again. 'I did some checking during the short time I had before coming here. Brewster's relationship has apparently foundered, probably because of the pending court case; his lover is apparently the type who doesn't care to be associated with criminals! So maybe Brewster just decided to try and salvage at least part of his life and try to walk away. I have a feeling your father will let him do that.'

So did she, once she had spoken to her father. 'He's certainly going to be ecstatic at the return of this.' She touched the statement as if she still couldn't believe the money was actually there, within her father's grasp.

Patrick said, 'He's gone back to Gerry's house, if you want to take it to him.'

This time Lilli didn't feel that sickening lurch in her stomach at the mention of the relationship between his sister and her father. Maybe she was getting used to the idea...

'And you?' Patrick suddenly asked her. 'How do you feel about it?'

She gave a glowing smile. 'Wonderful! Daddy has his money back, and it looks as if all the publicity a court case would have engendered can be avoided as well. It's— But you don't look too pleased, Patrick.' She suddenly realised he looked grimmer than ever. 'Do you think there's something wrong with the return of the money?' She looked down at the bank statement. 'Is Andy playing some sort of cruel joke on us all? Do you—?'

'Relax,' Patrick advised. 'The money is in a bank account in your name. It's yours. But it means the two of us have some serious talking to do once you've seen your father,' he added firmly.

Lilli looked startled. 'We do...?'

'One day, Lilli,' he bit out. 'Do you realise that if Brewster had returned that money to you just one day earlier you wouldn't now be my wife?' He looked at her intently. 'Would you?'

All the colour drained from her face as the force of his words hit her. One day... If Andy had come to see her the day before her marriage to Patrick, then he was right—there would have been no wedding. She wouldn't now be Patrick's wife. Never would have been!

She couldn't speak as this sickening realisation hit her.

'Exactly,' he grated, standing up. 'I really do have some things to do at the moment, Lilli. But we'll talk about this later at the hotel.'

Lilli sat and watched him go, her eyes dark green pools. Exactly what were they going to talk about? Not divorce? Did Patrick realise, with the return of this money, that they should never have been married at all? Did none of last night and this morning matter to him? Did he want to end their marriage before it had even begun?

CHAPTER TWELVE

'BUT this is wonderful!' Her father's delight was obvious as he smiled broadly. 'Absolutely marvellous!'

'But is it?' Gerry said slowly, looking at Lilli. 'Lilli doesn't look too happy.'

Her father turned to her too now, noticing the paleness of her face. 'Lilli?' he said warily. 'Brewster didn't say or do anything to upset you, did he?'

'No,' she dismissed with a shaky laugh.

'There aren't any hidden conditions attached to the return of this money, are there?'

She had come in a taxi straight to Gerry's house, knew she had to put her father's mind at rest as soon as possible. But inside she was still in shock from Patrick's enigmatic comments before he'd left her, couldn't actually remember the taxi journey here.

'No hidden conditions,' she assured her father wryly. 'I think Andy was quite relieved to get rid of it; a life of crime doesn't seem to have brought him too much happiness!'

'Then—'

'Where is Patrick, Lilli?' Gerry interjected. 'Richard said he came to join you at the hotel…?'

'He did.' She avoided the other woman's gaze: Gerry saw far too much! 'But he had some business to attend to,' she added brightly.

'Did he?' Gerry returned sceptically.

Lilli still didn't meet her sister-in-law's eyes. 'He said he did, yes.'

'But...?'

'Really, Gerry.' Lilli gave a light laugh, although no humour reached the dull pain in her eyes. 'You know Patrick—if he says he has something else to do, then he has something else to do.'

'I do know Patrick,' his sister acknowledged softly. 'We've always been very close. He more or less brought me up, you know.'

'Yes, he told me about that,' Lilli replied, those moments of intimacy between them seeming a lifetime away.

'Did he?' Gerry nodded her satisfaction with that. 'Then you must realise that the two of us know each other rather better than most brothers and sisters, that we've always had an emotional closeness?'

Lilli gave the other woman a puzzled glance. 'I don't understand where all this is leading to—'

'It's leading to the fact that Patrick is in love with you,' Gerry told her impatiently. 'And I have a feeling— a terrible feeling!—that because of this—' she held up the bank book and statement '—Patrick is going to do something incredibly stupid!'

Lilli was quick to protest, 'Patrick isn't in love with me, and—'

'Oh, yes, he is,' the other woman assured her with certainty.

'—he never does anything "incredibly stupid",' Lilli finished determinedly. 'Unless you count marrying me in the first place,' she added bitterly.

'Lilli, exactly what has Patrick said to you?' Gerry probed.

Lilli stood up and turned away from both her father and the other woman. 'Apart from more or less saying we should start talking about a divorce?' she said fiercely. 'Not a lot!'

'A divorce?' her father echoed incredulously. 'But you were only married yesterday! He can't be serious—'

'They were married yesterday, Richard,' Gerry cut in gently. 'But today the reason for Lilli marrying Patrick—that money—' she gestured in the direction of the bank book '—was made null and void. That is the reason Patrick believes you married him, isn't it, Lilli?'

She was starting to resent Gerry again; this was none of her business, even if she was Patrick's sister! '*It is* the reason I married him,' Lilli came back; she didn't believe either of these two could seriously have ever been fooled into believing otherwise!

'So you're going to agree to a divorce?' Gerry watched her shrewdly.

Lilli felt ill just at the thought of it, knowing she must have once again gone pale. 'If that's what Patrick's wants, yes.'

'And what do *you* want?' the other woman persisted.

'You know Patrick; I don't think I'll have a lot of say in this one way or the other!'

'Lilli, your father told me Patrick said he hadn't raised a fool.' Gerry spoke plainly. 'But at this moment you're being extremely foolish!' she added caustically.

'I don't think I asked for your opinion!' Lilli felt deep resentment.

'And now you're being very rude,' her father said sternly, moving forward to put his arms about Gerry's shoulders. 'Gerry is trying to help you—'

'I don't need—or want!—her help,' Lilli told him forcefully, her hands clenched at her sides at this show of solidarity from the couple. The last thing she needed at this moment was to have their relationship pushed in her face. She felt as if her whole world was falling apart already, without that!

'Calm down, Richard.' Gerry put a soothing hand against his chest as he would have exploded angrily. 'Lilli is hurt and upset—and God knows we all do stupid things when we feel like that! I think it's time, Richard,' she opined slowly, 'that Lilli heard about some of the stupid things I did in the past—don't you?'

He looked down at her uncertainly. 'I—'

'It's time, Richard,' Gerry repeated firmly. 'Unless you want Lilli to make the same mistake I did? Because, believe me, these two are even more stubborn than we are, and at this moment, basically because she's here and Patrick isn't, I think Lilli is more open to reason.'

Lilli's father glanced across at his daughter uncertainly, Lilli steadily returning his gaze. She had no idea what all this was about, and she wasn't sure she wanted to know either. But she did know that when she got back to the hotel Patrick was going to talk about their future— or lack of it!—and anything that delayed that happening was acceptable!

'Very well.' Her father finally gave his agreement. 'But listen carefully, Lilli. And try not to judge,' he added almost pleadingly.

'Do I need to sit down for this?'

'Yes,' her father confirmed, going to the drinks tray on the side dresser. 'You're also going to need this.' He handed her a glass of brandy. 'We all are!' He handed another glass to Gerry, and kept one for himself.

Lilli sat, although she made no move to drink the brandy, putting the glass down on the table beside her chair, looking up expectantly at Gerry.

The other woman looked apprehensive at her sceptical expression. 'Your father is right, Lilli—you aren't going to like what you hear,' she said. 'But please try to understand; this isn't being done to hurt; I'm doing this for an altogether different reason.'

'I'll try,' Lilli conceded dryly.

'Lilli—'

'Leave it, Richard,' the other woman told him lightly. 'Lilli makes no pretence of doing anything other than disliking me, and at least it's honest. It isn't what I would like, but it's honest.' She walked over to the blazing fire, suddenly seeming to need its warmth. 'Six years ago I met a man I fell very much in love with,' she began. 'Unfortunately, the man was married— We haven't all led neatly packaged lives, Lilli,' she added at Lilli's derisive expression. 'The man was married. Unhappily—I know, aren't they all?' she acknowledged self-deprecatingly. 'But in this case it was true. I had seen the two of them together, knew that the wife was involved with someone else. And I—I fell in love with the husband. And he loved me in return.'

'But your marriage only lasted a couple of months,' Lilli pointed out. 'Hardly the love of a lifetime!' she said scathingly, wondering why she was being told all this.

'Because I didn't marry the man I loved!' Gerry returned curtly. 'There were complications. The man had a child. At fifteen, not a very young child, I'll admit, but a child the father loved very much. And there were reasons why—why this man couldn't leave his wife and child.'

'Once again, there always are,' Lilli returned without interest, this was an all-too-familiar story, surely…?

Gerry drew in a harsh breath. 'But in this case the wife threatened to completely alienate the child from the father if he dared to leave her—'

'But I thought you said she was involved in an affair, too?'

'She was,' Gerry rasped. 'And if things had been— different she had intended leaving her husband! But the woman became ill, seriously so, and her—lover decided he didn't want to tie himself to a woman dying of cancer.'

Lilli had become suddenly still, her eyes wide now as she stared at Gerry. 'Go on...'

'Your father and I were deeply in love, Lilli,' Gerry told her emotionally. 'We had intended being together. But he—he left it too late to agree to giving your mother a divorce. She had been diagnosed as terminally ill, her lover left her, and suddenly all she was left with was a broken marriage. And her daughter.' Gerry swallowed hard. 'She was determined to hang onto both of them— at any cost.'

Lilli could hardly breathe, felt suddenly numb.

'Your parents' marriage began to deteriorate after your brother died, Lilli,' the other woman continued huskily. 'Your father buried himself in his work—and loving you. And your mother went from one affair to another. And the love they had once felt for each other turned to a tolerant contempt. By the time I met your father four years later they were living completely separate lives, with you as their only common ground.'

Lilli looked at her father with pained eyes, couldn't believe she could have been so blind to her parents' loveless marriage. Or perhaps she hadn't... She had known they spent little time together, that her mother could be verbally vicious to her father when she chose to be, but she had always put that down to the pain of her illness. Now she could see that perhaps it had been that they simply didn't love each other any more...

'Daddy…?' She looked at him emotionally now.

'I'm sorry, Lilli. So sorry.' He gripped her hands tightly. 'But it's all true. In fact, there's so much more. Your mother had asked me for a divorce before she found out about her illness, was going off with this other man—'

'Richard…!' Gerry looked at him uncertainly.

He shook his head, his gaze still on Lilli. 'It's time it all came out, Gerry. Your mother was leaving us, Lilli. She had told me she was going, asked me for a divorce—on her terms, of course. She wanted a huge settlement of money, and in return she would leave you with me. The man she was involved with was ten years younger than her, and he didn't want Caroline's fifteen-year-old daughter cluttering up their lives.'

'Mummy was leaving me behind,' Lilli said dazedly.

'Yes,' he replied. 'And I was happy to give her the money if I could keep you. Then she found out she had cancer…' His expression darkened. 'And everything changed!'

'Lilli!' Gerry came to her side as she swayed where she sat. 'No more of that, Richard,' she said briskly. 'I only wanted to try to explain a little…'

'I've misjudged you,' Lilli realised flatly, reaching out blindly to clasp the other woman's hand—blindly because her eyes were full of tears. 'Patrick knows all of this, doesn't he?' She realised only too well now what he had meant when he'd said her father had been protective of her to the point of stupidity! She looked up at her father now. 'You gave up your chance of happiness because you didn't want to lose me,' she said brokenly.

'You had already been through so much when we lost Robbie—'

'You gave up the woman you loved—Gerry—' she

looked at the other woman as the tears began to fall down her cheeks '—so that Mummy wouldn't destroy all our lives. And you…' She tightly squeezed Gerry's hand. 'You married someone else on the rebound.' She recalled her father's words… 'An angry and upset Gerry is a force to be reckoned with!'

'Oh, Lilli!' Gerry moved to hug her. 'Don't make the same mistake. Please!'

She pulled back slightly. 'You mean Patrick?'

'I mean my stubborn, arrogant brother,' Gerry confirmed. 'It runs in the family, I'm afraid. Your father went out of my life five years ago because I was too stubborn to listen to him. I married—disastrously—to spite him. I loved him, wanted to be with him, and although I understood what he was doing it was impossible for me to stay in his life. My marriage was a mess, and within a couple of months I had to admit I had made a terrible mistake.' She grimaced at the memory. 'Don't do something stupid like I did, Lilli. I know Patrick; he would never have married you if he didn't love you.'

'When he asked me to marry him it was because he said I had the qualities he wanted in his wife, in the mother of his children—'

'He probably believed it when he said it too.' Gerry shook her head with affectionate exasperation. 'But it's all nonsense. Patrick is in love with you— Yes, he is, Lilli,' she insisted firmly even as Lilli opened her mouth to deny it. 'Do you love him? The truth, Lilli. It's the day for the truth,' she went on throatily.

Lilli took a deep breath. 'I— Yes!' The word was virtually forced out of her. It was one thing to admit to herself how she felt, quite another thing to admit it to someone else. Even someone she realised she had completely misjudged… God, Gerry should have been the one resenting her all this time, not the other way around. So many years wasted... And what Gerry was saying to her now was, did she want to waste as many by giving up on Patrick without a fight? But Gerry had known Richard loved her, whereas Patrick didn't love Lilli at all...

'Then what do you have to lose by telling him so?' Gerry sat back, her expression encouraging. 'Your pride? Oh, Lilli!' She held her hand out towards the man she loved, straightening to stand at his side. 'My pride, after I made such a mess of things, cost me years I could have spent with your father. Long, lonely years, when I went out with lots of men who meant nothing to me, men who, because of their own male pride, would never admit to anyone that those relationships were never physical. I've been so lonely, for so long, without your father, Lilli; but thank God he came back and claimed me once he was free to do so!'

'And—thank God—she let me!' Lilli's father added with feeling.

Lilli smiled shakily up at the two of them. 'So when are the two of you getting married?'

'As soon as you and Patrick agree to be our witnesses,' her father told her.

Patrick... A shadow passed over her face, her smile, emotional as it was, fading.

'I'm ordering you to stay away from him, Lilli,' her father told her expectantly.

Her smile returned, a little wanly, but it did return. 'That won't work this time, Daddy. I—' She broke off as the telephone began to ring, Gerry going to answer it.

'Good afternoon, Patrick,' she greeted once he had identified himself as the caller. 'Richard is ecstatic over

the news, and— Yes, Lilli is still here.' She glanced
across the room at a now tense Lilli. 'Well, we're all
just about to sit down and enjoy a celebratory glass of
champagne— Yes, I know it's your honeymoon,' she
answered him smoothly. 'But it's Christmas too. And
we all have something to celebrate—why don't you
come and join us—?' Gerry suddenly held the receiver
away from her ear, wincing as the loudness of Patrick's
voice down the receiver could now be heard by all of
them, although the words themselves were indistinct.
'Well, it's your choice, of course. Lilli will be back
later.' Gerry looked down at the receiver, shrugging before placing it back on its cradle. 'I'll give him twenty
minutes.' She grinned.

'For what?' Lilli frowned, having been frozen in her
seat since she realised it was Patrick on the telephone,
her hands still shaking slightly.

'For him to get here.' Gerry grinned her satisfaction.
'And you doubted he loves you! Patrick never shouts,
Lilli. He's never needed to. The softer he talks, the more
anxious people are to do what he wants. But he's shout-
ing now, Lilli—and it's because I deliberately gave him
the impression you wouldn't be going back to the hotel
until later this evening.' She laughed, glancing at her
wristwatch. 'Eighteen minutes, and counting!'

Lilli was sure the other woman was wrong. As his
sister, she might know Patrick very well, but she had no
knowledge of him as a husband. There was no way
Patrick would come to her...

And she wasn't going to him yet either, wasn't ready
for that, readily falling in with her father's suggestion
that they have the champagne after all. Anything to delay going back to the hotel. And discussing their divorce...

'To the two of you.' She toasted her father and Gerry with pink champagne. 'May you be happy together at last.' She owed them this much, owed them so much more than she had ever realised.

Her marriage to Patrick meant she was no longer a child, and she was learning all too forcefully what Patrick had said all along: things were never just black and white. No one was to blame for the triangle that had evolved six years ago, not even her mother. Maybe it wasn't emotionally fair, but, faced with a sure slow death, her mother had clung to the things that she still could, and that included her husband and daughter. Given the same circumstances, Lilli wasn't sure she would have done the same thing, but it was what had happened, and it was over now. It was time to shut the door on that, and start again.

For all of them, it seemed…

She swallowed down her feelings of apprehension with the champagne. Time enough to face all that later; right now was the time to let her father celebrate. And for him and Gerry to be allowed to be happy with each other at long last.

'Hmm, three minutes early,' Gerry suddenly murmured after another glance at her watch. 'He must have broken several speed limits to get here this fast at this time of the day—and on Christmas Eve!' She smiled across at Lilli. 'I just heard Patrick's car in the driveway.' She listened again. 'Patrick entering the house,' she added ruefully as the front door could be heard slamming loudly shut. 'Patrick entering the room,' she announced before turning to face him, a glowing smile lighting up her face. 'Patrick, what a surprise!' she greeted warmly. 'You decided to join us, after all.'

He didn't even glance at his sister, all his attention

focused on Lilli as she stood near the fire. 'I thought you were coming back to the hotel once you had spoken to your father,' he grated accusingly.

Her hand trembled slightly as she held onto her champagne glass. 'We were celebrating,' she said with soft dismissal.

'Richard and I were just going off in search of another bottle of champagne,' Gerry said lightly. 'Weren't we, darling?' she prompted pointedly.

'Er—yes. We were,' he agreed somewhat disjointedly, frowning at Lilli and Patrick.

Patrick returned his gaze coldly. 'Pink, of course,' he said. 'It's Lilli's favourite.'

'How well you know your wife,' Gerry drawled, lightly touching his cheek as she passed him on her way to the door. 'We shouldn't be too long,' she assured Lilli gently in passing.

The room suddenly seemed very quiet once the other couple had left, closing the door softly behind them, even the ticking of the clock on the fireplace suddenly audible.

Lilli could only stare at Patrick. Dear God, he looked grim. Her hands began to shake again as she tightly gripped the glass.

'But not for much longer, hmm, Lilli?' he suddenly exclaimed as he strode further into the room, dark and overpowering in black denims and a black sweater. 'Will I know you as my wife?' he added at her puzzled frown.

Something seemed to snap inside her at that moment, a return of the old Lilli through the fog of uncertainty, pain, truth—so much truth, it was still difficult to take it all in!—and she faced Patrick unflinchingly as she carefully placed her glass down on the table behind her. 'I thought we had an agreement that our marriage was for life,' she reminded him haughtily—every inch Elizabeth Bennett at that moment. But she was neither Just Lilli nor Elizabeth Bennett any more, she was Lilli Devlin—and she was about to fight for what she wanted! 'The agreement—verbal though it might have been— was binding on both sides. You can't just opt out of it when it suits you, Patrick.' She still didn't believe that Patrick loved her—it would be too much to hope for!— but if she could remain his wife, who knew what might happen in the future...?

'When it suits me—!' he exploded furiously, a nerve pulsing erratically in the hardness of his cheek. 'It doesn't *suit* me at all to have my wife walk out on me the day after our wedding! Even Sanchia waited a little longer than that.'

'Forget Sanchia,' Lilli returned. 'I am not her, am nothing like her. And I'm not walking out on you.'

'I have just spent most of the day, the day following our wedding, at the hotel on my own,' he bit out. 'I would say that's walking out!'

'Rubbish,' she snapped back. 'I spent all of the morning and part of the afternoon, at the hotel with you,' she reminded him, a blush to her cheeks as she remembered those hours of intimacy. 'We've been apart maybe three hours at the most—'

'And look what happened in those three hours!' he said disgustedly.

'What, Patrick? What happened during that time?' she challenged. 'My father had his money returned to him. What does that have to do with us, with our marriage? You told me last week that it wasn't mentioned during the proposal or the acceptance; so what bearing does this afternoon's events have on our marriage? Well?' she pressed after several seconds of tense silence.

He gave a snort. 'Everything!'

She became suddenly still, looking at him carefully. 'Why?'

'Oh, for God's sake, Lilli.' He paced about the room. 'It may not have been mentioned, but we both know how relevant Brewster giving the money back is to us; you admitted as much yourself earlier this afternoon when I asked you!'

She thought back to their conversation after Andy had left, to what Patrick had said, because she hadn't said anything! 'And just how did I admit it, Patrick?' she asked softly. 'I don't believe *I* said anything.'

'You didn't have to,' he groaned. 'The look on your face when you realised how close you had come to not marrying me spoke for itself; you went white!'

She drew in a deep breath. Pride, Gerry had told her, had cost her six years of happiness with the man she loved...

'Are you interested in why I went white, Patrick?' she said.

'I know why you went white,' he ground out, glaring at her. 'You missed keeping your freedom by twenty-four hours!'

Lilli steadily met his tempestuous gaze, unmoved by the fierceness of his expression. 'You're partly right—' She ignored his second snort of disgust in as many minutes, choosing her words carefully. 'I realised,' she said slowly, 'how narrowing I had avoided not marrying you—'

'Then we don't have a problem, do we, because—?'

'Be quiet, Patrick, and let me finish what I'm saying!' She glared at him. 'And listen, damn it! I said ''how narrowly I had avoided *not* marrying you'' —because if Andy had come back into our lives two days ago *you* would have been the one to call off the wedding. Wouldn't you?' she persisted.

'I—'

'Not me, Patrick,' she continued unwaveringly. 'I wouldn't have called it off, because I *wanted* to marry you!' The last came out in a rush, Lilli holding her breath now as she waited for his reaction.

He continued to look at her, but some of the fierceness went out of his expression, uncertainty taking its place.

And uncertainty wasn't an emotion Lilli had ever associated with Patrick before...

'Why?' he said bluntly.

She swallowed hard. Could she really just tell him—? Pride, Gerry had called it. And look what it had cost the other woman in terms of real happiness...!

She drew in a deeply controlling breath. 'Because I love you!' Once again the words came out in a rush, and it was her turn to look uncertain now. 'I know you don't love me,' she continued hurriedly at Patrick's stunned expression. 'That you decided never to love again after Sanchia—'

'As you said earlier—forget Sanchia,' he dismissed harshly. 'As far as I'm concerned she ceased to exist the day she decided to destroy our child because she believed pregnancy would ruin her figure—'

'Patrick, no!' Lilli gasped disbelievingly. How could anyone destroy another human life for such selfish reasons? The life of Patrick's child... Which was why he had asked her if she wanted children... Why he had made such a point of telling her she would look beautiful when she was pregnant...! 'Oh, Patrick...!' Her voice broke emotionally as she went to him, her arms going about his waist as she rested her head against his chest.

'You said you loved me...?' he said quietly.

He stood a little apart from her, his own arms loose at his sides, his expression distant as she looked up at him. 'Not the past tense, Patrick.' She shook her head firmly. 'I do love you. Very much. And I do not want a divorce,' she added determinedly. 'I told you before, you aren't going to have everything your own way—'

'I don't want a divorce either!' His voice rose agitatedly, moving at last, his arms coming tightly about her waist. 'I thought you did. I thought— Lilli, I know what I said to you when I asked you to marry me.' He looked intently down at her. 'I was trying to protect myself, trying—' He shook his head in self-disgust. 'I lied, Lilli. I—'

'You don't tell lies, Patrick,' she reminded him softly, hope starting to blossom somewhere deep inside her, too deep down yet to actually flower, but it was there nonetheless...

'Lilli. Just Lilli. *My* Lilli.' His hands cupped either side of her face as he raised it to his. 'That first night at the hotel, as you lay sleeping in the bed— Don't look like that, Lilli,' he admonished gently. 'You were beautiful that night. I lay beside you for hours just watching you.' He smiled as she looked startled. 'You were— are—so beautiful, and yet as you slept you looked so vulnerable. By the time morning came I had decided I wanted to spend the rest of my life waking up with you beside me. I didn't recognise those feelings as love then, but—'

'Love?' she echoed huskily, that hope starting to flower now, to grow and grow, until it filled her.

'Love, Lilli. I fell in love with you that night. Although I certainly didn't recognise it as such.' He grimaced. 'Only that I wanted you with me for the rest of my life. But when I came out of the bathroom that morning you had gone...'

'I felt so embarrassed by what I had done.'

'I realise that,' he nodded. 'It was the shock of my life, only a matter of hours after that, to discover you were actually Richard Bennett's daughter. With all the complications that entailed—'

'I know about my mother, Patrick,' she interrupted. 'And about Gerry and my father. I— We've all made our peace.'

'Have you? I'm glad. Gerry's life was such a mess five years ago, and for years I harboured very strong feelings against your father for causing that unhappiness. And then two months ago Gerry took him back into her life, and I— I didn't take the news too well initially. Maybe I was a bit over-zealous—businesswise—where your father was concerned, because of that. Part of me wanted him destroyed in the way he had destroyed my sister's life,' he admitted heavily.

'And you hated me because I was his daughter,' Lilli said knowingly.

'I didn't hate you.' His arms tightened about her once again. 'I could never hate you. I was not—pleased to discover you were his daughter.'

'You believed I had slept with you deliberately,' she reminded him teasingly.

'Only for a matter of a few hours. I was so damned angry when I found out who you really were that it seemed the only explanation for the way you had left the party with me—'

'I had just seen my father with Gerry,' she told him. 'I was angry and upset, and although I didn't know you were Gerry's brother the two of you seemed close, and so I—I decided to go with you to spite her. Not very nice, I'll grant you, but at the time I just wasn't thinking straight. I got the shock of my life when I woke up that morning in a hotel bedroom and heard you singing in the adjoining bathroom!'

'Well, of course I was singing,' he grinned. 'I had just found the woman I wanted to spend the rest of my life with!'

'And I thought I had spent the night making love with you and couldn't even remember it!' she recalled with a groan.

'I know, love,' he said. 'That was obvious when I came to your house later that day.'

'And you let me carry on believing it!' she reproved exasperatedly.

'Don't be too angry with me, Lilli.' He kissed her gently on the lips. 'It was the fact that we hadn't made love that made me realise I had made a mistake about that. When I sat and thought about it later, if you really had set out to trick me that night, you would never have allowed yourself to go to sleep in the way that you did, and you certainly wouldn't have left the hotel so abruptly. I also realised, as I sat angrily churning all this through my mind, that our night together actually made things less complicated rather than more so. It enabled me to ask you to marry me,' he explained at her questioning look, 'to point out all the advantages of such a marriage, without ever having to admit how I felt about you. I didn't want to love anyone, Lilli, but— What I feel for you is like nothing I have ever known before. I want to be with you all the time. To make love with you. To argue with you—we do them both so well!' He smiled. 'I've never felt like this before, Lilli,' he told her intently. 'I love you so very much.'

She believed him! Patrick loved her. And she loved him.

And if either of them needed any further proof of that then the kiss they shared was enough, full of love and aching passion—enough to last a lifetime.

Lilli's eyes glowed, her cheeks were flushed, her lips bare of gloss, when she looked up at him some time later. 'Would you really have let me go?' she prompted huskily.

He frowned. 'If it was what you wanted,' he said slowly.

No, he wouldn't. She knew him too well already to actually believe that. 'Without a fight?' she teased.

'No,' he admitted dryly.

She laughed softly, hugging him tightly. 'I'm so glad you said that—because I wouldn't have gone without kicking and screaming either!'

His answering laugh was full of indulgent joy. 'We're never going to part, Lilli. I'll do everything in my power to make you happy.'

'Just continue to love me,' she told him. 'It will be enough. I—'

'Can we come back in yet?' Gerry looked cautiously around the door she had just opened. 'Only the champagne is getting warm!'

'Do come in.' Lilli held her hand out towards the other woman. 'Let's drink the champagne and make a toast.' She smiled glowingly at her father as he came in carrying the tray with the champagne bottle—pink, of course!—and another glass. 'To a wonderful Christmas and New Year for all of us,' she announced as they all held up their glasses, sure in her heart that every year was going to be a happy one from now on. For all of them.

'How could you do this to me?' Patrick groaned tragically. 'I'll never survive!'

Lilli laughed at his comical expression, very tired, but filled with a glow that shone from deep inside her. 'You'll survive only too well,' she said knowingly. 'Now there will be three of us to love and spoil you.'

'Twins!' Patrick looked down into the cribs that stood next to the hospital bed, gazing in wonder at the identical beauty of the babies that slept within them. 'And both girls,' he added achingly. 'I'm going to end up spoiling all of *you*!'

Lilli smiled at him indulgently. Their daughters had been born fifty-five and fifty-one minutes ago, respectively, and Patrick had been at her side the whole time she had been in labour. As he had been at her side during the whole of the last year...

Lilli had been right; this past year had been the happiest of her life. And she knew it had been the same for Patrick, that the birth of their beautiful daughters on New Year's Eve had made it all complete.

'Think how poor Daddy felt.' She gave a happy laugh. 'James Robert was born on Christmas Day!' No one, it seemed, could have been more surprised than her father when Gerry had presented him with a son a week ago.

It was probably the celebrating that had been going on ever since the birth that had brought on Lilli's own slightly premature labour. But it hadn't been a difficult birth, and their darling little girls were worth any pain she might have felt.

'Now all we have to do is think of names for them both,' Patrick said a little dazedly.

He was right. They hadn't even known she was expecting twins, and because they had been absolutely convinced the baby she carried was a boy they hadn't chosen any girls' names at all.

'Is there room for three more in there?' Her father stood in the doorway, his baby son in his arms, Gerry at his side. 'Or are the Devlins taking over?' he added teasingly.

Lilli's family was complete as her father, Gerry and her new little brother came into the room.

Since she and Patrick had admitted their love for each other, Lilli had been convinced that every new day was the happiest of her life. But as she looked at all her family gathered there together, all so happy, she knew this was definitely their happiest day. Yet...

A WINTER
LOVE STORY

BY
BETTY NEELS

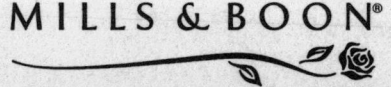

MILLS & BOON®

CHAPTER ONE

CLAUDIA leaned up, took another armful of books from the shelves lining the little room, put them on the table beside her and sneezed as a cloud of mummified dust rose from them. What had possessed her, she wondered, to take on the task of dusting her great-uncle William's library when she could have been enjoying these few weeks at home doing as she pleased?

She picked up her duster, sneezed again, and bent to her task, a tall, slim but shapely girl with a lovely face and shining copper hair, which was piled untidily on top of her head and half covered by another duster, secured by a piece of string. Her shapely person was shrouded in a large print pinny several sizes too big, her face had a dusty smear on one cheek and her nose shone. Nevertheless she looked beautiful, and the man watching her from the half-open door smiled his appreciation before giving a little cough.

Claudia looked over her shoulder at him. There was nothing about him to make her feel uneasy—indeed, he was the epitome of understated elegance, with an air of assurance which was in itself reassuring. He was a big man, very tall and powerfully built, not so very young but with the kind of good looks which could only improve with age. His hair was pepper and salt, cut short. He might be in his late thirties. Claudia wondered who he was.

'Have you come to see Great-Uncle William or my mother? You came in through the wrong door—but of course you weren't to know that.' She smiled at him kindly, not wishing him to feel awkward.

He showed no signs of discomfort. 'Colonel Ramsay.' His commanding nose twisted at the dust. 'Should you not open a window? The dust…'

'Oh, they don't open. They're frightfully old—the original ones from when the house was built. Why do you want to see Colonel Ramsay?'

He looked at her before he answered. 'He asked me to call.'

'None of my business?' She clapped two aged tomes together and sent another cloud of dust across the room. 'Go back the way you came,' she told him, 'out of the side door and ring the front doorbell. Tombs will admit you.'

She gave him a nod and turned back to the shelves. Probably someone from Great-Uncle William's solicitor.

'I don't think I like him much,' said Claudia to the silent room. All the same she had to admit that she would have liked to know more about him.

She saw him again, not half an hour later, when, the duster removed from her head and her hands washed, she went along to the kitchen for coffee.

The house was large and rambling, and now, on the edge of winter, with an antiquated heating system, several of its rooms were decidedly chilly. Only the kitchen was cosy, with the Aga warming it, and since there were only her mother, Mrs Pratt the housekeeper, Jennie the maid and, of course, Tombs, who seemed to Claudia to be as old as the house, if not older, it was here that they had their morning coffee.

If there were visitors Mrs Ramsay sat in chilly state in the drawing room and dispensed coffee from a Sèvres coffee pot arranged on a silver tray, but in the kitchen they all had their individual mugs. However, despite this democratic behaviour, no one would have dreamt of sitting down or drinking their coffee until Mrs Ramsay had taken her place at the head of the table and lifted her own special mug to her lips.

Claudia breezed into the kitchen with Rob the Labrador at her heels. Her mother was already there, and sitting beside her, looking as though it was something he had been doing all his life, was the strange man. He got to his feet as she went in, and so did Tombs, and Claudia stopped halfway to the table.

She didn't speak for a moment, but raised eloquent eyebrows at her mother. Mrs Ramsay said comfortably, 'Yes, I know, dear, we ought to be in the drawing room. But there's been a fall of soot so the fire can't be lighted. And Dr Tait-Bullen likes kitchens.'

She smiled round the table, gathering murmured agreements while the doctor looked amused.

'Come and drink your coffee, Claudia,' went on Mrs Ramsay. 'This is Dr Tait-Bullen who came to see Uncle William. My daughter, Claudia.'

Claudia inclined her head, and said, 'How do you do?' in a rather frosty manner. He could have told her, she thought, instead of just walking away as he had done. 'Uncle William isn't ill?' she asked.

The doctor glanced at her mother before replying. 'Colonel Ramsay has a heart condition which I believe may benefit from surgery.'

'He's ill? But Dr Willis saw him last week—he didn't say anything. Are you sure?'

Dr Tait-Bullen, a surgeon of some fame within his profession, assured her gravely that he was sure. 'Dr Willis very wisely said nothing until he had a second opinion.'

'Then why isn't he here now?' demanded Claudia.
'You could be wrong, whatever you say.'

'Of course. Dr Willis was to have met me here this
morning, but I understand that a last-minute emergency
prevented him. I have been called in as consultant, but
the decision concerning the Colonel's further treatment
rests with his doctor and himself.' He added gently, 'I
was asked my opinion, nothing more.'

Mrs Ramsay cast a look at Claudia. Sometimes a
daughter with red hair could be a problem. She said carefully, 'You may depend upon Dr Willis getting the very
best advice darling.'

Claudia stared across the table at him, and he met her
look with an impassive face. If he was annoyed he
showed no sign of it.

'What do you advise?' she asked him.

'Dr Willis will come presently. I think we should wait
until he is here. He and I will need to talk.'

'But is Great Uncle William ill? I mean, really ill?'

Her mother interrupted. 'Claudia, we mustn't badger
Dr Tait-Bullen.' She looked round the table. 'More coffee for anyone?'

Claudia pushed back her chair. 'No, thank you,
Mother. I'll go and get on with the books. Tombs knows
where I am if I'm wanted.'

She smiled at the butler and whisked herself out of
the room, allowing the smile to embrace everyone there.

Back in the library, she set about clearing the shelves,
banging books together in clouds of dust, wielding her
duster with quite unnecessary vigour. She had behaved
very badly and she was sorry about it—and a bit puzzled
too, for she liked him. What had possessed her to be so
rude? She had behaved like a self-conscious teenager.
She ought to apologise. Tombs, she knew, would come

and tell her what was happening from time to time, so
when the doctor was about to leave she would say something polite…

She spent a few minutes making up suitable
speeches—a dignified apology, brief and matter-of-fact.
She tried out several versions, anxious to get it right.
She was halfway through her final choice when she was
interrupted.

'If those gracious words were meant for me,' said Dr
Tait-Bullen, 'I am flattered.'

He was leaning against the door behind her, smiling
at her, and she smiled back without meaning to. 'Well,
they were. I was rude. I was going to apologise to you
before you left.'

'Quite unnecessary, Miss Ramsay. One must make al-
lowances for red hair and unpleasant news.'

'Now you're being rude,' she muttered, but went on
anxiously. 'You really meant that? Great Uncle William
is seriously ill? I can see no reason why I shouldn't be
told. I'm not a child.'

He studied her briefly. 'No, you are not a child, but
Dr Willis and I must talk first.' He came into the room,
moved a pile of books and sat down on the table. 'This
is a delightful house, but surely rather large for the three
of you?'

He spoke idly and she answered him readily. 'Well,
yes, but it's been in the family for a long time. Most of
the rooms are shut up, so it's easy enough to run. Tombs
has been here for ever, and Mrs Pratt and Jennie have
been here for years and years. The gardens have got a
bit out of hand, but old Stokes from the village comes
up to help me.'

'You have a job?'

'I did have. Path Lab assistant—not trained, of course,

just general dogsbody. But London's too far off. I've applied for several jobs which aren't so far away so that I can come home often.'

He said casually, 'Ah, yes of course. Salisbury, Southampton, Exeter—they are all within reasonable distance.'

'And there are several private hospitals too. I didn't much like London.' She added chattily, 'Do you live there?'

'Most of my work is done there.'

She supposed that he hadn't added to that because Tombs had joined them.

'Dr Willis has arrived, sir.' He looked at Claudia. 'Mrs Ramsay is in the morning room, Miss Claudia. Jennie has lighted the fire there for the convenience of the doctors.'

'Thank you, Tombs.' She glanced at the doctor. 'You'll want to go with Tombs. I'll come presently—I must just tidy myself.'

Left to herself, she took off her pinny, dragged a comb through her hair and went in search of her mother.

Mrs Ramsay was with the two men, making small talk before they began their discussion of their patient's condition. She was still a strikingly beautiful woman, wearing her fifty years lightly. Her hair, once as bright as her daughter's, was streaked with silver, but she was still slim and graceful. She was listening to something Dr Willis was saying, smiling up at him, her hand on his coat-sleeve. They were old friends; he had treated her husband before his death several years ago, and since he was a widower, living in a rather gloomy house in the village with an equally gloomy elderly housekeeper, he was a frequent visitor at the Ramsays' house.

He looked up as Claudia joined them.

'My dear, there you are. Come to keep your mother company for a while? Are we to stay here, or would you prefer us to go to the study?'

'No, no, stay here. There's a fire specially lighted for you. Claudia and I will go and see to lunch.' She paused at the door. 'You will tell us exactly what is wrong?'

'Of course.'

In the dining room, helping her mother to set the lunch, Claudia asked, 'Is Great-Uncle William really very ill, Mother?'

'Well, dear, I'm afraid so. He hasn't really been very well for some time, but we couldn't persuade him to have a second opinion. This Dr Tait-Bullen seems a nice man.'

'Nice?' Claudia hesitated. 'Yes, I'm sure he is.' 'Nice,' she reflected, hardly described him; it was far too anaemic a word. Beneath the professional polite detachment she suspected there was a man she would very much like to know.

They were standing idly at the windows, looking out into the wintry garden, when Tombs came to tell them that the doctors had come downstairs from seeing their patient.

Dr Willis went straight to Mrs Ramsay and took her hand. He was a tall, thin man, with a craggy face softened by a comforting smile as he looked at her. He didn't say anything. Claudia saw her mother return his look and swallowed a sudden surprised breath. The look had been one of trust and affection. Don't beat about the bush, Claudia admonished herself silently. They're in love.

There was no chance to think about it; Dr Tait-Bullen was speaking. Great Uncle William needed a triple bypass, and without undue loss of time. The one difficulty, he pointed out, was that the patient had no intention of agreeing to an operation.

Claudia asked quickly, 'Would that cure him? Would he be able to lead a normal life—be up and about again?'

'The Colonel is an old man, but he should be able to live the life of a man of his age.'

'Yes, but…'

'Claudia, let Dr Tait-Bullen finish…'

'Sorry.' She flushed and he watched the colour creep into her cheeks before he said, 'I quite understand your anxiety. If Dr Willis wishes, I will come again very shortly and do my best to change the Colonel's mind. I feel sure that if anyone can do that it will be he, for they have known each other for a long time. I can but advise.'

He glanced at the other man. 'We have discussed what is best to be done—there are certain drugs which will help, diet, suitable physiotherapy…'

'I'm sure you have done everything within your power, Doctor,' said Mrs Ramsay. 'We will do our best to persuade Uncle William, and if you would keep an eye on him?' She looked at Dr Willis. 'That is, if you don't mind, George?'

'I am only too glad of expert advice.'

'Oh, good. You'll stay for lunch, Dr Tait-Bullen? In half an hour or so…'

'I must return to London, Mrs Ramsay. You will forgive me if I refuse your kind invitation.'

He shook hands with her, and then with Dr Willis. 'We will be in touch.'

'Claudia, take Dr Tait-Bullen to his car, will you, dear?'

They walked through the house together, out of the door and across the neglected sweep of gravel to where a dark grey Rolls Royce stood. Claudia stared at it reflectively.

'Are you just a doctor?' she wanted to know. 'Or someone more important?' She glanced at his quiet face. 'Mother called you Doctor, so I thought you were. You're not, are you?'

'Indeed, I am a doctor. I am also a surgeon...'

'So you're *Mr* Tait-Bullen. You're not a professor or anything like that, are you?'

'I'm afraid so...'

'You might have said so.'

'Quite unnecessary. Besides, being called a professor makes me feel old.'

'You're not old.'

He answered her without rancour. 'Thirty-nine. And you?'

She had asked for that. Anyway, what did it matter? 'I'm very nearly twenty-seven,' she told him.

He said smoothly, 'I am surprised that you are not yet married, Miss Ramsay.'

'Well, I'm not,' she snapped. 'I've not met anyone I've wanted to marry.' She added pettishly, 'I have had several proposals.'

'That does not surprise me.' He smiled down at her, thinking how unusual it was to see grey eyes allied with such very red hair. He sounded suddenly brisk. 'You will do your best to persuade the Colonel to agree to surgery, will you?'

When she nodded, he got into his car and drove away. His handshake had been firm and cool and brief.

Claudia went back to the morning room and found her mother and Dr Willis deep in talk. They smiled at her as she went in, and her mother said, 'He's gone? Such a pleasant man, and not a bit stiff or pompous. Dr

Willis has been telling me that he's quite an important surgeon—perhaps I shouldn't have given him coffee in the kitchen.' She frowned. 'Do you suppose Uncle will take his advice?'

'Most unlikely, Mother. I'll take his lunch up presently, and see if he'll talk about it.'

Great-Uncle William had no intention of talking to anyone on the subject. When Claudia made an attempt to broach the matter, she was told to hold her tongue and mind her own business. Advice which she took in good part, for she was used to the old man's irascible temper and had a strong affection for him.

He had been very good to her mother and to her when her father died, giving them a home, educating her, while at the same time making no bones about the fact that he would have been happier living in the house by himself, with his housekeeper and Tombs to look after him. All the same, she suspected that he had some affection for them both, and was grateful for that.

It was a pity that on his death the house would pass to a distant cousin whom she had never met. That Uncle William had made provision for her mother and herself was another reason for gratitude, for Mrs Ramsay had only a small income, and after years of living in comfort it would have been hard for her to move to some small house and count every penny.

They would miss the old house, with its large rooms and elegant shabbiness, and they would miss Tombs and Mrs Pratt and Jennie too, but Claudia supposed that she would have a job somewhere or other and make a life for herself. Somewhere she could get home easily from time to time. Her mother would miss her friends. Especially she would miss Dr Willis, always there to cope with any small crisis.

The days went unhurriedly by. Claudia finished turning out the library and turned her attention to the rather
battered greenhouse at the bottom of the large garden.
The mornings were frosty, and old Stokes, who came up
from the village to see to the garden, tidied the beds and
dug the ground in the kitchen garden, leaving her free
to look after the contents of the glass house.

It contained a medley of pots and containers, filled
with seedlings and cuttings, and she spent happy hours
grubbing around, hopefully sowing seed trays and nursing along the hyacinths and tulips she intended for
Christmas.

And every day she spent an hour or so with her great-
uncle, reading him dry-as-dust articles from *The Times*
or listening to him reminiscing about his military career.
He still refused to speak of his illness. It seemed to her
anxious eyes that he was weaker, short of breath, easily
tired and with an alarming lack of appetite.

Dr Willis came to see him frequently, and it was at
the end of a week in which he could detect no improve-
ment in his patient that he told Mrs Ramsay that he had
asked Mr Tait-Bullen to come again.

He came on a dreary November morning, misty and
damp and cold, and Claudia, busy with her seedlings, an
old sack wrapped around her topped by a jacket colour-
less with age, knew nothing of his arrival. True, she had
been told that he was to come again, but no day had
been fixed; he was an exceedingly busy man, she'd been
told, and his out of town visits had to be fitted in whenever possible.

He had spent some time with the Colonel, and even
longer with Dr Willis, before talking to Mrs Ramsay,
and when that lady observed that she would send Tombs

to fetch Claudia to join them, volunteered to fetch her himself.

Studying the sack and the old jacket as he entered the greenhouse, he wondered if he was ever to have the pleasure of seeing Claudia looking like the other young women of his acquaintance—fashionably clad, hair immaculate, expertly made up—and decided that she looked very nice as she was. The thought made him smile.

She had looked round as he opened the door and her smile was welcoming.

'Hello—does Mother know you're here?' And then, 'Great Uncle isn't worse?'

'I've seen the Colonel and talked to your mother and Dr Willis. I've been here for some time. Your mother would like you to join us at the house.'

She put down the tray of seedlings slowly. 'Great Uncle William won't let you operate—I tried to talk him into it but he wouldn't listen...'

He said gently, 'I'm afraid so. And the delay has made an operation questionable.'

'You mean it's too late? But it's only a little more than a week since you saw him.'

'If I could have operated immediately he would have had a fair chance of recovering and leading a normal quiet life.'

'And now he has no chance at all?'

He said gravely, 'We shall continue to do all that we can.'

She nodded. 'Yes, I know that you will. I'll come. Is Mother upset? Does she know?'

'Yes.' He watched while she took off the deplorable jacket and untied the sack and went to wash her hands at the stone sink. The water was icy and her hands were grimy. She saw his look. 'You can't handle seedlings in gloves,' she told him. 'They are too small and delicate.'

'You prefer them to dusting books?' he asked as they started for the house.

'Yes, though books are something I couldn't possibly manage without. I'd rather buy a book than a hat.'

He reflected that it would be a pity to hide that glorious hair under a hat, however becoming, but he didn't say so.

Her mother and Dr Willis were in the morning room again, and Mrs Ramsay said in a relieved voice, 'Oh, there you are, dear. I expect Mr Tait-Bullen has explained…'

'Yes, Mother. Do you want me to go and sit with Great-Uncle?'

'He told us all to go away, so I expect you'd better wait a while. Mr Tait-Bullen is going to see him again presently, but he doesn't want anyone else there.' She turned as Tombs came in with the coffee tray. 'But you'll have coffee first, won't you?'

They drank their coffee while the two men sustained the kind of small talk which needed very little reply, and presently Mr Tait-Bullen went back upstairs.

He was gone for some time and Claudia, getting impatient, got up and prowled round the room. 'I don't suppose he'll come again,' she said at length.

'There is no need for him to do so, but the Colonel has taken quite a fancy to him. Mr Tait-Bullen calls a spade a spade when necessary, but in the nicest possible way. What is more, his patients aren't just patients; they are men and women with feelings and wishes which he respects. Your great-uncle knows that.'

Mr Tait-Bullen, driving along the narrow roads which would take him from the village of Little Planting to the

M3 and thence to London, allowed his thoughts to wander. He and the Colonel had talked about many things, none of which had anything to do with his condition. The Colonel had made it clear that he intended to die in his own bed, and, while conceding that Mr Tait-Bullen was undoubtedly a splendid surgeon and cardiologist, he wished to have no truck with surgery, which he considered, at his time of life, to be quite worthless.

Mr Tait-Bullen had made no effort to change his mind for him. True, he could have prolonged his patient's life and allowed him to live for a period at least in moderate health, but he considered that if he had overridden the Colonel's wishes, the old man would have died of frustration at having his wishes ignored. They had parted good friends, and on the mutual understanding that if and when Mr Tait-Bullen had a few hours of leisure he would pay another visit as a friend.

Something he intended to do, for he wanted to see Claudia again.

He went straight to the hospital when he reached London; he had an afternoon clinic which lasted longer than usual. He had no lunch, merely swallowed a cup of tea between patients. It was with a sigh of relief that he stopped the car outside his front door in a small tree-lined street tucked away behind Harley Street, where he had his consulting rooms.

It was a narrow Regency house in a row of similar houses, three storeys high with bow windows and a beautiful front door with a handsome pediment, reached by three steps bordered by delicate iron railings. He let himself in quietly and was met in the hall by a middle-aged man with a craggy face and a fringe of hair. He looked like a dignified church warden, and ran Mr Tait-

Bullen's house to perfection. He greeted him now with a touch of severity.

'There's that Miss Thompson on the phone, reminding you that she expects to see you this evening. I told her that you were still at the hospital and there was no knowing when you'd be home.' Cork lowered his eyes deferentially. 'I trust I did right, sir.'

Mr Tait-Bullen was looking through the post on the hall table. 'You did exactly right, Cork. I don't know what I would do without you.' He glanced up. 'Did I say I would take her somewhere this evening? It has quite slipped my mind.'

Cork drew a deep breath through pinched nostrils. In anyone less dignified it would have been a sniff. 'You were invited to attend the new play. The opening night, I believe.'

'Did I say I'd go? I can't remember writing it down in my diary.'

'You prevaricated, sir. Said if you were free you'd be glad to accept.'

Mr Tait-Bullen picked up his case and opened his study door. 'I'm not free, Cork, and I'm famished!'

'Dinner will be served in fifteen minutes, sir. The young lady's phone number is on your desk.'

Mr Tait-Bullen sat down at his desk and picked up the receiver. Honor Thompson's rather shrill voice, sounding peevish, answered.

'And about time, too. Why are you never at home? It's so late; I'll go on to the theatre and meet you there. The Pickerings are picking me up in ten minutes.'

Mr Tait-Bullen said smoothly, 'Honor, I'm so sorry, but there is absolutely no chance of me getting away until late this evening. I did tell you that I might not be free; will you make my excuses to the Pickerings?'

They talked for a few minutes, until she said, 'Oh, well, you're not much use as an escort, are you, Thomas?' She gave a little laugh. 'I might as well give you up.'

'There must be any number of men queueing up to take you out. I'm not reliable, Honor.'

'You'll end up a crusty old bachelor, Thomas, unless you take time off to fall in love.'

'I'll have to think about that.'

'Well, let me know when you've made up your mind.' She rang off, and he put the phone down and forgot all about her. He had a teaching round the next morning and he needed to prepare a few notes for that.

He ate the dinner Cork set before him and went back to his study to work. He was going to his bed when he had a sudden memory of Claudia, her fiery hair in a mess, enveloped in that old jacket and a sack. He found himself smiling, thinking of her.

The first few days of November, with their frosty mornings and chilly pale skies, had turned dull and damp, and as they faded towards winter Great-Uncle William faded with them. But although he was physically weaker there was nothing weak about his mental state. He was as peppery as he always had been, defying anyone to show sympathy towards him, demanding that Claudia should read *The Times* to him each morning, never mind that he dozed off every now and then.

His faithful housekeeper's endless efforts to prepare tasty morsels for his meals met with no success at all. And no amount of coaxing would persuade him to allow a nurse to attend to his wants. Between them, Claudia, her mother and Tombs did as much as he would allow them to. Dr Willis, inured to his patient's caustic tongue, came daily, but it was less than a week after Mr Tait-Bullen's visit when Great-Uncle William, glaring at him from his bed, observed in an echo of his former commanding tones, 'I shall die within the next day or so. Tell Tait-Bullen to come and see me.'

'He's a busy man...'

'I know that; I'm not a fool.' The Colonel looked suddenly exhausted. 'He said that he would come.' He turned his head to look at Claudia, standing at the window, lingering after she had brought Dr Willis upstairs.

'You—Claudia, go and telephone him. Now, girl!'

She glanced at Dr Willis, and at his nod went down to the hall and dialled Mr Tait-Bullen's number. Cork's dignified voice regretted that Mr Tait-Bullen was not at home.

'It's urgent. Do you know where I can get him?' She added, so as to make things clear, 'I'm not a friend or anything. My great-uncle is a patient of Mr Tait-Bullen's and he wants to see him. He's very ill.'

'In that case, miss, I will give you the number of his consulting rooms.'

She thanked him and dialled again, and this time Mrs Truelove, Mr Tait-Bullen's receptionist, answered.

'Colonel Ramsay? You are his niece? Mr Tait-Bullen has mentioned him. He's with a patient at the moment. Ring off, my dear; I'll call you the moment he's free.'

Claudia waited, wondering if Mr Tait-Bullen would have time to visit Great-Uncle William or even to phone him. She supposed that he was a very busy man; he could hardly be blamed if he hadn't the time to leave London and his patients to obey the whim of an old man who had refused his services. Then the phone rang, and she picked it up.

'Yes,' said a voice in her ear. 'Tait-Bullen speaking.'

This was no time for polite chit-chat. 'Great-Uncle William wants to see you. He says he's going to die in a day or two. He told me to phone you, so I am, because he asked me to, but you don't have to.'

She wasn't sure if she had made herself clear, but apparently she had. Mr Tait-Bullen disentangled the muddle with a twitching lip and answered her with exactly the right amount of impersonal friendliness.

'It is very possible that your great-uncle is quite right. I'm free this evening; I will be with you at about seven o'clock.'

He heard her relieved sigh.

'Thank you very much. I'm sorry if I've disturbed your work.'

'I'm glad you phoned me.'

She could hear the faint impatience in his voice. 'Goodbye, then.' She rang off smartly, and then wondered if she'd been rather too abrupt.

He arrived punctually, unfussed and unhurried. No one looking at his immaculate person would have guessed that he had been up since six o'clock, had missed his lunch and stopped only for the tea and bun his faithful Mrs Truelove had pressed upon him. Dr Willis was waiting for him, and they spent a few minutes talking together before they went up to the Colonel's room. Dr Willis came down presently. 'They're discussing the merits of pyrenaicum aureum as opposed to tenuifolium pumilum...'

Mrs Ramsay looked puzzled. 'Is that some new symptom? It sounds alarming. Poor Uncle William.'

'Lilies,' said Claudia. 'Two varieties of lily, Mother.'

Dr Willis patted her mother's arm. 'Don't alarm yourself, my dear. Your uncle is enjoying his little chat. It was good of Mr Tait-Bullen to come.'

'But he's not doing anything to help Uncle…'

But that was exactly what he *was* doing, reflected Claudia, although she didn't say so. Instead she asked, 'Do you suppose he will stay for supper? Mrs Pratt can grill a couple more chops.'

But when he joined them presently, he declined Mrs Ramsay's offer of supper, saying that he must return to London.

'I hope we haven't spoilt your evening for you—caused you to cancel a date?'

Claudia noticed that he didn't answer that, merely thanked her mother for her invitation. 'If I might have a word with Dr Willis?'

They left the two men, returning when they heard them in the hall.

Mrs. Ramsay shook hands. 'We're so grateful to you. Uncle did so wish to see you again—although I'm sure you are a very busy man.'

He said gravely, 'The Colonel is going to die very soon now, Mrs Ramsay; he is content, and in no pain, and in Dr Willis's good hands.'

He turned to Claudia. 'I was bidden to tell you to read the editorial in *The Times* before he has his supper.' His hand was firm and cool and comforting. 'He's fond of you, you know.'

He left then, getting into his car and driving back to his house to eat the meal Cork had ready for him and then go to his study and concentrate on the notes of the patients upon whom he would be operating in the morning. Before that, he paused to think about the Colonel. A courageous old man hidden behind that crusty manner. He hoped that he would die quietly in his sleep.

Great-Uncle William died while Claudia was still

reading the editorial. So quietly and peacefully that it wasn't until she had finished it that she realised.

She said softly, 'You had a happy talk about lilies, didn't you, Uncle William? I'm glad he came.'

She bent to kiss the craggy old face and went down-stairs to tell her mother.

CHAPTER TWO

THE Colonel had been respected in the village; he had had no use for a social life or mere acquaintances, although he had lifelong friends.

Claudia had very little time to grieve. Her mother saw the callers when they came, arranged things with the undertaker and planned the flowers and the gathering of friends and family after the funeral, but it was left to Claudia to carry out her wishes, answer the telephone and make a tidy pile of the letters which would have to be answered later.

Dr Willis was a tower of strength, of course, but he was more concerned with her mother than anything else, and Mrs Ramsay leaned on him heavily for comfort and support. She needed both when, on the day before the funeral, the cousin who was to inherit the house arrived.

He was a middle-aged man, with austere good looks and cold eyes. He treated them with cool courtesy, expressed a token regret at the death of the Colonel and went away to see the colonel's solicitor. When he returned he requested that Mrs Ramsay and Claudia should join him in the morning room.

He stood with his back to the fire and begged them to sit down. Already master of the house, thought Claudia, and wondered what was coming.

He spoke loudly, as though he thought that they were deaf. 'Everything seems to be in order. The will is not yet read, of course, but I gather that there are no surprises in it. I must return to York after the funeral, but

I intend to return within two or three days. Monica—my wife—will accompany me and we will take up residence then. My house there is already on the market. You will, of course, wish to leave here as soon as possible.'

Claudia heard her mother's quick breath. 'Are you interested as to where we are going?'

'It is hardly my concern.' He eyed Claudia coldly. 'You must have been aware for some time that the house would become my property and have some plans of your own.'

'Well,' said Claudia slowly, 'whatever plans we may have had didn't include being thrown out lock, stock and barrel at a moment's notice.' When he started to speak, she added, 'No, let me finish. Let us know when you and your wife will arrive and we will be gone in good time. What about Tombs and Mrs Pratt and Jennie? I understand that they have been remembered in Uncle William's will.'

'I shall, of course, give them a month's wages.' He considered the matter for a moment. 'It might be convenient if Mrs Pratt remained, and the girl. It will save Monica a good deal of trouble if the servants remain.'

'And Tombs?'

'Oh! He's past an honest day's work. He will have his state pension.'

'Have you any children?'

He looked surprised. 'No. Why do you ask?'

She didn't answer that, merely said in a matter-of-fact voice, 'Well, that's a blessing, isn't it?' Then she added, 'I'm glad you're only a distant cousin.'

He said loftily, 'I cannot understand you…'

'Well, of course you can't. But never mind that. Is that all? We'll see you at dinner presently.'

She saw him go red in the face as she got up and urged her mother out of the room.

In the hall, her mother said, 'Darling, you were awfully rude.'

'Mother, he's going to throw Tombs out, not to mention us. He's the most awful man I've ever met. And I'm sure Mrs Pratt and Jennie won't want to stay. I'm going to see them now.'

She gave her mother a reassuring pat on the shoulder. 'Why don't you go and phone Dr Willis and see what he says?'

Over a mug of powerfully brewed tea, she told Tombs and Mrs Pratt and Jennie what her cousin had said. They listened in growing unrest.

'You'll not catch me staying with the likes of him,' said Mrs Pratt. She looked at Jennie. 'And what about you, Jennie, girl?'

'Me neither.' They both looked at Tombs.

Claudia hadn't repeated all her cousin had said about Tombs, but he had read between the lines.

'I'll never get another place at my age,' he told them. 'But I wouldn't stay for all the tea in China.'

He turned a worried old face towards Claudia. 'Where will you and madam go, Miss Claudia? It's a scandal, turning you out of house and home.'

'We'll think of something, Tombs. We've several days to plan something.'

'And Rob?'

'He'll come with us. I don't know about Stokes...'

'I'll see that he gives in his notice,' said Tombs. 'What a mercy that the Colonel isn't here; he would never have allowed these goings on.'

'No, but you see this cousin of his has every right to do what he likes. If you intend to leave when we do, have you somewhere to go? Mother's on the phone to Dr Willis, who may be able to help. If not then we will all put up at the Duck and Thistle in the village.'

'I could go home,' ventured Jennie. 'Me mum'll give me a bed for a bit.' She sounded doubtful, and Claudia said, 'Well, perhaps Dr Willis will know of someone local who needs help in the house. I think we'd all better start packing our things as soon as the funeral is over.'

She found her mother in the morning room. It was cold there, for the fire hadn't been lighted, and Mrs Ramsay was walking up and down in a flurried way.

'Mother, it's too cold for you here, and you're upset.'

'No, dear, there's nothing wrong—in fact quite the reverse. Only I'm not sure how to talk to you about it.'

Claudia sat her parent down on the sofa and settled beside her.

'You talked to Dr Willis? He had some suggestions? Some advice?'

'Well, yes…'

'Mother, dear, does he want to marry you? I know you're fond of each other…'

'Oh, yes we are, love, but how can I possibly marry him and leave you and the others in the lurch? At least…'

'Yes?' Claudia had taken her mother's hand. 'Do tell. I'm sure it's something helpful. He's such a dear; I'll love having him for a stepfather.'

Mrs Ramsay gave a shaky little laugh. 'Oh, darling, will you really? But I haven't said I'd marry him.'

'But you will. Now, what else does he suggest?'

'Well, it's coincidental, but his housekeeper has given him notice—wants to go back to her family somewhere in Lancashire—so Mrs Pratt could take over if she would like the job. And he knows everyone here, doesn't he? He says it should be easy to find a place for Jennie.'

'And Tombs?'

'George said he's always wanted a butler. His house is quite small, but there would be plenty for Tombs to do. And he'd love to have Rob... Only there's you, darling.'

'But, Mother dear, I'll be getting a job. I've already applied for several, you know, and none of them are too far from here. I can come for holidays and weekends, if George will have me.'

'You're not just saying that to make it easy for the rest of us?'

'Of course not. You know that was the plan, wasn't it? That I should come here for a week or two while I looked for something nearer than London?'

She didn't mention that she had had two answers that morning from her applications, and both posts had been filled. There was still another one to come...

'Well, Claudia, if you think that's the right thing to do. We shall go and tell Tombs and the others.'

'Yes, but no one had better say a word to Mr Ramsay. When do you see Dr Willis—no, I shall call him George if he doesn't mind?'

'After the funeral. He thought it best not to come here.'

'Quite right too. We don't want Cousin Ramsay smelling a rat. Mother, you go to the kitchen; I'll hang around the house in case he comes looking for us.'

Later at dinner, Mr Ramsay made no mention of their plans; he had a good deal to say about the various alterations he intended making in the house. Monica, he told them, was a woman of excellent taste. She would have the shabby upholstery covered and the thick velvet curtains in the drawing room and dining room torn down and replaced by something more up-to-date.

'The curtains were chosen by Great-Uncle William's mother,' observed Mrs Ramsay, 'when she came here as a bride.'

'Then it's high time that they were removed. They are probably full of dust and germs.'

'Most unlikely,' said Claudia quickly. 'Everything in the house has been beautifully cared for.'

He gave her an annoyed look. He didn't like this girl, with the fiery hair and the too ready tongue. He decided not to answer her, but instead addressed Mrs Ramsay with some query about the following day.

It was after the last of the Colonel's friends and acquaintances had taken their leave, after returning to the house for tea and Mrs Pratt's delicious sandwiches and cakes, that Mr Potter, the Colonel's solicitor, led the way across the hall to the morning room. He had been a friend of the family for years, and his feelings had been hurt when Mr Ramsay had told him that he would no longer require his services.

His father and his father before him had looked after the Ramsays' modest estate, but he was old himself and he supposed that Mr Ramsay's own lawyer would be perfectly capable. He said now, 'If someone would ask Tombs and Mrs Pratt and Jennie to come in here.' He beamed across at Dr Willis. 'I had already asked you to be present, George.'

He took no notice of Mr Ramsay's frown, but waited patiently until everyone was there.

The will was simple and short. The house and estate were to go to Cousin Ramsay, and afterwards to his heirs. Mrs Ramsay was to receive shares in a company, sufficient to maintain her lifestyle, and Claudia was to receive the same amount, but neither of them could use the capital. Tombs received five thousand pounds, Mrs Pratt the same amount, and Jennie one thousand pounds. Claudia heard Cousin Ramsay draw in a disapproving breath at that.

Mr Potter put the will back in his briefcase and said, suddenly grave, 'If I might have a word with you, Mrs Ramsay, and Claudia, and you, Mr Ramsay?'

When the others had gone, he said, 'I am afraid that I have bad news for you; the company in which the shares were invested and destined for you Mrs Ramsay, and you, Claudia, has gone bankrupt. I ascertained this the day before the Colonel died, and I intended to visit him on that very day. There is nothing to be done about the terms of the will, but perhaps you, Mr Ramsay, will wish to make some adjustment so that Mrs Ramsay and Claudia are not left penniless.'

He saw no sign of encouragement in Mr Ramsay's stern features. Nevertheless he persisted. 'Their incomes would have been small, but adequate. I can advise you as to the amount they would have been. One wouldn't expect you to make good the full amount, but I'm sure that a small allowance for each of them...' His voice faded away under Mr Ramsay's icy stare.

Claudia saw the painful colour in her mother's face. 'That is very thoughtful of you, Mr Potter, but I think that neither mother nor I would wish to accept anything from Mr Ramsay.'

Mr Ramsay looked above their heads and cleared his throat. 'I have many commitments,' he observed. 'Any such arrangement would be quite beyond my means.'

Mr Potter opened his mouth to protest, but Claudia

caught his eye and shook her head. And, although the old man looked bewildered, he closed it again.

It was Mrs Ramsay who said, in a voice which gave away none of her feelings, 'You'll stay for supper, Mr Potter? I remember Uncle William promised you that little painting on the stairs, which you always admired. Will you fetch it, Claudia?'

She smiled at Mr. Ramsay. 'It is of no value, and one must keep one's promises, must one not?'

Mr Potter refused supper and, clutching the picture, was escorted to his car by Claudia. 'It is all most unsatisfactory,' he told her. 'Your great-uncle would never have allowed it to happen. How will you manage? Surely even a small allowance—'

Claudia popped him into the car and kissed his cheek. 'I'll tell you a secret. Mother is going to marry Dr Willis and I've my eye on a good job. We haven't told Mr Ramsay and we don't intend to. And Tombs and Mrs Pratt and Jennie are all fixed up. So don't worry about us.'

He cheered up then. 'In that case I feel very relieved. You will keep in touch?'

'Of course.'

She waved and smiled as he drove off, then went back into the house. Despite her cheerful words she would hate leaving the old house, although she told herself sensibly that she would have hated staying on there with Mr Ramsay and his wife, who would doubtless alter the whole place so much that she would never recognise it again.

Later, in her mother's bedroom she said, 'You'll have to marry George now, because I told Mr Potter you were going to.'

'But, Claudia, there's nothing arranged…'

'Then arrange it, Mother dear, as quickly as you can. There's something called a special licence, and the vicar's an old friend. Now, what's to happen when we leave? Is George giving us beds, or shall we go to the Duck and Thistle?'

'George wants me to go and see him tomorrow morning. I think he has something planned. Will you stay here, in case Mr Ramsay wants to talk to us about something?'

'Not likely. But I'll be here. Take Rob with you, Mother; *he* doesn't like dogs.'

Mr Ramsay spent the next morning going from room to room, taking careful note of his new possessions. The kitchen and its occupants he ignored; they could be dealt with when he was satisfied with his arrangements. He kept Claudia busy answering his questions about the furniture and pictures, all of which he valued.

'We shall sell a good deal,' he told her loftily. 'There are several pieces which I think may be of real value. But these...' He waved an arm at a pair of Regency terrestrial and celestial globes in one corner of the morning room. 'I doubt if they'd fetch more than a few pounds in a junk shop.'

Claudia, who happened to know that they were worth in the region of twenty thousand pounds and had been in the family for well over a hundred years, agreed politely.

'And this clock—Monica has no liking for such old-fashioned stuff; that can go.' He pointed to a William the Fourth bracket clock, very plain and worth at least two thousand pounds.

He brushed aside a stool. 'And there are all these around. I have never seen such a collection of out-of-date furniture.'

The stool was early Victorian, covered with petit-point tapestry. Claudia didn't mention its value, instead she said politely, 'There is a very good firm at Ringwood, I believe—a branch of one of the London antiques dealers. But I expect that you would prefer to go to someone you know in York.'

'Certainly not. I am more likely to get good prices from a firm which has some knowledge of this area.'

Claudia cast down her eyes and murmured. If and when he sold Great-Uncle William's family treasures, and she could find out who had bought them, she might be able to buy one or two of them back. She had no idea how she would do this, but that was something she would worry about later.

She knew the elder son of the antiques dealer at Ringwood; he might let her buy things back with instalments. Which reminded her of the letter she had stuffed in her pocket that morning. The post mark was Southampton, and it was the last reply from the batch of applications she had sent. Perhaps she would be lucky...

She was roused from her thoughts by Mr Ramsay's sharp, 'Where is your mother?'

She looked at him for a moment before replying. She wondered if she dared to tell him to mind his own business, but decided against it.

'Well, she will have gone upstairs to check the linen cupboard with Mrs Pratt—a long job—then she told me that she would be taking Rob for his walk and doing some necessary shopping in the village. She should be back by lunchtime. I don't know what she will be doing this afternoon.'

He gave her a suspicious glance. 'I wish to inform her of my final plans for moving here.'

'Well, I am going to the kitchen now to see about lunch.'

But first she went into the hall and out of the side door at its end, taking an old coat off a hook as she went and making for the glass house.

The letter was a reply to her application for the post of general helper at a geriatric hospital on the outskirts of Southampton. She had applied for it for the simple reason that there had been nothing else advertised, and she hadn't expected a reply.

Providing that her references were satisfactory, the job was hers. Her duties were vague, and the money was less than she had hoped for, but on the other hand she could start as soon as her references had been checked. It would solve the problem of her immediate future, set her mother's mind at rest and put a little money into her pocket.

She didn't see her mother until the three of them were sitting down to lunch, but she deduced from the faintly smug look on that lady's face that her talk with Dr Willis had been entirely satisfactory. It wasn't until they left the house together to take Rob for another walk that they were able to talk.

'When's the wedding?' asked Claudia as soon as they had left the house.

Her mother laughed. 'Darling, I'm not sure. I won't marry George until you're settled...'

'Then he'd better get a licence as soon as he can. I've got a job—in Southampton at one of the hospitals. I had the letter this morning.'

Mrs Ramsay beamed at her. 'Oh, Claudia, really? I mean, it's something you want to do, not just any old job you're taking to make things easy for us?'

To tell a lie was sometimes necessary, reflected

Claudia, if it was to a good purpose, and surely this was. 'It's exactly what I'm looking for—quite good money and I can come back here for weekends and holidays, if George will have me?'

'Of course we'll have you.' Her mother squeezed her arm. 'Isn't it strange how everything is coming right despite Uncle William's horrid cousin? And George has found a place for Jennie—they were looking for someone up at the Manor, so she will still keep her friends in the village and see Mrs Pratt and Tombs if she wants to.'

'Good. Now, when will you marry?'

'Well, as soon as George can get a licence.'

'You'll stay with him, of course?'

'Mrs Pratt and Tombs will be with me.'

'Mr Ramsay wants to talk to you about his plans. He didn't say anything at lunch…'

'Perhaps this evening.'

He was waiting for them when they got back. 'Be good enough to come to my study?' he asked Mrs Ramsay. 'I dare say Claudia has things to do.'

Dismissed, she went to her room; there were clothes to pack and small, treasured ornaments she had been given since childhood to be wrapped and stowed in boxes. As soon as Mr Ramsay went back to York Dr Willis would come and load up his car and stow everything they didn't want in his attics.

She hoped that the new owner of the house would stay away for several days, for they all intended to be gone, the house empty of people, by the time he and his wife arrived. He had said nothing to Tombs or Mrs Pratt, nor to Jennie; perhaps he expected them to stay on until he saw fit to discharge Tombs. He was arrogant enough to suppose that Mrs Pratt and Jennie would be only too thankful to remain in his service.

Since it was teatime, she went downstairs and found her mother in the morning room. There was no sign of Mr Ramsay, and at her questioning look Mrs Ramsay said, 'He's gone to see the vicar. He's going to York tomorrow afternoon and returning with Monica in two days' time. I am to tell Mrs Pratt and Jennie that they are to stay on in his employment—he hasn't bothered to ask them if they want to—and I'm to dismiss Tombs.'

'Why doesn't he do his own dirty work?' demanded Claudia. 'What else?'

'He avoided asking me where you and I were going; he made some remark about us having friends and he was sure we had sufficient funds to tide us over until we had settled somewhere.'

'Mother, he's despicable. Does he know about you and George?'

'No, I'm sure he doesn't, for he made a great thing of offering to send on our belongings once we had left.'

'Have you had a chance to tell Tombs?'

'No, I'd better go now; if he comes back, come and let me know.'

Not a word was said about their departure during dinner, and the following day Mr Ramsay got into his car and drove himself back to York.

'You may, of course, remain until the day following our return,' he told Mrs Ramsay. 'Monica will wish to be shown round the house.' He looked over her head, avoiding her eyes. 'Kindly see that Tombs has gone by the time we return.'

He turned back at the door. 'It will probably be late afternoon by the time we get here. Tell Mrs Pratt to have a meal ready and see that the maid has the rooms warm.'

Mrs Ramsay lowered her eyes and said, 'Yes,' meekly. She looked very like her daughter. 'I'm sure that if you think of anything else you will phone as soon as you get home.'

They waited a prudent hour before starting on their packing up. He was, observed Claudia, the kind of man who would sneak back to make sure that they weren't making off with the spoons. They collected their belongings, taking only what was theirs, and presently, when Dr Willis drove up, loaded his car. Mr Ramsay had said two days before he returned, but to be on the safe side they had decided to move out on the following day.

Dr Willis would have taken them all to his house for supper, but they refused and, while Mrs Pratt got a meal for them, began on the business of leaving the house in perfect condition. Tombs was set to polish the silver, Jennie saw to the bedrooms, and Claudia and her mother hoovered and dusted downstairs. After supper, tired but happy, they all went to bed.

They were up early in the morning, making sure that there was nothing with which the new owner could find fault, and as soon as the morning surgery was over Dr Willis came to fetch them to his house. He had to make two journeys, and Claudia left last of all, wheeling her bike and leading Rob on his lead. Mr Ramsay had a key—he had taken care to have all of the keys in his possession—but she had a key to the garden door which she had kept. She wasn't sure why and she didn't intend to tell anyone.

Dr Willis's housekeeper had already left, and Mrs Pratt slipped into the kitchen as though she had been there all her life, taking Tombs and Jennie with her.

'There are an awful lot of us,' worried Mrs Ramsay

as they ate the lunch the unflappable Mrs Pratt had produced.

'The house is large enough, my dear, and Jennie goes to her new job tomorrow.'

'And I go to mine in a day or two,' said Claudia.

'You're quite happy about it?' he asked her kindly. 'There's no hurry, you know.'

'It sounds just what I'm looking for. When will you marry? I'd like to come to the wedding.'

'Darling, we wouldn't dream of getting married unless you were there.'

'Within the week, I hope,' said George. 'Very quiet, of course, just us and a few friends here at the church. I've put a notice in the *Telegraph*.'

Everyone in the village knew by now that there was a new owner at Colonel Ramsay's house. Those that had met him didn't like him overmuch. The postman, who had been spoken to sharply by Mr Ramsay because he whistled too loudly as he delivered the letters and had been discovered drinking tea in the kitchen, had promised that any letters would be delivered to the doctor's house. The village considered Mr Ramsay an outsider, for he had made no effort to be pleasant. Even the vicar, a mild and godly man, pursed his lips when his name was mentioned.

There was a letter for Claudia the next morning. Her references had been accepted for the post of general assistant and she should present herself without delay to take up her duties. The list enclosed was vague about these, but the off duty seemed fair enough. She was to have two days a week free and the money was adequate. There was accommodation for her within the hospital.

She wrote back at once, accepting the post, and saying that she would present herself for duty in the early evening of the following day. Feeling pleased that things were turning out so well, she went away to unpack and repack what she would need to take with her.

Dr Willis drove her to Southampton after lunch the following day, and that same afternoon, as dusk was gathering, Mr Ramsay came back to take possession of his new home. An arrogant man, and insensitive to other people's feelings, he had taken it for granted that he would be received suitably—the house lighted and warm, a meal waiting to be put on the table, Mrs Ramsay there to show his wife round, Jennie to see to the luggage. He got out of the car and surveyed the dark, silent house with a frown before unlocking the door.

It was obvious that there was no one there. Monica pushed past him, switched on the lights and looked around her. She saw the letter on the side table and opened it. Mrs Ramsay wrote politely that as Mr Ramsay had requested they had left the house. And, since neither Mrs Pratt or Jennie wished to work for him, they had also left. There was food in the fridge, the fires were laid ready to light and the beds were aired and made up.

Monica laughed. 'You told them you wanted them out, and they've gone. I wonder where they went?'

'It's of no consequence. We can get help from the village easily enough, and I had nothing in common with either Mrs Ramsay or that daughter of hers.'

'A pity about the servants...'

'Easily come by in a small place like this—they'll be only too glad to have the work.'

'There was a butler, you said.'

'Oh, he was too old to work. I dare say he has found himself a room or gone to live with someone. He'd have his pension.'

His wife gave him a long look. 'You're a heartless

man, aren't you? You'd better bring in the luggage while I find the kitchen and see what there is to eat.'

Dr Willis left Claudia at the door of the hospital with some reluctance. The place looked gloomy and down at heel, and he was sorry that he hadn't found out about it before. True, geriatric hospitals were usually the last ones to get face lifts—probably inside it was bright and cheerful enough, and she had wished him goodbye very happily, with the promise that she would be at the wedding. She poked her head through the open window of the car.

'I know that you and Mother will be happy. You really are a very nice man, George.'

She picked up her case and went into the hospital.

She knew she wasn't going to like it before she had gone ten yards from the door, but she ignored that. A tired-looking porter asked her what she wanted, told her to leave her case and follow him and led her down a long passage. He knocked on the door at the end of it. The label on the door said 'Hospital Manager,' and when the porter opened the door in answer to the voice inside, she went past him into a small austere room.

It was furnished sparsely, with a desk and chair, two other chairs along one wall, and a great many shelves stuffed with paper files. The woman behind the desk had a narrow, pale face, a straight haircut in an unbecoming bob and small dark eyes. She looked up as Claudia went in, pursing her mouth and frowning a little.

'Miss Ramsay? It's too late for you to do much for the rest of the day. I'll get someone to show you your room and take you to where you will be working. But if you will draw up a chair I will explain your schedule to you.'

Not a very good start, reflected Claudia, but perhaps the poor soul was tired.

Her duties were many and varied and rather vague. She would work from seven o'clock until three in the afternoon three days a week, and her free day would follow that duty, and for the other three days the hours would be three o'clock in the afternoon until ten o'clock at night.

'The off duty is arranged so that you are free from three o'clock before your day off, and not on duty until three o'clock on the day following.'

Two nights at home, thought Claudia, and felt cheered by the thought.

She asked politely, 'Am I to call you Matron?'

'Miss Norton,' she was told, in a manner which implied that she should have known that without being told. She was dismissed into the care of a small woman with a kind face and a bright smile, who told her that her name was Nurse Symes.

'You're on duty in the morning,' she told her. 'Ward B—that's on the other wing. First floor, thirty beds. Sister Clark is in charge there.'

She paused, and Claudia said encouragingly, 'And…?'

'She's terribly overworked, you know—we can't get the staff. She doesn't mean half she says.'

'Tell me, what exactly do I do? General assistant covers a lot of ground, and Miss Norton was a bit vague.'

'Well, dear, there aren't many trained nurses, so you do anything that's needed.'

They got into the lift at the back of the hall and stepped out on the top floor, went through a door with

'Private' on it and started down another corridor lined with doors.

'Here we are,' said Nurse Symes. 'Quite a nice room, and the bathrooms are at the end. There's a little kitchen too, if you want to make tea.'

The room was small, with a bed, a small easy chair, a bedside table and a clothes cupboard. It was very clean and there was a view of chimneypots from its window. There was a washbasin on one corner, and a small mirror over the wide shelf which served as a dressing table. A few cushions and photos and a vase of flowers, thought Claudia with resolute cheerfulness, and it would be quite pretty.

'We'll go to the linen room and get you some dresses. You'll get three, but of course you'll wear a plastic apron when you're on duty.'

The dresses—a useful mud-brown—duly chosen and taken to her room, they began a tour of the hospital. It was surprisingly large, with old-fashioned wards with beds on either side and tables with pot plants down the centre. The wards were full, and most of the patients were sitting in chairs by their beds, watching television if they were near enough to the two sets at either end of the wards.

Most of them appeared to be asleep; one or two had visitors. Claudia could see only one or two nurses, but there were several young women shrouded in plastic pinnys, carrying trays, mops and buckets and helping those patients who chose to trundle around with their walking aids.

It wasn't quite what she had expected, but it was too early to have an opinion, and first impressions weren't always the right ones.

*   *   *

It was Cork who folded the *Telegraph* at the appropriate page and silently pointed out the notice of the forthcoming marriage between George Willis and Doreen Ramsay to Professor Tait-Bullen as he ate his breakfast.

He read it in an absent-minded fashion, and then read it again.

'Interesting,' he observed, and then, 'I wonder what will happen to the daughter? Staying on at the Colonel's house, I suppose.'

He thought no more about it until that evening when, urged by some niggling doubt at the back of his mind, he phoned Dr Willis. His congratulations were sincere. 'You will be marrying shortly?'

'In four days' time. Mrs Ramsay is here with me, so are Mrs Pratt and Tombs. Jennie, their maid, went to the Manor to a new job this morning.' George added drily, 'They were turned out by the new owner.'

The professor asked sharply, 'And the daughter—Claudia?'

'Fortunately she found a job at Southampton, in a hospital there—geriatrics. Didn't like the look of the place, but they wanted someone at once.'

'You mean to tell me that this man turned them all out? Is he no relation?'

'A cousin of sorts.'

'Extraordinary.' The professor had a fleeting memory of a lovely girl with red hair and decided that he wanted to know more. 'I'm going to Bristol in a couple of days. May I call in and wish you both well?'

'We'd be delighted. And if you can come to the wedding we should very much like that.'

Mr Tait-Bullen put down the receiver and sat back in his chair. With a little careful planning there was no reason why he shouldn't go to the wedding.

CHAPTER THREE

BY THE end of her first day at the hospital Claudia knew exactly what a general assistant was: a maker of beds, carrier of trays, bedpans, and bags of bed linen. And when she wasn't doing this she was getting the old and infirm in and out of bed, finding slippers, spectacles, dentures, feeding those who were no longer able to help themselves and trotting the more spry of the ladies to the loo.

It was non-stop work, and, going off duty soon after three o'clock, she was thankful that she was free until seven o'clock the next morning and that by some miracle she would have her day off on the day following that. The whole day, she thoughtful joyfully, and not on duty until the afternoon after that. She got into her outdoor clothes and hurried out to the nearest phone box.

Her mother and George were to be married in three days' time; she would be able to go to the wedding, although she would have to leave Little Planting directly after the ceremony. The bus service between Romsey and Southampton was frequent; it was just a question of getting from Romsey to Little Planting and back again.

She would be met, declared her mother; any of their friends in the village would be glad to collect her. 'Phone me tomorrow and let me know what time the bus gets to Romsey. And don't worry about getting back to Southampton, there'll be someone to give you a lift. You're happy there, Claudia?'

'Yes,' said Claudia, 'I'm sure I shall be happy.' She

45

was so convincing that her mother observed happily to
George that Claudia sounded perfectly content, and
wasn't it lucky that she should be free for the wedding?

Claudia went back to the hospital and had a cup of
tea with some of the other girls, then went to her room,
kicked off her shoes and curled up on the bed. Her feet
ached and she was tired. It had been a hard day's work,
but it wasn't only that; she felt sad and lonely and uncertain of the future. She was prepared to stay in this
job for as long as it took to save enough money for her
to train in something which would allow her more freedom. Enough money for her to have nice clothes, and a
holiday. A career girl.

It would have to be something to do with computers,
shorthand and typing and a knowledge of the business
world. A receptionist, mused Claudia, a nine-to-five job
with free weekends so that she could go and stay with
her mother and George from time to time. And, of
course, a nicely furnished flat, and friends to entertain
and to be entertained by. She might even meet a man
who would fall in love with her and marry her...

Mr Tait-Bullen's handsome features imposed themselves upon her wishful thinking, but she brushed them
away. One didn't cry for the moon, and she was never
likely to meet him again. Even if she did, she wasn't
sure if he had noticed her as a woman. She wondered
what he was really like behind that impersonal, impassive face. Probably quite nice...

A thump on the door brought her back to reality, and
when she called, 'Come in,' a girl opened the door. One
of those on the afternoon shift.

'Oh, good, you're here. The other two are out and
Sister sent me. Mrs Legge—that's the one with the
Zimmer walker—fell over and she's broken a leg and an

arm. She'll have to go to the City General with a nurse, and that only leaves Sister and me and we're up to our eyes. Could you come back on duty for an hour or two, just until someone can be found to take over?'

Claudia crammed her feet back into her shoes. It would be, after all, a way of passing the empty evening.

She stayed on the ward for more than two hours, and was sent off at last with the promise of extra time off when it was convenient. She ate supper with several of the other girls, watched television for half an hour and then went to bed. She was too tired to think much. Someone had to look after those old ladies...she would be an old lady herself one day, but hopefully loved and cherished by a husband. Someone like Mr Tait-Bullen, she decided, half asleep.

By the end of the following day she had realised that—never mind what Miss Norton had told her—the off duty was very much in the hands of the ward sister. It was possible, one of the other assistants told her, to have five days in a row of seven o'clock duty, or several days of afternoon shift with no more than an hour or two's notice.

So she wasn't altogether surprised when she was told that she would have an afternoon shift before her day off. That meant she wouldn't be able to go home until the following morning. Still, that would give her all the day before the wedding, and she had already told her mother that she would have to leave directly after the ceremony. She caught the first bus in the morning, after phoning her mother, and found Tombs waiting for her at Romsey. He was driving the doctor's car—a battered old Ford, long ago pensioned off in one corner of the garage, but used in emergencies. It wasn't a long drive, and Tombs filled it with gossip about Mrs

Ramsay, the wedding and how well they had settled in at the doctor's house. Indeed, he seemed to have shed several years; Claudia hadn't seen him as happy for some time, and she was glad of that; she had known him all her life and he was part of it. They talked about the wedding at some length, and he said, 'It is a great pity that you have to return so soon, Miss Claudia. Mrs Ramsay tells me that you have a very good job.'

She enlarged upon that, drawing upon her imagination rather more than was truthful, and was rewarded by his satisfied, 'We all want you to be happy, Miss Claudia.'

At the doctor's house she was greeted by her mother and borne away to inspect the wedding hat, give her opinion of the outfit to go with it and listen while her parent told her of the plans for the wedding.

'Very quiet, of course, but that's how we want it. George can't get away for a week or two, but then we're going down to Cornwall. He has a cottage at St Anthony—that's a bit further on from Falmouth. But we'll be back for Christmas, of course. Will you be able to come home?'

'I don't know, Mother. The off duty is made out a week or two at a time, and it has to be altered from time to time. I'll certainly do my best.'

Christmas was still five weeks or more away; anything could happen…

The wedding was to be at eleven o'clock in the morning. A fellow doctor had come over from a neighbouring village to keep an eye on the practice until the evening, and Mrs Pratt had arranged luncheon for the few friends who had been invited. Tombs, to his tremendous delight, was to give the bride away, and Miss Tremble, who had played the organ for more years than anyone could remember, had insisted on playing for the service.

Claudia, in the grey suit she had had for rather longer than she would have wished, perched a velvet beret on her bright hair and took herself off to the church, leaving her mother and Tombs to follow in George's car.

The handful of friends who had been invited were completely swallowed up by the villagers, who had turned out to a man and woman to see the doctor they respected and liked marry Mrs Ramsay. Claudia, sitting in the front pew greeting those she knew, turned round, craning her neck to see who was there. Almost everyone, except of course Mr and Mrs Ramsay, but they wouldn't have been welcome anyway. She turned round again and looked at George's upright elderly back, and then turned her head once more, this time with everyone else, to watch her mother coming down the aisle, her hand on Tombs' arm.

It was a short, simple service, but what it lacked in grandeur it made up for in warmth and friendliness as the congregation surged down the aisle after the happy pair. Claudia, hemmed in by well wishers and friends she hadn't seen for some time, looked around her as she waited patiently to leave the church.

At the back of the church Mr Tait-Bullen, towering over those around him, was looking at her. He wasn't smiling, but that didn't prevent her from feeling pleasure at the sight of him. She made her way towards him and held out a hand.

'Hello, how nice to see you here. Did George invite you?'

He took her hand, shook it briskly and gave it back to her. 'I invited myself. I saw the notice in the *Telegraph* and, since I am on my way to Bristol, George kindly suggested that I might like to come to the church.'

They were outside now, everyone getting into cars or walking back to the doctor's house.

'You're coming to the house?'

'Yes.' Without asking her, he opened the car door and popped her in. 'Are you still at the Colonel's house? George said something about you leaving...'

He didn't sound very interested, so all she said was, 'Yes, we have all left.'

'And you?'

'Oh, I've got a job at Southampton. I'm going back this afternoon.'

They had reached the doctor's house, and Mr Tait-Bullen parked the car, opened her door and followed her inside. They were separated almost at once by other guests, and, feeling let down that he had evinced so little interest in her, Claudia wormed her way to where her mother and George were standing.

She kissed them both. 'I know you're going to be happy,' she told them. 'And this is a lovely wedding; everyone here wants you to be happy too.'

Her mother beamed at her. 'Darling, it's such a wonderful day. Must you go back so soon?'

'I'm afraid so. I'm on duty at three o'clock. I must get to Romsey in time to catch the bus, it goes at a quarter past the hour. Could Tombs take me?'

'Of course he can. And if he can't there are plenty of people here who wouldn't mind running you over to Romsey.' Her mother frowned. 'I meant to have fixed something up, but there was so much to do and think about...'

'Don't worry, Mother. And it will be a pity to take Tombs away; he's being so useful here. I'll get Tom Hicks from the garage to run me over.'

It was ten minutes or so later when she went back to

the buffet with the plate of canapés she had been handing round, that she found Mr Tait-Bullen beside her. He
took the plate from her, put it back on the table and
handed her a glass of champagne. He said pleasantly,
'I'll drive you to Southampton. When do you want to
leave?'

'But you're not going to Southampton; you're going
to Bristol. You said so.'

'Indeed I am, but I have ample time to take you back
on my way. At what time do you need to leave here?'

'I'm on duty at three o'clock. I was going to catch a
bus from Romsey. There's really no need—it's very kind
of you, but you'll miss the rest of the reception.'

Looking at him, she could see that he was taking no
notice of what she was saying. He said now, 'If we leave
at half past one that should give us ample time.
Presumably you will need time to get ready for whatever
job you are in.'

'I'm a general assistant at a geriatric hospital. It's near
the docks.'

She spoke defiantly, as though she expected him to
argue with her, but all he said was, 'You'll have to guide
me. Do you like your work?'

'Yes. I've only been there for a short while. It's—it's
very interesting.'

The vicar joined them then, and presently she excused
herself and went to talk to Mr Potter, who asked her
worriedly if she was managing.

'I hear you have work at Southampton. Providential,
my dear, providential. I have been worried about you
and your mother, and can only be thankful that things
have turned out so well for you both.'

'Oh, everything is splendid,' said Claudia. 'And Dr
Willis has been so kind and thoughtful to all of us.'

'You have not seen Mr and Mrs Ramsay since they returned to the house?'

'No, and I don't want to.' She patted his arm. 'We don't need to worry about them any more, Mr Potter. We hated leaving the house, but we couldn't have stayed even if he had suggested it.'

She wandered round the room then, talking to other guests, most of them old friends who had known her for years. But she kept her eye on the clock, and when she saw that it had just struck one, she went in search of her mother and George, wished them goodbye, assured them that Mr Tait-Bullen was driving her back, and promised to come again just as soon as she had a free day.

Then she got her case and went into the hall. Tombs was there, talking to Mr Tait-Bullen as he shrugged himself into his coat.

'Ah, there you are, Miss Claudia. I was just saying you'd be here dead on time, and so you are.'

'Tombs, it's been a lovely wedding, and I'm sure you did a great deal to make it so. I'll be back when I get a day off. Take care of yourself, won't you? I've seen Mrs Pratt and Jennie.'

'Bless you, miss,' said Tombs, and opened the door for them. 'A safe journey.'

Claudia settled herself in the comfortable seat. 'Do you know how to get onto the Romsey road? Through the village and keep straight on, then turn left at the crossroads. Then it's a right-hand fork. The roads are narrow.'

He said thank you so meekly that she was emboldened to say chattily, 'We're so glad that George gave Tombs a job. He'd been with my great-uncle for years and years. I don't suppose there are many like him...'

Mr Tait-Bullen, not a man for small talk, gave a grunt.

And, since he had nothing to say, Claudia observed, 'Are you one of those people who don't like to talk while they are driving? I dare say it takes quite a lot of concentration, especially in a car like this one.'

Mr Tait-Bullen, whose work demanded powers of concentration well beyond the average, gave another grunt.

Claudia, not one to give up easily, took a look at his profile. It looked severe. 'Oh, well, if you don't want to talk…' She turned her head to look out of the window. 'Probably you're tired.'

'No, I am not in the least tired. Claudia, tell me your off duty for next week…'

'Whatever for?' When he didn't answer, she said, 'Oh, well…' and told him. 'But it gets changed at the last minute very often. There don't seem to be enough staff…'

'It is not, I believe, the most popular form of nursing.'

'Oh, I can quite see that, and I'm not even a nurse.'

'You say that you will be free at three o'clock on Friday? I shall call for you shortly after that and we will spend the rest of the day together.'

'Oh, will we? Have I been asked?'

'Ah, forgive me. I presumed that you would like to see me again, just as I would like to see you.'

'Well!' exclaimed Claudia. 'Whatever next…?'

'Just so. That is what I wish to find out.'

A remark which needed to be thought about and still remained puzzling.

'Well, thank you,' said Claudia, deciding to ignore his remark for the moment. 'But don't be annoyed if my off duty's been changed.'

'I don't think you need worry about that.'

They were threading their way through the outskirts

of Southampton. 'Tell me where I should turn off?' he said.

It was half past two when he stopped before the hospital entrance. He got out to open her door and walked with her into the entrance hall. He handed her case over, and when she put out a hand shook it briefly.

'Thank you for the lift.' She smiled up at him and he smiled in return, a slow, gentle smile so that he looked quite different from the rather silent reserved man she had thought him to be. And the smile warmed her loneliness, making the future full of unexpected hope. It wasn't until then that she realised how much she needed a friend.

When she had gone, Mr Tait-Bullen strolled over to the old-fashioned porter's lodge. He was there for several minutes, until its elderly occupant led him away down a long, dreary corridor, knocked on a door and ushered him inside.

Claudia didn't exactly forget him for the rest of the day; he was there at the back of her mind, almost smothered in her non-stop chores. The old ladies were such a cruel contrast to the pleasures of the morning she could have wept with pity for them. Not that weeping would have helped in any way: cups of tea, endless trundles to the loo, mopping up after the inevitable accidents, making beds and the back-breaking task of getting elderly frail bodies back into bed... By ten o'clock, when she went off duty, her mother's wedding seemed part of a dream.

She fell into bed and was instantly asleep. In the morning, after a quick shower, she got into the brown dress and went down to her breakfast, her spirits fully restored. And they stayed that way all day, despite the hundred and one setbacks and Sister's sharp tongue.

Claudia forgave her that, for coping with forty old ladies, keeping them clean and tidy and well fed, was no easy task. Claudia, putting clean sheets on a bed for the ump-teenth time, considered Sister a splendid woman, even if she had no time to waste on being friendly.

All the same, it was difficult not to feel hard done by when that lady told her that her Friday off duty would be altered; she was to go on the afternoon shift instead of the morning. She wouldn't be able to go out with Mr Tait-Bullen after all, and there was no way of letting him know. She hoped that he wouldn't be too annoyed about it; not to annoy him was suddenly important. Not that it mattered any more. He would go away and not bother to see her again. That thought left her feeling sad.

She was going off duty the next day when Sister called her into the office.

'You'll take your original off duty on Friday.' She sounded cross. 'There will be an extra nurse here for a couple of days, so there will be no need for you to change.'

'I shall be free at three o'clock on Friday?' asked Claudia, just to make sure.

'I've just said so, haven't I? You young girls are all alike, never listening to a word that is said to them.'

Claudia begged her pardon in a suitably humble voice, and once out of the office did a few dance steps along the corridor. Maybe the future wasn't going to be so bad, after all.

Friday dawned wet and cold. Claudia, deep in her morning chores, found the time to look out of the windows in the hope that the weather would improve. It did no such thing. Indeed a nasty wind had sprung up. It would have to be the grey suit and a raincoat—both suitable for the conditions out of doors, but hardly likely to inspire Mr Tait-Bullen to take her anywhere fashionable for tea.

She thought that three o'clock would never come, and even if it did, would she get off duty punctually? She did, hurrying through the hospital to her room, in a panic that she would be called back at the last moment.

Once there, she didn't waste a second—tearing out of the brown uniform, racing to the shower room before someone else got there, dressing with the speed of light. He had said shortly after three o'clock, but if she didn't show up within fifteen minutes of that time she hardly hoped that he would wait much longer. It was already five minutes over time as she gained the entrance hall, out of breath, and with her hair bundled up underneath the velvet beret. There had been no time to do more than powder her nose and put on some lipstick. She didn't look her best, she worried. He would take one look at her and decide that he was wasting his time...

Mr Tait-Bullen, leaning his length against a marble bust of a bewhiskered Victorian dignitary, entertained no such thought. He watched her slither to a dignified walk as she crossed the hall and reflected that she was the most beautiful girl that he had ever set eyes on. Even in the unbecoming garment in which she was swathed. But then she would look mouthwatering in a tablecloth with a hole cut for her head.

None of these interesting thoughts showed on his face as he went to meet her.

'Hello,' said Claudia, her smile so enchanting that he had difficulty in keeping his hands to himself. 'I haven't kept you waiting? I was so afraid that you might think I wasn't coming.' She plucked a bright lock of hair which had escaped her brush and tucked it behind an ear. 'I haven't done my hair properly.' She searched his calm face. 'I'm not dressed up either. You don't mind?'

'No, I don't mind. You look very nice.'

A tepid compliment which satisfied her; he had smiled at her when he had made it, which gave her a comfortable feeling that he had meant exactly what he had said.

'Shall we have tea first? I thought we might drive into the country for dinner later.'

'That would be lovely. Nowhere grand—I'm not dressed for it. I mean, I didn't know if we would be going out this evening—I was in a hurry so's not to miss you…' She paused, aware that she was babbling.

He said gently, 'There's a nice quiet hotel at Wickham. But tea first.'

He drove into the heart of Southampton and took her to a small quiet tea room tucked away in a side-road where he was able to park the car. The place was half-full, warm and pleasantly lighted, and they sat down at a table in the window curtained against the gathering dark of the late afternoon.

They ate hot buttered teacakes, and Claudia, urged to do so, sampled the creamy confections the waitress brought, and all the while Mr Tait-Bullen kept up an undemanding flow of small talk, calculated to put her at her ease so that presently, warm and nicely full, she answered his carefully put questions with less caution than she might have done.

Yes, it was hard work, she admitted, but the other girls were friendly and most of the old ladies were dears. 'Although there are one or two who are a bit difficult…'

'In what way?'

'Oh, they don't mean to be. They get cross, but I'd get cross if I had to sit in a chair because I couldn't do anything for myself. You see, they don't seem to have anyone to look after them—if they had daughters or someone, or sons or husbands who could look after them…'

'That might be difficult in a household with children, or where everyone goes out to work.'

'Yes, I know. Only it would be nice.'

Her hand was lying on the table, and he saw that it was rough and rather red. He said lightly, 'I dare say you have a lot of mopping up to do.'

'Oh, yes. All the time.' She smiled suddenly. 'It's not the cool hand on the brow kind of work—more like a charwoman—plastic pinnys and mops and buckets.'

'You intend to stay there?'

'When I've saved up enough money I shall train for something…' She saw his raised eyebrows. 'Well, I don't know what yet.' She paused. 'I'm talking too much. Will you tell me about you?'

'I live and work in London. I have a house there, and Cork, who has been with me for a long time, looks after me. I have patients in several hospitals and hold clinics in each of them. I have a private practice, and I operate twice a week—sometimes three times. I travel round the country from time to time if I'm wanted for a consultation or to operate.'

'You have lots of friends?'

'I have a few old friends and acquaintances, yes. I'm not married, Claudia.'

She went pink. 'I should have asked you that ages ago, shouldn't I? I did want to, but I—well, I don't know you well enough…'

'We must do something about that. At what time do you have to be back?' And when she told him he said, 'Good, we'll drive to Evershot for dinner. It's a pleasant drive, even in the dark, and we have no need to hurry.'

At her uncertain look, he added, 'Don't worry, it's a quite small hotel. At this time of the year it will be half-empty, and it isn't somewhere where one needs to dress up.'

They went back to the car then, and he drove through the heavy evening traffic until they had left the city behind, taking the secondary roads through the New Forest. Mr Tait-Bullen drove slowly, stopping from time to time to allow the ponies to cross the road ahead of him, and a badger to amble along, refusing to be hurried. He drove for the most part in silence, an easy, undemanding silence in which there was no need to talk for the sake of uttering.

Claudia sat cocooned in warmth and comfort and watched the road unwind ahead of them in the car's headlights. She hadn't felt so quietly happy for a long time.

Evershot was a sizeable village, and even on a dark, wintry night looked charming. The hotel was charming too—not large, but delightfully furnished, warm and welcoming. They went to the bar and sat over drinks, then dined on crab ravioli with ginger, breast of duck with potato straws and tiny brussels sprouts, and pear tatin with cinnamon ice cream. Claudia ate it all with a splendid appetite, sharpened by the wholesome, rather stodgy fare offered at the hospital.

She sat back, savouring the last mouthful of ice cream. 'That was lovely—and do you know it was just luck that I was free this afternoon? Sister changed my duty to the afternoon shift, and then she changed her mind. It was a miracle...'

Mr Tait-Bullen, who had engineered the miracle, agreed that indeed it was.

They sat over their coffee and Claudia, gently en-

couraged by her companion, talked. There was not much
time to talk at the hospital—really talk. On duty conversations were confined to cheerful chat with those of
the patients who welcomed it, and only that when there
were a few minutes to spare. And off duty, although she
got on well with the other girls, the inclination was either
to go out or to sit in front of the television. But now she
allowed her tongue full rein, vaguely aware that later on
she would regret it but happy now, saying whatever
came into her head. She paused briefly.

'Am I boring you?'

'No. I do not think that you will ever bore me,
Claudia. I have to go away for a couple of days. When
I return I should like to take you out again.'

'Oh, would you? I'd like that too.' She beamed at him.
'We get on well together, don't we? I didn't think I
would like you when we met, but I've changed my
mind.'

'I hoped that you would. As you say, we get on well
together.'

He drove her back presently, saw her into the hospital
and, under the porter's interested eye, bent to kiss her
cheek. It wasn't until she was in her room that she realised that he hadn't said anything more about seeing her
again.

Claudia, brushing her fiery locks, stopped to stare into
the small mirror above the little dressing table.

'You're a fool,' she told her reflection. 'Whatever he
said, he must have been bored out of his mind. I must
have sounded like a garrulous old maid. No wonder he
didn't say when he would want to see me again.' She
put down the brush and got into bed, suddenly sad; she
liked him and felt at ease in his company. If only she
hadn't behaved like an idiot. Living in London, obvi-

ously a successful man in his profession, and presumably comfortably off, she thought gloomily, he would have his pick of elegant women who had a fund of witty and amusing talk and knew when to hold their tongues...

Two days later she was on the afternoon shift. It was drizzling outside, with a mean wind, and the thought of a morning doing nothing by the gas fire in the recreation room was tempting. Then Claudia thought of the long hours on the ward until the late evening, buttoned herself into her mac, tied a scarf over her hair, found her gloves and sensible shoes and made her way to the side door the hospital staff used. A brisk walk would do her good...

She was crossing the back of the hall when the porter called after her.

'I've been ringing round for you,' he grumbled. 'You're to go to the visitors' room.'

'Me? Why?'

'How should I know? That's the message I got and I'm telling it to you.'

'Yes—well, thank you!'

She turned round and went the other way along the wide corridor from which the boardroom, the manager's office and the consultants' room opened.

'Mother,' she said, suddenly afraid of bad news, and opened the door.

The room didn't encourage visitors. It was a dark brown, with shiny lino on the floor and a hideous glass lantern housing a stark white bulb glaring down onto the solid table beneath it. Chairs were arranged stiffly around the walls, and, half lost in the massive fireplace, there was a very small gas fire. Watching her from the other side of the table was Mr Tait-Bullen.

Claudia slithered to a halt. 'Oh, it's you.' And then,

aware that perhaps that had sounded rude, added, 'What I meant is, I didn't expect you.' He smiled then, and she smiled back. 'I was just going out for a walk.'

When he didn't speak, she asked, 'Are you on your way somewhere or are you on holiday?'

'I'm on my way back to London.'

'Well, what luck I'm on afternoon duty.' She flushed. 'What I mean is, you could have called in and I would have been working.' She hurried on, because it sounded as though she expected him to take her out. 'I expect you're anxious to get back home...'

'In which case I should have driven straight back to London...'

'But you didn't know if I was free...'

'Yes, I did. I phoned up first to find out. I have to go away again for a couple of days, and I wanted to see you before I go.'

'Me? Why? Mother's not ill, or George? Did they ask you to come?'

'No, they are both, as far as I know, in the best of middle-aged health.'

He smiled at her, a slow, warm smile. 'Claudia, before I say anything more, will you answer me truthfully? Are you happy here? Are you content to be, eventually, a career girl and, if not, will you tell me what you really wish for?'

'Why do you want to know?' she asked, and, when he didn't answer, went on, 'Well, all right—no, I'm not happy here. I'm truly sorry for the old ladies, but I miss the garden and the village and being out of doors. We're well looked after, you know, but I feel trapped.' She had lost herself in her own thoughts. 'And I suppose I wish for what every woman wants—a home and a husband and children.'

'Not love?'

'That too, but I think that isn't granted to everyone—
I mean, the kind of love that doesn't mind being poor
or neglected or kept hidden, and will love and cherish
despite that.' She stopped suddenly. 'Why did you make
me say all that?'

He didn't answer her at once, but stared at her across
the table, seeing a rather untidy figure, her bright hair
escaping from the scarf, enveloped in her sensible mac.

'Will you marry me, Claudia?' he asked quietly.

At her astonished look, he said, 'No, don't say anything for a moment or two. You see, I think we might
have a successful and happy marriage. I need a wife and
you long for freedom. We could help each other in many
ways; I have no doubt that you will be an excellent
housewife and hostess, and a companion I shall always
enjoy, and you could be free to spread your wings in
whichever direction you wish to fly.

'I haven't said that I love you, nor do I expect you to
tell me that. There's time enough for us to get to know
each other. And I shan't hurry you. But it seems to me
that to marry as soon as possible would be the sensible
thing to do. You will need to give a week's notice at the
hospital, but there is no reason why we shouldn't marry
before Christmas.'

Claudia opened her mouth to speak, and shut it again,
reflecting on what he had said. It all sounded so sensible,
so calmly thought out. And he didn't love her. On the
other hand he must like her, if he intended to marry her,
and she would enjoy having a household of her own—
meeting people, making friends, being there when he
wanted a companion. And she liked him; she liked him
very much.

Mr Tait-Bullen asked quietly, 'You would like to

think about it? I shall quite understand if you dislike the idea, but I shall be disappointed. You see, Claudia, I have been honest with you. I have not promised love and endless devotion, but I have offered you what I hope will be a happy and contented life together. We like the same things, don't we? And laugh at the same jokes. We would be good companions and friends. That, I think, is more important than a sudden and uncertain infatuation.'

He was right, of course. It was, she told herself, a sensible and sincere offer of marriage made by one of the handsomest men she had ever met, and a man she liked wholeheartedly. She didn't know much about him, but, as he had said, getting to know each other was something they could do in their own good time. She would be a good wife, just as she was instinctively aware that he would be a good husband.

She looked across the table at him, standing there with no sign of impatience.

'Yes, thank you, I should like to marry you.' She laughed suddenly. 'I don't know your name...'

He came round the table and put gentle hands on her shoulders. 'Thomas,' he said, and bent to kiss her. 'Thank you, Claudia.'

CHAPTER FOUR

CLAUDIA looked up into his quiet face. 'What do we do next?'

Mr Tait-Bullen suppressed a smile. A girl after his own heart; no coy smiles and fluttering of the eyelashes, no girlish whispers. Claudia obviously liked to meet a situation, when she encountered it, head-on.

'If you will give in your notice today? Phone me this evening—I'll be in Edinburgh; I'll give you my number—let me know the soonest you can leave and I'll fetch you.'

'Where will I go?'

'To George Willis. We'll marry there if you would like that. I'll get a special licence—remind me to ask you for some particulars when you phone. Your mother?'

'I'll phone her.'

'A pity that I have to go back to town this morning; I could have called in at Little Planting. I'll telephone her this evening.'

He was holding her hands in his. 'This must be the most unlikely place in the world in which to receive a proposal of marriage.'

'I don't think that matters at all. I mean, moonlight and roses wouldn't have been suitable, would they? Not for us.'

He frowned a little. 'You will be happy, Claudia? I am a good deal older than you...'

'I like you just as you are, Thomas. Please don't change any of you. We shall be happy together.'

'I must go. Forgive me, there isn't even time to give you a cup of coffee.'

She went with him to the hospital entrance and he kissed her again, a light kiss which meant nothing, although she hadn't expected it to, got into his car and drove away.

It was a few moments before she moved—back into the hospital, intent on doing what Thomas had suggested, not noticing the porter's interested stare. She must compose a suitable letter and then take it to Miss Norton, and she must do it at once, so that when Thomas phoned that evening she could tell him when she could leave. And she must phone her mother...

She wrote her letter of resignation and presented herself at Miss Norton's office, inwardly quaking; could she be prevented from leaving? She hadn't signed a contract, and she was paid weekly, all the same she wasn't absolutely sure...

Fifteen minutes later she closed the office door behind her with a sigh of relief. Miss Norton hadn't been very pleased. Indeed, she had read Claudia a lecture on young women who were irresponsible and said she hoped that she had given marriage serious thought, but she hadn't refused to let Claudia go. She was, she had pointed out, scrupulously fair in such matters; if a girl wasn't happy in her work then she was entitled to leave. Normally, said Miss Norton severely, after a reasonable period. Claudia had hardly given herself time to settle down, but in the circumstances she could, of course, leave.

Claudia had thanked her and asked if she could leave two days earlier, since she would have her week's days off due. Miss Norton had looked affronted but she had agreed.

Claudia got into her mac again and went to telephone her mother; there was a phone in the hospital, but it was in a passage and in constant use; to discuss anything other than the weather was impossible.

Her mother was delighted, surprised as well. 'Darling, I didn't know that you and Mr Tait-Bullen—Thomas—were so close. I'm delighted, and I'm sure George will be too when I tell him. What are your plans?'

Claudia inserted all the money she had, and explained. 'And we want to have a very quiet wedding, Mother. Thomas is getting a special licence and we'd like to marry at Little Planting. I'm leaving in five days; Thomas will fetch me. May I stay with you and George until the wedding? It'll only be for a day or two.'

'Of course, darling. And we must do something about clothes…'

Claudia, with an inward eye on her scanty wardrobe, agreed.

The rest of the day passed in a dream; since she was happy, she wanted everyone else to be happy too, coaxing smiles from even the most cantankerous of the old ladies, clearing up unmentionable messes, changing sheets, trundling round the ward with the tea trolley, the supper trolley and at the end of the day having to listen to a lecture from Sister, who, apprised of her leaving, took it as a personal affront.

It was after ten o'clock by the time she left the ward—too late to go to the phone box at the end of the road. Besides, the passage where the hospital phone was was empty so late in the evening. She rang the number Thomas had given her and waited, half afraid that he wouldn't answer.

His voice sounded strangely businesslike.

'It's me,' said Claudia, heedless of grammar. And she added quite unnecessarily, 'You told me to ring you up, but I haven't kept you up, have I?'

Mr Tait-Bullen, studying the notes of a patient he was to operate on the next day, assured her that she hadn't.

'You saw Miss Norton?'

'Yes, I may leave in five days' time—actually, it's four days now. That's a Friday.'

'In the morning? You're actually free to leave after duty on Thursday?'

'Yes, but I must pack my things and give my uniform back…'

'I'll come for you at nine o'clock on Friday morning, Claudia.'

'Thank you, but don't you have to work?'

He said gently, 'Oh, yes, but not until the afternoon, I'll drop you off at Little Planting on my way back. Now, tell me—where were you born, how old are you, have you any other names besides Claudia, and are you British by birth?'

She told him in a matter-of-fact voice, sensing that he hadn't time to waste on idle talk. She hesitated before she said, 'My other name is Eliza…' and waited for him to laugh.

But he didn't. All he said was, 'That's a nice old-fashioned name. You must be tired, my dear. Get to bed and sleep well. I'll see you on Friday.'

'Good night, then,' Claudia said, and hung up. It would have been nice if he had said something like, I miss you, or, I'm looking forward to seeing you. But he wouldn't pretend to feelings he didn't feel; she quite understood that. Theirs would be a sensible marriage, she reflected, undressing and falling into bed, there would be no false sentiment.

The following afternoon she took herself off to the shops; she hadn't much money, but it was essential that she had something suitable in which to be married. Luck was on her side; she found a small dress shop going out of business and selling up at half price. Claudia thrust aside a wish to wear white chiffon and a gauzy veil and tried on a plainly cut dress and jacket in fine wool. It was in a misty blue, with a grey velvet collar and cuffs, and fastened with a row of velvet buttons. And when the saleslady found a charming hat in matching velvet, Claudia decided that she need look no further.

'It's for a special occasion?' enquired the sales lady.

'Well, yes—my wedding.'

Which prompted the sales lady, who had a sentimental heart under her smart black dress, to make a special price. And that meant that there was enough money left to buy gloves and shoes—and some essential underpinnings from Marks and Spencer.

Well pleased with her purchases, Claudia went back to the hospital—too late for tea and too early for supper, but that didn't matter. She tried everything on once more and spent a long time trying out various new hairstyles, none of which pleased her. Perhaps once she was married she would be able to go to a good London hairdresser and have it expertly cut.

The days dragged; Friday was never coming, and she had ample time to wonder if she was about to make the mistake of a lifetime. A letter or a phone call from Thomas would have cleared up her uncertainty, but there was nothing. He had told her that he would see her on Friday and with that she had to be content. She had phoned her mother again, and that lady, agog with maternal delight, had told her that she was to go with her to Salisbury and get a few clothes. 'Our wedding present to you, darling. Have you bought anything yet?'

Claudia described the dress and jacket.

'They sound just right. Aren't you excited? And will you have a honeymoon?'

'No. Thomas can only take a day off—we'll go later.'

On the Thursday she bade the old ladies goodbye, leaving a vase filled with chrysanthemums on one of the tables, wishing she could have done more to brighten the ward. Sister wished her goodbye in an ill-humoured way, and then surprised her by saying, 'A pity you are leaving; the old ladies liked you.'

And the other girls were friendly—laughing and joking and asking her to send photos of the wedding.

'Well, it's not that kind of wedding,' she explained. 'Just us and a few family and no one else...'

'Who'd want anyone else but him, anyway?' declared one of the girls, who had seen Mr Tait-Bullen leaving the hospital. Everyone laughed and Claudia got out a bottle of sherry and a packet of biscuits. It seemed the right moment for a farewell party.

She was ready and waiting long before nine o'clock the next morning. Supposing Thomas had changed his mind? Had a breakdown, an accident, been called away to an emergency? She sat, as still as a mouse, wrapped in the mac, since it was raining again, her hair glowing in the gloomy entrance hall.

Mr Tait-Bullen knew exactly how she felt the moment he set eyes on her.

He nodded to the porter and reached her before she could get to her feet, his eyes searching her face. What he saw there reassured him, and he smiled.

'I can see that I am marrying a treasure. Do you know that the one virtue a medical man longs for in a wife is punctuality? You see, he is never punctual himself…'

'I was a bit early. I wasn't sure—that is, I thought that perhaps…' She met his steady gaze. 'No, that's not quite true—I knew you'd come.'

'Of course. Do you have to see anyone? You've said your goodbyes?'

And, when she nodded, he picked up her case and together they left the hospital.

They were clear of Southampton, driving through a dripping countryside, before he said, 'If you will agree, we can be married on Monday. I'll come down to Little Planting on Sunday evening, and we can marry in the morning and drive back in the afternoon.'

He had a list on Tuesday, but there would be Monday evening in which to show Claudia her new home. Cork had confided plans for a splendid supper, and Mr Tait-Bullen had left his devoted servant icing a cake for tea. It wasn't the kind of wedding that Cork would have liked for his master, but he was determined to make it as bridal an occasion as possible.

And that reminded him of something. He brought the car to a gentle halt and fished around in a pocket.

'Ours must be one of the briefest engagements ever known,' he observed, and opened the little velvet box in his hand. The ring it contained was a sapphire, a rich, sparkling blue surrounded by diamonds and mounted in gold. He picked up Claudia's left hand, resting in her lap, took off her glove and slipped the ring on her finger.

'Oh, it's beautiful—and it fits.' Claudia's sigh was one of pure delight. 'Thank you, Thomas.' She stared at it, incongruous on her roughened hand with its short, clipped nails. She would have to do something about that before the wedding.

She looked at him and saw that he was studying her hand. She said quite awkwardly, 'We did wear gloves whenever we could, but sometimes it just wasn't possible.'

His smile was kind. 'It was my grandmother's engagement ring. She left it to me with the wish that I would give it to the girl I married.'

'She was fond of you?'

'Indeed, she was; we were the best of friends.'

'You miss her?'

'Yes, we all do—my mother and father, my two sisters and younger brother. You will meet them all at Christmas…'

Claudia said faintly, 'Oh, shall I? Do they all live in London?'

'No, Mother and Father live in Cumbria, a small village called Finsthwaite, at the southern end of lake Windermere. It is rather remote but very beautiful, close to the heart of Grizedale Forest but not too far from Kendal. My sisters are married. Ann—she's the elder—lives in York; her husband's a solicitor. Amy and her husband live near Melton Mowbray; he's a farmer. James is at Birmingham Children's hospital—a junior registrar.'

'They won't be coming to our wedding?'

'Mother and Father—the rest of the family you'll meet at Christmas. We shall spend it at Finsthwaite.' He added casually, 'They'll be delighted to welcome you into the family.'

'They don't know me. They might not like me…'

'You will be my wife,' said Thomas.

A fact which she could not dispute.

Tombs, beaming widely, opened the door to them when they reached George's house. He shook Claudia by the hand, and then Mr Tait-Bullen, wished them happy and led them across the hall to the sitting room. Her mother was there and embraced Claudia warmly before offering a cheek for her future son-in-law.

'Such a surprise,' she told them. 'We're all so excited. George is in his surgery but Tombs has gone to fetch him. We had no idea...'

Nor had I, thought Claudia, but she didn't say so. 'We thought we'd be married on Monday...'

'Darling—but you haven't any clothes, and I must have a new hat at least, and who is to be invited? Such short notice...'

'Thomas would like his parents to come, Mother.' Claudia looked at him and felt a touch of peevishness at the sight of him standing there, looking faintly amused.

'May they do that, Mrs Willis? We both want a quiet wedding, and I can't spare more than a day. We would like to marry in the morning, then drive back to London, which would give us the rest of the day together.'

'Of course, you poor dears—scarcely more than a few hours to be together.'

'We shall make up for that later on,' said Mr Tait-Bullen soothingly.

He turned as George came into the room. 'We do hope we haven't spoilt any plans you and Mrs Willis may have made...'

Dr Willis kissed Claudia and shook hands with him. 'We don't go away until the end of next week, and even if we had plans we would be delighted to upset them for such a happy occasion. Staying for lunch, I hope?'

Tombs had brought in the coffee tray, and Mrs Willis

poured while Claudia, glad of something to do, handed around cups and saucers and biscuits.

'I must get back. I've a clinic this afternoon and patients to see this evening.'

Claudia, sitting beside her mother, watched Thomas, perfectly at ease, everything arranged as he had wished, calm and self-assured, listening to George explaining the difficulties of being a GP's wife. He made no attempt to mention his own work; she guessed that it was just as time-consuming and demanding.

She went out with him to his car presently, and he stood for a minute, looking down at her. 'I'll see you on Sunday evening. My mother and father will be with me in their own car. We'll put up at the Duck and Thistle.'

He took her two hands in his. 'Quite sure, Claudia?'

She said steadily, 'Yes, Thomas. It's a bit unusual, isn't it? Getting married like this. But if we're sure, and it's what we want, there's no point in mulling it over for months, is there? And I don't suppose that if we were engaged for a long time we'd see much of each other— I mean, get to know each other better—for you would be working and I'd be bogged down in plans for the wedding.'

'What a sensible girl you are, Claudia.' He bent and kissed her, a brief, friendly kiss, before getting into his car and driving away.

Back in the sitting room, her mother said, 'Darling, we're all so happy for you. He's just right for you and so handsome. You'll have a delightful life together. I can hardly believe it—there we were a few weeks ago, with not a penny piece between us and no roof over our heads, and look at us now. I'm here with George, and so very happy, and you'll be happy too with Thomas.'

She paused to look at Claudia. 'Clothes—you must have some new things…'

'I've told you about the dress and jacket, and the hat, and I've bought one or two other things. Enough to go on with. I expect I'll get some new clothes when we're in London. There hasn't been time, and Thomas knows that.' She added carefully, 'You see, there didn't seem much point in waiting—my job in the hospital wasn't quite what I thought it would be, and Thomas wanted me to leave as soon as possible.' She smiled suddenly. 'So did I.'

Mrs Willis started to say something, and then stopped. Instead she observed, 'I expect Thomas fell in love with you the first time you met…'

'It happens all the time,' said Claudia. 'Look at you and George.'

'Well, dear, for George, yes. But it took me a long time to discover that I loved him. And I dare say if it hadn't been for that awful Ramsay cousin, and us being turned out of the house, I might never have discovered how I felt.'

'What a good thing it happened that way, then. Though it was horrid, wasn't it? Do you hear or see anything of him and his wife?'

'No, dear. They keep themselves very much to themselves, and the village isn't friendly towards them.' Mrs Willis sighed happily. 'How nice that we don't have to think about them any more. Now, on Monday I thought that we would have a buffet lunch. Mrs Pratt is longing to prepare a feast for you. A pity that it is to be such a quiet wedding.' She glanced at Claudia. 'You don't mind?'

'No, Mother, I'm happy to do whatever Thomas wants. If we had decided to marry later on, we wouldn't have seen much of each other—he's busy all day most days. At least I shall see him when he comes home in the evenings.'

A remark which satisfied her mother, just as Claudia had meant it to.

Claudia woke early on Monday morning. It was still dark outside as she got out of bed, wrapped herself in her dressing gown and crept downstairs. The light was on in the kitchen and Mrs Pratt was there, carefully lifting tiny vol-au-vents from a baking sheet onto one of Dr Willis's best china dishes. Tombs was there too, sitting by the Aga, polishing wine glasses.

'No, no. Don't move,' said Claudia as he started to get up. 'I thought I'd make a cup of tea.'

Mrs Pratt beamed at her. 'You should still be in your bed, Miss Claudia. I dare say you're excited. It isn't every day a girl marries. The kettle's boiling, if you'd like to make tea...'

'We'll all have a cup. You're both coming to the church, aren't you?'

'Wouldn't miss it for all the tea in China, Miss Claudia,' said Tombs. 'Me and Mrs Pratt are that pleased. Took to the doctor the moment we set eyes on him, didn't we?'

Mrs Pratt, whipping something delicious in a bowl, agreed. 'A handsome pair you'll be—though it's to be hoped you won't let him see that old dressing gown, Miss Claudia. Warm and cosy it may have been at one time, but it's past its best...'

Claudia warmed the teapot and had a sudden moment of doubt. Surely Thomas would have realised that she had had no time to buy a lot of clothes? And would he mind anyway? She had gained the impression that her appearance wasn't something he found important. True, he had told her that she looked nice...

'I shall go shopping in London.' She turned to smile at Mrs Pratt. 'I'll leave this dressing gown behind!'

The three of them drank their tea in a friendly silence, and Rob, rousing from sleep in his basket, came to join them.

'I'll let him out and take the tea up as I go,' said Claudia.

'Begging your pardon, Miss Claudia,' said Tombs, at his most stately. 'You will do no such thing. That is a morning task for myself.'

'Oh, Tombs,' cried Claudia. 'I'm going to miss you and Mrs Pratt.'

She finished her tea and went to the garden door with Rob, who lumbered out into the garden. She stood watching him and looked at the sky, beginning to lighten. It had been a frosty night, and her breath drifted away in soft swirls. It was going to be a lovely winter's day. A good omen? She hoped so.

Rob came in then, making for the warmth of the Aga, and she went back to her room.

It was growing lighter by the minute. She went to the window, opened it wide and leaned out, breathing the cold air. At the other end of the village Thomas was sleeping—his parents too. They had come at teatime—Thomas in his Rolls Royce, his father driving a Daimler. She had seen them arrive from her bedroom window and hurried downstairs, her hair very tidy for once, wearing a dark green jersey dress which she had had for so long it had become quite fashionable again.

It was essential to make a good impression; Thomas's parents might live miles away, but they were bound to meet occasionally. She hadn't allowed herself to speculate about them, she'd only hoped that they would like her.

Thomas's mother had come in first, pausing to smile at Tombs, but before she reached Claudia, Thomas had been there, bending to kiss her cheek, putting an arm round her shoulder.

'This is Claudia, Mother—Father.' And they had both shaken her hand and kissed her warmly, so that her vague doubts had vanished.

Thomas's father was an elderly edition of his son, still very upright, grey-haired and handsome. His mother was almost as tall as Claudia, and still a beautiful woman, with a beauty she had allowed to age gradually, without excess make-up or tinted hair. Her face wrinkled in all the right places, and her hair was grey and simply dressed. But her eyes were still young—vivid blue and smiling. She was well dressed too, in an understated and slightly old-fashioned way. Claudia had liked her at once.

It had been easy after that first meeting. Her mother and George had joined them, and the evening had been pleasant. Neither of the Tait-Bullens had badgered her with questions; they had talked about the wedding in a soothing manner, remarked upon the charm of the village and told her something—but not much—of their own home. And she had had no chance to talk for more than a few moments to Thomas. Only as they had been leaving to go to the Duck and Thistle had he asked her kindly, 'Cold feet, Claudia?'

'Certainly not,' she had answered him indignantly, and then, looking into his face, seeing the casual friend-liness in it, had added softly, 'No, I promise you, Thomas.'

Someone was coming down the lane from the village.

She withdrew her head and then poked it out again; in the dim light of dawn Thomas was coming through the open gate and up the short drive. He stopped under her window.

'Come for a walk?' he invited.

How could he have known that that was the very thing she most wanted to do?

'Five minutes,' said Claudia, and closed the window.

There were trousers and an old sweater in the cupboard; she put them on over her nightie, tied back her hair, cleaned her teeth and went down to the kitchen; her wellies were there, with socks stuffed inside them. Under Tombs's and Mrs Pratt's astonished gaze, she put them on, bundled on one of the coats hanging behind the kitchen door, blew them a kiss and went out into the garden round the house to where Thomas was waiting.

He took her arm and walked her briskly along the lane, away from the village. 'No gloves?' he asked, and took his own off and put them onto her cold hands. 'This isn't quite the usual behaviour of the bride and groom on their wedding day...'

'But it isn't a usual kind of wedding, is it?'

The lane petered out into a rough track, its rutted surface frost-bound, and as they walked Thomas began to talk—a nicely calculated jumble of odds and ends about his work, and information about his home, his friends... 'I hope you will like them—most of them are married...'

'Have you had any girlfriends? I'm not being nosy, but if I were to meet them I'd have to know who they are, wouldn't I?'

Mr Tait-Bullen didn't pause in his stride. He said briskly, 'Naturally I have been out and about with several woman acquaintances, but they have never been more than that, Claudia.'

'Have I annoyed you by asking? I don't expect to know about your life, but I don't want to be taken un-awares. Anyway, I don't suppose you've had much time to fall in love.'

'I'm not sure if time is needed when one falls in love. I imagine it happens in the blink of an eye. I can promise you that I have had neither the inclination or the time. I have always been too busy. But I shall enjoy being mar-ried to you; we shall be good friends and companions and above all we like each other. Liking the person you marry is as important as loving them.'

'I'm sure you're right,' said Claudia, 'although we can't be quite certain, can we? I mean, you'd have to be married to someone you loved and didn't like...'

They had been walking uphill; now they paused to watch the first rays of a wintry sun creep over the countryside. They stood and watched for a moment, and Claudia said, 'Nice, isn't it?' She added slowly, 'That's the only thing. I expect I'll miss this for a bit.'

'Yes, I can understand that. I thought we might look around for a small house not too far from here, where we can spend weekends. It's an easy run up to town.'

He had flung an arm round her, and she turned within its comfort so that she could see his face. 'Oh, Thomas, that would be lovely. But would you like that, too?'

'Very much. We will wait till after Christmas and then go house-hunting. There are plenty of villages between here and the M3.'

The sun was above the horizon now, and Claudia said reluctantly, 'We'd better go back. We're not dressed for the wedding, are we?'

Mr Tait-Bullen took a good look at her. 'No. I like the hair, but you look all the wrong shape...'

'Well, I didn't stop to dress—only an old sweater and

trousers over my nightie. And I don't know whose coat this is—I took it from the back door.'

'And you still contrive to look beautiful,' he told her, and then turned her round smartly and marched her back.

He left her at the kitchen door, bending to kiss her quickly. 'Don't be late,' he said, and walked away as she opened the door.

'Your ma is in a fine state,' said Mrs Pratt. 'Miss Claudia, whatever possessed you to go gallivanting off like that? Looking like a scarecrow, too.'

Claudia flung her arms round her old friend's neck. 'It was lovely—a kind of ending and a beginning, if you see what I mean.' She skipped to the door and flew upstairs to shower, then put on her dressing gown again and went down to breakfast.

Mrs Willis submitted to her hug. 'Darling, you shouldn't have gone off like that—you and Thomas aren't supposed to see each other until you meet in church, and Mrs Pratt says you looked like a bag lady…'

Claudia helped herself to toast. 'It was lovely. We watched the sun come up. Mother, I'm so happy!'

And Mrs Willis, happy herself, leaned across the table and patted her daughter's arm. 'Oh, love, I do understand. So does George. He was called out just before you came downstairs—old Mrs Parson's grandson cut his arm on a bottle.'

'George will be back in time for the wedding?'

'Don't worry, dear, he will. It's only a matter of a few stitches.'

Claudia, casting a critical eye over her reflection, wished for a brief moment that it was white chiffon and yards of veiling and not the blue outfit she was looking at. She had dressed with care, taken pains with her face and her hair, and arranged the hat at the most becoming angle. She supposed that for a quiet wedding she looked all right.

Supposing it didn't work out well? Thomas was so sure that it would, and so was she, but that hadn't prevented last-minute doubts creeping in. Did all brides feel as she did? she wondered. Wondering if they were making the biggest mistake of their lives? Or was that because she was marrying Thomas after such a short time in which to know him?

She turned away from the mirror and went to look out of the window; she couldn't even see the Duck and Thistle from it, but it was only a few minutes' walk away. Was Thomas standing at his window as full of doubts as she was, perhaps wishing that he had never set eyes on her?

Her mother, coming into the room, broke into her thoughts. 'Darling, just look at this—Thomas doesn't know what you're wearing, so the flowers are white—isn't it gorgeous?'

The bouquet she was offering Claudia was truly bridal; white roses very faintly tinged with pink, lilies of the valley, hyacinth pips, orange blossom, little white tulips and miniature white narcissi nestling in a circle of green leaves. It made up for the lack of white chiffon; just looking at it made her feel like a bride.

A very quiet wedding, Thomas had said, but that hadn't prevented everyone in the village who could get to the church from going to see Claudia married. But they understood, sitting at the back of the church quietly so that Claudia and Thomas were unaware of them, knowing that they wanted a quiet wedding. Only as they left the church did she become aware of smiling faces and voices wishing them luck and happiness.

Back at George's house, they drank the champagne which Mr Tait-Bullen had thoughtfully provided, and presently sat down to an early lunch, waited upon by Tombs at his most majestic. Mrs Pratt, refusing to be discouraged by the brief notice she had had of the wedding, had sat up late and got up early in order to provide a feast worthy of the occasion.

Cheese soufflés, each in their own small ramekin, followed by salmon *en croûte*, watercress salad and potato straws, and, following that, Tombs carried in the wedding cake. Not quite in the traditional manner, perhaps—Mrs Pratt hadn't had time for that—but she had iced a fruit cake and ornamented it with silver leaves, searched for at length in the village shop, and arranged it on one of George's much prized Coalport plates, which he kept under lock and key.

'Nothing but the best for Miss Claudia,' Mrs Pratt had told him, standing over him while he took the plate from the glass cabinet where it was displayed.

It was a pleasant meal. No one made a speech, although they did drink the bride and groom's health, with Tombs and Mrs Pratt summoned from the kitchen, well pleased with their efforts, beaming at them from the door.

It was Thomas, refilling their glasses, who said, 'My wife and I thank you both for giving us such a delightful lunch; it has made our happy day even happier.'

They had coffee in the drawing room, and presently Thomas said, 'I think we should be going, Claudia.' He looked at George. 'We both thank you for making our wedding such a happy occasion. Once we are settled in we do hope that you will come and visit us.' He turned to his mother and said, 'And of course you and Father. But we shall be seeing you at Christmas.'

'We look forward to that, Thomas.'

It took quite a while saying goodbye to everyone. Thomas put the luggage in the car and then waited with no sign of impatience while Claudia went from one to the other. Tombs and Mrs Pratt had to be bidden goodbye, messages left for Jennie, and Rob hugged. But finally there were no more goodbyes to be said, and she went out to the car with Thomas and got in beside him. It wasn't until they had driven for a mile or two that she said in a small voice, 'It has all been so sudden...'

He touched her hand briefly. 'Don't worry, Claudia, I shan't hurry you. Think of us as being engaged, if that makes you feel happier...'

'Well, I dare say it would, but I won't. We're married, aren't we? Once I get used to that everything will be fine.' She added quickly, 'Don't think I'm regretting it; I'm not. I'm very happy—only a bit out of my depth.'

'You may have all the time in the world to find your feet. I have to work tomorrow, but on Wednesday I shall be home in the morning—time for us to talk.'

He was on the motorway now, driving fast through the already fading light.

'Cork will have tea for us and we shall have this evening together. I enjoyed our wedding, Claudia, and I hope you did too?'

'Oh, yes, I did. And the flowers—they were glorious. They made me forget that I was wearing an ordinary outfit. I felt as though I was in white chiffon and a veil— a real bride.'

'But you were a real bride, my dear. You looked beautiful...'

A remark which lifted her spirits, so that for the rest of the journey she was utterly happy.

CHAPTER FIVE

THOMAS'S description of his home in London had been
vague; Claudia had gathered that he lived near his consulting rooms in a terraced house, and she had pictured
a typical London house—solid, mid-Victorian, with
rather a lot of red brickwork. And, since she knew very
little of London, her visits having been confined to brief
shopping expeditions and the occasional visit to a theatre, she'd visualised a busy road, noisy with traffic and
not a tree in sight.

When Thomas stopped before his home, got out and
opened her door, she got out too and stared around her.
It was quite dark by now, but the street lighting was
shining onto the elegant houses standing back from the
tree-lined pavement. He took her arm and led her up the
three steps to the door being held open, giving a glimpse
of a softly lighted hall.

'Ah, Cork,' said Mr Tait-Bullen. 'Claudia, this is
Cork, who looks after me so well and will doubtless do
the same for you.' He put a hand on the other man's
shoulder. 'My wife, Cork.'

Claudia offered a hand and smiled into the craggy
face, and Cork allowed himself a pleased and relieved
smile in return. A nice young lady, he saw at once, just
right for his master.

'May I wish you both every happiness?' he observed
solemnly. 'And I shall hope to give you as much satisfaction, madam, as the master.'

'Very nicely put,' said Mr Tait-Bullen, busy taking

85

Claudia's coat and gloves and tossing them and his own coat onto one of the chairs flanking the side table.

Cork allowed himself another smile. 'Tea will be brought to the drawing room in five minutes, sir.'

He melted away, and Thomas took Claudia's arm and led her through a door—one of three leading from the hall.

The room was large, with its windows overlooking the quiet street. There was an Adam fireplace, with two sofas and a maple and rosewood library table arranged before it, a Regency writing table under the window and a magnificent Chinese lacquer display cabinet facing the window. There were comfortable chairs too, upholstered in the same burgundy velvet as the curtains draping the window. And small lamp tables here and there, too, piled with books and magazines. A lovely room, restful and lived in.

Claudia felt instantly at home in it—a good augur for the future? she wondered, smiling at Cork, coming in with the tea tray. He didn't return the smile. She appeared to be a nice young lady, at first sight a suitable wife for his master, but time would tell, and he was a man who did nothing hastily. She might want to interfere in his kitchen...

Claudia had seen the prim set of his mouth. If Cork was anything like Tombs then she would need to tread carefully for a while. It had taken her quite a time to win over Tombs, but once she had he had become her firm friend and ally. She sat down in the chair Thomas had offered her and composedly poured their tea, as though she had been doing it for years.

Mr Tait-Bullen, leafing through his post, observed her from under his lids. He had known instinctively that she was the right wife for him: taking things in her stride, accepting each new challenge as it arose, fitting into his life without fuss. And he liked her; he liked her very much.

He considered himself beyond the age of falling in love, and he had no intention of doing so. His work was all-engrossing. The way of life that he had chosen suited him very well; he had no doubt that Claudia would accept that. They had similar tastes. She would be free to make her own friends, and whenever they had the time they would spend a day or so in the country. He must remember to do something about that...

Cork came back presently, removed the tea things and ushered her upstairs. The staircase was narrow, and curved against the end wall of the hall, and Claudia stopped to admire it. She ran a hand over its mahogany banisters, gleaming with polish. 'Lots of elbow grease,' she reflected out loud, and Cork gave her a respectful look.

'Nothing beats it, madam.' He allowed himself the ghost of a smile.

Her room was at the back of the house, overlooking a long, narrow garden. Even in winter it looked charming, with a tracery of leafless trees grouped here and there. Doubtless in the spring there would be crocuses and daffodils around them, and bright flowers in the summer.

She turned from the window and found Cork still standing at the door. 'The bathroom is through the door on the right, madam, and beyond that is the Professor's room. Tomorrow, if you wish, I will conduct you round the house.'

'Oh, please, Cork. And if you will tell me anything that I should know—advise me. You will know exactly how the—the Professor likes things done.'

'I trust so, madam.'

When she was alone she took stock of the room and could find no fault with it. The bed was a satinwood four-poster, curtained and covered with a gossamer-fine ivory silk patterned with forget-me-nots, and the bow-fronted chest was of the same wood. There was a satin-wood and mahogany mirror on the mahogany sofa table under the two windows, and a tallboy in exquisite mar-quetry. On either side of the bed were delicate little side tables, each with a china figure bearing a rose-coloured lamp. There was a wall cupboard too, she discovered, and beyond the further door a bathroom to be drooled over. She peeped round the door in the bathroom too: another bedroom, furnished more plainly, but with the same beautiful old pieces.

It was something she hadn't thought about; that Thomas had comfortable means had always been appar-ent, but this house of his was full of treasures. Had he inherited them? she wondered. Or did he collect old and valuable furniture as a hobby?

She went downstairs presently, determined to find out.

Thomas looked up from his letters as she went into the room. 'Is your room all right? Most of the furniture here was left to me by my grandmother, who had it from her husband's family—they had an enormous old house in Berkshire. I loved it when I went to stay with her as a boy, and I still do.'

'So do I, and it's just right for this house, isn't it?'

'I think so, and I'm glad you agree. This place isn't large but the period's right.'

'I was wondering—you know, while I was upstairs—if you collected old furniture or something like that?'

'No, but when we have found the house we like in the country we will spend time finding exactly the right furniture for it. I'm seldom free for any length of time, so it may take months.'

Lying in the four-poster, nicely drowsy, Claudia reviewed her wedding day. They had spent a happy evening together, talking like an old married couple, disagreeing pleasantly from time to time, discovering that they agreed about most things which mattered. Cork had served them with a splendid dinner—watercress soup, roast pheasant with all its trimmings, a dessert of his own devising—a concoction of ground almonds and whipped cream, angelica and crystallised fruit—and finally coffee in a very beautiful silver coffee pot, poured into paper-thin cups. They had drunk champagne, too, with Cork toasting them gravely and wishing them long life and happiness.

She had gone to bed quite happily. Wasn't there a song 'Getting to Know You'? That was what they were doing, wasn't it? Taking their time like two sensible people, but instead of getting engaged for a time before they married, they had married first.

'Let us give ourselves time to get to know and understand each other,' Thomas had said, and she had agreed. Life spread before her, undemanding and rather exciting. Tomorrow, she thought sleepily, she would go over the house with Cork, taking care not to encroach on his orderly life. She would wait for him to make the first suggestions as to what she should or should not do; later on, when he had accepted her, it would be for her to make suggestions...

Breakfast was at half past seven. When Thomas had suggested that she might like hers in bed, or later in the morning, she had told him that, no, she liked getting up early and would breakfast with him. She had seen his faint frown and hastened to add, 'Don't worry, I won't talk!'

In the morning she was as good as her word. Beyond a cheerful good morning she stayed silent, eating the scrambled eggs Cork put before her and following that with toast and marmalade. Thomas left before she had finished, dropping a hand on her shoulder as he went past her chair.

'I may be late home...'

'How late is late? Does Cork have a meal ready for you whatever time it is?'

'Yes. But I'll do my best to be here by eight o'clock. If I'm held up I'll phone, or get someone to do it for me.'

He had gone. She heard him speak to Cork in the hall before he went out to his car. She had finished breakfast when Cork came to clear the table.

'You will wish to see over the house, madam?'

'Yes, please, Cork. When it's convenient to you. I'm sure you have your day organised. I'd like to telephone my mother and write a letter or two, so will you let me know when you are ready? Does someone come in to give you a hand?'

'Mrs Rumbold comes each morning except Saturday and Sunday. A reliable, hardworking person, and entirely trustworthy. If it suits you, I will bring you coffee at ten o'clock, after which I shall be free to take you round the house.'

'Thank you, Cork. Ought I to meet Mrs Rumbold?'

'Certainly, if you wish, madam. I will bring her to you—she comes at nine o'clock.'

Claudia had a long and satisfying conversation with her mother, declaring herself to be entirely happy and promising a full description of the house later. She put

the phone down as Cork came in with Mrs Rumbold—
a stout lady with small dark eyes in a round face, a great
deal of hair, in a most unlikely shade of ebony, and a
wide smile.

Claudia got up and shook hands, and murmured suitably, and Mrs Rumbold's vast person quivered with
cheerful laughter.

'Lor' bless me, ma'am, it's a great treat to see another
female in the house. A bit of a surprise, but Mr Cork
tells me as 'ow you and the Professor 'as known each
other a while.'

Claudia smiled and said that, yes, indeed that was so.
Cork coughed, a signal for Mrs Rumbold to take her
departure, declaring that she'd do her best, same as always, and had never given Mr Cork cause to complain…

'I'm sure you haven't, Mrs Rumbold…'

She had her coffee presently, this time from a small
silver coffee pot and a much larger cup, delicately patterned with roses. It looked so fragile that Claudia was
in two minds as to whether to drink from it. But she did.

She went for a walk after lunch, finding her way round
the quiet streets, lined by similar houses, going to the
nearest main road to study the bus timetables. There
were no large stores close by, although she did find a
row of small shops tucked away behind an elegant row
of houses. The kind of shops she was used to—selling
wools and knitting needles and high-class green-
groceries, an antiquarian bookshop, a tiny tea shop—
very elegant—and at the end a dusty, rather shabby little
place selling small antiques and a variety of odds and
ends.

She spent some time looking in its window, and then
walked back, thinking about her morning. Cork had been
very helpful, but she felt he was still suspicious of her.

He had shown her every nook and cranny of the house, every cupboard... The house was bigger than she had thought at first: three storeys high and every room charmingly furnished. Cork had a room and bathroom behind the kitchen in the semi-basement, and she had no doubt that it was comfortably furnished too.

The kitchen was very much to her own taste; a cheerful red Aga, a vast old-fashioned dresser along one wall, filled with plates and dishes, a square wooden table in the centre of the room, around which were an assortment of comfortable, rather shabby chairs, and pots and saucepans neatly stacked on the shelves on the walls. There were checked curtains at the window and a thick rug before the Aga. It reminded her of Great-Uncle William's kitchen... She reached the front door and rang the bell, reminding herself that she must ask Thomas for a key.

Thomas didn't get home until almost eight o'clock. She saw that he was tired and, beyond answering his queries as to how she had spent her day, she forebore from chattering. They dined in a companionable silence, and, since it was by then getting late in the evening, she said that she was tired and would go to bed if he didn't mind. It had been the right thing to say, but she tried not to mind when she saw the relief on his face.

Still, he bade her goodnight and kissed her cheek, then reminded her that he was free in the morning and they would go shopping. 'I shall open an account for you at Harrods and Harvey Nichols, and arrange for an allowance to be paid into your bank. But tomorrow we will shop together.'

He took her first to Harrods the next morning, accompanying her to the fashion floor, telling her to buy what-

ever she liked and making himself comfortable in one
of the easy chairs scattered around.

'You mean a dress and coat, and things like that?'
asked Claudia. 'How much may I spend?'

'One dress will hardly do. Buy several—and certainly
a winter coat and anything else you like. Don't look at
the price tags, Claudia.' He smiled at her. 'Buy all you
need for the next few weeks; we shall be going out a
good deal, I have no doubt...'

'Dinner dresses,' breathed Claudia, and her eyes sparkled.

'Certainly, and a couple of dresses for dancing—the
hospital ball and so on. And something tweedy for the
lakes. I shall take you walking.'

'You don't mind waiting here?'

'Not in the least. Come and show me what you buy
from time to time, if you like.'

So Claudia, guided by a majestic saleslady in black
crêpe, went shopping in earnest. She had had nothing
new for some time, and her present wardrobe was sparse
in the extreme, but that didn't prevent her from knowing
exactly what she needed to buy.

A beautifully tailored winter coat in dark green, a
tweed skirt with a matching soft leather jacket, a twinset
in cashmere, peat-brown, a jersey dress in soft blue and
another in dove-grey, and, at the sales lady's suggestion,
a handful of silk blouses and another cardigan. She had
shown most of these to a patient Mr Tait-Bullen, then
gone with him to the restaurant for a cup of coffee before
embarking on the choosing of a crêpe dress in old gold,
and another in a green patterned silk jersey. She would
have bought a little black dress, but when she mentioned
her intention to Thomas he begged her not to. 'They're

not for you,' he told her. 'Get something with a waist and a wide skirt.'

Which wasn't much to go by. Anxious to please him, she spent some time looking for such a garment, and found it at last. Blue again—a smoky blue—with long sleeves and a modest neckline, and a tucked bodice cinched in at the waist by an embroidered belt, the skirt was several layers of chiffon, and it showed off her splendid figure. She paraded before him in it and saw that he approved.

'Would you like me to stop now?' she asked him.

'No. No. Let us by all means get the basics. What else do you need?'

'Well, evening dresses. I won't be long...'

She knew what suited her and she didn't dither, although there was a magnificent black taffeta she longed to own... She chose instead a russet taffeta with a tucked bodice, shoestring shoulder straps and a wide skirt which rustled delightfully as she walked. And a honey-coloured crêpe, very simple in cut.

'I've bought masses of clothes,' she told Thomas finally. 'I do hope....'

'We'll have lunch, and, if you haven't made me bankrupt, we will go to Harvey Nichols.'

'But I've bought masses of stuff.'

'Undies, dressing gowns, shoes, boots, a Burberry—a hat for church on Christmas Day?'

She stared up at him with wide eyes. 'You think of everything.'

'No, my dear, but you forget I have sisters, and I have from time to time accompanied them on shopping expeditions.'

'Oh, well, if you don't mind.'

'No, I don't mind,' said Mr Tait-Bullen, and thought how very pretty she looked.

They lunched at Harvey Nichols, in the basement bar-restaurant because Claudia declared that she was too full of excitement to eat much. All the same, gently urged on by Thomas, she managed grilled salmon and a salad, and apple tart, and, thus fortified, spent the next hour or so adding to her wardrobe. Having approved of the Burberry, boots, and shoes, Thomas left her in the undies department.

'I'll look around for presents for the family,' he told her, 'on the ground floor.' He glanced at his watch. 'An hour? I'll be waiting by the main entrance.' He smiled down at her happy face. 'Don't hurry.'

She lost herself in the delights of the lingerie department, but she remembered that he had said an hour. Laden with carrier bags, she went punctually to the ground floor and found him waiting.

He looked at the bags. 'They can be delivered with the other things,' he suggested.

She shook her head. 'I can't bear to part with them,' she told him seriously. 'You have no idea how lovely...'

'Shall we go home for tea?' he asked in a matter-of-fact way, which stopped her short.

They had their tea, and then an hour or so sitting together talking about nothing in particular. There would be more Christmas presents to buy, he warned her. And would she like to go to Little Planting before Christmas?

'I can spare a Sunday, if you would like that. And don't forget the hospital ball next week. You will be bound to get any number of invitations for us both from the people we meet there. I rely on you to deal with them. There is a certain amount of hospital social life, and you will probably be roped in for some charity or other. Don't take on too much...'

They were halfway through dinner when he was called away. He went quickly, warning her that he might be late back.

As he went he dropped a kiss on her cheek. 'I enjoyed our day together,' he told her.

'Me too. Only I've spent an awful lot of your money...'

'Our money,' he said quietly. 'It was a great pleasure.'

She sat in the drawing room that evening, leafing through magazines, thinking about her delightful day. Thomas had been a splendid companion too. Patient, and interested in what she had bought. Of course, she quite understood that as the wife of a well-known cardiologist she needed to be well turned out—he wouldn't want her to meet any of his friends and colleagues wearing the shabby tweeds and woollies she had always worn at Little Planting.

She got up and took a look at herself in the Georgian giltwood mirror. Perhaps she should have her hair cut and styled? Go to a beauty parlour and learn how to apply make-up? She tended to forget anything but lipstick; there had seemed no point in it when she lived with Great-Uncle William. On the sparse occasions when she'd gone out to dinner she had dashed powder over her nose, added lipstick and done her best with her hands, so often grubby from gardening. She would remedy this, she promised herself, so that Thomas need never feel ashamed of her.

The long case clock in the hall had struck eleven, and he still wasn't back. She went to the kitchen and found Cork sitting there, reading the evening paper.

She said quickly, 'No, no. Don't get up, Cork. I think

I'll go to bed. Do you wait up or does the Professor let himself in? And does he need anything? A drink? Or sandwiches?'

'I wait up, madam. There is coffee, and there are sandwiches if he should require them. I'm sure he would wish you to take your normal rest.'

'Yes, well…I'll go to bed, then. Thank you, Cork.'

'Thank you, madam, and goodnight.'

He held the door for her and didn't return her smile. She went up to her room, still not sure if he approved of her or not. She must have been a surprise to him, and doubtless he wondered if she was going to interfere. She didn't intend to; perhaps she'd do the flowers, discuss the food with him, and then later on, when he had accepted her, he might allow her into the kitchen.

Thomas was already at breakfast when she went down in the morning. He looked as he always did, immaculate in his sober grey suit and silk tie, but there were lines in his face…

She wished him good morning. 'When did you get home?' she asked.

'Round about one o'clock. I didn't disturb you?'

'No, no. Do you often get called out? I thought specialists and consultants could more or less please themselves.'

Mr Tait-Bullen looked surprised. 'We're just the same as any other medical man. We go when and where we're needed.'

'And you are going to the hospital this morning?'

'No, first to one of the private hospitals. I operated there a couple of days ago, and I must visit my patient there first. Then to the hospital, and a clinic after lunch, and then private patients at my consulting rooms.'

'Will you come home for lunch?'

He shook his head. 'I'm afraid not. I may be back in time for tea, though.' He glanced at her. 'You'll be all right?'

'Yes…'

'I should have warned you that I'm away a good deal.'

He left the house presently, and, since Cork informed her that it was Mrs Rumbold's day for turning out the drawing room, she guessed quite rightly, that they would like her out of the house.

'I thought I'd explore a bit,' she told him. 'Hyde Park and perhaps Kensington Gardens…'

'A pleasant walk, madam. Lunch at one o'clock?'

'Yes, please. Something on a tray will do.'

She had put on the tweed skirt and one of the silk shirts, and, since it was drizzling with a chilly wind, she donned the Burberry and the boots. The Burberry had a little matching hat, which she crammed onto her hair with no regard to her appearance, so that copper strands escaped. She took her new shoulder bag, her expensive leather gloves, bade Cork goodbye and left the house.

There weren't many people about as she made her way to Marble Arch. Cork, that paragon of servants, had thoughtfully provided her with a small street map, and it wasn't until she reached Marble Arch that there was much traffic and the first sight of Christmas shoppers.

She crossed the road into the park, following the Serpentine, enjoying the quiet emptiness, for there was scarcely anyone else to be seen. She was halfway to Rennie's Bridge, which would lead her to Kensington Gardens, when she saw a very small dog sitting under the bushes some yards from the path. He didn't bark, nor did he take any notice of her, and she walked on, supposing that its owner was somewhere nearby. But an hour later, as she came back the same way, he was still there.

There was no one in sight; she crossed the grass and bent down to take a closer look.

It was a very small dog indeed—a puppy, pitifully thin and shivering with cold. It made no sound as Claudia touched his matted coat with a gentle hand; it only looked at her with terrified eyes, cringing away from her. He was tied by a thin rope to a thicket behind him, and she could see that the rope was tight around his throat. If he'd tried to run away he would have choked.

She opened her bag, found the small folded scissors she always carried with her and began to saw through the rope. It took time, but the puppy didn't move, and when at last he was free she scooped him up and tucked him into the front of her Burberry, where he shivered and shook but made no effort to escape.

'You poor little scrap,' said Claudia. 'You're coming home with me, and I'll make sure that you're never frightened nor hungry again.'

It was only as she reached the house that she wondered what Thomas would say—or Cork!

He had seen her coming along the street and had the door open before she had a chance to get out her key.

She didn't beat about the bush. 'Cork, I found this tiny dog tied to a tree in Hyde Park. He's starving and cold...'

Cork peered at the small creature. 'The Professor has said on various occasions that he intended to get a dog, madam. Perhaps, a box with an old blanket by the Aga?'

'Oh, Cork, may he stay just until he's warm? And I thought a little warm milk... I'll have him as soon as I've got my things off.'

'If I might suggest, madam, you allow him to rest quietly for a period while you have lunch. By then we shall be able to see if he is recovering.'

So the puppy was settled in a cardboard box and covered warmly, and Claudia fed him with warm milk. Although he cringed still, he looked less terrified.

He was asleep when she went to fetch him after lunch. 'Thank you for having him in the kitchen, Cork, I won't let him bother you.'

'I have no doubt that when he is feeling more himself he will be a nice little dog. I'm partial to dogs, madam.'

Claudia beamed at him. 'Oh, are you, Cork? So am I.'

She took the little beast with her to the sitting room beside Thomas's study—a charming little room, where she chose to sit and have her meals when Thomas was away from home—and he fell asleep by the warmth of the fire, twitching and whimpering in his sleep. And when Cork brought her tea tray he handed her a small jug. 'Egg and milk, madam,' he explained. 'Perhaps a few spoonfuls from time to time…'

They inspected the sleeping puppy and decided that he looked a little better.

'As soon as I dare, I'll clean him up a bit,' said Claudia. 'He's stopped shivering…'

She went to her room presently, and changed her blouse and skirt for one of the jersey dresses, not bothering overmuch about her face and hair. She was feeding the puppy, kneeling by the box, rather untidy about the head, when Thomas came quietly to join her.

She scrambled to her feet when she saw him. 'Thomas, I'm so glad you're home. Come and see what I found this morning…' She paused while Cork placed a tea tray on the rent table by the easy chair where Mr

Tait-Bullen often sat. 'I'll pour your tea. Have you had a busy day?'

He could see that for the moment his day would have to take second place to whatever it was in the box which had given her eyes such a sparkle and her cheeks such a fine colour.

'And what did you find?' He went over to the box and got down on his hunkers to take a better look.

'Cork says you always wanted a dog...'

Mr Tait-Bullen choked back a laugh. 'Oh, indeed I have.' He put a gentle finger on the skinny little body. 'Lost? Starved? Probably ill-treated. Where did you find him?'

'Sit down and drink your tea and I'll tell you. Then you can examine him, can't you?'

He drank his tea and ate the toast she offered him, and listened without interrupting. 'And Cork has been marvellous. I thought he would mind—I mean, a grubby little dog in this lovely house—'

'Our house,' he interrupted her gently.

'Well, of course it is, but you know what I mean, don't you? Please may we keep him? I don't know what kind of a dog he is, but I dare say he'll be handsome when he's older.'

Mr Tait-Bullen studied the puppy thoughtfully. 'There is always that possibility,' he agreed. 'Let's have a look at him.'

Claudia was surprised to see that the puppy accepted Thomas's gentle hands feeling his poor, bony frame, with no more than the whisper of a whine.

'Starved and kicked around, but I can't feel any broken bones. I'm on nodding terms with the local vet; I'll get him to come round and take a look.'

'May we keep him? You don't mind?'

'No, I don't mind. Cork was right. I have often said that I would like a dog.' He didn't add that the dog he had had in mind was a thoroughbred Labrador.

They dined presently, and tended to the puppy's needs, and later that evening the vet came. He was a youngish, thickset man, with a great deal of black hair and a face one could trust.

'Thomas, what's all this about a dog? Where did you get it?'

'Come and meet my wife. It was she who found the creature.'

The two men crossed the hall to the sitting room, where Claudia had gone to feed the puppy.

The vet shook hands. He had heard about Tait-Bullen's unexpected marriage, and, glancing at Claudia, he considered him to be a lucky fellow. Beautiful and charming—nice voice too.

He said out loud, 'I must get Alice—my wife—to call on you. Now, where's this dog?'

He took his time going over the puppy's small frame. 'No bones broken. Several swellings, though—he's been kicked. And just look at these paws—he's been tied up somewhere and tried to escape. Poor little beast.'

'Any idea what breed?' said Mr Tait-Bullen.

'Take your pick. He'll never be a large dog, nor perhaps a handsome one, but I guarantee he'll be a faithful companion to you both. I'll give him a couple of jabs while I'm here. As to food and exercise…'

He outlined suitable treatment. 'And a run in the garden is all he'll need for several weeks—that and frequent small meals.' He looked at Claudia. 'You will be busy, Mrs Tait-Bullen.'

'I've time enough to look after him, and I shall enjoy it. You'll have a cup of coffee?'

He stayed for a while, idly chatting, and presently Thomas went with him to the door. 'You've a charming wife, Thomas. You must come to dinner one evening.'

'We'll be delighted.'

He went back to the sitting room, where Claudia was kneeling by the puppy's box. She looked up as he went in. 'Thomas, thank you. Perhaps he's not the kind of dog you wanted, but he'll be such fun to have.'

Mr Tait-Bullen contemplated the skinny creature, sitting up now and no longer cowering, knowing that he was among friends. Under the dirt and mud his coat was black. His ears were far too large for his small foxy face, and he had a long, thin tail of which any rat would have been proud.

'I have no doubt that he will grow into the most unusual type,' he observed gravely.

'That's what I thought,' said Claudia happily. 'I like the vet. Are all your friends as nice?'

'I hope you will think so. You will meet a good many of them at the ball.' He went to sit in his chair, stretching his long legs to the fire. 'I'm sure you have a grand gown to wear among your purchases, or would you like to look for something else?'

'I have a gown. It's not grand, but I think it's suitable for your wife, if you see what I mean?'

'I trust your judgement, Claudia. You have excellent taste.'

Claudia went to bed with the pleasant feeling that it had been a happy day; they got on so well together, she reflected, and there was so much to talk about, so much that they intended to do together. Every day, she was discovering, she was finding out something else about Thomas that she liked; she hoped that he felt the same about her. She curled up and closed her eyes. Tomorrow was another day; she wondered what it would bring.

Fortunately for her peace of mind she wasn't to know *who* it would bring!

CHAPTER SIX

THE day began well. Thomas had no need to leave the house until nine o'clock, so they had leisure to clean up the puppy, anoint his battered little paws and brush his coat while he lay on Claudia's lap.

'What shall we call him?' she asked. 'A nice English name, since I found him in Hyde Park.'

'Since you found him you must choose his name.'

'Yes, well...' She thought for a moment. 'Harvey—that's easy to say, isn't it?'

Harvey cocked an ungainly ear; he was beginning to look more like a dog every minute.

Mr Tait-Bullen went presently, promising that he would be back for tea unless some emergency turned up.

'Oh, good,' said Claudia, with such transparent pleasure that he turned to look at her. She met his gaze with a look of faint enquiry. 'You look surprised. But teatime is one of the nicest parts of the day, isn't it? You can tell me what you've been doing and I'll listen...'

Mr Tait-Bullen discovered to his surprise that the idea appealed to him.

At four o'clock Cork arranged the tea things on a small table in the drawing room, and, since Mr Tait-Bullen had phoned to say that he would be home shortly after half past four, Claudia carried Harvey in his box from the sitting room and set it near the open fire. She had been out walking again, and was still in the tweed skirt and a blouse, but she had tidied her hair and powdered her nose and put on a pair of elegant kid slippers. She was sitting admiring them when Thomas came in.

He crossed the room and dropped a quick kiss on her cheek. 'How very cosy it is here. Cork's bringing the tea.'

He sat down opposite her. 'You have had a happy day? Harvey is doing well?'

'He's better. Look at him, Thomas. He's almost like a normal puppy.'

Harvey took this as a compliment and waved his tail.

'You don't mind him being in here? I don't think he'll get out of his box.'

'I don't imagine he could do much harm even if he did. He certainly looks more like a dog.' Thomas stretched an arm and tickled Harvey behind one ear. 'I must let John know how he's getting on. I dare say he'll want to see him again.'

Cork brought in the tea then, and buttered muffins in a dish, a fruit cake and a plate of paper-thin sandwiches. He arranged everything just so, and stood back to admire his handiwork.

Claudia said, 'Thank you, Cork, it all looks delicious. I hope you're going to have your own tea now?'

'Thank you, madam, yes. Dinner at the usual hour? You won't be going out again, sir?'

'I hope not, Cork.' And, as Cork slid through the door, Thomas added, 'I've a mass of paperwork to sort out. A quiet evening at home to get that done will be delightful.'

Claudia, pouring tea, agreed placidly. If she had been looking forward to an evening in his company, she didn't utter the thought aloud.

They were inspecting the fruit cake when the front doorbell was rung. And, before either of them had time to speak, Cork opened the door and stood aside to let someone in.

Mr Tait-Bullen got to his feet, his face expressionless, and his pleasant, 'Why, Honor, how nice to see you,' giving nothing away of his feelings.

Claudia stood up too, recognising in an instant that here was someone she wasn't going to like and who wasn't going to like her. But she smiled, a bright social smile, and then looked enquiringly at Thomas.

'My dear, let me introduce Honor Thompson. Honor, my wife, Claudia.'

Claudia offered a hand. 'Do sit down and have a cup of tea. I'll get Cork to bring a fresh pot...'

Honor sat on the sofa facing the fire, throwing off her coat to reveal a black dress—very short, very smart and undoubtedly very expensive. It showed off her long legs and her very slim body.

No shape at all, thought Claudia, and wondered if Thomas admired women who looked like beanpoles. She was suddenly aware of her own curves, and busied herself with the fresh tea Cork had brought in, listening with half an ear to Honor's rather loud voice complaining that she had had no idea that Thomas was getting married and why hadn't he told her. 'You must have known what a shock it would be to me.'

She glanced at Claudia, who handed her a cup and saucer. 'I expect you and Thomas are very old friends,' Claudia remarked. 'But, you see, we didn't tell anyone except our families. It was a very quiet wedding.'

'Well, I for one shan't forgive you easily, Thomas,' said Honor, and she leaned forward to lay a hand on his arm.

Mr Tait-Bullen got up and put his cup and saucer on the table without answering her, and she flushed angrily.

'Of course, I don't suppose you know much about Thomas. You can't have known each other long.' She gave Claudia a sly look.

'Long enough to know that we wanted to be married,' said Claudia, in a matter-of-fact voice which robbed the question of drama. 'You live in London?'

'Of course. Where else is there?'

'You don't care to travel?' asked Claudia guilelessly. 'I mean, around England? Perhaps all your friends live here?'

'I hate the country. I adore the theatre and dining out and dancing.' She gave a little trill of laughter. 'I can see that Thomas will have to change his ways now that he is a married man.'

'I expect most men do,' said Claudia cheerfully. 'And I don't suppose they mind or they wouldn't marry, would they?' She smiled at Thomas. 'Don't you agree, Thomas?'

'Wholeheartedly. Honor, take a look at our addition to the household.'

He bent and picked up Harvey, tucked him under an arm and went over to where Honor was sitting.

She eyed Harvey with dislike. 'You aren't serious? It's a horrid little stray. He must be filthy, and he's hideously ugly...'

'He's a brave little dog. We call him Harvey—he'll probably grow into something quite splendid. He's still rather grubby, but he's been ill-treated—look at this sore on his shoulder, and under his paws...'

Honor shrank back. 'Don't come any nearer with the nasty little brute...' She stood up. 'I must go. I'm going out this evening.' She turned a cold eye on Claudia. 'Nice meeting you, Claudia. I dare say we shall see each other around—that is, if you go out much socially.'

She didn't shake hands, and she didn't shake hands with Thomas either, since he was still holding Harvey. She reached the door as Cork, summoned by the bell-push by the fireplace, opened it and ushered her out.

It wasn't until he had returned and carried away the tea tray that Claudia said, 'I hope you're grateful that I married you. She would have eaten you alive in a couple of years. Are all your girl friends like that?'

Mr Tait-Bullen had gone back to his chair with Harvey curled up on his knee. He had expected a reproachful comment, or at least coolness and hurt looks, and he was taken aback by Claudia's cheerful question. Taken aback and, he had to admit, amused.

'I only now begin to realise what a treasure I have married. I am indeed grateful that you are my wife; calm, good sense and not a single sulky look. I can assure you that I have never had any intention of marrying Honor, although I suspect that she had the intention of marrying me. And I have had no girlfriends. Oh, I have taken Honor out from time to time, and other women too, but on a strictly platonic basis. I have not been in love for a very long time. If that were so, I would have told you.'

'Oh, my goodness, I didn't mean to pry. It's none of my business. All the same, I'm glad that it's me you married.'

'And so am I. Now, let us forget the woman and talk about other things which matter. I can be free next Sunday; shall we go down to Little Planting? Will your mother and George be home?'

'Yes, they only went away for a few days because they want to spend Christmas at home, and Mother enjoys all the preparations, you know—the tree and paper chains and holly and presents. She always managed to make it a lovely time when we lived with Great-Uncle William.'

'Then we will go, and take Harvey with us. Do you want to shop for presents?'

'I could go tomorrow…and what about your family? Should we not buy more presents for them?'

'I can't spare the time; if I give you a list, will you do your best for us both?'

It was the kind of question that required nothing more than a meek answer.

She went shopping the next morning; Thomas had left the house early, and she found no one when she went down to breakfast, but by her plate was a list of names scrawled in his unreadable writing. A long list, starting with his mother and ending with someone called Maggie, with brackets beside her name requesting warm slippers, size six! His father wasn't mentioned—presumably he bought that present himself. She added Cork's name, and Mrs Rumbold's. Probably Thomas gave them money, but a personal gift was always nice to have…

She found a cashmere stole for her mother-in-law, silk scarves for his sisters, and a small leather case containing razor, hairbrush and a variety of small necessities which a man might need when travelling. And then she decided that scarves weren't enough for his sisters; she added a small silver photo frame and a little enamelled box. There were nephews and nieces too; she spent a happy hour in the toy department of Harrods.

Thomas got home in the early evening, and she saw at once that for the moment at least he had no wish to look at what she had bought. He had greeted her in his usual manner, given her a drink, poured one for himself and gone to sit in his chair. Harvey had climbed out of his box and wriggled his way on to his knee, and Thomas now stroked the small creature gently.

'You have had a pleasant day?' he asked presently.

'Yes, thank you. But you don't want to hear about it for the moment, do you? Do you want to talk about your day? I dare say I won't understand the half of it, but I'll be a pair of ears.'

He laughed then. 'Claudia, you are so understanding. It is as if we had been married for years—you are such a comfortable woman to come home to. And at the end of the day sometimes a pair of ears is what I most want.'

He began to talk: a difficult diagnosis, a long list in Theatre, a post-operative patient who wasn't progressing as well as he should, and always a backlog of patients who needed his skill.

Claudia listened to every word. There was quite a bit she didn't understand, but that didn't matter; she was intelligent enough to have a good idea as to his working day.

Presently she asked, 'Do you have a team working with you?'

'Yes, a splendid one. My senior registrar is a most dependable man, and I have two junior registrars and a couple of young surgeons—you'll meet them all at the ball. And a splendid theatre sister too.'

Claudia felt a faint flicker of something which she didn't recognise as jealousy. All she knew was that she felt regret that *she* couldn't be his theatre sister, working beside him.

Thomas smiled across at her. 'Have I bored you? You must tell me if I do.'

'No, I like to know something of your work. I'm really interested.'

Cork came to tell them then that dinner was on the

table and Thomas said, 'You must tell me what you have bought...'

She spent the next day shopping for her mother and George, and Tombs, Mrs Pratt and Jennie. It was nice having enough money to choose presents without having to bother too much about their price. Thomas had given her a very generous allowance, and told her carelessly not to worry if she spent too much, but she reminded herself that she hadn't married him for his money. Indeed, she admitted, she would have married him if he were penniless. The thought surprised her, and left her feeling disquieted.

The day after that was the hospital ball. Anxious to present as pleasing a picture as possible, Claudia spent most of the afternoon doing her nails, washing her hair, and experimenting with make-up. But by teatime she had decided that her usual dash of powder and lipstick would do. As for her hair, after a tiring hour pinning it into a variety of elaborate styles, she decided to twist it into a chignon—a simple style which suited her lovely face and which required no fuss. She suspected that Thomas would dislike it if she were to fidget about her appearance.

He had expected to be home early, but Cork had carried away the tea things and there was no sign of him. They had planned to have a light meal before going to the ball, and when she heard the clock strike seven she went along to the kitchen with Harvey trotting beside her.

'Cork, what is best to be done? We are to leave here by half past eight, and the Professor will want time to change. Would it be a good idea if you served a meal in the sitting room? We were going to have grilled soles, weren't we? Could they be saved for tomorrow? And could you give us soup and an omelette? Then whatever time he comes in we could eat when he is ready?'

'I have been thinking along those lines, madam: a plain omelette with a small salad, and I have prepared a sustaining soup with fresh-baked rolls.'

'Cork, that will be simply splendid. I'm going up to dress...'

Thomas came home half an hour later and Claudia, fresh from her bath and ready save for getting into her dress, wrapped her dressing gown round her and went down to meet him.

He looked tired after his long day, but he said cheerfully, 'Hello—did you begin to think I wasn't coming home?'

'Well, we were getting a bit anxious.' He hadn't kissed her, but she told herself that it didn't matter a bit. 'Would you like a meal at once, or do you want to change first?'

'I see that you aren't dressed yet.' He eyed her pretty pink quilted dressing gown. 'Shall we eat now?'

'Cork has a meal ready for us; we're having it in the sitting room. How well he looks after you, Thomas.'

He looked at her sharply. 'And you, too?'

'Heavens, yes! He's a treasure.' She led the way into the sitting room, scooping up Harvey as they went. He was still a somewhat battered little animal, but now that he found himself among friends, he was full of a desire to please.

Cork offered the soup, and presently the omelette, looking gratified when Thomas observed that it was exactly the meal he needed. Cork, having overheard Claudia's praise of him, murmured that it was madam who had suggested it. It was an unusually generous remark on his part, but he was becoming aware that

Claudia had no intention of ousting him from his position in the household. In fact, he was beginning to like her.

The meal eaten, they went away to dress, and half an hour later met again in the drawing room. Claudia, in the cream chiffon, wasn't sure if Thomas would find it grand enough, but she need not have worried.

He watched her cross the room. 'Delightful, Claudia. Exactly right. You look charming.' He took a box from the table beside him. 'Will you wear these?' he asked. 'I think they will go very well with the dress.'

He offered pearls, a double row with a diamond clasp, and to go with them earrings, pearl drops set in a delicate network of diamonds.

'My goodness,' said Claudia, 'they're magnificent, Thomas.' She touched the pearls with a gentle finger. 'I'm almost afraid to wear them.' She smiled at him. 'Thank you very much.'

She stretched up and kissed his cheek, and he took the necklace from her and fastened it round her throat.

'My grandmother left them to me with the advice that they should be given to my wife when I married.'

'She must have loved you,' said Claudia, and swallowed disappointment; they weren't a present from Thomas—not something he had wanted to buy for her, to give her as a present; he was merely carrying out his grandmother's wishes.

She said rather too brightly, 'I'm ready if you want to leave now.'

He gave her a thoughtful look, which she met with an equally bright smile. He looked distinguished in his black tie; the formal suit, cut by a master tailor, emphasised his height and size. He was a handsome man, she reflected, who ignored his good looks and had not an ounce of conceit. He was high-handed at times, perhaps, and capable of a fine rage, she suspected, but, like so many large men, gentle.

Cork, with Harvey tucked under an arm, saw them from the house, and it was only when they were driving through the quiet streets towards the busy heart of the city that Claudia felt the first pangs of nervousness.

'I don't know anyone…'

She felt his large, comforting hand on her knee for a moment. 'Don't worry, my dear, you will soon have more friends and acquaintances than you can imagine.'

'Oh—are you very well known, Thomas?'

'Well, I do visit a number of hospitals, and have done for some years now.'

He turned the car into the hospital forecourt, parked and helped her out.

He nodded to one of the porters standing at the entrance, and one of them got into the car and drove it away as they went in.

After that Claudia found herself in a sort of dream world. Thomas led her from one hospital dignitary to the other, a hand under her elbow guiding her, and when the formalities were over he took her onto the dance floor. He danced well, in an unspectacular way, guiding her effortlessly through the crowded hall, talking casually from time to time, putting her at her ease so that presently she found herself dancing with a variety of partners and enjoying herself.

From time to time she glimpsed him dancing, partnering his colleagues' wives, she supposed, slightly older women, well dressed and self-assured, but once or twice she saw that he was dancing with pretty girls, who laughed up into his face as though they had known him for years…

She was about to take to the floor with a stout, bearded man, whom she vaguely remembered having been introduced to, when Thomas slipped a hand under her elbow.

'The supper dance,' he observed mildly. 'You don't mind, Harry, if I claim my wife?'

The bearded man laughed. 'It wouldn't make a scrap of difference if I did, Thomas, but I shall lie in wait for you, Mrs Tait-Bullen!'

'Who was that?' asked Claudia, accepting a plate of vol-au-vents and a glass of wine. 'I've met him, haven't I?'

'Yes, he's the consultant pathologist and an old friend.' He smiled. 'You're enjoying yourself? I've been showered with compliments about my bride.'

She went pink. 'Oh, have you? People are very kind.'

'I have been told how beautiful you are—and you are, Claudia, that dress is exactly right.'

Somehow that last bit spoilt the compliment.

'You have been dancing with some very pretty girls. Of course, you must know all the nurses.'

He fetched her a little dish of ice cream before he replied.

'Not quite all. You see, I meet only ward sisters and staff nurses, and then our conversation is purely professional, but once a year at this ball the senior staff dance with those of the nursing staff they work with on the wards or in Theatre or the clinics. I don't know who started the idea, but the custom is handed down from one generation of doctors to the next.'

A remark which she found reassuring.

It was well past midnight when they got back home. Cork had left hot chocolate on the Aga, and they sat drinking it while Harvey snoozed in his basket.

'A very pleasant evening,' observed Mr Tait-Bullen, 'and you have won all hearts, Claudia.'

'It's nice of you to say so, but it's only because I'm a nine-days wonder.'

He laughed. 'What a matter-of-fact girl you are.' He took her mug from her. 'And a sleepy one, too. I must leave the house by seven o'clock, so don't get up until you have had your sleep. I should be home for tea.'

'Oh, good.' She yawned, and rubbed her eyes like a child. 'It was a lovely evening, and it was lovely to dance.'

He got up and hauled her gently from her chair. 'Indeed it was.'

He opened the door and gave her a gentle shove. 'Off to bed, and sleep well.'

She hesitated a moment, but he held the door open, smiling a little, so she wished him goodnight and took herself off to bed, feeling vaguely unhappy.

She woke late, and when she went downstairs Cork was waiting for her with Harvey scampering at his heels.

'You slept well, madam? I have set breakfast in the sitting room by the fire. A most inclement day, I'm afraid. I am to tell you from the Professor not to venture too far in this weather.'

Claudia peeped out of the window. Indeed, it looked horrid outside—dull and grey with an unremitting drizzle.

'It looks awful, Cork, but Harvey must have his run…'

'Perhaps a brisk turn in the garden, madam. There is always the chance that the weather will improve.'

'Well, I hope it does, for we are going to Little Planting on Sunday. We'll take Harvey with us.' She poured her coffee. 'Cork, you do have a day off each week, don't you?'

'I have two half-days, madam, and such free time as I can arrange without upset to the running of the house.'

He sounded cagey, and she added hastily, 'I'm sure you have it all worked out, Cork. But I just thought that it would be a chance for you to have a day to yourself while we are out.'

'Thank you, madam. I shall avail myself of your offer...'

'I expect that you have family and friends to visit?'

'Indeed, I have. At what time will you be leaving on Sunday, madam?'

'Quite early, I believe, and we shan't be back here until after tea.'

She finished her breakfast and spent the morning tying up presents, considerably hampered by Harvey. When, after lunch, the drizzle ceased, she got into her mac, tied Harvey into his waterproof jacket, and led him out for a quick walk. On the way home she stopped to look in the windows of the little shops she had found. The wool shop had a pretty knitting pattern in the window, with a basket of wools every colour of the rainbow. She already had a present for her mother, but there was no reason why she shouldn't give her another one. She scooped up Harvey, tucked him under her arm and went into the shop.

In the end shop, in amongst the glass and silver bits and pieces, she found a small porcelain model of a dog, the spitting image of Harvey, just right for Thomas's desk. She went home well pleased with her finds, and found Thomas sitting by the drawing room fire reading the papers.

'Oh, how lovely; you're home. No, don't get up. I'll tell Cork I'm back and we'll have tea.'

When she had poured the tea and offered him sandwiches she asked, 'Have you had a busy day?'

Mr Tait-Bullen bit into a buttered scone. 'Much as usual.' He offered Harvey a bit of scone, and didn't see the disappointment on her face. He seemed to shut her out of his working life sometimes. Perhaps he thought that she was not really interested. He added, 'You have created quite a sensation, you know...'

'Me? Didn't I behave like a consultant's wife? Shouldn't I have danced so much?'

'You behaved beautifully, my dear, and everyone is enchanted by you. I was inundated with invitations. I can see that we have a busy social winter ahead of us.'

'Do you mind that? If you do, I'll make excuses.'

'No, you mustn't do that. I rely on you to organise our leisure, and several of the invitations will be for you alone, I imagine—coffee mornings and tea parties.'

He finished his tea, and, with the remark that he had work to do, went to his study. Harvey went with him and she was left sitting alone. She had declared rather too quickly that she had letters to write, and he had nodded casually with the remark that they would meet at dinner.

He had told her before they married that he wanted a companion. It seemed to her that he had forgotten that— or was it that she bored him? She told herself not to be silly, allowing imagination—and, it must be admitted, a modicum of self-pity—to take over.

But she forgot all that when at dinner he suggested that they leave early on Sunday morning so that they might take a look at some likely villages not too far from Little Planting.

'Is there any particular village you fancy? We might at least look around us, so that after Christmas we can house-hunt in earnest.'

'Would we spend the weekends there?'

'Whenever possible, and any free days that I can manage. Somewhere not too far from a good road back to town.'

'Well, there's a lovely little village—Child Okeford—south of Shaftesbury, close to Blandford, and only a mile or so from the main roads. Years ago I used to go there with Mother, she had an old schoolfriend living there, but she moved away. I dare say it's changed. I must have been nine or ten years old.'

'Then we will have a look at it before we go to Little Planting. If we leave really early we should have plenty of time to look around.'

They left at eight o'clock. It still wasn't full daylight, and the streets were Sunday morning quiet. The presents were packed in the boot, and Harvey, wrapped in an old shawl, slept peacefully on the back seat. Claudia felt her spirits soar as she got into the car. She was wearing the leather jacket over a silk shirt and a tweed skirt, and leather boots which had cost so much that she felt quite faint when she thought about it. But they were worth every penny—as supple as velvet and exactly matching the colour of her jacket.

She would have liked to draw Thomas's attention to them, but he seldom noticed what she wore, although he never failed to tell her that she looked nice. But he didn't *look*, she reflected, not at her, not to see her in detail, as it were. She dismissed the thought as unworthy; he was a kind and thoughtful husband and they got on famously.

They reached Child Okeford an hour and a half later.

There was a pale watery sun now, and the village still slept under it. In another hour there would be church, and people setting off in their cars or going for a country walk, but for the moment they had the place to themselves.

'Could we park and look around?' asked Claudia.

They left the car in the centre of the village and, with Harvey on his lead, began to explore.

'It hasn't changed much,' said Claudia. 'The village shop's still there, and the pub.' They paused to admire the church and walked the length of the main street, stopping to explore the narrow side turnings. It was a charming place, its cottages well kept, with one or two bigger houses standing back from the road. They had gone its length when Claudia saw a narrow lane leading away from it, half hidden by high hedges.

'Let's take a look, Thomas...'

The lane curved, and they passed two cottages with their doors opening directly onto the lane, and then round the next curve they saw another cottage, quite large, standing behind hedges. There was a 'For Sale' board beside its old-fashioned wrought iron gate.

It must have been empty for some time, for the windows were uncurtained and the garden was woefully overgrown.

Claudia looked at Thomas, and he opened the gate and they walked up the brick path to the solid door under the thatched porch. There were windows on either side, and small windows above, tucked away under the thatch.

Claudia went to peer through one of the windows. 'The kitchen,' she said. 'There's another window at the side, and two doors. Come and look, Thomas.'

She went round the side of the cottage and found a door, and, at the back, more windows. A quite large room and next to it a room which took up the whole of the other side of the cottage. She bent to peer through the letterbox. 'There's a staircase,' she told Thomas, but when she turned round he wasn't there. He was by the gate, writing down the address of the house agents.

'Oh, Thomas, do you like it? I mean, well enough to want to see inside?'

Mr Tait-Bullen put away his notebook and walked up the path to join her.

'Yes, I like it, too. The agent is a local man—Blandford—supposing we go and see him? I'll phone him from the car—he might even come here to us.'

'Now? This morning? Oh, Thomas...'

He looked at her, smiling a little. Her cheeks were flushed and her eyes shone with excitement. He had the sudden urge to wrap her in his arms and kiss her. The thought took him by surprise; it was as though he was seeing her for the first time.

'Now, this morning,' he assured her, and nothing in his level voice showed his feelings.

They went back to the car and he phoned from there. The agent was willing to drive to meet them at the cottage. He would be with them in half an hour, he assured them.

'Shall we phone your mother?' suggested Thomas. 'Tell her that we may be a little later than we intended?'

That done, they went back to the cottage, and while they were waiting poked round the garden. It was quite large, and there was a rough track at the side of it which led to a sizeable barn.

'The garage?' asked Claudia hopefully. 'And, look, there was a greenhouse there and a summer house...' She clutched his arm. 'Oh, Thomas.'

The agent was middle-aged and fatherly, wearing

comfortable country tweeds and carrying a bunch of
large keys. When Mr Tait-Bullen apologised for disturbing his Sunday, he made light of it. 'Come inside,' he
invited. 'It's solid enough, roof was thatched a couple
of years ago, brick and cob walls, the usual mod cons;
the old lady who lived here went into a nursing home
six months ago, but she kept the place in good order.'

He opened the door with a flourish and stood aside to
let them in.

The hall was narrow, with a staircase along one wall.
There were three doors, and Claudia opened the first one.
The room was large, with windows both at the front and
the back of the house, an inglenook and open beams.
Claudia rotated slowly, seeing the room in her mind's
eye just how it would look—an open fire, comfortable
chairs, little tables with lamps on them, bookshelves. She
crossed the hall, taking Thomas with her. The room on
the other side of the hall was smaller, with cupboards
on either side of an old-fashioned grate and more open
beams.

'The dining room,' she breathed happily, and went
into the kitchen. A quite large room, with an old-
fashioned dresser and windows on either side of a door
to the garden. And upstairs, leading off the small landing, were three rooms, two of them small but the third
of an ample size. There was a bathroom too, rather old-
fashioned, but the plumbing, the agent assured them, was
up-to-date.

Claudia wandered round on her own while the two
men talked quietly in the hall, and presently Thomas
went in search of her. She was hanging out of a bedroom
window, planning the garden in her mind's eye.

'You like it? I've made an offer; he'll let me know
tomorrow when he's contacted the owner.'

Claudia flung her arms round his neck. 'Thomas, oh, Thomas!' And she kissed him. She hadn't kissed him like that before, and she drew back at once, rather red in the face. 'Sorry—I got carried away.'

Mr Tait-Bullen didn't allow the normally calm expression on his face to alter. The kiss had stirred him, but all he said was, 'Let us hope that we are able to buy the place.'

She reminded herself that he was not a man to be easily aroused from his habitual calm. But he liked the little place; she could see that. They would furnish it together and spend happy weekends there and get to know each other.

CHAPTER SEVEN

CLAUDIA'S mother came to meet them as they stopped before George's door.

'Darling, what kept you? You haven't had an accident?' She looked anxiously at Thomas. 'All you said was that you were unexpectedly delayed... But come in, do, there's coffee and mince pies...'

It had been a happy day, reflected Claudia, sitting beside Thomas as he drove back to London in the early evening. Such a lot of cheerful talk, presents to exchange, Tombs and Mrs Pratt to visit, a walk after lunch with Rob and Harvey, and, of course, the cottage to be discussed while the men exchanged views on medical matters.

Claudia, with her mother's enthusiastic help had had the place metaphorically furnished, the curtains hung and the garden dug and in full bloom by the time they got into the car. She'd still been thinking about it as Thomas began the journey home.

'Blue and white checked curtains in the kitchen, and that white china with blue rings round it—you know the kind I mean?'

'I can't say that I do, but I shall leave such matters to you—if and when the cottage is ours.'

She felt a stab of disappointment. Furnishing the little place together would have been fun. She reminded herself that he was a busy man, and that any free time he had he would want to spend in a way to please himself.

125

She said, 'It was a lovely day, Thomas, thank you for bringing me. Harvey enjoyed himself too.'

They didn't talk much more on the way back. Thomas replied cheerfully enough to her remarks, but she sensed indifference. A polite indifference, but all the same it was there, like an invisible wall between them. It was a relief to get home and find Cork waiting for them in the warm, well lighted hall.

He led Harvey away to the kitchen for his supper, and Claudia, casting off her jacket, followed him.

'Have you had a pleasant day, Cork?'

'Yes, thank you, madam. I trust that you had an enjoyable trip?'

'Yes, yes, we did.' She would have liked to tell him about the cottage, but perhaps Thomas might not like that.

Cork, spooning Harvey's supper into a dish, said civilly, 'Would supper in half an hour suit you, madam?'

She said that yes, that would be fine, and wandered away out of the kitchen and up to her room to tidy herself. When she went downstairs presently there was no sign of Thomas.

Cork met her in the hall. 'The Professor has been called away—an emergency—he will phone you as soon as he is able. He had no time to say more, madam.'

Claudia stood in the hall looking at him, saying nothing, so he added, 'I'll serve you supper at once—there's no knowing when he will be back, madam.'

'All right, Cork. Let's hope it's nothing that will keep him away for too long.'

She ate her solitary meal and then went to sit in the drawing room, with Harvey for company. The evening was well advanced by now, and there had been no message. She sat there, pretending to read, her ears stretched to hear the sound of his return or a phone call, but there was neither. At midnight she took Harvey to his bed in the kitchen, and bade Cork goodnight after being told that he would wait up— 'The Professor wouldn't want you to lose your sleep, madam,' he said, and was interrupted by the phone.

He answered it, and then handed it to Claudia.

'Go to bed, Claudia. I shall probably be here for most of the night. Sleep well—I'll have a word with Cork.'

She handed the phone to Cork, who listened with an expressionless face. His 'Very well, sir' was uttered in a disapproving voice, and when he rang off he said, 'I am not to wait up, madam. I'll lock up as soon as you are upstairs.'

There was nothing else to do but wish him goodnight, give Harvey a quick cuddle and go to her room.

She had expected to stay awake, waiting for Thomas's return, but she fell asleep almost at once to wake hours later, not knowing why she had wakened. The house was quiet, but all the same she got up, peered at her clock and saw that it was almost four o'clock. She got into her dressing gown and slippers and crept downstairs, and as she reached the hall, the front door opened very quietly and Thomas came in.

He closed the door equally quietly before he spoke. 'Shouldn't you be in bed?'

Disappointment at his terse greeting turned her pleasure at seeing him to peevishness. 'Of course I should,' she snapped. 'I'm not in the habit of wandering round the house at this hour. I woke up—I don't know why…'

She started towards the kitchen. 'I'll get you a drink; you're tired.'

'Nothing to drink, thank you, but I am tired. Go back

to bed. I'll go to bed myself as soon as I've put my bag away.'

She felt a childish wish to burst into tears. He was behaving as though he wished she wasn't there. She turned to go upstairs again, and then paused.

'At what time will you want breakfast?'

He was already at his study door. 'The usual time.'

'But it's after four o'clock!'

He didn't answer, but went in and shut the door. Now that there was no one to see, she allowed unhappy tears to trickle down her cheeks as she went upstairs.

As for Mr Tait-Bullen, he sat down at his desk and allowed all kinds of thoughts to fill his head. The sight of Claudia, standing in the hall in her pink gown, her hair in glorious wildness with that look on her face, had disturbed him deeply. When he had envisaged being married to her he hadn't imagined anything like that. She was Claudia, a girl he admired and liked, a perfect companion and a wife whose company he would enjoy without any of the hazards of being in love with her.

Being in love was something he had lost faith in years ago, when he had given his heart to a woman and it had been thrown back to him. Not that his heart had been broken, not even cracked—indeed, he had remained happily heart-whole ever since. But, since then, falling in love had been something in which he didn't believe.

And now, suddenly, he had discovered that that wasn't true.

Claudia, crying her eyes out in the comfort of her bed, fell asleep at last, and woke a few hours later looking much the worse for wear. She still looked beautiful, but her eyelids were pink and so was the tip of her delightful nose; she disguised the pinkness with expensive cream

and powder guaranteed to work miracles, happily unaware that they made no difference at all, and went down
to breakfast, rehearsing a few polite remarks about the
weather as she went, just to let Thomas see that their
unfortunate conversation earlier that morning was to be
ignored.

He was already at the table, the post scattered around
his plate. He got up as she went to the table and wished
her good morning in a brisk voice which warned her that
he didn't wish to talk, so she discarded the weather and
replied even more briskly. Cork, offering coffee, buttered eggs and fresh toast, returned to the kitchen quite
worried, for he had allowed himself to approve of his
mistress after a doubtful start. She didn't interfere, but
at the same time she had made it her business to know
exactly how the house was run—without interfering. She
was looking unhappy, and he was uneasy.

'If it was anyone else but the Professor,' he told
Harvey, 'I'd have said it was a tiff, but he's not one to
waste his time on anything as silly. Very polite he is this
morning, too—in a rage, no doubt. And she's been crying…'

Harvey looked sympathetic and allowed his ears to
droop, so that Cork felt constrained to offer him a couple
of nicely crisped bacon rinds.

Mr Tait-Bullen studied Claudia from beneath lowered
lids; she had been crying, but it seemed best not to mention that, for she wore a haughty expression which
warned him off. It was hardly the moment to tell her
that he had fallen in love with her. Claudia, being
Claudia, would probably turn on him and tell him not to
talk nonsense.

He said mildly, 'I hope to be home for tea today.'

Claudia said, 'Very well, Thomas,' and, since she was

anxious to be friends, even though they weren't on the
best of terms at the moment, added, 'Is there any shopping you need? Have we all the presents for your family?'

'If you would check the list? Have we remembered
Mrs Rumbold?'

'Yes—a cardigan. Would you mind if I added a box
of chocolates? A big box tied with ribbon…'

'By all means.' He got to his feet. 'I'll see you later.
Enjoy your day.'

It was her last chance to find a present for Thomas.
It was a pity that he had everything. She had the little
figure of the dog like Harvey, but that wasn't enough.
She spent an anxious morning peering into shop windows; a tie wasn't enough, besides, he might not like
it—all the same she bought one in a rich silk—dark,
glowing colours in a subdued pattern.

Looking at a display of photo frames gave her an idea.
She chose a small one in silver and took it back home,
found one of the photos which Tombs had taken at their
wedding and inserted it. It wasn't a very good photo,
but they had both been laughing—perhaps it would remind him that they had declared their intention of making their sensible marriage a success!

She was in the drawing room, bent over a piece of
tapestry she had bought, of roses on a creamy back-
ground which, when finished, would become a cushion
cover, when Thomas came home. She saw with relief
that he was his usual calm self, and they had tea together, talking casually—Christmas, his work, Harvey's
progress, Christmas again—and later, after dinner, they
sat together in the drawing room, she with her tapestry,
he with the evening papers and his medical journals. Just
like an old married couple, thought Claudia contentedly.

She must remember not to bother him when he had had a hard day.

It was almost dark when she took Harvey for his evening trot the next day. It was cold, but dry, and a brisk run in the park would do him good. There were few people about—most were shopping frenziedly for Christmas. She kept to the main paths and decided to keep Harvey on his lead. He was an obedient little beast, but if he were frightened by something he might run off in a panic. She had turned back towards the road when two youths passed her, and then turned and followed her. She didn't dare look round, but she picked up Harvey and quickened her pace. The road wasn't more than a few minutes' walk away, and there would be other people...

Only there weren't—there was no one in sight!

She could feel they were close to her now. Should she run for it, scream, or turn and confront them? She spun round and found them within inches of her.

Mr Tait-Bullen, arriving home earlier than he had expected, found the sitting room and drawing room empty. Cork, coming to meet him in the hall, wished him good evening, adding that Mrs Tait-Bullen had taken Harvey for a run in Hyde Park.

'I did suggest that it was a bit dark, sir, but she said that they both needed a breath of fresh air. She usually goes there from the Bayswater Road.'

'Then I'll go and meet her,' said Mr Tait-Bullen, and got into his overcoat again. 'Explain to her if she gets back first, Cork.'

The streets were almost empty and he walked fast, which was a good thing, for he had no sooner got to the park than he heard Harvey's shrill bark.

It was quite dark now, but he could see Claudia and the two youths. As he reached them she landed a nicely placed kick on one of the youth's shins and he yelped with pain.

'Let's 'ave the dog and break 'is neck for him…'

Thomas didn't waste time in talk. He knocked the pair off their feet, begged them in a terrifyingly quiet voice to be off before he called the police, and turned his attention to Claudia.

The youths scrambled to their feet and ran off, and Claudia said in a rather shaky voice, 'Oh, thank you, Thomas. They were going to hurt Harvey.'

Thomas's quiet voice was harsh. 'They were going to hurt you, too. It was foolish of you to come here at this time of day; you have only yourself to blame.'

He had turned her round and was marching her back, out of the park, into the lighted respectable streets with their sedate houses and infrequent passers-by.

She hadn't expected that; she had expected sympathy, kindly concern, enquiries as to whether she had been frightened or hurt. The fact that he had only uttered the truth made no difference. Rage and delayed fright made her shiver. He was an inhuman monster! Scathing remarks she would have liked to make in reply remained unuttered, for they were walking too fast for her to talk; his hand on her arm urged her forward, but it didn't feel friendly.

Mr Tait-Bullen, aware of her thoughts, remained silent. The wish to sweep her into his arms, Harvey and all, was strong, but if he did that, and kissed her, things might get out of hand. Rather, let her dislike him for the moment than be frightened off by a love she hadn't expected or asked for.

Indoors once more, he took Harvey from her, took off

her coat and gloves, sat her down in the drawing room and put a glass in her hand.

'Drink this; it will make you feel better.' He sounded like a friendly family doctor.

'What is it?'

'Brandy. You don't like it, but drink it—there's a good girl.'

She tossed it back, caught her breath, whooped, was slapped gently on the back and burst into tears.

'I'm not crying,' said Claudia fiercely. 'It's this beastly brandy.'

He forebore from comment, only smiled a little and went away to take off his own coat. Cork was hovering in the hall. 'Madam isn't hurt? An accident?'

'Thugs. No, she isn't hurt—only frightened and shocked.'

'I'll bring in the tea at once.'

'Splendid, and give Harvey a biscuit or a bone. He's been frightened, too.'

Cork, quite shaken, glided away, to return within a few minutes with the tea tray and Harvey.

He arranged the tea things on a table convenient to Claudia, murmured his regrets at her unpleasant adventure, assured her that the crumpets were freshly toasted and took himself off. His mistress certainly didn't look quite the thing; she was usually as neat as a new pin, but now her hair was decidedly untidy and she was crying. He hoped that the master would comfort her in the proper fashion.

Claudia, in a haze of brandy, took the handkerchief which Thomas offered and mopped her face and blew her nose.

'I'll go and tidy myself,' she muttered, and started to get out of her chair.

'No need. You look very nice as you are.' Thomas's voice was soothing, and at the same time matter-of-fact. 'I'll pour the tea; the brandy will wear off if you eat something.'

He was regretting his harshness in the park; he had been afraid for her when he had first caught sight of her with the youths and fear had made him angry. He must repair the damage as quickly as possible.

He gave her tea, and put a crumpet on a plate and set it on the small table by her chair. He said cheerfully, 'You know, you had me scared for a moment—those boys can be so rough. Will you promise me not to go into the parks—any of them—once it is dusk?'

'All right—you were so angry...'

'Yes, but it was anger which spilled over from those thugs, and I had no right to blame you. Life at Little Planting is free from such unpleasant encounters—you weren't to know...'

It was going to be all right again, thought Claudia. They were back on their friendly footing once more. She bit into her crumpet. 'I should have used my head,' she conceded.

They didn't hurry over their tea; Thomas led the talk round to Christmas, and their journey north. 'There are some splendid walks,' he told her, 'and there is a special beauty in winter. I'm looking forward to showing you something of the countryside.'

'I'll bring my boots...'

'And something warm to wear. Have you had time to tie up all the presents?'

She nodded. 'Yes, and I've put in one or two extra things—some chocolates and a scarf and some scent, just in case we've missed someone out, or someone turns up who isn't expected.'

Nothing had changed, reflected Claudia, going to bed after a quiet evening with Thomas. True, he hadn't said much, but just having him there, sitting opposite her, was nice...

They were to drive up to Finsthwaite on Christmas Eve. A long drive but, as Thomas pointed out, they would be on a motorway for almost the whole distance: the M1 as far as Birmingham, then the M6 until they left it, just before Kendal, and took the road to the lower end of Lake Windermere and, a few miles further on, Finsthwaite—a matter of just under three hundred miles. He would go to the hospital in the morning, and they should be able to leave London by mid-afternoon—a little over four hours' driving; once out of town and on the motorway, it would be a straightforward run.

Claudia packed carefully, made sure that the presents were stowed in the big box Cork found for her, and collected Harvey's basket, tins of food and his favourite bone. She would travel in the leather jacket, with a tweed skirt and a cashmere sweater—suitable garments if they were to go walking. She took her winter coat, too, for she was sure they would go to church, and added a little velvet hat, one of the jersey dresses, the green patterned dress, silk shirts and cardigans, sensible shoes—her boots she would wear—and a pair of elegant slippers. She wanted Thomas to be proud of her...

They left at three o'clock. The afternoon was already turning into a raw, cold evening, but the shops were lighted, there were Christmas trees and coloured lights and, as they drove out of the city, pavements packed with last-minute shoppers.

'I love Christmas,' said Claudia happily. 'And people look so happy... I hope Cork will have a good time.'

'I fancy he will. His widowed sister comes for Christmas Day, and on Boxing Day some old friends of his come to lunch and stay until the evening.'

'Oh, good.'

She stayed silent then, while he threaded his way through the streets until they were on the M1.

'We'll stop this side of Birmingham for a cup of tea and allow Harvey a breath of air. There's a service station.'

After that he was mostly silent, but it was a friendly silence, and Claudia had a good deal to think about. His family—she had met his parents, but only briefly at the wedding. Supposing his mother had decided that she didn't like her? And his sisters… She began to compose a series of suitable topics of conversation.

The Rolls swept with silent speed towards Birmingham. There wasn't much traffic going north, and nothing impeded its progress. The service station lights loomed ahead of them and they parked and got out, glad of a few minutes to stretch their legs while Harvey aired his tail and then, tucked under Claudia's arm, went with them to the restaurant.

Thomas found a table, told her to sit down and went away to fetch their tea. Watching him coming back, with a tray of tea things and a plate of buttered teacakes, Claudia thought that Cork would have a fit if he could see his master now.

They didn't waste time, but drank the strong hot tea, ate the teacakes and, since there was no one to see for the moment, Claudia gave Harvey a saucer of milk, tucked a paper napkin under his small chin and fed him the last of the teacakes.

'Are we going to stop again?' she asked.

'If necessary. I'd like to get off the motorway before we do, but if you need to stop say so.'

'I was thinking of Harvey,' said Claudia primly.

Mr Tait-Bullen suppressed a chuckle. 'Of course. But with luck he'll sleep for a few hours.'

They were bypassing Liverpool in just over an hour; in another hour they were off the motorway and through Kendal. There the road was still good, but narrow in places, with long stretches of dark countryside and few villages—Grigghall, Croathwaite, Bowland Bridge, and then nothing until they rounded the end of the lake at Staveley. Now the road had become a narrow lane, running between trees.

Finsthwaite was a small village: farms, a cluster of cottages, a village store and post office, the church, and a village school lower down a gentle slope. A short walk away there was Grizedale Forest. It was a little paradise, but now shrouded in darkness, save for a few lighted windows, and then, unexpectedly, a lighted Christmas tree by the church.

Thomas drove through the village, turned into an open gateway and stopped before the house where he had been born; it was a nice old house, built of grey stone, with light streaming from its windows and its solid door flung open before they were out of the car.

Claudia need not have worried about her welcome. She was drawn at once into the family circle, kissed and hugged, helped out of her coat, then carried away by Ann and Amy to warm herself by the log fire in the drawing room and be plied with delicious coffee.

'Just to warm you up,' said Ann. 'Dinner will be in about half an hour. Don't change.' She hesitated. 'Well, perhaps you'd rather. Did you have a good trip here?

Thomas is such a good driver. A pity it was dark, but I don't suppose you could come any earlier?'

When Claudia had finished her coffee they took her up the wide staircase at the back of the hall and along the gallery above it. 'You're here, Thomas's dressing room is next to it, and there's a bathroom. I expect he'll be up presently. Come down as soon as you can; we've still got to put the presents round the tree.'

They left her then, in the high-ceilinged big room. The furniture was big too: a vast brass bed, a tallboy and a mighty wardrobe in mahogany, and an old-fashioned dressing table with a great many little drawers and a triple mirror standing in the window. Despite the heavy furniture the room was charming, with its sprigged wallpaper, thick cream carpet and chintz curtains and bedcover, and two bedside tables, each with a rose-shaded lamp.

Claudia opened the door in the further wall and saw the bathroom beyond, and another door on its opposite side which she opened too. The dressing room.

She went back then, unpacked her case, which someone had brought to the room, and changed into the patterned jersey. She did her hair and her face and then sat down on the bed. She was suddenly nervous of going downstairs. Thomas had no right to leave her alone...

There was a tap on the door and Thomas came in. He took one look at her and sat down beside her on the bed. 'Feeling a bit overpowered?' he asked, and put an arm round her shoulders. 'Don't—they are all so delighted to see you. Come down; Father's waiting to open the champagne and James wants to kiss you under the mistletoe!'

They went down to the drawing room together, and Claudia stifled a wish that Thomas had been the one who wanted to kiss her. A silly wish, she reflected. He wasn't a demonstrative man… Hadn't he told her that before they married? That he had no interest in being in love, that he had loved once, but never again? And she had accepted that.

Everyone was in the drawing room—a square room with two windows overlooking the front garden. It had panelled walls, and chairs that were roomy and very slightly shabby, but the furniture was solid and beautifully kept, the chairs covered in a dark red damask which matched the curtains, and a vast sofa before the stone fireplace, which housed a roaring log fire. The room was warm—warm with content and happiness and love; there was no doubting the affection Thomas's family had for each other, although it wasn't on display.

They drank their champagne and presently crossed the hall to the dining room. It was panelled, like the drawing room, and had a vast mahogany table surrounded by Victorian balloon back chairs, a William the Fourth pedestal sideboard, which took up almost all of one wall, and a magnificent giltwood side table. There were a number of paintings on the walls—Claudia supposed that they were family portraits—dimly lit by wall sconces.

The table had been decked for Christmas, with a centrepiece of holly and Christmas roses, a white damask cloth and napkins, and heavy silverware. When the soup was served Claudia recognised Coalport china.

She was hungry and dinner was excellent: game soup, roast pheasant and a chocolate and almond pudding. She wasn't sure what she was drinking; all she knew was that she was very happy and enjoying herself. And Thomas, sitting beside her, had once or twice put his hand over hers, which gave her a warm glow inside.

They arranged the presents round the tree after dinner.

'We all go to church in the morning,' Amy told her. 'But perhaps you and Thomas would like to go to the midnight service? It's only a short walk to the church and it's a lovely service. We always went, but now we have the children we stay at home. They still wake in the night sometimes, and we like to be there.'

'How many have you?'

'Two, and another one in the spring. Ann has one so far.' She smiled. 'They're such fun, but an awful lot of work.'

Claudia went to sit by her mother-in-law then, until that lady declared that it was time they all went to bed. 'You still have the children's stockings to fill,' she reminded them. 'Breakfast at eight o'clock. Church at half-ten.'

'I'm taking Claudia to the midnight service,' said Thomas quietly, and smiled across the room at her.

'Then we'll leave the side door unlocked. I'll tell Maggie to leave coffee on the Aga, and there are sandwiches in the fridge if you feel hungry.'

There was a leisurely round of goodnights as the party broke up, leaving Claudia and Thomas sitting by the fire.

'Well?' he asked. 'Are you going to like my family?'

'Yes, very much. I've never had more than Mother—and Father, of course, but he died several years ago. I think it must be wonderful to be one of a large family.'

'Indeed, it is. We don't see a great deal of each other, but we make a point of meeting for important occasions. Amy and Ann are happily married—Jake and Will are sound men—and I suppose James will marry in due course.'

'Your mother and father aren't lonely so far from you all?'

'No. They are happy to be together. Mother has her garden, Father sits on various committees, and they both enjoy walking. Besides, there is quite a social life here, even in the winter.'

He glanced at the walnut long case clock. 'Would you like to walk to church? It's only a question of five or ten minutes.'

'I'll go and get a coat.'

It would be cold outside. She put on her winter coat and the little velvet hat, found gloves and sensible shoes, and went back downstairs to where Thomas was waiting for her in the hall.

He took her to a door beyond the staircase and opened it onto the night. There was a clear sky, alight with stars and a dying moon, and he walked her along a path leading from the side door of the house to a small gate which led onto the lane.

'The church is below the village,' he told her, and took her arm. And round a bend she saw its squat tower close by. There were other people making their way there, too, and when they reached the church she saw that it was already almost full. Thomas made his unhurried way to a pew in the front, stopping to greet people he knew and introduce her, but presently she had time to glance around her. The church was small, rather cold, but scented with the evergreens and holly and Christmas flowers which decorated it. She liked it, and she enjoyed the service, simple and peaceful.

They walked home later, and Claudia said, 'It's Christmas Day...'

Thomas stopped. 'Ah, yes, and we have no need to wait for the mistletoe.' He hugged her close and kissed her, and then let her go rather abruptly. He had very nearly lost his self-control.

Claudia had enjoyed the kiss very much; if she hadn't been taken by surprise she would have kissed him back, but he had released her before she had the chance. Perhaps later...

The house was in darkness as they went quietly through the side door and into the kitchen. It was a thoroughly old-fashioned one, with a huge dresser along one wall, a big scrubbed table with ash and elm Windsor chairs around it, and two elbow chairs on either side of the Aga. The floor was of flagstones and there was a rag rug before the Aga. Harvey was fast asleep in his basket, and curled up on one of the chairs was a large tabby cat.

Thomas fetched two mugs and poured their coffee. 'Maggie has been with us for a lifetime,' he told her. 'She's a really marvellous cook. We all love her, and the children can't be kept away from her when they come to stay. She has plenty of help, of course, but both maids have gone home for Christmas Eve. They'll be here in the morning, and go again after lunch. There's an ancient man who does the heavy work in the garden; he should have been pensioned off years ago, but the people round here don't retire.'

'Would you rather live here than in London?'

'This is my home, and I love it, but my work is in London and that is my life. I am fortunate enough to be able to have both.' He glanced at her. 'You like living in London, Claudia?'

'Oh, yes, you have a lovely home, and the parks are close by.'

'I've bought the cottage at Child Okeford. We'll go down to see it in the New Year. It seems pretty sound, but it will need painting and some small alterations.'

'You've bought it? Oh, Thomas, how splendid. Did you forget to tell me?'

'I didn't know myself until this morning, when the agent phoned. You're pleased?'

'Yes. Oh, yes. You're pleased, too?'

'Yes!' He got up and took her mug. 'It's very late. Go to bed, my dear, you have had a long day.'

'And a very happy one.' She leaned up and kissed his cheek. 'This is such a lovely Christmas.'

For a second time that evening Thomas very nearly lost his self-imposed restraint.

Claudia went down to breakfast in the morning to a chorus of greetings and good wishes. The children were there too. Ann's small son was in a high chair, but Amy's two—little girls—were sitting at table. There was a lot of noise and laughing while they ate, and afterwards, before they all went to church.

Claudia could see that Thomas was on excellent terms with his nephew and nieces. He would be a splendid father, only it seemed that he had no desire to be one. Perhaps in a few years' time, when they had grown closer to each other... She shut the thought away; he had married her for companionship and because he wanted a wife to order his household and entertain his friends. Their marriage was a sensible one, based on friendship and compatibility, and a genuine liking for each other.

The church was warmer now, and there were even more people there. She stood between Thomas and his mother and sang the carols, and told herself that she was the luckiest girl on earth.

CHAPTER EIGHT

CHRISTMAS dinner was at midday, so that the children could share it—turkey and Brussels sprouts, roasted potatoes, braised celery, cranberry sauce—nothing had been overlooked. Then the Christmas pudding, set alight with great ceremony, and last of all mince pies. They drank champagne again, and then coffee before going to the drawing room to open their presents. The children first, of course, before they went for their afternoon naps, and for a while the room was awash with coloured paper, ribbon and toys.

Presently it was the grown-ups' turn. Everyone was there, including Maggie, the two maids and the gardener, and they collected their gifts first, drank a glass of sherry and went off to the kitchen to enjoy a splendid high tea.

Mr Tait-Bullen Senior handed out the presents, and very soon the room was just as untidy as when the children had been there. Claudia, looking round her, thought how delightful the room looked, with the lighted tree and the gaily covered presents, the roaring fire and the soft lamplight. She wished that her mother and George could have been there, too, although when she had phoned her mother that morning that lady had sounded in the best of good spirits. She caught Thomas's eye and smiled—a wobbly smile, for she was on the verge of tears—and he came to sit by her, taking her hand in his large, cool one and giving it a friendly squeeze.

'You haven't opened all your presents...'

'No. There are so many and they're all so lovely.' She

picked up a small box and tore away the paper. A jeweller's box, blue velvet and quite small. She looked at the tag then, and said, 'Oh, Thomas, it's from you....' She opened it and looked at the earrings bedded in white satin—sapphires in a network of gold and diamonds.

'Oh, Thomas...'

'Go on, kiss him,' said Amy, who had been watching. 'You're in the family now.' They had all turned to look, smiling and nodding, so she kissed him, very pink in the cheeks, feeling shy.

Thomas didn't kiss her back. She thought he might have done, with everyone watching, but he took the earrings out of the box and fitted the hooks neatly into her ears. She got up then, and went to admire the earrings in the gilt mirror opposite the fireplace, and that gave her time to let the blush die down and regain her composure.

She still had more presents to open, so she went back and sat down again on the massive sofa beside Thomas and started to open them. A gorgeous silk scarf from Harvey, who was sitting at her feet and muttered sleepily when she thanked him. A leather writing case from her in-laws—red leather with her initials. Gloves and scent and a jewel case from Thomas's sisters and brother. She went round thanking everyone, and being thanked, and when she sat down again Thomas was opening his presents. He had a great many, but he saved hers till the last, quietly approving of the tie. When he unwrapped the photo frame he said nothing for a few moments.

'It's a kind of reminder,' said Claudia quickly. Perhaps he didn't like it; perhaps he thought it was a silly, sentimental thing to have done.

'I shall put it on my desk at my consulting room,' he

told her quietly, 'so that everyone can see what a beautiful wife I have.'

'That wasn't why I did it,' she told him. 'I thought it would remind you...' She paused to get it right. 'It's difficult to explain...'

'Then don't try, Claudia. I think I understand and I shall treasure it.'

The presents had all been opened by now, and everyone was sitting round, content to do nothing for the moment.

'Shall we go for a quick walk?' Thomas pulled her to her feet.

'Yes, dear, take Claudia towards the forest,' his mother said. 'Tea will be a little later because of the children. Be back by five o'clock.'

So Claudia fetched her coat, tied her new scarf over her head, got into her boots and went down to the hall where Thomas, coated but bare-headed, was waiting.

They went out of the side door again, and along the lane towards the church, and then turned away along a rough track which took them almost at once into the forest. It was a perfect late afternoon, the sky in the west a blaze of red and yellow, the rest of the heavens already darkening, lights from the village and outlying farms twinkling.

'It's been such a lovely day,' said Claudia as they walked along arm in arm. 'I feel happy, don't you, Thomas?'

He didn't answer that, but observed, 'It would be hard to be unhappy here. Some places are meant to be happy in—I think the cottage at Child Okeford will be such a place.' He looked down at her face, rosy with the cold. 'What are we going to call it?'

'Why, Christmas Cottage, of course.' She went on

happily. 'We'll have a cat—at least, he'll have to live with us in London and go to and fro like Harvey... Should we have brought Harvey out with us?'

'Harvey is sleeping off a much too large dinner. I'll give him a run after tea.'

'Your parents haven't got a dog? I know Maggie has a cat...'

'Jasper, our Labrador, died a month or so ago. He was old and a devoted friend. In a while, when they are over his death, I've arranged for a puppy—another Labrador—to join the family.'

'Oh, Thomas, how kind. They must miss him terribly.' She stopped to stare into his face in the gathering dusk. 'You think of everything, don't you?'

'I do my best.' He reflected that he hadn't thought of falling in love...

They walked back presently, to eat Christmas cake and drink tea from delicate porcelain tea cups round the fire while the children sat at a small table eating an early supper. They had had an exciting day and were inclined to be peevish. Amy and Claudia went to sit with them, coaxing them to eat their peanut butter sandwiches, the little fairy cakes Maggie had made for them, which followed the Marmite toast, and to drink their milk.

When they were borne off to bed there were plaintive requests for Daddy to tuck them up and read them a story. They were taken upstairs then, and presently Amy and Ann came down again. 'Now it's your turn,' Amy told the men, and as they went away she said laughingly to Thomas, 'Just you wait; it'll be your turn next. I don't know why fathers read bedtime stories better than mothers, but be prepared for it!'

Thomas said mildly, 'What do you suggest? That I start re-reading Hans Anderson? A bit out of date, I dare say. How about the *Wind in the Willows*? My favourite when I was a small boy.'

The conversation became general then, and Claudia joined in, avoiding Thomas's eye. She supposed that there would be a good many such remarks, but, since they didn't seem to disconcert Thomas, she must learn to treat them in a light-hearted manner.

She had married him so quickly there hadn't been time to foresee the small pitfalls, but as long as he didn't mind, she wouldn't allow it to bother her.

Everyone went away to dress presently, and when she came downstairs there were guests, invited for a drink—local people who, it seemed, had known Thomas and his family for years. They accepted her as one of the family at once, but the talk inevitably turned to reminiscences, so that she felt an outsider despite everyone's efforts to include her in their talk. But she did her best, and Thomas's hand on her arm reassured her.

When the last guest had gone, they went in to supper. A buffet—the vast sideboard laden with bowls and dishes filled with Maggie's delicious food: smoked salmon, salads of every kind, a ham on the bone, stuffed eggs, chicken pie, miniature hot rolls. Claudia allowed Thomas to fill her plate and found herself sitting by James.

'Pity you have to go back tomorrow. I suppose Thomas can't be away for more than a few days. Time he took a holiday. He doesn't need to work quite so hard, you know.'

'Yes, I do know, but he loves his work, doesn't he? It's important to him.'

'He's good, of course, you know that. You should see him in Theatre…'

'And people like him, I think. He came to see my

great-uncle, you know—that's how we met...' She paused, remembering that she hadn't much liked him then. 'They got on awfully well together. People do things for him, too, don't they?'

James chuckled. 'Well, he can be a bit hoity-toity if he can't get what he wants—in the nicest possible way, mind you. And in no time they are all doing exactly what he wants!'

But it was something Ann said which made her vaguely uneasy.

'You're so right for Thomas. We've all hoped he would marry, but for years and years—ever since he had that miserable love affair with that girl who went off with a tycoon from South America—he's been considered a splendid catch. Not that he's bothered about that. I don't suppose you've met a woman called Honor Thompson? She'll be livid when she hears that he's married...'

'I've met her,' said Claudia in a carefully level voice.

'You have? I expect Thomas told you about her. She's one of the persistent ones. Don't let her worry you, though. He doesn't care tuppence for any of them. He's always known what he wanted from life and now he's got you.'

Was that why Thomas had married her? she wondered. To be a barrier against wishful partners? Someone who wouldn't spoil the even tenor of his life by demanding undying love? Really, it was a sound idea! An undemanding relationship, the tolerance of good friends towards each other, shared pleasures—and they did like the same things. He could have married Honor, or any other of his women acquaintances if he had wished, but he had chosen her. Well, she was quite prepared to be the wife he wanted. And just let Honor try any of her tricks, Claudia thought waspishly.

They didn't leave until after lunch on the following day. In the morning they had gone for another walk, taking one of the paths which led into the heart of the forest. They had talked about Christmas, and plans to come again, perhaps for Easter, or perhaps he could persuade his parents to visit them.

'The cottage should be quite ready by then, and I'm sure they would enjoy it. We will go down there as soon as possible and see what needs doing. I'm sure you have some ideas, and the place will need painting and decorating.'

'And furnishing.' Claudia's eyes sparkled. 'Curtains and things.'

It had been a most satisfactory morning, she reflected, and began a leisurely round of goodbyes. Christmas had been two wonderful days; she liked Thomas's family, and she loved the countryside around his home and the comfortable old house. She hoped that they would come again, but she doubted if Thomas could spare the time to drive up frequently. She got into the car with real regret, made sure that Harvey was comfortable on his blanket on the back seat, and turned to give a final wave.

It was still light, although the day was fading. She looked around her at the country as Thomas drove back to join the motorway, and, since he didn't speak other than to ask her if she was comfortable, she stayed silent.

They were approaching the motorway when he said, 'We'll stop for tea just before Birmingham, but do tell me if you want to stop before then.'

Her, 'Yes, Thomas,' was the epitome of wifely obedience.

It was quite some time before he said, 'You're very quiet?'

'Well, I thought that's what you wanted. I'm sure you have a great deal to think about...'

'For instance?' He sounded amused.

'Your work and your patients, and perhaps you are wishing you were back with your family and that Christmas was just beginning and not over.'

He didn't comment on that. 'You enjoyed your Christmas?'

'Oh, I did. I loved every minute of it, and I like your parents and your sisters and brother.'

'They like you, Claudia.'

They stopped for tea at a service station, took Harvey for a brisk walk around the car park and resumed their journey, speeding along the motorway, talking of this and that. And Claudia had the feeling that even while he talked Thomas's mind was on something else.

'Are you worried about something?' she asked. 'You don't have to talk if you don't want to. I shan't take umbrage.'

He laughed then. 'I'm not worried, Claudia.' He began to talk about plans for Christmas Cottage, and she felt as though she had been snubbed. It had been nicely done, but whatever it was, she wasn't to be told about it.

London was empty of traffic; Boxing Day was a family visiting day and many people were indoors. Later they would return to their own homes, but just now it was quiet.

Cork opened the door and they went in to a welcoming warmth and a faint but delicious smell from the kitchen. He welcomed them with grave pleasure, fetched the cases and then announced that dinner would be in half an hour if that suited them.

'Excellent,' said Thomas. 'I'll take Harvey for a run.' Which left Claudia to go to her room and tidy herself and unpack before going down to the drawing room. Thomas wasn't there, but Harvey was sitting before the fire looking drowsy.

'I gave Harvey his supper, madam,' said Cork, coming silently into the room. 'The master's in his study; he will be joining you presently.'

'Thank you, Cork. Have you had a happy Christmas?'

'Very pleasant, madam. I trust that you enjoyed yourself?'

'Very much. The country was beautiful.'

Cork went away, and she fetched her tapestry and began to stitch. It was a bit of an anticlimax after the cheerful racket that had been such fun. Only yesterday, she thought, and it seems like weeks ago already.

Mr Tait-Bullen, coming into the drawing room some minutes later, paused for a moment in the doorway; Claudia looked delightful, sitting there working away at her embroidery. It seemed to him that she had always been there; it was hard to think of the house without her in it. He wondered what she would say if he were to tell her that he had fallen in love with her, but he thrust the temptation aside. He thought she was happy and content, and he must have patience; in time she might come to love him, but until then they must stay good friends. It was lucky that he had more than enough work to keep him busy.

He sat down opposite her and observed mildly, 'I've a good deal of work on my hands for the next week or so, but we might go down to Child Okeford next Sunday and take a good look round. You might like to spend an hour or two with your mother.'

'Yes, I would, and I'm longing to see the cottage again. You don't have to go away, do you?'

'In a couple of weeks I have a seminar in Liverpool— two days or so.' He gave her a thoughtful look. 'I'm afraid you will be on your own a good deal, Claudia.'

'Oh, I don't mind that,' she said cheerfully. 'I've all those coffee mornings and tea parties to go to—with people I met at the hospital ball—and plans for the cottage.'

'Ah, yes. You must decide how you want it furnished...'

'Well, you must decide too, for you'll be living there as well, whenever we get the chance.'

They spent the rest of the evening together. 'Like an old married couple,' said Cork to himself. 'They ought to be out dancing or whatever. It isn't right.'

Such an idea hadn't entered Claudia's head. She was perfectly content, sitting there, making heavy weather of the tapestry while Thomas immersed himself in a pile of medical journals. It was nice, she reflected, that they enjoyed each other's company but made no demands on each other.

Soon after ten o'clock she folded her work, declared that she was tired and took herself off to bed, after giving Harvey a hug and bestowing a friendly goodnight on Thomas as he got up to open the door for her. His manners were beautiful, she reflected as she went upstairs, and he was unfailingly kind. She heaved a sigh, not knowing quite why.

She didn't see a great deal of him for the next few days. He was away early in the mornings and didn't get home until early evening; there was a good deal of flu, he told her, and his registrar was off sick.

'Take care!' said Claudia. 'Are there many off sick at the hospital?'

'Amongst the nursing staff, yes—quite a few of the medical staff, too. And, of course, the wards are all full...'

There was nothing she could do to help, but she took care to see that a meal was ready when he got home, with welcoming warmth and no disturbances if he wanted to work. As for herself, her days were nicely filled. Walks with Harvey, such shopping as Cork allowed her to do, coffee with various of the ladies she had met at the ball and most afternoons spent reading though not always understanding some of the medical books in Thomas's study. But it was necessary that she had some idea of his work, and now was no time to bother him with any questions. If ever he chose to talk to her about work, at least she would have some idea of what he was talking about.

There was also the New Year to look forward to— only a day away—and all being well they were to go out to dinner tonight, and dance the New Year in. Claudia washed her hair, did her nails and massaged in a cream guaranteed to improve the complexion. That she had no need of it was quite beside the point.

She took Harvey for a long walk in the afternoon and returned home, thankful to be out of the damp cold, looking forward to tea round the fire. She let herself in, dried Harvey and took off her outdoor things, then went to sit down in the small sitting room. It was already past the usual teatime, but she supposed that Cork had forgotten the time. After half an hour she went to the

kitchen, vaguely uneasy. Cork ran the house like clock-
work. Perhaps he had had to go out for some reason...

He was huddled in a chair by the Aga, with a white
face and shivering.

'Cork, you're ill.' She put a hand on his forehead and
felt its heat. 'You must go to bed at once.' When he
protested feebly, she added, 'No, please do as I say.'
She saw that the effort to get out of the chair was too
much for him, so she heaved him up and helped him to
his room, sat him on the bed, took off his shoes and
pulled the bedclothes over him. 'Now, lie still, there's a
good man. I'm going to get you a drink.'

There was bottled water in the fridge; she filled a jug,
found a glass and took them to his room, gave him a
drink and tucked the bedclothes round him.

'Your tea, madam,' croaked Cork. He closed his eyes.

'Don't give it a thought. Go to sleep if you can. I'm
going to find a warm water bottle for you. As soon as
the Professor gets home he'll come and see you. I expect
it's the flu.' She cast a worried glance at him. He really
looked ill; thank heaven Thomas would be home early.

She went to the kitchen and made a pot of tea. Cork
wouldn't have any, although he drank some more of the
water, so she went back to the kitchen and drank her
own tea. She ate some of the sandwiches on the tray,
fed Harvey, and, since they wouldn't be going out to
spend the evening, peered into the fridge and the cupboards, collecting the makings of a meal.

She was still there when Thomas came home. Harvey
ran into the hall to greet him, and as the dog came into
the kitchen, with Thomas behind him, she dropped the
potato she was peeling and ran to him, quite forgetting
to be calm and sensible.

'Thomas, I'm so glad to see you. Cork's ill. I've put

him to bed but he's so hot and shivery.' She tugged at his sleeve. 'Do come and see what's wrong.'

Mr Tait-Bullen's features displayed nothing but calm assurance. He said in an unhurried manner, 'This wretched flu, I expect. I'll take a look.' He paused on his way. 'You didn't take his temperature?'

'Well, no. His teeth were chattering so much I was afraid he would break the thermometer.'

He nodded and went out of the kitchen and into Cork's room, and Claudia peeled the last of the potatoes. There was plenty of food in the fridge; she had chosen salmon steaks to go with the potatoes, frozen petit pois and there was a cabbage in the sink to clean and cook. Dull fare for Old Year's Night, but with Cork ill, food didn't seem very important.

'It will have to be cheese and biscuits afterwards,' she told Harvey, 'and I just hope he likes it.'

'He'll like it,' said Thomas, from somewhere behind her. 'Cork has the flu, but he's not too bad. I've given him paracetamol and I'll go back presently and settle him down. We've plenty of orange juice and cold drinks, I presume? That's all he'll need for a while...'

'Poor man. Now, just you sit down and I'll make a pot of tea. Supper won't be very exciting, but it'll be food...'

Mr Tait-Bullen sat, watching his wife trot to and fro, her glorious hair getting very untidy, her lovely face flushed. She might look a bit disorganised, he reflected, but she was efficient and quick. A pot of tea was placed before him, with the sandwiches, now rather dry, and a dish of the little cakes Cork was so clever at baking.

'If you don't mind waiting for dinner, I'll go and see to Cork.'

'My dear girl, he would rather die. He needs to be undressed and put to bed—washed and so on.'

'Oh, well, I'm quite able to do that, you know.'

'Of course you are. All the same, I think it is better if I see to him while you get our dinner. By all means see to his drinks and any food that may take his fancy.'

He got to his feet. 'I'll check the post and be back very shortly.'

He was as good as his word. 'We'll eat here, shall we?' he asked, taking off his jacket. 'I'll see to the table presently.' He didn't wait for an answer, but went to Cork's room and shut the door.

Claudia drank another cup of cooling tea, offered Harvey a biscuit, because he was being such a good boy, and turned her attention to the salmon. She was a good cook; if she had known that she was to cook the meal that evening she would have thought out a dinner worthy of the occasion, but it would have to be a simple meal. She thought with regret of the pretty dress she had laid out ready to wear this evening, the delicious supper they would have had, the excitement of toasting the New Year. What could they have for a pudding? she wondered, and began to squeeze oranges for poor Cork.

Thomas came back presently, put on his jacket and then started to lay the table. It took some time, since he had to search for everything in drawers and cupboards, but the end result was as elegant as if Cork had done it himself. He took a bowl of hyacinths from the windowsill and put it at the centre of the table, arranged silver and glass just so, and went to look in the fridge. Cork, that admirable man, had put a couple of bottles of champagne in it earlier that day. Thomas opened one, filled a glass and took it to Claudia.

'I'm sorry—you must be disappointed that we can't

go dining and dancing with the rest of the world,' he told her. 'We'll make up for it later on.'

Claudia took a good drink of champagne. 'I don't mind a bit; I'm so sorry for Cork.' She wrinkled her nose. 'Why does champagne make you feel so uplifted?'

'A good question.' He topped up her glass. 'Something smells good.'

Claudia drained the cabbage, chopped it fine, added nutmeg and a squeeze of lemon and put it on the dish Thomas had got from the dresser. She had creamed the potatoes with plenty of butter and milk and dished up the peas; now she laid the salmon on two warmed plates and took it to the table.

'Not very exciting, I'm afraid,' she said. 'But there's a nice piece of Stilton for pudding!'

Mr Tait-Bullen, who had snatched a sandwich for his lunch, cleared the plate. 'You're a good cook,' he told her. 'What a treasure I have married.'

Claudia went pink. 'Well, I can't cook anything fancy. Great-Uncle William didn't hold with spending a great deal of money on what he called "elaborate food" so I became good at fancying up sausages and things.'

'Tell me more about your great-uncle,' suggested Thomas and filled her glass again.

And Claudia, nothing loath, her tongue nicely loosened by the champagne, told—until she stopped suddenly. 'I'm being boring. It's all the champagne—you should have stopped me...'

Mr Tait-Bullen, enjoying himself, made haste to assure her that he hadn't been in the least bored. 'After all, we know very little about each other even now.'

While she made coffee he went to look at Cork.

'Sleeping like a baby. Now, let us discuss the cottage. As soon as Cork is better, we will spend a day at Child

Okeford, see what is to be done and get hold of a builder. We had better find a gardener too, to get the place into some shape before we can take over. I'll get hold of the estate agent—he may be able to recommend someone. We will try not to alter the place too much, but the barn will need a secure door and a firm run-in for the car. Had you thought of anything you wanted changed or added to?'

Claudia shook her head. 'I loved it as it was. Will it take long, the necessary repairs and the garden?'

'It shouldn't do. We can choose carpets and furniture once we have all the measurements. A local firm, I think, don't you? Sherborne or Shaftesbury.'

'Carpets and curtains,' said Claudia happily, 'and comfortable furniture. Thomas, it will cost an awful lot of money…'

'Probably, but it will be our second home, won't it? We mustn't spoil the ship for ha'porth of tar.'

They washed the dishes together then, and in no time at all, it seemed, it was five minutes to midnight.

Cork was still asleep. Thomas came back into the kitchen, filled their glasses and went to stand by her. As the clock struck midnight they toasted the New Year, and then he took the glass from her hand, put it with his on the table and bent to kiss her. An unhurried, gentle kiss, quite different from his usual rather brisk salute, it stirred something inside Claudia's person, and she stared up into his face, vaguely puzzled.

He was as calm as he always was. 'A Happy New Year, my dear.'

'You too, Thomas.' She paused. 'You're quite happy, aren't you? I mean, with us being married? We're good friends, aren't we? And I promise I'll not get in your

way—with your work, you know. When we married I
hadn't thought of all the things which could go wrong.'

He had seen the puzzled look; his Sleeping Beauty
was beginning to wake up. He said in a matter-of-fact
manner, 'I'm very happy, Claudia. Getting married was
something I should have done years ago—to you, of
course!'

'Well, you didn't know me, did you? Do you have to
go to the hospital tomorrow—no, today?'

'No, unless I'm needed. Supposing we go down to the
cottage?'

'But we can't leave Cork.'

He took the phone out of his pocket and dialled.

'A male nurse will be along at eight o'clock; he'll
stay with Cork until we get back. He's a good man—
kind and trustworthy.'

'But won't he be on duty?'

'No, he has days off, and he'll be glad of the fee.'

'Oh, won't anyone mind?'

He smiled and shook his head, and she said, 'Are you
so important that you can do things like that?'

'I must admit to having a certain amount of clout.'

'Well, it would be marvellous. All day? We must take
a notebook and pen and a tape measure. But only if Cork
feels better…'

'Of course. Now, go to bed, Claudia. If we're to leave
early you'll need your beauty sleep.' He added, 'You
don't need any beauty sleep, actually. You're already as
beautiful as it is possible to be.'

A remark so unlike Thomas that she stopped to stare
at him. Then, 'It's all that champagne,' she told him.
'You're looking at me through rose-coloured spectacles.'

Thomas only smiled, and he didn't kiss her as she
went past him. She was quite disappointed.

Mr Tait-Bullen saw to Cork, locked up and took himself off to his study. He still had reports to read, patients' notes to examine, his workload to be checked. Harvey went with him, to snooze on his shoes until Thomas went to his bed after a last visit to Cork, who, while still very much under the weather, was prepared to stay alive after all.

Claudia woke soon after six o'clock and went down to the kitchen to make tea. She peeped at Cork, made him another jug of lemonade, laid the table and went back to dress. A day at the cottage meant sensible clothes: the leather jacket, a sensible tweed skirt and a pullover. She made short work of her hair, did almost nothing to her face, and went back downstairs. She could hear the murmur of voices from Cork's room as she set about frying bacon and eggs and making toast, and presently Thomas came in with a short, middle-aged man.

He wished her good morning and added, 'This is Sam Peverell, my dear. Sam, my wife. We'll have breakfast as soon as it's ready. You know what to do for Cork, and you can reach me on my mobile, of course, if you need me. We should be back in the early evening.'

Claudia piled plates with bacon and eggs and made more toast. 'I'll put your lunch ready for you, Mr Peverell, and a tray for tea. There are oranges and lemons in the fridge, and milk and yoghurt. So will you help yourself?'

'Certainly, Mrs Tait-Bullen.' He turned to Thomas. 'Phone calls, sir?'

'I'll put on the answering machine. But get hold of someone at the hospital if you're worried.'

'It's very kind of you to come, Mr Peverell,' said Claudia. 'On your day off, too. We're awfully grateful.'

'No problem, Mrs Tait-Bullen. My wife's gone to her

mother's, and the girls are spending the day with friends.'

'You have daughters?'

'Two, fourteen and sixteen, and you wouldn't believe what a worry they are…'

Mr Tait-Bullen sat back, listening to Claudia charming Sam—a martinet on the ward, a splendid nurse and reputed not to have much of an opinion of young women. *His* Claudia, he reminded himself, who was a delight to the eye and the ear and whom he loved.

They left well before nine o'clock, and, since the streets were almost empty after the night's celebrations, they were on the motorway in no time at all. They stopped at a service station after more than an hour's driving, had coffee and allowed Harvey a brief stroll before resuming their journey. Claudia felt a little thrill of excitement as Thomas turned the Rolls into the network of small lanes which would lead them to Child Okeford. Supposing they didn't like the cottage now that they had the leisure to look it over?

'Where's the key?' asked Claudia, a bit late in the day.

'I'm to fetch it from the end cottage as we pass.'

The village was quiet, its inhabitants no doubt sleeping off the excesses of the previous night, but when Thomas knocked on the cottage door he was soon given the key; several keys, in fact.

The cottage looked a bit forlorn, for it was a dull morning with the hint of rain, but Claudia, seeing it in her mind's eye with roses round the door, curtains at the open windows, the garden full of flowers, skipped inside the moment Thomas had the door open.

They went slowly from room to room, checking them with the particulars which the estate agent had sent. The cottage was in good heart, its small windows secure and solid, large cupboards, the stairs sound. The kitchen would need cupboards and shelves, and an Aga, and its flagstone floor cleaned, but the vast stone sink was something Claudia wanted to keep.

They went round a second time while Claudia argued the merits of porridge-coloured carpeting against different colours in each room. Thomas listened patiently, told her to have whatever she liked and suggested that they went and looked round the garden. It was larger than they had first thought, and there were apple trees forming a screen between the garden and the open fields beyond.

'We can grow vegetables,' said Claudia, quite carried away, 'and there's space for a little greenhouse, and we could have a small summer house in that corner, so that you could have somewhere quiet to go.'

Thomas agreed gravely, waiting to see if she would suggest a swimming pool, but she didn't. She did suggest a rockery, and a little pool where frogs might live.

They went to the village pub presently, and ate a ploughman's lunch and emptied a pot of coffee between them. The cottage was every bit as delightful as they remembered it—better, even, for now they had explored it from bottom to roof.

'I'll get on to the agent tomorrow,' said Thomas, 'and get things started.'

He glanced at his watch. 'Do you want to see your mother and George as we go back?'

'May I? Is there time? And what about Cork?'

'I'll check when we go back to the cottage. We must lock up properly.'

Claudia beamed at him across the pub table. 'Oh, Thomas, I'm so happy…'

CHAPTER NINE

CLAUDIA'S glow of happiness lasted until they were back home. They had called at George's house, had tea with him and her mother, and stayed for a while. Claudia and her mother had a lot to say to each other, but, mindful of Cork, she'd got up at once when Thomas suggested mildly that they should go. It wasn't for a while that she'd realised Thomas was rather silent. She'd stopped talking then, sitting quietly beside him, still happy, her thoughts busily occupied with the cottage.

It wasn't until they were home again, and Sam Peverell had given his report, pocketed his fee and gone home, and she had been to see Cork and gone to the kitchen to get a meal, that she realised that Thomas, after seeing Sam Peverell off home and spending a short time with Cork, had gone to his study and shut the door.

It was as if he had erected an invisible barrier between them. She told herself that he was probably tired or had work to do, and that the faint air of reserve would have disappeared by the time their supper was ready.

Lamb chops, sprouts, potatoes and mint sauce. Plain fare indeed, but it was already after seven o'clock and she still had to cook... She rummaged around in the cupboards, found what she wanted, made an apple pie and popped it in the oven and then made an egg custard for Cork. He was feeling more himself, assuring her that he would be on his feet in another day or so, adding, with a touch of suspicion, that he hoped she could find everything she wanted in the kitchen.

'Oh, indeed I could, Cork, and I've been careful to put everything back where it belongs.' She gave him a motherly smile. 'We do miss your lovely cooking.'

Cork, still pale and poorly, nevertheless looked smug at that.

The first few days of January went swiftly by; Claudia enjoyed them, for she was kept busy shopping and cooking, and although Mrs Rumbold came each day there was always something to be done: the flowers to arrange, the phone to answer, bills to pay. She was careful to ask Cork's advice about most things, and in a few days, when he was feeling better, he sat by the Aga, warmly wrapped, and advised her about the best methods to cook their meals.

She found this rather tiresome, since she was a capable cook, but she knew that he meant it kindly and nothing would have induced her to snub him. And Cork, for his part, acknowledged the fact that she was an ideal mistress, never encroaching on his preserves while asserting a gentle authority. The master was a lucky man.

The master was a busy man too, away early in the morning and for the most part not back again until the early evening. He made time, though, to visit Cork, and spent what leisure he had in Claudia's company, although she sensed his reserve towards her. She tried to remember if she had said or done something to annoy him and wondered if she had disappointed him in some way. One day, she promised herself, when he wasn't away from home so much, she would ask him.

Cork, back on his feet once more, took over his normal duties again. He made her a little speech of thanks with the voice and manner of a benevolent person, making it quite clear that, much though he had appreciated her help, he no longer required it. Claudia, thrown back onto her own resources, took long walks with Harvey, drank coffee with various of the wives she had met at the ball, and ploughed her way through the books in Thomas's study, not understanding them by half but feeling that by doing so she was bridging the gap which she felt was between them.

It was something of a relief when he told her that he had to go to Liverpool for two or three days, and would she like to visit her mother?

'I can drop you off on my way, and then why not bring your mother back here for a day or so? There's the possibility that I may go on to Leeds and have to spend the night there.'

'I'd like that, Thomas. I'll phone Mother; I'm sure she'd love to come, and we might do some shopping.'

'Yes, well, take her to Harrods or Harvey Nichols and use our account.'

He looked so kind when he said it that she was tempted to ask him if there was anything wrong, but she didn't; he had come home later than usual and he looked tired.

Harvey was to stay with Cork, for she intended to stay only one night at George's house; she and her mother could return by train and they would spend two days together. Her mother hadn't seen Thomas's home, and Claudia was longing to show it to her. They could have a good gossip and shop. She got into the car two days later, on a still dark morning, and Thomas drove out of town, leaving Cork and a protesting Harvey behind.

'I hope Harvey won't pine,' said Claudia, 'and that

Cork will take care of himself…all alone,' she added doubtfully.

'I should imagine that he is pleased to see the back of us. He now has the opportunity to take a nap when he feels like it, and rearrange everything around the house to his satisfaction. He will spoil Harvey, bully Mrs Rumbold, and probably drink my port.'

She laughed. 'He'd never do that; he's your devoted slave.'

'And yours, I fancy. I'll phone you this evening, but don't worry if you don't hear from me after that. I'll let you know when I'm coming home.'

They didn't talk much, just casual remarks from time to time, and although Thomas was friendly it was as though the real Thomas was hidden behind this pleasant man sitting beside her. She could say something about that now, she supposed, but then changed her mind. He wouldn't want to be bothered when he had the seminar ahead of him to think about.

They reached George's house by mid-morning and, despite her mother's pleas that he should stay for lunch, he was on his way again after a cup of coffee. Claudia went with him to the car and he kissed her lightly as he got in. She poked her head through the window as he was about to drive off.

'Do be careful, Thomas, and I hope everything is successful.'

Her face was very close to his, and he drew back with a jerk, an action which sent a cold shiver down her spine. She stood back, fighting sudden tears. It was as though he couldn't bear her near him. When he got home again they would have to talk…

She enjoyed her day with her mother and George.

That they were quietly happy together was evident, and Mrs Pratt and Tombs were, in their own way, just as happy. George drove them over to Child Okeford one evening, and they looked round the cottage. She hadn't got the key, but the builders had already started on the repairs and they peered through the windows and explored the garden. George pronounced it a nice little property, and her mother could find no fault with it.

She bore her mother off to London the next day. Thomas had phoned on the previous evening, expressed the hope that she was enjoying herself and warned her that he might not phone her for a couple of days. He had sounded friendly, but even over the telephone she'd imagined she could hear the constraint in his voice.

Her mother was delighted with the London house. She professed herself overwhelmed with its comfort and luxury, and Cork's perfections. Claudia took her walking in the park with Harvey, and the next day went shopping with her. George had given her money with which to buy herself something she liked, and Claudia, mindful of Thomas's suggestion, persuaded her mother to accept a cashmere twinset, and the wool skirt which went so well with it...

Thomas had told her not to expect to hear from him for a day or so, but all the same she was disappointed that there was no word from him. She had to explain this to her mother, who said roundly, 'The poor man; it's time he slowed down. After all, he's a married man now; his work is important, but so is his married life.'

Claudia said cheerfully, 'He loves his work, Mother, but once the cottage is ready we shall be able to spend weekends there, away from his patients.'

She took her mother to the station the following morning and saw her onto the train. Feeling suddenly lonely, Claudia lingered at the station entrance, trying to decide whether she would join the taxi queue or walk home. She could cross the road and go through Hyde Park— quite a long walk, but it would fill in her morning.

She had left the park, crossed Park Lane and was walking along Brook Street when she came face to face with Honor.

She summoned a social smile and a hello, and went on walking, but Honor put out a hand so that she was forced to stop.

'Claudia—it is Claudia, isn't it? How delightful to meet you again. I've been away; I can't stand London at this time of year. I phoned Thomas at his rooms before I left, and he told me that you were very occupied getting ready for Christmas. Such a bore, having to go all that way to the Lakes just for a couple of days.'

'I enjoyed it,' said Claudia. 'Nice to see you again. I really must get on…'

Honor didn't let go of her arm. 'My dear, you can spare half an hour, surely? Let's have a cup of coffee…?'

Against her will, Claudia agreed. Perhaps Honor really was an old friend of Thomas's, in which case she shouldn't be rude—besides, Honor was making herself pleasant.

Over coffee, after a witty account of her holiday in Italy, Honor began asking questions put so casually it was difficult to ignore them.

'Thomas is away?' she asked. 'Off on one of his jaunts?'

'Well, it's not a jaunt. He's in Liverpool, and probably going on to Leeds.'

'Has he taken Emma with him?' Honor gave Claudia a sly glance. 'His secretary goes everywhere with him. A beautiful creature—very efficient and very sexy. Of course, now he's a married man, I expect he's more discreet.'

'I haven't the least idea what you're talking about.'

Honor said quickly, 'Oh, my dear, I'm sorry. I quite thought you knew. After all, it isn't as if you and Thomas are desperately in love—anyone could see with their eyes that neither of you are...' She paused as Claudia got to her feet.

'You're talking rubbish, and spiteful rubbish at that,' said Claudia. 'If making mischief is all you know how to do, I pity you.'

'You're upset,' said Honor. 'Naturally. You don't have to believe me, but if you ring Thomas's rooms I'm quite sure that Emma won't be there.'

'I'll do no such thing,' said Claudia. 'Goodbye, Honor, I hope we don't need to meet again.'

Honor had a parting shot. 'You wouldn't dare find out for yourself,' she laughed. 'But I shouldn't be surprised to hear that Thomas won't be home for a few more days.'

Claudia didn't answer that, but walked out of the elegant café where they had been sitting and then walked all the way home.

This gave her time to remember every word Honor had said, and to assure herself over and over again that nothing would induce her to phone his rooms—a nasty, low-down action not to be contemplated.

She hardly touched the lunch Cork had ready for her; she took Harvey for his afternoon walk, and the moment she got back picked up the phone.

Mrs Truelove answered. After an exchange of pleasantries, she said that, no, Emma wasn't there. 'She doesn't come in when the Professor is on one of his trips. A most efficient girl,' enthused Mrs Truelove, 'quite indispensable.'

Claudia chatted for a few minutes before putting down the phone. Mrs Truelove hadn't asked her why she had rung, and she hoped that she wouldn't wonder about it later. She felt mean and wicked and disloyal, but no more so than Thomas...

'I hate him,' said Claudia to Harvey, and burst into tears. She didn't hate him, she loved him, and what a time to discover it.

Before she'd made that shattering discovery it wouldn't have mattered about Emma—after all, he had never said that he loved her or was likely to do so. Theirs was to be a sensible marriage, wasn't it? So he was free to do what he liked, wasn't he? She knew that he would never be unkind to her, would always be a friend, even be a little fond of her and share at least some of her life, but now, with the discovery that she loved him, that wouldn't do.

This was something they would have to talk about. She would never tell him that she had fallen in love with him, but she would make sure that he wasn't having second thoughts about their marriage. And he would be home the next day.

She had pecked at her dinner and was poking her needle in and out of her tapestry when Thomas phoned. He would be delayed for another day, perhaps two, he told her. 'I'm in Leeds; I'll come home as soon as possible.'

She said, 'Yes, Thomas. Goodnight,' and hung up on

him. If she had said more she would have burst into tears.

The next day seemed endless. She filled it with walks and arranging the flowers and trying to eat the delicious little meals Cork had set before her, but by the evening she was restless, and at ten o'clock she decided to go to bed. The day had been long enough, and there was all tomorrow to get through before Thomas got home.

'Bed,' she told Harvey, and started towards the kitchen with him, but in the hall he stopped and rushed to the door, barking furiously, and a moment later Thomas came in.

He closed the door gently behind him, bent to fondle Harvey and looked at Claudia, standing speechless. She had rehearsed all the things she was going to say to him but she couldn't remember a word of them. She said, 'Hello,' and then, 'You said you'd be home tomorrow.'

'I'm home today because something's wrong, isn't it? You were upset when I phoned last night.'

He was taking off his coat as he spoke, and Cork, coming into the hall, greeted him with grave pleasure, took the coat, enquired if he would like a meal or drinks and then went away, taking Harvey with him.

'Cut the air with a knife, I could,' Cork told the little dog. 'What's up, I'd like to know. Well, we'll have to leave them to it, won't we? And hope it comes out in the wash.'

Harvey, accepting a biscuit, wagged his ridiculous tail.

Claudia found her voice. 'Would you like a meal, or something to drink?'

Thomas smiled briefly. 'Cork just asked me; you couldn't have been listening. And, no, I don't need anything. What I do need is to know why you sounded as you did last evening?'

Claudia, playing for time, asked, 'How did I sound?'

'Don't waste time, Claudia. You were upset, angry—too angry to speak to me. Why?'

He took her by the arm, marched her into the drawing room and shut the door. 'Let us sit down...'

He sounded friendly, and reassuringly calm, and she longed to fling herself at him, feel his arms around her, but first she must know about this secretary of his. She wouldn't mention Honor, for he might dismiss her as a malicious gossip bent on making mischief, and perhaps she was, but Mrs Truelove was quite another kettle of fish.

'Where do you go when you aren't at a hospital? I mean, do you have friends or stay at a hotel—in the evenings when you're free.'

If she had been looking at him she would have seen the sudden stern set of his mouth and his cool stare, but she wasn't, so she plunged on, getting muddled and resenting his calm silence. 'Don't you meet people you know? Or—or have a meal out, or something?'

She did look up then, and sat up straight at the sight of his cold anger.

He said in a quiet, icy voice, 'Are you accusing me of something, Claudia? Perhaps you should be more explicit.'

She had gone too far now to stop. Besides, she had to know... She steeled herself to look at his expressionless face. 'Your secretary, Emma—she wasn't at your rooms. Mrs Truelove said that she was never there when you were away...'

Mr Tait-Bullen crossed one long leg over the other.

He said mildly, 'You wish to know where she was for some reason?'

'Yes, well, I think you should have been honest about it. I know it doesn't matter, because we—we don't love each other, but I am your wife.'

'Let me get this quite clear. You have been told by someone that when I go away Emma goes with me, so when I'm not working we can—er—live it up together.'

He spoke quietly, but Claudia flinched at the contempt in his voice. 'And who told you this?' He smiled thinly. 'I'll give you credit for not imagining it for yourself.'

'Of course I didn't imagine it,' said Claudia hotly. 'It never entered my head. I met Honor...'

'And you believed her?'

She peeped at his face. He was in a splendid rage, but he was controlling it with an iron will. She said recklessly now, knowing that she had cooked her goose with a vengeance, 'Not quite. I tried not to think about what she had said, but she told me Emma wasn't at your rooms—she laughed and said I didn't dare to find out for myself... So I did. I phoned Mrs Truelove and she told me that Emma wasn't there.'

'I see.' He got to his feet. 'Our marriage may not be quite as other marriages, Claudia, but I thought that we shared a mutual trust, and I hoped that our liking might have turned into something deeper in time. It seems as if I was wrong. This is something which must be put right as soon as possible. If you are unhappy, and I think you are, you must make up your mind what you want to do. Take your time, and we'll talk again later.'

He walked to the door. 'And now I must do some work. Goodnight, Claudia.'

She said in a squeaky voice, 'Thomas, are you very angry?'

He smiled then. 'Yes, my dear.' It was a bitter smile.

She heard him whistle to Harvey and then shut his study door, and she went up to her room, reflecting that he still hadn't told her if Emma had been with him.

The night seemed endless, and by the end of it she hadn't had a single sensible thought. She would never be able to tell Thomas that she loved him now. Not that she would have done, she contradicted herself, but they would have made something of their marriage, because loving him, even secretly, would have made it worthwhile. Something would have to be done, but she had no idea what.

She went down to breakfast, her pale face carefully made up. It didn't conceal her puffy eyelids or her pinkened nose, and Thomas, bidding her good morning in his usual voice, had difficulty in restraining himself from picking her out of her chair and carrying her off somewhere quiet, where he could tell her how much he loved her. But of course that wasn't possible; she had demonstrated only too clearly last night that her feeling for him wasn't strong enough to overcome her doubts.

He said in his usual calm way, 'I shall be away all day. Could dinner be a little later? I've a meeting at the hospital, and I'm not sure how long it may last.'

He finished his breakfast, wished her a pleasant day and went away, leaving her to feed Harvey with her neglected toast.

She was trying to decide what to do when the phone rang, and she went to answer it.

'Mrs Tait-Bullen? This is Emma, the Professor's secretary. Mrs Truelove told me that you had asked for me.

I'm sorry I wasn't here; when the Professor goes away he allows me to go home—I live in Norfolk—at least, my parents do. I'm getting married in the summer, and there's such a lot of planning to do; was there something I could do for you?'

Claudia, astonished at herself, heard her own voice saying the first thing which came into her head. 'Emma, how nice of you to phone. I just wondered if you had any ideas about a wedding present? I've seen some lovely china... The Professor says I should make it a surprise, but perhaps there's something you would like to choose? A dinner set, or something for the house? Will you think about it and let me know?'

She rang off presently, Emma's thanks ringing in her ears. But she forgot that immediately. What a fool she had been; with her stupid outburst yesterday evening she had destroyed any chance of Thomas ever falling in love with her. He must despise her. They would have to go on living together, outwardly friendly, while she ate her heart out for him, and he would treat her with a distant courtesy which would chill her to the bone.

She suddenly couldn't bear it any longer. Thomas would be at his consulting rooms until ten o'clock; she picked up the phone and dialled.

Mrs Truelove answered her. The Professor had just seen a patient. If Mrs Tait-Bullen would wait a second, she would get him to come to the phone before she ushered in the next one. She came back to the phone very quickly.

'I'm so sorry, the Professor asked me to say that he is unable to talk to you at the moment. I was also to tell you that he would be late home this evening and that you weren't to wait up for him.'

The dear soul sounded worried, and Claudia hastened to say that it wasn't important and that she had expected him not to be home early. 'It was nothing important,' she added, 'really, it wasn't.' As though repeating it would convince her, as well as Mrs Truelove.

Her normal common sense had been taken over by a kind of recklessness. To stay quietly at home waiting for his return and then probably be met by his cold stare and refusal to talk was impossible. She swept upstairs, changed into a tweed skirt, a sweater and the leather jacket, pulled on boots, found scarf, gloves and a handbag and went in search of Cork.

'I'd like to go for a drive in the Mini,' she told him. 'Would you fetch it round from the garage for me, Cork, while I take Harvey for a quick walk?'

Cork put down the silver he was polishing. The Mini lived in the garage in the mews behind the house, for his use and as a second car if it was needed. It was kept in good order, ready for the road at a moment's notice, and there was no reason why Claudia shouldn't drive it. All the same, he felt doubtful.

'I could drive you, madam. The traffic's very heavy...'

'I've been driving for years,' Claudia told him, which wasn't true; she had used Great-Uncle William's old car from time to time, driving him to friends, before he took to his bed, and her mother to the nearest supermarket, but now fright and rage and bitter unhappiness had made her pot valiant. 'I won't take Harvey. I've had a message to say that the Professor won't be back until very late this evening, so something on a tray will suit me. I'll be out to lunch.'

She fastened Harvey's lead, gave Cork a reassuring

smile and went for a brisk walk, going over in her mind the route she must take to get her onto the motorway. It was still early, and the morning rush was at its height, but it was coming into the city; traffic going out of it would be much lighter.

When she got back Cork had the Mini at the door. He was still uneasy, but he received Harvey, begged her to take care as she drove away and went indoors. He wasn't a man to say much, but he voiced his doubts to Mrs Rumbold.

'Don't you worry, Mr Cork,' said that lady comfortably. 'You just said she'd had a message about him not being home early. Like as not she told him where she was going.'

Cork took comfort from that. At least Claudia had looked confident as she had driven away.

She might have looked confident, but several times during the next hour she wished herself anywhere but behind the wheel of the Mini. She was a good driver, but London traffic was something she hadn't had to deal with, and it was daunting. Only the despairing urge to get away from Thomas as far as possible kept her going.

She followed the route Thomas had taken, driving steadily, thankful at last to turn into the country roads from the motorway. It was after midday when she turned the little car from Child Okeford's main street and down the lane to Christmas Cottage.

The dry morning had clouded over, and it was drizzling. The cottage looked forlorn, although she could hear voices from within. She got out of the car and opened the front door.

There were several men working there and she stood, forgetful of her worries for a moment, marvelling at the amount of work which had been done. The walls were plastered and the woodwork painted, and two men were laying an oak floor in the sitting room.

She wished them good afternoon, told them who she was and asked if she would be in the way if she looked round.

No one minded, and one of the men led her from room to room, pointing out what had been done and what was still needed.

The plumbing was done, he pointed out, but none of the bathroom fitments had arrived yet. 'Nor yet the stuff your husband ordered for the kitchen.'

'You've been so quick....'

'Well, seeing as how there's not much work around at this time of year, and us being paid on the nail, we got started right away. Staying in the village, are you, missus?' She crossed her fingers and fibbed. 'No, I just came down to have a look on the way to visit my mother. I expect my husband and I will be coming down at the weekend if he's free.'

'Busy man, isn't he? The house agent told us he is a famous doctor.'

'Yes, he is.' She couldn't bear to think of Thomas. 'Look, I'm going to the pub for lunch, and then I want to look round the village. What time do you go?'

'We'll pack up as soon as the flooring's down—can't do much outside with this rain. About three o'clock, I should say.'

'Well, if I'm not back before you go, thank you for letting me see round. I've a key, but you'll lock up, won't you? The car won't be in the way if I leave it there? I'd like to have a walk.'

'Right you are, missus.'

They parted the best of friends, and Claudia went back to the village main street and went into the pub. It was almost two o'clock, but the landlord found coffee and sandwiches for her and, when she told him who she was, came and sat at the table while she ate, giving her a friendly insight into the village and the people who lived there. By the time she had finished her leisurely meal it was already dusk, and almost three o'clock.

She made her way back to the cottage and found the men loading their van, ready to leave. It was obvious they expected her to leave too, so she got into the Mini, reversed it into the lane so that the van could pass and waved them on. She stayed where she was, though, until they had been gone for a few minutes, then drove back and parked the car at the side of the cottage, found the key and went in.

The electricity had been turned on, but there was only one naked bulb in the kitchen. Someone had left an old wooden chair there and she sat down. Her sudden spurt of recklessness had worn itself out. She had been a fool to come, but she had wanted to see the place where she had hoped that they were going to be happy. She hadn't thought beyond that. 'I'll sit here for a bit,' she said out loud, 'and presently I'll drive back. Perhaps Thomas will let me explain.'

Mr Tait-Bullen saw the last of his private patients out, got into his car and went to the hospital, where he had a clinic and ward round waiting for him. He would be finished by teatime, and then he would go home and he and Claudia could talk. There was a great deal to be talked about. Their sensible marriage wasn't working out; after only a few short weeks she had let him see that she didn't trust him. All the same, he was going to tell her that he loved her...

The ward round went smoothly, and the clinic wasn't quite as busy as usual. He saw his new patients, giving them his meticulous attention, and then, waiting for the first of his old patients, he phoned Cork.

'Is Mrs Tait-Bullen home, Cork?'

'Sir—a good thing you called. I was getting that worried. She took the Mini early this morning, and said she wouldn't be back for lunch. Didn't say where she was going.'

'Took the Mini? Did she seem upset, Cork?'

'Worked up, as it were, sir. Left Harvey with me, said you wouldn't be home until late, and that she'd have something on a tray.'

'I see, Cork. I'll be home as soon as I can. She may have decided to go and see her mother. Phone Mrs Willis, will you, and find out? Don't ring me here as I shall leave as soon as I can.'

He put the phone down, deliberately dismissing Claudia from his mind while he looked through the patients' notes to see if there was anyone whom he should see. There wasn't; he could safely leave them to the registrar.

It was too early for the evening rush hour, and he took short cuts.

Cork was hovering in the hall when he went in, and said at once, 'She's not at Mrs Willis's. I shouldn't have let her go.'

Thomas gave him a reassuring pat on the shoulder. 'Nonsense, Cork. You weren't to know that she would be gone for so long. Besides, I think I know where she is.'

Cork brightened. 'You do, sir? I'll get your tea...'

'Later, Cork. I'll bring her back in the car. The Mini can be fetched later.'

Mr Tait-Bullen drove out of London a good deal faster than Claudia had done, and once on the motorway put his large, well-shod foot down, sliding past traffic, a sleek, dark shadow, there one minute, miles away the next. He had taken time to go to Claudia's room before he left the house, and had seen with satisfaction that she had taken no clothes with her. Indeed, all the usual things a girl would put carefully into her handbag before a day out were strewn on the dressing table. Her driving licence was there too. He had smiled when he saw it. His Claudia had left the house without her usual common sense.

He was forced to slow down once he left the motorway; all the same he made the journey in record time. He slid the car slowly up the lane and its lights showed him the Mini. He turned off his own lights and got out of the car, and saw the faint glow of light from the kitchen. He had brought Harvey with him; now he tucked the little beast under one arm, one hand over his muzzle to muffle his bark, and went into the house.

Claudia was still on the wooden chair. She was sitting very untidily and she was fast asleep, her head at an awkward angle. She would be stiff and cramped when she woke.

He stood looking at her, loving her very much, and Harvey, suddenly realising who it was sitting there, gave a small, pleased yelp. Claudia opened her eyes.

She stared up at Thomas for a few moments, eased her stiff neck away from the chair and said in a wondering voice, 'Thomas, dear Thomas. I thought I'd never see you again.'

He put Harvey down then, and stooped and swept her into his arms. He was tired, and he had been very worried, but now that didn't matter. He said slowly, 'You said "dear Thomas"...'

'Well, you are. Only I didn't know, and now it's all such an awful muddle...'

'No, it's not, my darling. You see, I love you. I've loved you for quite a while now. Just when I have despaired of you ever loving me, you called me dear Thomas.'

'Oh, you are, you are. I must have been blind or something. I think I've loved you for a long time too, only we both thought the other one didn't, didn't we?'

Mr Tait-Bullen listened to this muddled speech with delight. 'Dear love, you couldn't have put it more clearly.'

He bent and kissed her in a way which proved how right she was. 'Were you running away?' he asked, and bent to kiss her again. 'Because if you try to do so again, remember to take your driving licence with you.'

'I'll never do it again, Thomas. Thomas, you do love me? Really love me?'

'My dearest love, I would not wish to live without you.'

Claudia kissed him. 'We have the rest of our lives together,' she said, 'and we'll come here whenever we can, won't we? And be happy together—with Harvey, of course.'

'And a handful of sons and daughters, my darling. Harvey will need young company...'

'He has us.'

'Yes, and I have you too, Claudia.'

She peered up into his face. The bland calm wasn't there any more; she saw the man she loved, the man who had been there all the time.

'We're going home now,' said Mr Tait-Bullen.

ONE WICKED NIGHT

by

Jo Leigh

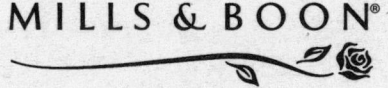
MILLS & BOON®

Thanks to Birgit Davis-Todd and
Huntley Fitzpatrick for giving me a shot!

1

THE FIRST THING Michael Craig saw was her leg. Long, sleek and clad in a high-heeled black shoe, it was a leg that would have stopped him even if he hadn't been on the lookout for her. It was a leg that deserved attention.

He waited impatiently for the rest of the woman to emerge from the limousine. If the leg was this good, perhaps the rest of her was also more enticing than her grainy newspaper photograph had led him to believe. Shifting a bit to his left to get a better view, he watched as Emma Roberts leaned forward, her long straight dark hair obscuring her face. But only for a moment. She stood, and the hair fell back so he could see her profile. He wasn't close enough for details, but from here, she seemed attractive. Not quite as beautiful as the leg had promised, but not bad.

As she turned and he got a look at her from the front he revised his original assessment yet again. She looked younger than twenty-eight. Her somewhat severe black suit seemed incongruous on her, as if she were playing dress up. He looked once more at the newspaper photo in his hand. In it, Emma's hair was pulled back in a bun. That was the difference, of course. He hoped she would wear it back tonight. It would be a lot easier to do what he had to if she didn't look so innocent.

He watched her as the bellman came over and got her bags from the trunk. She stood very straight, with her toes pointed slightly out, a sure sign that she'd studied ballet. He'd gone out with a dancer once. Amazingly limber.

Emma turned to look at the twenty-six-story hotel before her. Then she turned his way and he saw she was smiling. Was it the architecture that pleased her? Or was it the fact that she was on an all expenses paid vacation courtesy of her company? Or maybe she'd never been to New Orleans before. He hoped she hadn't. He'd like to show her the city for the first time. Even if he didn't have enough charm to do the job, the city did. New Orleans could seduce the hardest hearts. Emma wouldn't stand a chance.

She walked toward the big glass door, but paused before entering. Slowly turning, she looked back at the limo, the street and finally she turned his way. He thought about ducking back, but what was the point? She didn't know him. There was no reason for her to think of him as anything but part of the scenery.

But that's not what happened. When her gaze came to him, it lingered. Just for a moment. In that moment, Michael got a strange feeling in the pit of his stomach. It had been a mistake, seeing her like this. He should have just waited until dinner and gone ahead with his plan. He wasn't sure, but he thought the strange feeling might just be guilt. No, he was probably wrong about that. There was no room for guilt in business. He who ends up with the most toys wins and Michael was determined to end up with the most toys. Including Emma Roberts.

EMMA LOOKED AROUND the elegant dining room and saw she was the only single party in the place. Single party. Party of one. Talk about oxymorons. She'd never felt less like a party girl, which was yet another example of how her dreams got her into trouble every time.

This was supposed to be the night of her life. She'd won this trip to New Orleans as Employee of the Year at Transco Oil. All expenses paid, dinner at this five-star restaurant, even the company jet to wing her from Houston and back again. Well, she made a lousy Cinderella. She'd been so excited—looked forward to this trip for weeks—and now, all she felt was lonely. Prince Charming must have had other plans.

She took another bite of salad, then stared at the flickering candle on her table. It was better than staring at the couples around her, all of whom seemed to be spectacularly, demonstratively, in love.

The tap on her shoulder startled her, but then she remembered she'd asked the waiter for the sommelier. She turned. And nearly choked on her lettuce. The wine steward was the single best-looking man she'd ever seen. He made the Diet Coke guy look like Barney Fife. The sommelier's dark hair was slightly wavy and thick and a bit long around the collar. His eyes sparkled, and he smiled elegantly with perfect teeth. And his jaw—she'd never been big on jaws before—but this one changed her forever.

"Ms. Roberts?"

Boy, he was good. How had he found out her name? She nodded, wanting him to speak again so she could get another shiver from that baritone voice of his.

"From Transco Oil?"

"Wow," she said. When he smiled, she realized she'd said it aloud. "I mean, wine. Wine, you know. To drink."

"Yes, I've heard of it." He said it gently, teasing. Then he snapped his fingers and at once a man wearing a corkscrew on a chain around his neck was at his side. "Puligny Montrachet, *s'il vous plaît*, Pierre."

Emma blinked. Twice. If Pierre was the sommelier... "Who are you?" she asked the man with the remarkable jaw.

"I'm Michael Craig. I read about you in the *Chronicle*. Congratulations on winning your prize. You must be very pleased."

Blinking seemed appropriate again. "You recognized my picture from a Houston paper?"

"Yes, of course. I never forget a pretty face."

That did it. The fantasy he'd created vanished as she realized the beautiful man was a liar. "Well, thank you," she said, now just wishing he'd leave. Hoping he couldn't see the rush of heat in her cheeks.

"You're quite welcome." He walked around the table and put his hand on the chair across from her. "I'm afraid I've been stood up. I see you've already ordered, but if it's not too presumptuous of me...may I join you?"

"I...uh..."

"Thank you."

He sat down, but not before she got a good look at his tuxedo. She'd never seen anything like it before. At least not in person. It fit him perfectly, accentuating his broad shoulders and slim waist. Good grief, who in their right mind would stand up this man?

"I was supposed to go to the opera with three men from Oklahoma. One of them goes by the name of Bubba Jorgenson. What a night it would have been, eh?"

Despite her earlier wish for Prince Charming to appear, Emma tried to figure out how to politely tell him that she'd rather dine alone. She was always fascinating to men who lived only in her mind. With the real thing, however...? On the other hand, he sure did improve the view. What the heck. One dinner with a beautiful liar wouldn't kill her. "Bubba Jorgenson? It's not a name one would forget."

Michael smiled. Oh, heavens. It was enough to set her heart racing. Why hadn't she listened to her friends? They'd begged her to go for a makeover, to get her hair done, to buy some new clothes. But no. She had waved all the poofery aside, and now here she was with Adonis himself, while she felt like a charwoman. Well, maybe not that bad. Although next to Michael, Cindy Crawford would get a complex.

"Now, you need to tell me what you did to become Employee of the Year. That's quite an honor."

If she hadn't been watching him, listening to the tone of his voice, she would have been certain he was being sarcastic.

"You really recognized me from that silly photo? I would barely recognize the president from a picture in the newspaper."

"Yes, I really did. The article is in my briefcase up in my room. If you'd like, I can go get it and show you."

She shook her head. "No, that's okay. I believe you...I think."

"Emma Roberts, head of research at Transco Oil of Houston was named Employee Of The Year at this year's annual meeting."

Emma recognized the words from the article. He'd memorized it verbatim.

"Philip Bailey, president and CEO of the privately owned natural resource company made the announcement on the heels of a disappointing third quarter...."

"Stop," she said, holding out her hand. "You win."

"Good. Then as my reward, I get to hear you answer my question."

"What question?"

"I asked what you did to win this grand prize."

"Oh, right. Well, it wasn't all that hard," she said. "All I had to do was show up for a full day's work every weekday for the past three years."

"That's real dedication."

She laughed. "That's real desperation."

"They don't pay you well at Transco?"

"Sure. The salary is fine. Except for the fact that I'm sole support for my mother and a sister who's in college."

The smile left, and his brow creased, which somehow made him better looking. "I'm sorry. That must be hard for such a young woman."

She shrugged, and sipped some water. After she put the glass down, she managed a smile of her own. "It's just life. No different from anyone else's. Well, maybe Madonna, but who'd want her problems?"

He laughed, and she knew right then if he asked her to make love with him right here on the dining room table, she'd say yes. Or at least maybe.

"It seems to me what you do must be very different from anyone else," he commented. "From what I read, I imagined your job would require someone unique."

"Actually, I head up the research department at Transco. My team and I coordinate resource exploration, expeditions and long-term feasibility studies." She felt her shoulders relax now that she was in familiar territory. "It's exciting."

"Not many people say that about their work. You must really enjoy it," he said.

"I do. I work with three of the best researchers in the business. We don't punch a time clock, we each have an area of expertise, and we get the job done."

"Satisfaction in a job well done," he said, his focus not on her any longer, but somewhere far away. "That's it, isn't it? What it's all about."

"You speak from experience?"

He was with her again. His eyes, a light hazel that contrasted with his tan skin, weren't dreamy anymore. They were serious, and interested and scanning her with acute intelligence. "I like to think so."

"What do you do?"

"I'm a businessman. But we're not here to talk about me. This is your night."

As if to emphasize his point the sommelier arrived just then and went through the ritual of wine acceptance with Michael. The label was examined, the cork popped, the liquid poured, then tasted. Emma and the steward waited for the nod of approval, and when it was given, her glass was filled.

Michael lifted his for a toast. "To a very lovely Employee of the Year," he said.

She lifted her own. "Bottoms up." She sipped just as he did, their gazes locked over their respective brims. By the time the wine reached her stomach, she was a goner. Before she could stop it an image of him taking off that Armani tux slid into her mind. The promise of what lay beneath elevated her temperature and kick-started her pulse.

"I'll have what the young lady is having," Michael said.

She hadn't noticed the waiter approach until she heard Michael speak.

"Would you like to begin with the salad, sir?"

"No, Emma will be fine."

Emma jolted back, then realized he'd said *entrée*, the *entrée* would be fine. The heat increased until she could feel her cheeks burn pink.

Michael turned to her when the waiter had gone. "Will you excuse me for a moment? I have to make a phone call."

She nodded and watched him walk away, wishing he would lift up the back of his tux so she could get a gander at what was underneath.

After he disappeared behind the door leading to the phones, she signaled the maître d'.

"Yes, ma'am?"

"The gentleman I'm sitting with. Do you know him?"

"Mr. Craig? Yes, of course. He comes here often."

"So he's not a crazed ax murderer or something?"

The maître d' laughed, and Emma felt her shoulders relax. "No, ma'am. He's a very good customer, and well-known in the hotel. I don't believe you have anything to worry about."

"Thank you," she said.

He nodded and walked away.

"But I'm not so sure," she whispered.

Then Michael appeared, and she was stunned once more at his elegance. It was ridiculous, really. He was just a man. Just like any other man. Uh-huh.

He sat down, flipping his napkin once and laying it on his lap. "This research," Michael said, as if there hadn't been a break in the conversation. "It's a lot of geology, isn't it?"

"That's my specialty. I have a master's degree in environmental geology. I look for alternate methods of oil extraction with an emphasis on preservation."

"That explains why Transco isn't doing too well."

"Oh?" He really did pay attention to the business section.

"Sure. They're not a slash-and-burn company. They have a stake in the planet. That costs money."

"But it's worth it, don't you think?"

"Of course. Up to a point."

"What point is that?"

"When they stop making a profit."

"Sometimes a profit isn't the goal," she said.

"It has to be. Or the job doesn't get done. The company goes under. No more responsible company watching out for the earth. It's a simple equation." He lifted his glass.

"It's only simple when you don't care."

The wine didn't make it to his lips. "A smart girl like you, and you think caring has something to do with success?"

"Don't you care about anything?"

"One thing only." He smiled again, but this time she wasn't so taken in by his looks that she didn't notice the slight sadness that came with it. "Profit."

"That's a strict master."

"I'm a practical man, Emma. I know that the best intentions without money remain intentions."

"A practical man in an Armani tuxedo? I don't think so."

"Pretty *and* observant," he said. "Very good."

"Well?"

"It's an investment. Plain and simple."

"It doesn't hurt that it makes you look superb, though, does it?"

"You think so?"

"No. *You* think so."

"Touché. But I'm disappointed. I was hoping the suit would give me bonus points."

"Don't worry. I think you're very pretty. Honest."

"Then spend the night with me."

That got her attention. She opened her mouth, then closed it again.

He laughed. "No, I didn't mean that. I meant the evening. We'll take a walk around Jackson Square. Maybe a ride in a carriage." He leaned forward and covered her hand with his. The sensation made her inhale quickly. Just looking at his hand, so wide and broad and masculine, made her feel suddenly feminine and cared for. It wasn't a feeling she was accustomed to.

"Please, Emma. New Orleans at night is quite something."

The waiter arrived, and Michael took his hand away. She couldn't have been less hungry, even though her scallops in wine sauce smelled wonderful. She wanted Michael to touch her again. Just once more. How had she gone so long without feeling like this? But still, he was a stranger. And she was, after all, Emma. "I don't think so. But thank you."

"You're worried. Which is a wise thing to be. These are dangerous times."

"Yes, I know."

"How can I convince you that I'm not like the times?"

"You? Not dangerous? There's no way I could ever be convinced of that."

He smiled and she found herself leaning forward.

"I have references," he said.

"What kind?"

"The manager of the hotel for one."

She shook her head. "Unless the manager is a woman, it's not going to be enough."

"Ah, so you think I have designs on you, is that it?"

A quick heat filled her cheeks and she looked away. What on earth had she been thinking? A man like that wanting her? Oh, sweet mercy she'd stuck her foot in it this time.

"Of course, you'd be correct," he said, his voice low, soft, intimate.

She gathered her courage and met his gaze once more. "Really?"

He laughed. "Why do you sound so surprised?"

"Because you're you, and I'm me."

The look he gave her was one she'd seen a hundred times before. She'd baffled him. He didn't know what to make of her. He found her...curious. It was her mouth, of course. Her inability to think before she spoke. Her foolish insistence on telling the truth had run off more men than she cared to think about, and now she was going to run off this magnificent specimen.

"Now, Emma, are we really so different, you and I?"

She laughed. "Yes."

"Why? We're both businesspeople. We're both in a city that isn't our home. We're intelligent, single and we both like scallops."

"Oh, well, I'd forgotten about the scallops. You're right. We're practically twins."

"And we both appreciate your sarcastic sense of humor," he said with a wry smile.

"Sorry. I don't mean to be—"

"Don't apologize. I do like it."

"You like smart-ass remarks?"

He nodded. "Much better than polite indifference."

"That puts the pressure on."

"Hmm?"

"Most of the time I don't think of the right smart-ass remark until the next day."

"Then it's a good thing I'm here for the whole weekend."

Emma went for her wineglass again. She concentrated on bringing it to her lips with a steady hand. Sipping, not gulping. Lord, was she out of her league here. The only thing she knew about men like Michael Craig was that they didn't go out with women like Emma Roberts. They dated beauty queens and fashion models. Not environmental researchers.

Finally, the light dawned. She swallowed a bigger gulp of wine than she had planned, and coughed, but thank God she didn't spit all over the table. The girls! Her three very nosy, very clever assistants at Transco had set this all up. It had to be. He was a paid escort! Of course. It all made sense now.

Ever thorough, the girls must have alerted the staff here at the hotel to play along. No wonder they'd wanted her to get the makeover. She was going to kill them on Monday. Imagine, hiring an escort to keep her company.

Now she looked at Michael with different eyes. Critical eyes. He must have cost a fortune. Richard Gere himself couldn't have played the part more convincingly. He was stunning, smooth, a good conversationalist. He even talked business like a professional. She had to hand it to them, they'd hired the best.

The only thing was, she didn't know what to do

now. Or how to feel. Should she be insulted? Or grateful?

"What's going on in that pretty head of yours?" Michael asked.

Should she play her hand? Let him know she'd figured out this little charade?

He leaned forward slightly. His gaze traveled over her face, feature by feature. She watched carefully for some indication of what he really thought of her. If this assignment was distasteful, or pleasant. She couldn't bear the former. He may be a paid escort, but he was still a man.

"I've been too forward, haven't I? I've made you uncomfortable."

She shook her head. "No, it's all right. You're just doing your job."

He leaned back. "My job?"

Emma decided right there that she wasn't going to let on. She was Cinderella, right? This was her night at the ball, and Michael was her Prince Charming. So he came with a price tag. What didn't these days? Knowing her friends, they'd checked him out up one side and down the other. She was safe, at least in the Boston Strangler sense of the word. But was it wise to play this fantasy out? To let herself be a princess for a weekend?

"Emma, what do you mean?"

"I was trying for smart-ass," she said. "But I got cryptic instead."

His eyes narrowed. "I'm not sure I understand."

"It's okay. It's nothing."

"You're not what I expected," he said, after a long pause.

She wondered briefly what the girls had told him about her. Probably extolled her virtues as a geologist and researcher. And, knowing them, they'd probably told him that she hadn't been on a date since the Hindenburg disaster. "What did you expect?"

"Someone a little more serious, a little more sedate."

"A scientist, right? Pocket protector. Thick glasses. Perhaps wearing an 'X-Files' T-shirt?"

He laughed. "No. Just not...you."

"You don't know the first thing about me, Mr. Craig."

"You're wrong, Emma. I've learned quite a bit so far."

"Oh?"

He moved his hand to hers once more. The touch undid her, made her stomach tighten, and she found herself crossing her legs.

"You're very bright," he said. "Maybe too bright for your own good. Because you're smart enough to see through the veneer, aren't you? You have things all figured out. You assume I want something. Well, you're right. I do. I want your company. No strings attached. I want to walk through New Orleans and see it through your eyes. I want to listen to your smart-ass remarks. And your laughter. Emma, come with me. Be mine, just for tonight."

It was now or never. She could put an end to the farce and tell him she knew he'd been hired to seduce her. Or she could let herself be seduced. She needed time to think it over, but of course there wasn't time. He wanted an answer. Now.

"All right," she said.

He cocked his head a bit to the side. "Really?"

She nodded. It was her night, wasn't it? So what if he was a hired prince? She wouldn't let it matter. Tonight, she would be Cinderella. Her real life would be there tomorrow, and a hundred tomorrows after that.

2

MICHAEL FELT inordinately pleased with himself. This was going better than he'd expected. While Emma wasn't exactly his ideal woman when it came to looks, she was pretty in her own way, and a quick thinker, which made his task very pleasant.

She didn't suspect a thing, that much he was sure of. Although for a moment there, he'd been afraid she was going to turn him down. It was clear she wasn't used to his kind of attention. She wore her skepticism like a cloak, and that, he thought, was going to be his biggest hurdle. Getting her to accept and believe that she was the most desirable woman in all of New Orleans wouldn't be easy. Luckily, he wasn't going to have to do too much acting.

He watched her sip her wine. He found himself wanting to touch her long and lovely throat. By caressing her hand, he'd already discovered how remarkably soft her skin was. Caution reigned, however, and he held back. He wasn't here to enjoy himself. He was here to find out about Transco Oil. To get the final details that would make his takeover of the company a fait accompli. Period.

If he did his job right, he'd have everything he

needed by the end of the night. Emma would be sadder, but wiser, and he'd be quite a bit richer.

"This is my first time in New Orleans," she said. "Can you believe it? I've lived in Houston all my life, and I've never come down here. I just kept meaning to."

"Then I'll show you the city."

"You're from here, then?"

He shook his head. "No, I live in Houston now. But I made it a point to visit New Orleans very early on."

"A real mover and shaker?"

"I don't procrastinate. Don't believe in it."

Emma played with a scallop on her plate for a minute. "So you just go after what you want? Just like that?"

He smiled. "Yep."

"How often do you succeed?"

He held back his first answer. Instead, he said, "Very often. But not always."

She put down her fork and touched her wineglass with her fingertips. He watched the way her hand moved, surprised at the delicate slip of her wrist. He hadn't thought she would be so slim. Or that he could be so taken by the small gesture.

"Do you still want what you can't have?" she asked quietly.

"No. Never. If it can't be mine, I walk away. No regrets."

"We're more alike than I'd imagined."

"How?"

"I walk away, too. Only I don't have the 'no regrets' part down yet. I envy you."

"Don't." He leaned forward, no longer able to watch her hand without touching it. He held it gently and rubbed her palm with his thumb.

"Why not?" she asked. "The regrets are the painful part."

"They're also the human part."

She looked away from his gaze to the interplay of their hands in the center of the white tablecloth. He continued to caress her palm and she watched the flickering candlelight play shadowy tricks.

"You surprise me, too," Emma said. "I thought I had you pegged. Now I'm not so sure."

He pulled away from her and took hold of his glass. "Ms. Roberts, I have the feeling you know exactly who I am." Then he turned, and signaled the waiter.

"Dessert for you and the lady, sir?" The waiter, who looked a little like John Lennon, leaned a bit forward, as if the answer to his question was a matter of great importance.

Michael looked at Emma, and she shook her head no. "We'll just take the bill," he said.

"That's already been taken care of, sir."

Once more, Michael turned to Emma. "Ready?"

This time she nodded yes.

Michael left a generous tip on the table, and then held Emma's chair for her. When she rose, the top of her head reached the bottom of his chin. He figured she must be about five foot five. Again, the delicacy of her body surprised him. She wore a soft pastel dress that clung to her as she walked, and beneath it he could see the outline of a slim, but womanly, figure.

She'd worn her hair down, and as he'd predicted it was making things more complicated. Just seeing how it framed her face, how it made her seem so pure and sweet, brought back that little niggling sensation he'd felt this afternoon. That wouldn't do. He thought of his profit and loss statement. His portfolio. There, that was better.

He put his hand on the center of her back, and he felt her body quiver at the touch. That was better, still. He was in control once more. Emma might be nice to touch, but he had an agenda, and that was all that mattered.

THE AIR OUTSIDE the restaurant was sultry and infused with the smell of the sea. It caressed Emma's face and arms and legs, and made her feel exotic and soft. She was incredibly aware of Michael's hand on the small of her back. It was warmer than human touch was supposed to be, the heat infiltrating her body and stirring her blood. She wanted him to move his hand away, and keep it there forever. She wanted to be safe, and yet she wanted adventure. Michael, she was sure, was more adventure than she'd had in her whole life.

"Let's walk this way," Michael said, nodding toward the river.

They walked slowly, Michael setting the pace. Many people were out on such a balmy night, most of them couples. Everyone seemed to be touching—holding hands, arms around waists or shoulders. The sound of a saxophone wafted softly from somewhere.

Emma didn't want to think that he was touching her because he had to. She wanted to believe that his hand was there because he needed to touch her, as much as she needed to be touched. Perhaps it was. Perhaps she'd been wrong about him. What if... What if he were really just a businessman who'd seen her picture in the paper? Stranger things had happened. Not to her, of course, but Ripley had made a whole career of oddities and coincidences. So why wasn't she allowed one night with a real prince?

Michael stopped her. He didn't say anything or take her arm, he just slowed and stopped, and her rhythm was his, so she paused as he did. With his free hand, he pointed out to where the Mississippi met the Gulf, to a cruise ship ablaze with lights. Floating over the black water, it was a ghost ship come from far away, and its otherworldly beauty moved her inexplicably.

"Ever been on a cruise?" Michael asked.

"No. Nothing like that."

"You should go. It's really something being out in the middle of all that water."

"Where did you go?"

"Barbados."

"Wow."

"Yeah."

"I used to dream about Barbados when I was a kid," she said. "It always seemed like a magical place."

He laughed, but it held no humor. She heard derision, cynicism, and she wondered why. It hadn't seemed an odd statement to her.

"I didn't know there was an island called Barbados when I was a kid. And I certainly didn't know about magic."

"Where are you from?"

"California. East Los Angeles."

"I've never been there, either. I'd love to go, though."

"Not to East L.A. you don't."

"Why?"

"It's a ghetto. A barrio to be more exact. You wouldn't want to get a flat tire out there."

They walked a few steps forward, until they reached the high metal barrier that separated the sidewalk from the shoreline. Michael took his hand away and leaned forward, resting on his elbows. Her back felt chilled, and she thought briefly of encouraging him to walk some more on the chance that he'd touch her again. Instead, she leaned forward too, mimicking his stance.

"Tell me," she said. "Tell me about when you lived in the barrio."

He didn't speak for a long while. Just stared at the slow moving ship. Finally, he turned to look at her. "You don't want to know," he said. "There was nothing pretty about it."

"That's all right. I don't need pretty."

She could see his frown in the moonlight. "It wasn't much. A typically dysfunctional family. Gangster friends, bad schools. The whole nine yards."

"But look at you now."

"Yeah. I've scraped my childhood off my shoes, all right."

"But?"

The saxophone grew louder for a moment, as if a door had opened letting the sound escape. Then it grew quiet again, and melancholy.

Michael stood up sharply. He coughed, and looked around, checking, she thought, for witnesses to his moment of indiscretion. "The carriages are just down the road," he said. "Let's see if we can get one."

He led her down the street toward some wonderful old Spanish buildings, and a small square with several horse-driven carriages waiting at the curb. He didn't touch her again, and she felt that whatever magic had been swirling between them had left with her question. And darn it, she wanted it back.

There were a lot more people by the carriages. A

lot more women to stare at Michael. She couldn't blame them. He was an extraordinarily handsome man. He held himself tall and straight, with a confidence that was palpable. Why would a man like him need to make a living as a paid escort? Maybe she had been wrong.

"There's one. It looks like a nice horse, doesn't it?" He pointed to a bay mare pulling a black carriage. The driver was an old man with sparse white hair, combed to perfection over a big bald patch.

"Very nice," she said.

They approached the calash and the old gentleman gave them a big, semitoothless grin. "Come on up, folks. Thirty minutes for fifteen dollars."

Michael held Emma's hand as she climbed into the black carriage. She sat on the small leather seat, amazed at how tiny the space was. She would be right up against Michael. Touching. Oh, my.

She expected him to follow, but instead, he walked to the front of the buggy. He reached into his pocket and took out a bill, she couldn't see the denomination, and held it out for the driver. They spoke briefly, but she couldn't hear the exchange. The old man nodded, smiling broadly once more, and then Michael climbed in beside her.

She had been correct in her assessment of the size of the seat. His whole left side pressed against her right side from shoulders to knees.

Before she could acclimatize to this intimacy, the carriage jolted, and she jerked forward. Michael's arm went out to stop her, landing squarely across her chest. His hand, positioned to protect her from a nasty carriage accident, lay on her breast.

Then the ride smoothed, and he withdrew, leaving her breathless. It wasn't on purpose, she assured herself. He was being gallant, trying to save her from hitting her head. But she was reminded of the time Alex Trent, her high school boyfriend, had used the same maneuver in his father's Chrysler, claiming the brakes weren't to be trusted. She'd stopped Alex posthaste, but she certainly wouldn't cry foul tonight if the horse came to a jarring halt.

Michael looked at her, a bit flustered at what he'd done.

She smiled. "Was it good for you?"

Then he laughed. It was a good laugh. Strong. Low. Sexy as hell. "Very good."

"Glad to oblige."

His brow shot up.

"Once."

His grin melted the last of her willpower. Keeping her composure was a Herculean task, but she managed. It wasn't a good idea to let the gentleman know she wasn't thinking like a lady.

"The architecture is wonderful here, isn't it?"

She looked up, surprised that they were so far away from the square. "Where are we?"

"Headed someplace very special."

"I thought this carriage went to Jackson Square?"

"Not tonight."

She turned a bit so she was facing him. "Are you kidnapping me?"

"For an hour or two."

"Should I be worried?"

"Only about sudden stops."

It was her turn to laugh. It felt easy and right to laugh at Michael's jokes. To lean back and rest her head on the leather cushion. She was surprisingly comfortable with the feel of him so close. Enchanted by the *clop-clop* of the horse's hooves on cobblestone. Bewitched by the scent of jasmine and the soft silk of the sultry air. She decided right then that she wouldn't wonder any more about why Michael was here. She would just enjoy the fact that he was.

They rode along quietly for a long stretch. Emma looked at the old buildings, knowing she should be impressed and enthralled, but all she could think of was Michael. It was her night. The prize of prizes. So what if she would wake tomorrow in her old skin, with her old job, and her old house and her old problems. Tonight she was Cinderella, Princess Jasmine, Sleeping Beauty all rolled into one.

Michael looked at the smile that played on Emma's lips. She was having a good time, he thought. So was he, which was more to the point. Why hadn't he asked her more questions about Transco? She showed no hesitance in discussing the company, so what was he waiting for?

Something else was going on. With him, not her. It seemed very important to show Emma a good time.

Not an ordinary good time, but something unique, special. He wanted her to open her eyes wide with wonder. To see things she'd never seen before. What he didn't know was why.

Was this woman so different from any other? He'd gone out with models, actresses, legendary beauties. Emma couldn't begin to compete. He dealt regularly with female executives who were smart, savvy, elegant. Emma was more down-to-earth. There was just something about her. Maybe the ease with which she smiled. Or the gentleness of her voice. Perhaps it was her clear green eyes that seemed to hold no secrets.

Whatever it was, he'd better get over it. His window of opportunity was closing. By the end of the night, he needed to get all his questions answered.

He turned, prepared to broach the subject once more. Only Emma had captured a leaf from an overhanging tree, and was brushing it softly against the skin of her cheek. It was impossible to think of anything else. His questions flew away on the breeze as he watched her. She closed her eyes, smelled the leaf, smiled her Mona Lisa smile.

He became acutely aware of his body—the lower regions to be exact. Maybe he wouldn't go home tomorrow. What was one more day?

Emma focused on her surroundings, and seemed surprised to see they had entered a business district. The streets were bare and the buildings large and utilitarian. The beautiful architecture was saved for less industrious sections of town, but hidden inside one huge warehouse was a treasure. Michael silently urged the horse on. He wanted to get there, to stand up, to cool down. Being this close to Emma wasn't good for his blood pressure.

She'd grown puzzled. "This is the special place?"

"Just wait."

"Well, if you meant to confuse me, congratulations."

"Confusion wasn't the goal."

"What was?"

"Surprise."

At last he saw it. The warehouse was lit up, just as he'd requested in his phone call. A security guard stood outside the door. The carriage stopped.

"Mr. Craig?" The guard didn't really wait for an answer. He just turned and opened the door, then flipped on a bank of light switches. Michael was afraid his surprise would be spoiled, but they couldn't see anything from outside.

He climbed down, then held Emma's hand as she descended. He led her toward the entrance, then moved behind her. "Okay, this is it."

"What?"

He moved his right hand over her eyes. "Patience. Two more seconds." He walked forward, steering her toward the door. His body pressed against her back, feeling the curves of her slight figure.

Once she was inside, and the security guard had stepped out, Michael took his hand away.

Emma's gasp told him he'd scored big time.

"My God, what is all this?"

He looked at her, unable to quit smiling at his victory. "This is where all the Mardi Gras floats live when they're not in the parade."

He couldn't take his eyes off her. She was like a child, filled with wonder as she wandered among the huge papier-mâché figures. She touched the grapes on the Bacchus float, the intricate detail on a pirate ship. There were over a dozen floats in the huge room, each one capable of holding ten or twenty riders. Emma seemed tiny and delicate next to the monstrous cartoon figures.

Michael had been here once before, but the magic of the place hadn't lived until Emma walked inside. It was just as he'd hoped. He'd given her a gift, a rare treat, and he felt like Santa Claus on Christmas morning.

"This is unbelievable," she said, her voice echoing off the concrete walls. "I've never seen anything like it."

"I'm glad."

"How did you do this?"

"The man in charge is a buddy of mine. I called him from the restaurant."

She turned to him, the same astonishment she'd had for the floats now focused on him. "You planned this back in the restaurant?"

He nodded.

"But you didn't know me."

"Sure I did. You're the Employee of the Year. It's your special night."

She let her gaze wander slowly over the room, briefly scanning each individual float. Then she turned to him, walked close and went up on her toes. She kissed his cheek. "Thank you."

"No, thank you."

"What for?"

"I'm not sure."

She flushed a bit, her soft skin infused with a shade of pink he'd never seen before. He wanted to kiss her. Not the tiny peck she'd given him, but a real kiss. A world record kiss. It could be incredible. Or it could be a big mistake.

Emma felt as though nothing in her life would ever be the same. Her heart pumped loudly in her chest, and she wondered if Michael could hear the steady beat. She touched the painted shell of a Cupid pointing his arrow into the air. Tonight, she believed in Cupid. In Donner and Blizten, too. The Tooth Fairy was real, so were the Easter Bunny and Tinkerbell. She felt like Alice in Wonderland, except she had Michael as her guide.

How could this be happening to her? Although she hadn't tried it, she was quite certain that if she looked up the word *ordinary* in the dictionary, she would find her picture. And tonight was decidedly extraordinary.

She turned to Michael, shocked once more by the

look on his face. He was watching her. Just watching. Wearing a comfortable, appreciative smile.

"Why did you bring me here?" she asked.

"Don't you like it?"

"Of course. It's fabulous. I've never seen anything like it before."

"That's why."

She moved closer to him, really studying his expression, trying to find the answer he wasn't giving her. She reached with her hand, and touched his smile with her fingertips, expecting him to vanish like all her other dreams. But he was flesh and blood. A real live man, and she was awake, alive and she was suddenly very afraid that he was exactly who he said he was.

He took her hand in his, and brought her palm to his mouth. He kissed her once, sweetly, and she could feel the softness of his lips and the heat of his breath. His gaze caught hers in an unwavering stare. She froze, frightened, excited, and felt her own heat surge inside.

He moved her hand down, slowly, never blinking or looking away. He leaned forward, and she knew he was going to kiss her. She'd never wanted anything more than that kiss. Her eyes began to close.

But the kiss didn't come. Michael stopped just shy of her lips. He moved back sharply, looked away, and dropped her hand. "I'm sorry," he said. "I didn't mean to..."

"That's all right," she said, trying not to make too much of his change of heart.

"No. We barely know each other. I didn't mean to presume."

"You don't need to worry about that," she said. "Honest. I don't think the regular rules apply tonight. How can they, with the god of wine as a chaperone?"

"You may have a point. But I have a feeling even old Bacchus would want us to take things a little slower."

She flushed, amazed at her boldness, a bit embarrassed by it, too. "Of course." She turned away from him, unsure what to do or say. This was a first for her. She'd been with other men, well, two men. She hadn't felt this awkward with either of them. It was Michael that had her flummoxed. His beautiful suit, his rich, thick hair, those hazel eyes...and who could know what to do with those lips? It was all too much.

"Hey," he said, catching her hand. He waited until she faced him. "I said we'd take it slower. Not that we wouldn't take it at all."

If she were smart, she'd pull her hand away. Ask to go back to the hotel. Thank the man for a nice evening, and leave it at that. Then she would have her memories and a little bit of mystery to play with. The what-ifs would keep her happy for a long time.

On the other hand, if she played this out, there was a very real chance that it would end badly. That she would fall too hard, and the fall would break her heart. If she were smart, she'd run for her life.

But what had smart gotten her up to now? A stable job, responsibility for her whole family, nights filled with loneliness? Just once she'd like to throw caution to the wind and let the sparks fly.

Just once...

Just tonight.

3

MICHAEL WANTED Emma back in his arms. He wanted to kiss her more than he could have ever anticipated. She wanted the same thing, he could tell from her eyes, her disappointment when he'd backed away. But was it smart? Would it get him what he needed? Very probably. So why the hesitation?

It was the look in her eyes, of course. The innocence. The hope. The pure and simple sensuality that swirled just beneath the surface. He'd known from the beginning that he was going to hurt this woman. What hadn't occurred to him was that he might care.

Caring wasn't something that happened to him often. He thought about the gift his last girlfriend had given him. His briefcase. She'd had initials engraved in gold script. RB. Ruthless Bastard. He loved that briefcase.

So why was he acting the gentleman now? He could have Emma. Tonight. It wouldn't be a hardship, either. It didn't take a genius to see that she would be a wonderful lover, and that giving her pleasure would be an experience he'd not soon forget. Of all the times to get a conscience.

"What are you thinking?" she asked.

He realized he'd been staring for a long time. "That you're very beautiful," he said, startled, because it was true.

"I'm not, but thank you."

"What's this? Surely you can't mean you don't think you're pretty?"

She withdrew her hand from his. "Don't think I'm being rude, but if it's all the same to you, I'd rather not go there."

She turned from him, eyes lowered, and started walking toward the back of the warehouse.

Michael frowned. Clearly Emma was uncomfortable with her looks, which was a shame. He was accustomed to women who were secure in their beauty, who used their looks as a tool to get what they wanted. Admittedly, Emma wasn't in the Elle Macpherson category, but she was still a very attractive woman. It wasn't right that she didn't know it.

He followed Emma, watching her from the back. Her posture was so straight that his earlier notion that she'd been a dancer was reconfirmed. Only ballerinas walked with that funny little gait, and held themselves so tall. He'd like to see her dance. With that poetic soul of hers, she'd be good.

Poetic soul? What was he getting into here? He had some very specific questions he needed answers to, nothing more. As soon as he'd seen her picture in the paper, he'd realized the way to get those answers. He hadn't actually planned to take her to bed, nothing so concrete, but he wouldn't hesitate if that was his only option. After all, he was a ruthless bastard, wasn't he? So what was the problem? And why was he so concerned with the nature of Emma's soul?

She turned then, and he saw the hint of sadness on her face. Instead of the awed smile of just a few moments ago, her lips turned down in a slight frown. Her eyes seemed troubled, and the pink flush had left her cheeks.

He kept on walking until he was close enough to touch her. They stood directly beneath a huge pirate ship. Emma looked up at him, then her gaze lowered.

"Maybe we should go," she said, so softly he barely heard her.

"We can, but you haven't seen everything yet."

"That's okay. It's late."

"It's only late in the real world, Emma. Here, it's early."

Her gaze lifted, and met his. "I keep trying to keep the real world away. It has a nasty habit of not letting me."

"You don't have enough practice, that's all. But I do. And I'm a hell of a teacher."

She didn't respond. Instead, she studied his face unabashedly. Really examined him. From his forehead, slowly to his eyes, his nose, his mouth. It was hard not to look away. He wasn't used to such scrutiny. Most people were too intimidated to look him in the eye, let alone take the time to explore his face in detail.

"You aren't from an escort service, are you?"

"What?"

"My friends didn't hire you, did they?"

"I'm sorry, I don't know what you're talking about."

She nodded. "You're too handsome, for one thing. But more than that, you're too confident."

"Did I miss something?"

She smiled at him. "No. I did."

"Care to explain?"

She shook her head. Then she leaned forward, and slowly, very slowly, brought her lips to his. The kiss was so gentle, it was barely there at all. Just a whisper. But it still managed to knock him for a loop.

"What was that for?" he asked.

"That was for saying I was beautiful," she said, then she did it again. This time, the kiss was a bit more substantial.

"And that?" he murmured.

"Because you brought me here."

Once again, she leaned forward. This time, her lips lingered a moment, then two, before she broke it off. "That one was for joining me for dinner."

"I—"

She didn't let him finish. She closed her eyes and kissed him once more, but now there were no whispers. No delicate pressure from a poet. This time, she kissed him with a whole different kind of message. One he understood immediately.

His arms went around her back instinctively, pulling her close. The feel of her body pressed against his stirred him, and he wanted, no needed, to taste her fully. He parted his lips, and met no resistance. She was sweet and warm and moist, and her tongue explored his with matching intensity. He felt her arms go around his neck, and her head shifted a bit to the left, which made a perfect fit. He felt her muscles relax, her mouth become bolder. Then, she pulled back. She broke the kiss before he was ready, and he tried to hold her close, but her hands went to his chest and he let her go.

"What was that one for?" he asked, surprised at how low and gruff his voice sounded.

"That was because I wanted to," she said. "Now, I think we'd better go back."

He thought for a moment that she was asking him to take her back so they could pick up where she'd left off. But looking into her eyes, he knew that wasn't going to happen. She meant for him to take her back, and say goodbye.

"Are you sure?" he asked, reaching out with his hand to stroke her soft cheek.

She let him, but it didn't melt her resolve. "I'm sure."

"May I ask why?"

Her lips curled into a tiny smile. "No."

"May I guess?"

"If you want to."

"I think you're afraid, Emma. Afraid that I won't turn out to be a prince."

The color returned to her cheeks. He imagined that she would have that glow when they made love.

"I won't deny it," she said.

"You're right, of course. I'm no prince. I'm just a man." He moved his hand behind her head, and very gently pulled her closer. He kissed her then, still gentle. But she didn't have to tell him to stop. He was the one to pull back.

"What was that for?" she whispered.

"That was because I didn't expect you. Because I didn't expect this."

"I don't understand."

"I thought you'd be a diversion. Not a problem."

"A problem?" She stepped back a bit, just out of his reach, a smile playing about her lips. "I think I like that."

"Oh, really?"

She nodded. "I've never been anyone's problem before. Although I'm not so thrilled with being a diversion."

"We passed diversion way back at the restaurant."

She leaned against the pirate ship, and her dress pulled against her body. Her curves illustrated his point. She was a problem. He wasn't lying. He wanted her. Tonight. Now. But he wanted her in a way that put him at a disadvantage. That couldn't happen. "Come on," he said. "You're right. We should go back."

A flicker of disappointment crossed her face, but the smile didn't waver. "Right. Back to the real world."

He nodded, a little sadly. If things had been different, he would have liked to explore this world with her. Perhaps take her up into this pirate ship. Make love to her right under the eyes of Bacchus. But things weren't different. She was a means to an end. If he let his feelings get in the way, he could kiss Transco goodbye.

She walked next to him, taking one final look at all the floats as they headed for the door. Just before they went outside, she stopped, kissed his cheek, and said, "Thank you. It was the best present I've ever had."

That bothered him for the rest of the night.

EMMA AWOKE reluctantly. Her dreams had been filled with pirate ships and smiling gods. And Michael. He'd been almost as wonderful in her sleep as he had been in person. In some ways, better. No, she'd been better. She'd known what to say, how to act. She'd been as comfortable with Michael as she was with her business associates, and once her discomfort was gone, it had been easy to hear him say she was beautiful. That part of the dream stuck with her even after she got out of bed. The feeling of pleasure, instead of disbelief.

What was he doing right now? She turned on the shower and slipped off her nightgown. Was he awake? It was only seven. Of course he would be, she decided. A man like him wouldn't need much sleep. Perhaps, like her, he was climbing into the shower. Naked. Oh, my.

The warm water felt wonderful, and it was just the right pressure, too. Her shower at home was skimpy at best. She always felt as if she needed to run around in a circle to get wet. But this...this was luxury. She lathered up the washcloth and closed her eyes, letting herself enjoy the sensual feel of the rich soap on her skin. In a second, her thoughts turned once more to Michael, and they were definitely not G-rated.

She remembered his kiss, the taste of him as sharp and clear as if only a moment had passed, not a whole night. If only she could hold on to the memory, keep it this vivid. But that wouldn't happen. In time it would fade, become distant. More like something read in a book. Oh well. She could conjure it up now in exquisite detail. That would have to do.

Just to be a little daring she used the hotel shampoo instead of what she'd brought from home. It smelled delicious. When was the last time she'd changed shampoos? Or makeup? Or experimented with her hairstyle? Never, that's when.

She'd become an old woman. Not chronologically, but in her way of thinking. The girls had told her, but she hadn't listened. Of course, they had been a little obtuse. When Christie mentioned that Emma's makeup reminded her of a Seurat painting, it hadn't occurred to Emma that she meant it was a hundred years out of date.

When she got home, she was going to go for that makeover, dammit. Not because of Michael. Well, not just because of Michael. But because she'd had a taste of what it might be like to feel good about her looks, not just her research abilities. So what if there was no place in her life to meet men. She had to look at herself in the mirror every day, didn't she? Wasn't she worth feeling pretty?

She rinsed her hair, put on some conditioner, and for once, didn't even mind shaving her legs. Instead of the awful chore it usually was, she toyed with the idea of Michael touching her thigh. Her smooth thigh. She didn't nick herself, even once.

By the time she'd rinsed, stepped out of the shower, wrapped herself in the big fluffy hotel towel and gone to the closet to pick out something to wear, she'd decided that Michael or no Michael, she was going to have a magnificent day. A day so full of adventure, she'd never forget it.

MICHAEL WAS IN AND OUT of the shower in two minutes. While he shaved, he concentrated on nothing else. Just the razor. At least, that was his intention. But Emma intruded again.

He'd had a bad night. Which wasn't at all like him. He'd trained himself to get to sleep fast and hard.

That's why he didn't need as much sleep as other people. Four or five hours kept him feeling rested and healthy. It was simply a matter of turning his mind off. His secretary liked to call it a beta state of meditation, but he knew it was simply a matter of discipline. It didn't matter where he was, on an airplane, in a strange house, or even sitting up in some train station, he could be out in a flash. Except for last night.

Emma kept popping into his thoughts. Each time he forced her out, she came in another way. Sometimes it was her image. Another time, it was the sound of her voice, or the smell of her skin. She just wouldn't leave him alone.

By five-thirty, he'd figured out what he needed to do. Get his information, and get the hell out of Dodge. Get as far away from Emma and her distractions as he could.

He rinsed his face, then went back into his room to dress. Since he didn't know her well, he had no idea if she slept late or was an early riser. At first he'd assumed she'd sleep in; this was her vacation after all. But the more he thought about it, the more he was convinced she'd get up at her workweek hour. In either case, he was going to be in the lobby when she came down.

So it was settled. He put on his jeans and his Polo shirt, his shoes and socks, combed his hair, checked to make sure he had enough cash.

And thought about Emma.

WHERE THE HELL WAS SHE? Michael folded the newspaper he'd been trying to read for the last hour, and stood up. It was hard to maintain his nonchalance. He wanted her to think he just happened to be downstairs, just happened to be reading the paper, when she got off the elevator. But it was already seven, and no Emma. Maybe he should just call her, and invite her to breakfast. No, he'd already decided this was the plan, and he didn't like to deviate, even if it was inconvenient. He'd thought this through. She needed to be totally convinced that he had nothing on his mind but a relaxing day.

By the time he started asking her about Transco, she needed to be completely at ease. Not that he was going to ask her anything proprietary. He was more concerned with Phil Bailey and what he wanted. Emma would know. If he played his cards right, she would give him the formula that would convince Bailey to sell. Maybe he wanted to move to Hawaii. Or maybe he wanted to continue to be part of the research and development team. Michael had a feeling Bailey's biggest concern was his environmental work. Which could be dealt with. But Michael needed to know what Bailey's Achilles' heel was, and Emma was going to tell him. If she ever came down from her room.

He walked over to the gift shop window. From his position he could see the elevator doors, and he wouldn't look so damn conspicuous. Twice now, he'd gotten strange looks from bellmen.

The elevator dinged, and he held his breath. Emma walked out.

He turned, casually, and walked toward her. He didn't look at her again until he heard her say, "Michael!" Then he looked up.

Her smile knocked him out. She seemed so damn glad to see him. Her face lit up, her eyes shimmered. He couldn't help but smile back.

"What are you doing here?" she asked. "I thought you had to go back to Houston."

"I changed my plans."

"Oh? Did Bubba decide he liked the opera after all?"

Michael smiled briefly, then grew serious. "No. I stayed because of you, Emma."

Her easy grin froze, and her eyes widened. Lovely green eyes. Her hair was down again, too, which pleased him. Her jeans were faded, but fashionably so. They looked awfully good on her, as did the crisp blue blouse. Dammit, what was it about her that had him thinking like this?

"You don't mean it," Emma said. He could hear the hope in her voice.

"I certainly do. You, Miss Roberts, need a tour guide. I would like to apply for the position."

"You're hired," she said. Then she blushed.

He saw it start at her delicate neck and spread upward to infuse her cheeks with pink. It was going to be a good day. He took her hand in his, and mar-

veled again at her soft fragility. "Come on, Cinderella," he said. "Let's go find ourselves a pumpkin."

"Where are we going?" she asked, as he led her toward the street.

"Café du Monde of course. No trip to the Big Easy
would be complete without beignets and café au
lait."

"I've always wanted to go there."

"You let me know what you've always wanted,
Emma, and I'll make sure you have it."

She gave him a funny grin, but didn't say anything
more. He held the door open for her, and then followed her outside. Of course, his gaze moved south.
Yep, those jeans looked mighty good.

They passed on taking a carriage, and ended up
walking the dozen blocks to the open-air café at the
French Market. The lines were long, but that didn't
bother Michael. He really was enjoying himself. The
conversation was easy and light. She was excited
about visiting this landmark, and he saw it through
her eyes. With its tall pillars and green-and-white
striped awning, its shiny black ceiling fans whirring
above the sea of tables and chairs, it was to him the
very essence of New Orleans.

Full of delicious smells, laughing people, street
musicians just a step or two away, it made him feel at
home, even though he visited rarely. Seeing Emma's
delight made it all the sweeter.

Emma. Just like last night, he found her funny and
smart. It turned out to be easy to bring up Transco

and Phil Bailey, and by the time they'd found a table and were sipping the chicory coffee and eating the messy but delicious donuts, he had most of the information he needed. It was like shooting ducks in a barrel. Emma was open and honest, concerned about her boss, grateful, he thought, to be able to discuss her work with someone so sympathetic.

Another twenty minutes, and he knew how to strike, when to act, and what his bargaining chips were. Emma had given him all the ammunition he could have hoped for.

He excused himself for a moment and found a telephone. All during his conversation he kept thinking of Emma back at the table. When she found out, she was going to be devastated. She'd hate his guts. And he wouldn't blame her. The kindest thing he could do right now was leave. Tell her some emergency had come up, and he had to get back to Houston immediately.

But he couldn't. He finished the call and went back to her. For a long while he just sat there, listening to her talk and laugh. He wanted to spend the day with her. He wanted to show her New Orleans. He wanted to kiss her again.

"So what's next?" she asked, cocking her head slightly to the left.

He had to make up his mind. Now. Then he noticed she had a little speck of powdered sugar at the very edge of her mouth. He leaned forward and kissed that spot, tasting her sweetness. Then he leaned back to look in her eyes. Her pleasure gave him his answer. "This town is filled with magic, Emma. Let me show it to you."

4

EMMA RELAXED into Michael's arms. It was the best place she'd ever been, and she quietly sent pleas to whoever was in charge of street entertainers that the cellist on the corner would never stop playing. She knew the music, recognized the melancholy notes, but she couldn't recall the name of the piece. It didn't matter. Nothing mattered, except that she was here, Michael had his arm around her shoulder, and her head rested on his chest.

His scent filled her senses, forcing her to close her eyes. Indefinable, except for the hint of soap, the scent branded itself in her memory. Intoxicating, that's what he smelled like. Male and clean and rich and deep.

The morning had been ripe with new experiences. The city alone would have captivated her, but with Michael as her guide, each sight was even more special. Jackson Square, the French Quarter, the incredible hotels and quaint restaurants. The weekend would never be sufficient to see it all. On the other hand, she would be just as content to sit down in a back booth at Denny's for the rest of her stay, as long as Michael was there with her.

Her suspicions about him had vanished. He wasn't a paid escort, that much she'd determined when they'd talked this morning over coffee. His knowledge of the business world was born of experience. He knew a lot about oil exploration, which somehow didn't surprise her. It occurred to her that she still didn't know exactly what he did. She sighed. Maybe she'd ask. Later.

Right now, she had to concentrate on the way his hand, resting on her shoulder, rubbed back and forth, very gently.

"You about ready for the next stop?"

She looked up, seeing only his chin. Although she hated to move, she leaned back far enough so she could see his face. His smile did peculiar things to her stomach. Peculiar, nice things. "Sure," she said.

"Don't you want to know what the next stop is?"

She nodded, but there was no conviction in it.

He laughed. "Emma, what am I going to do with you?"

"Whatever you want," she said. Then she realized what she'd said and she winced. "Wait, that's not what it sounded like."

He shifted so that his other hand grasped her right shoulder, and he was looking at her straight on. "No?"

With those eyes staring at her, she couldn't lie. "Well..."

"That poses an interesting dilemma."

"It does?"

He nodded. "There are any number of things I'd like to do with you, Ms. Roberts."

"Oh, heavens."

"And then some."

She blinked, and then his lips turned up in a beguiling grin.

"Why do I feel like I've just stepped smack into the center of your web?" she asked.

"Hmmm. A spider, eh? Eight arms?"

"Legs, Michael. Legs."

"Oh, yeah. Forget it, then."

It was her turn to laugh. "Okay, so what is the next stop?"

He waggled his eyebrows. "Come with me."

Of course, she did. When his palm slipped over hers, she grasped it easily, as if their hands had always been meant to fit. Just walking down the street made her incredibly happy. One thing she noticed was how many people looked at them. Not just idle glances, but real looks, sometimes stares. The women were probably noticing how incredibly handsome Michael was, which made sense to her. But the men? Perhaps they were staring at Michael, too. New Orleans was a sophisticated city. The idea made her smile.

They turned corner after corner, going toward the outskirts of the Quarter. She was completely lost, but Michael seemed to know just which side street to take. The shops they passed all looked interesting to her, especially the costume shops and the little independent bookstores.

"Here we are."

She looked at the window display in front of her. There wasn't much there to clue her in to the type of shop it was, just a few books, and some New Age type crystals and such. Then she noticed the small wooden sign above the door. A voodoo shop! "You're kidding!"

Michael shook his head. "Nope. It's the real Mc-Coy."

"I've read about this stuff. About the plant extract in Haiti that paralyzes the victim so they appear dead, even when they're not. The doctors miss the faint heartbeat and bury the person, and when they come out of the stupor, they claw their way out of the grave. The real walking dead." She grabbed Michael around the neck and gave him a fierce hug. "This is so cool!"

"I had no idea you were going to like it this much," he said, grinning. "Maybe I shouldn't have brought you here. It might give you ideas."

She grinned right back. "Yeah. You'd better watch your step. I don't think you'd like being a zombie. They never get the best tables."

He wrapped his arms around her waist and brought her close. His laughter rumbled in his chest and she felt it all the way through her. Then he kissed her, long, slow and deep, and she knew right then that Michael Craig could have his way with her.

MICHAEL WATCHED EMMA. He watched as she crooked her head to the side to read the titles of the books in the cramped store. Funny how he'd known she'd like this place. He'd first been here three years ago, just for a few moments, at the request of his date. At the time, he'd thought the whole thing was silly, but now, through Emma's eyes, he saw the appeal. She was so eager to learn everything. To explore and feel and taste. He remembered a movie he'd seen once called *Awakenings*, with Robert De Niro and Robin Williams, in which De Niro awakened from a long state of disease-induced catatonia. How the character had seen life with a child's eye, a stranger's curiosity. That was how Emma looked at the potions and the books and the trinkets.

All he could think of was having that eager curiosity and excitement focused on him. In bed. Making love to Emma promised to be an experience he'd not soon forget. He had a distinct feeling she wasn't experienced. Not a virgin, he was pretty sure of that, but a novice. But oh, what a student she'd be. And how he wanted to be her teacher.

His conscience hadn't left him completely alone, although ever since he'd kissed the sugar from her lips this morning, there was really no choice in the matter. Emma would be his, and all he could hope for was that after it was all over, and she'd had a chance to see what he could do for the company, she'd forgive him and look back at today with affection. Hell, she was having a great time, she couldn't deny that. And things were only going to get better.

The hard part was holding back. Not jumping into a cab right now and racing to the hotel. He'd been in a constant state of arousal all day. Not the kind of arousal that had made him walk with his books in front of his lap back in junior high, but close. This was a little more subtle, and twice as maddening.

"Here," Emma said, holding out a little rag doll in one hand, a half dozen long hat pins in the other.

"What's this?" he asked, taking the voodoo doll from her.

"A present."

"Who's the victim?"

"I can't say for you, but I have quite a little list of folks who are suddenly going to get neck aches next week."

"Emma, I'm shocked."

She lifted her left brow. "Why?"

"You're so... I can't imagine you having any enemies."

"Sweet. You were going to say sweet, weren't you?"

"Yeah, I suppose I was."

"See that? If I didn't like you so much, that would have deserved a pin. Well, maybe not a pin. A little pinch."

"Why? What's wrong with being sweet?"

She sighed. "Nothing, I suppose. Unless that's all people see. I can be sweet, but that's not really me.

I'm a lot of other things, too. It's like being patted on the head."

"I see," he said. He did, too. Now that he thought about it, the term could be dismissive. "So, what would you like people to call you?"

"Ms. Roberts."

He smiled. "No, I mean an adjective. What would you like them to think about you?"

She was quiet for a moment. Staring at him, but not seeing him. "Funny," she said, her voice a lot quieter. "My first thought was that I wanted people to think I was smart. Then I changed my mind. But, now, no. I think I do want people to think I'm smart."

"Why not both?"

"Hm?"

"I said why not both? Smart *and* beautiful."

She blushed, confirming his guess. Now her gaze went down to the floor. "How did you know?"

"Because that's how I see you. Smart and beautiful. And sweet. So don't worry, Ms. Roberts. People aren't so narrow. Some are even pretty intuitive."

Emma reached up and touched him lightly on the cheek. Her wide eyes asked the question before she spoke. "Where in the world did you come from?"

He couldn't answer her. Instead, he pulled her tight to him, and kissed her. His arousal was no longer subtle.

SOMEHOW, THEY GOT BACK to the hotel. Emma wasn't sure how. They'd walked, but the streets had blended together. It could have been five blocks or fifty.

All she knew was that she was alone with the most exciting man she'd ever met, in his suite, sipping cognac, preparing to do something she'd never dreamed in a million years she would ever do. She was going to make love. To a man she barely knew. And she was going to relish every moment of it.

"Should I pour you another drink?" Michael asked as he walked to the couch with the bottle.

She shook her head. "No, thanks. I'm pretty tipsy now."

He crooked his brow. "Already?"

She nodded. "I'm not much of a drinker. Especially when it's the hard stuff."

He put the bottle on the coffee table and sat down next to her. Right next to her. Just like in the carriage ride last night, their bodies touching from shoulder to thigh. And just like last night, it took her breath away.

Michael stared at her, a small inscrutable smile on his lips. "Your face is wonderful," he said.

She felt her cheeks warm and she glanced away, but his fingers on her chin gently moved her head back until she was looking at him once more.

"Don't be embarrassed," he said, his voice so kind she knew he was speaking honestly. "I mean it. You're not hard to read, Ms. Roberts. Your eyes tell so much about you."

"What do they say now?" she asked, surprised at how bold and excited she felt.

He didn't answer for a moment. Then he leaned toward her, putting his lips gently on hers. He kissed her very lightly, then released the pressure, but he didn't pull away. Instead, he whispered, "They say yes." He moved that brief distance again, but this time, his kiss was anything but gentle.

She fell into his embrace, thrilled at his passion. Her body seemed electrified, as if his lips and hers together created something entirely new, alive, sizzling. She opened her mouth and when she tasted him, the sizzle skittered all the way through her.

This was so new, this kind of wanting. No one had told her it could be like this. She'd read about it, but always with an air of skepticism. Now she knew the fireworks they talked about were real.

He shifted on the couch, sliding his arm behind her, pulling her closer. Her hands cupped his face as she explored his taste and scent and feel. How had she gotten so lucky? She must have saved an orphanage in a past life or something. Nothing else could explain what she was doing in his arms.

She opened her eyes. To her surprise, his were open, too. He pulled slightly back, breaking the kiss. He swallowed, never moving his gaze from hers. "We can stop now, if you want," he said, his voice husky and low. "Because in another minute, I don't know if I'll be able to."

Taking in a deep breath, Emma moved her left

hand from his cheek and lowered it very slowly to his thigh. His gaze followed. She screwed up her courage and shifted her hand up and to the right. He clearly hadn't been kidding about his doubts. She felt him, thick and hard beneath her fingers. Moaning, he brought his hand to hers and pressed down as his gaze moved back up. "Are you sure?"

She nodded. "More than I've ever been about anything."

"Remember, Emma. I'm not a prince."

She closed her eyes and leaned forward. Just before her lips touched his, she whispered, "Oh, yes you are."

This time, it was her kiss. Her tongue darted into his mouth, tasting, licking. She felt a hunger so deep it could never be satisfied with just a kiss. When he broke away, she gasped. He rose to his feet, and held his arms out to her. Without a moment's hesitation, she went to him, and when he reached around and lifted her into his arms, she nearly expired from bliss.

He *was* a prince, if only for a day, and she was a princess. He carried her quickly, urgently, through the living room into his bedroom. She barely noticed the decor, except for the king-size bed. He laid her down gently, then stared at her for a long moment.

"What?" she asked, afraid that something was wrong.

"You're so beautiful."

"No," she said. "You are."

He sat down and brushed the side of her face with

the back of his hand. "Emma, what are you doing to me?"

"I don't know, but I think it's mutual."

He nodded. Then he leaned down and kissed her once on the lips. "I want you so much," he whispered. "But..."

"I want you," she said, not letting him finish. "Please."

"I can't promise you anything."

"I'm not asking for promises." She raised herself until she was on her knees next to him, never letting go of his gaze. Then she reached down and began to unbutton her blouse.

He never moved. He just watched her.

She'd never undressed like this in front of a man. Never so blatantly, with the lights on, on top of the covers. But she'd never felt this way with a man before. She wanted to do things with him she'd never dreamed of—well, that she'd never admitted she dreamed of. He was more a fantasy than a reality, and right now, she felt as if she were unreal, too. That this was a dream, a wish granted. She felt absolutely no shame, no hesitation.

The last button came undone, and she pulled her blouse off. His gaze shifted from her eyes to her breasts then back again. While he watched, she reached behind and undid the clasp of her bra. Slowly, teasing, she lowered the straps, then she took the bra away and dropped it over the side of the bed.

My God, here she was, half naked in front of him,

her nipples so tight she didn't have to look down to know they were erect. His hand came tentatively forward, almost as if he were afraid to touch her. Then she felt his palm on her right breast and she couldn't hold back her moan. She leaned forward, filling his hand.

His groan picked up where hers left off, and he moved closer to her on the bed. His other hand touched her, lightly playing over the sensitive flesh. He kissed her lips, then trailed down her cheek to her chin, to her neck, then her chest. She closed her eyes and arched her back as he reached her nipple. First, she felt his tongue, then the gentle suction of his mouth.

It was like nothing she'd ever felt before. Wanton and erotic beyond her imagination. She cupped the back of his head to keep him there, never wanting him to stop his ministrations. What was he doing to her? Such magical lips, such a talented tongue. She moaned and moved in an unconscious rhythm, pressing against him, and trying to ease the pressure between her legs.

When he broke away from her, her eyes flew open. Just in time to see him reach for the bottom of his T-shirt and pull it over his head.

She inhaled sharply at the sight of his chest. She'd only seen one other man who looked this good, and he'd been on television, so it didn't count. Michael was stunning. Broad muscled shoulders, pecs so firm she could bounce a quarter off them. Dark hair,

just thick enough to make him incredibly manly
without looking like a bear. His chest tapered to his
slim waist and as she watched, he undid his button-
fly jeans, his fingers fumbling in his haste. When he
stood to finish the job, she reached for her own jeans.
But she had to stop when he took his off. It was his
body. It stunned her, plain and simple. He was the
most gorgeous creature on the earth. Washboard
stomach, firm thighs, and...oh, my.

She swallowed. Then swallowed again. His erection required a moment of silence. Maybe two or
three.

He didn't let her look for long, though. Instead, he
came onto the bed, and helped her finish undressing.
She felt a moment of shyness, knowing she wasn't
half as beautiful as he was, hoping he wouldn't be
disappointed. But once she was naked, and he laid
her down on her back, her worry vanished. The way
he looked at her told her he was pleased. Pleased
and hungry.

"Oh, Emma. I had no idea."

"What?"

"You're exquisite."

"So are you."

He shook his head. "No. You don't understand."

"Tell me."

He reached out first, and ran his hand down her
stomach. She shivered at his featherlight touch. He
explored her slowly, touching her skin as if it were
the most delicate silk in the world. Closing her eyes,

she let the sensations take over. Each time his hand moved, her flesh caught fire. She felt his reverence, his appreciation, and for the first time in her life she felt beautiful. Really beautiful. It was his touch. And the sound of his breathing. The sigh that escaped as his palm lingered on her thigh.

Then she felt his lips replace his hand.

Emma spread her legs. She did so unconsciously, easily, as if it were the most natural thing in the world to reveal her most private self to this man. She opened her eyes briefly, and watched him move on the bed so that his body was no longer at an angle, but in line with hers. His smile when he caught her looking was half wicked, half dreamy, and then she couldn't see his smile anymore. His mouth was better occupied.

She gasped at his first touch. She had never been this sensitive, this ready. He used his fingers and his lips and his tongue to send her into a spiral of desire and heat. Her hands grabbed the bedspread, and then she was able to rock slightly, matching his rhythms. It was impossible to be silent. As her breathing deepened, she moaned long and low, the fire in her belly expanding until she was engulfed in flames.

She heard another sound. It was Michael, and he, too, was moaning his pleasure. It was almost too much for her to believe. How could gratifying her give him the kind of satisfaction she heard? But she couldn't think about that now, not when she was going crazy. Not when he did that right there.

Her head thrashed on the pillow, and all the muscles in her body tightened like bowstrings. Her pelvis lifted from the bed, and Michael rose with her. He never let up, not for a second, and then she was gone. Electrical spasms coursed through her body, one after the other, and she heard her voice, so loud, yet so far away, saying his name over and over.

He released her, and she collapsed, but in another second, he moved up, so he was poised on top of her. After a moment's pause, and the sound of tearing foil, his knees pushed hers apart. He found her gaze, locked on to her, and then, in one unbelievably intense motion, he thrust into her.

The spasms continued as he filled her so completely she felt as if she'd been made whole for the first time. Looking up at him, she felt awed that his need was so clear on his face. The desire, desire for *her*, shone in his eyes.

"Emma," he whispered. "What are you doing to me? I can't...."

Her arms went to his waist and her hips bucked in a dance she didn't know she knew. Gasping for air, she wrapped her legs around him so he could enter her farther. It was more than she could stand, and the spasms started again. Rich, deep, all the way to her soul, they rocked her and sent her mind adrift so that all that existed were sensations.

"I can't hold on," he said, his voice shaking. His

jaw muscles tensed, and she could see the cords in his neck. He looked as if he were in pain, the pressure was so great, and then he filled her to the brink, and he growled an animal growl that rumbled through his chest to hers.

Finally, he relaxed. Uncurling her legs, they settled into a new position, still joined, but touching in a different way. She could feel his rapid breathing, and knew hers was just as fast. He'd wrung her out like a rag, and all that was left of her were the echoes of her climax.

"Wow," she said.

He laughed, and she felt that, too. "You can say that again."

"I had no idea."

"Hm?" He shifted a bit, and for a second she thought he was going to move away, but he didn't. He just got more comfortable.

"I mean," she said, "that I've never had that happen before."

"What?"

"You know."

"No. Tell me."

She met his gaze to see if he was teasing her. He was. She pinched him lightly.

"Hey!"

"You deserved that."

"Why won't you tell me? Surely you can't still be shy. Not after what we just did."

"I am shy. I can't help it."

He lifted himself up on one elbow and looked at her sternly. "You are many things, Emma, but you're not shy. You can't fool me." He leaned down and kissed her, then he smiled. "You, my little one, are a wild woman."

"I'm not."

"Then who did I just have my way with?"

She giggled. "All right. So sometimes I can get a little carried away."

"Ha! If we'd gone on any longer, they would have had to carry me away on a stretcher."

"I bet you say that to all the girls."

His expression changed then. He grew serious, and somehow, darker. "No. Don't you dare think that. Ever."

She nodded, a sudden tightness filling her chest. "All right. I won't."

Then, as if a switch had turned on, his humor was back. "I hate to do this. I really do. But I have to move."

She sighed dramatically. "All right. If you must."

He kissed her quickly, then he did move, and she wanted him back immediately. But that wasn't going to happen. He wasn't hers, and she'd best remember that. This was a once-in-a-lifetime experience. He'd made it something she'd never forget.

Michael went into the bathroom and closed the door. While he took care of business, he tried to get control of himself. The guilt he felt was completely out of proportion to the deed. He'd given Emma several opportunities to back out, and she hadn't. On the contrary. She'd been more than willing. What had really caught him off guard was his own reaction to making love with her.

In all the years he'd been with women, nothing like that had happened to him before. Not the act of course, but the feelings that had come with it. It wasn't like him. Sure he enjoyed sex, but there had always been a small part of himself he held back. It was only prudent. He couldn't afford to let go completely. Yet that's just what he'd done with Emma. He'd never felt more exposed, more vulnerable, than when he'd been inside her.

The hell of it was that he wanted to go right back. One time wasn't enough. He had the sinking feeling that a hundred, a thousand times, wouldn't be. But that's all he was going to get. One time.

Come Monday morning, Emma Roberts was going to hate him. Sure, it would pass eventually, but while it lasted, it wasn't going to be pretty. Yesterday, that fact hadn't bothered him. Today, it mattered a lot. Too much. And that wasn't good.

It was time to let her go. To send her off, and forget her. He was a ruthless bastard, and now he was going to prove it.

5

EMMA BLINKED AWAKE. It was her first morning back in her own bed, and for a second she felt a little disoriented. Probably because of her dreams. *Michael.* He'd lived in her head now for three days. She had gone over every moment they'd spent together, flushing with heat when she got to Saturday night. There was even the bittersweet memory of their goodbye. He'd been perfect, said the right words, kissed her so tenderly. It had been hard not to ask if she could see him again, but she hadn't. She didn't want the cold hard truth to tarnish one second of her fairy-tale weekend.

But now she was back in the real world, and it was time to take off her glass slippers and put on her sensible shoes. All she had to do was get through the day. Then she could come back home, make an excuse to go to bed early, and she could meet him once more in her dreams. He would never change. He would never disappoint her. It would always and forever be the most perfect of weekends with the most perfect of men. No one could take that away from her.

Somehow, she managed to get up. As she got

ready, she realized nothing would ever be the same again. The simple act of washing her hair was different because his hands had done the task on Sunday morning. Lathering her body with soap was now a sensual act, instead of a brisk but necessary procedure. Drying her body made her aware of every place he'd touched and kissed. He'd altered the very fabric of her world, and she'd never see him again. But it was too late for regrets now. She'd have to be satisfied with having known him once.

"YOU'RE BACK!"

Emma smiled. It was good to see her friends. They all certainly seemed glad to see her, too. You'd think she'd been gone for a year, instead of a long weekend. Christie, Margaret and Jane. Her very own Three Musketeers. The best damn research team in the business, and so much more.

They ushered her into their spacious office. Their computers were all booted up and running. Usually, Emma was the first to arrive in the morning, but today, everyone had been here to greet her.

"Tell us everything," Margaret said, ushering Emma over to the couch. "Every detail."

"Wait till you hear what's been happening here," Christie said excitedly. "You won't believe it."

"You want coffee or tea?" Jane asked as she poured herself a cup of decaf.

Emma laughed. They'd all spoken at once, and she didn't know where to start. No, wait. She did. "Coffee, thanks." She could use another cup. It promised to be an interesting morning.

She took the cup from Jane, and waited until she'd gotten comfortable before she turned to Christie. "What do you mean? What's happened?"

Christie looked from Margaret to Jane, then settled her gaze on Emma. She waited just long enough, then said, "He's selling the company."

"What?" Emma put her cup down. "Who?"

"Phil, of course. Who do you think?"

"But when?"

"It started last night."

"On a Sunday?"

Jane nodded. "I found out because he called me."

"Why?"

"He needed some numbers. That's when he told me he'd been handed an offer."

"That's it? He was handed an offer and he took it, just like that?"

Margaret nodded. That was it, then. Margaret never guessed. She knew. At forty-five, she was the eldest of the group, and like a big sister, or a mother hen, she took great care of them all. Her advice was always thoughtful, her cautions legendary, and her heart as big as Texas. She even looked the part. Large in body, and in spirit, she wore her naturally graying hair in a conservative page boy. She dressed simply, but with a sense of style that was clearly her own.

Interestingly enough, Margaret and Christie, six years her junior and anything but conservative, were as close as they could be. Perhaps it was because Christie had lost her mother so young. And it didn't hurt that Margaret encouraged Christie to be herself, which included an eclectic taste in clothing; today she wore a short black mini skirt and a man's white shirt, which somehow managed to look great on her.

Jane, on the other hand, was more Laura Ashley than Todd Oldham. Almost six feet tall, Emma always envied her sense of grace. She was a beautiful, wonderful woman, and luckily, her husband Elliott treasured her.

Now all three of her dear friends were staring at her, watching for her reaction to this stunning news. They'd been a team for so long, what would they do if the new owners decided to make a change? It was too horrible to contemplate.

"Did Phil say who made the offer?"

"A company called MRC," Jane said. "We were going to look it up this morning, but we haven't had a chance yet."

"I've never heard of it," Margaret said. "That doesn't bode well."

"Maybe they'll keep Phil on to run things," Christie suggested. "Or you could talk him out of it. He'll listen to you, Emma."

Emma shook her head. She'd known for a long while that Phil wanted out. Africa and his safaris called to him. His photography had been his primary interest since she'd known him. This was just what he had been waiting for. However, she knew he cared a great deal about the company, and his employees. Surely he would see to it that everyone was provided for. "I'll go talk to him," she said, "but I doubt I can make him change his mind."

"You can't go yet," Jane said. "You didn't tell us about this weekend."

She felt an unbidden smile, completely uncalled for given the topic of conversation, spread over her face. Just the thought of Michael, and her special time with him, turned on the glow inside her.

"Wow," Christie said. "You aren't going anywhere till you explain that."

"I'll say," Jane piped in. "I need a fresh cup of coffee for this, I can tell."

Emma felt her cheeks warm. She'd toyed with the idea of keeping the weekend and Michael to herself. But that wasn't likely. These women were her best friends. They could read her like a book. Whether she wanted to tell them or not, they'd get it out of her. Of course, she wouldn't tell them *everything*.

"Go on," Margaret said, leaning forward in the big club chair. "We don't have all day."

Emma smiled again. "I met someone."

Her three cohorts exchanged surprised looks.

"Hey, it's possible."

"Of course it is. You're gorgeous and funny and brilliant." Jane gave her a playful swat on the leg. "You're the one who's been going for the world celibacy record. Which, I hope, is now out of the question."

"Jane!" Emma blushed fiercely.

Jane leaned back. "Thank God. Now, details."

"Just for that, I shouldn't tell you anything."

"But you will."

Emma sighed. It was true. Honestly, she could barely contain herself. If she didn't tell them soon, she felt like she'd burst. "His name is Michael."

"Michael what?"

"Craig. I met him that first night. He recognized me from my picture in the *Chronicle*. We had dinner together."

"That was quick," Margaret said.

"I know. Then he took me to see the floats from the Mardi Gras parade. In a carriage. And we kissed."

"Holy cow," Christie said. "What's he look like?"

Emma sighed again. "Only the most gorgeous man on three continents. Tall, dark, handsome. And his chest. My God."

"His chest?" All three women said it in unison.

"Yeah. His chest." Emma grinned.

For the first time ever, she'd shocked her team into silence. That tickled her.

"I hope this means you're engaged," Margaret said finally.

Emma laughed. "Nope. I'm never going to see him again."

"What? Where is he from?" Jane asked. "Who is he?"

"He's from right here in Houston. But I don't know that much more about him. He's a businessman. Smart. Stunning. The most elegant man I've ever met. It was just, I don't know, magic. A dream. A fairy tale. A once in a lifetime."

Margaret reached over and took Emma's hand. "I'm happy for you—if you're happy?"

Emma nodded. "I know, it's not like me. Not cautious, shy, workaholic me. But I tell you, Margaret, I felt like an honest-to-goodness princess this weekend, and I wouldn't change that for the world."

"Good." The older woman leaned back. "Maybe this will convince you that there's really no need to live like a nun."

Emma picked up her cup and sipped some coffee. "I don't know about that. But it sure is going to be a nice memory."

"Memory, shmemory," Jane said. "I say we find him."

Christie nodded. "Yeah. Why not? I'd bet he'd love to see you again, Em."

"He knows how to find me if he wants to," she said. "But he won't. It's okay. Honest."

Christie and Jane gave each other a look.

"Uh-uh, you guys," Emma said. "No sneaking into the computers. We've got other things to concentrate on. Like the new owners." With that, she stood. "I'm going to see Phil."

"Okay," Jane said, "but we want details when you get back."

Emma nodded. "Wish me luck."

EMMA STRAIGHTENED her skirt and checked her panty hose before she knocked on Phil Bailey's door. His "Come in," was immediate. Ellen, his secretary, had already buzzed ahead.

Emma walked into his office. The large room was an African museum. Pictures and artifacts lined the walls. Maps, only barely conceding the real business of Transco, got one small corner, and that was out of Phil's line of sight. His massive teak desk was neat, but that was only because it was early in the day. By the time Phil left, papers would be strewn everywhere. It was Ellen's lot in life to trail after her boss and keep him out of trouble. Emma wondered if he'd take Ellen with him when he left the company.

"Welcome home," Phil said.

She smiled. "It was a great trip. Thanks. But I understand you've had an interesting weekend yourself." She went over to the leather wing chair in front of his desk and sat down. It was a comfortable chair, and she was at ease. Phil was more than a boss. He was a friend.

She had to admit, he was the one who looked out of place here. Tall, lean, unkempt blond hair, and crooked wire-rimmed glasses had always made her think of him more as a professor than a CEO. He wore suits only when he was going to meet someone from out of the office. Most times, he was in khakis or jeans. Today, he was in his Brooks Brothers.

"Yep," he said. "But don't you worry. You're taken care of."

She tensed. "Taken care of? Does this mean it's a done deal?"

"As soon as I sign on the dotted line. Which should be in about ten minutes."

"But who is this company? What about my team? Are there going to be layoffs?"

He leaned forward and picked up a pen, not to write anything, just to keep his hands occupied. It was a habit of his, and it always told her when he was nervous.

"Your team is safe. You guys are a big part of this company, and frankly, you increased the value. So don't worry."

"What about..."

"There might be some layoffs. But I don't think so. At least not right away. But MRC does things a little differently than I do. They're a big company, and they're going to want to bring in some of their own people."

Emma sat silently for a moment, trying to digest the finality of the decision. She'd worked at Transco for five years. It seemed impossible that things were going to change so drastically.

"Phil, are you happy with your choice?" she asked him.

He looked her in the eyes. "Yeah. It was long past due. No one had offered the right package before. But this time, boy, they nailed every detail. They really did their homework. The kicker was the environmental impact research. I'd never have let it go if they hadn't agreed to keep that intact. With some minor modifications, they are." He crooked his head to the side and stilled his pen. "And they knew about you, too. Your reputation precedes you."

"My reputation? I don't understand."

"You were part of the package, Emma. Without you, there wouldn't have been a deal."

That puzzled her. There wasn't any reason for that. Researchers weren't that uncommon. She liked to pride herself on her job, but really, there was no cause to even mention her in this kind of deal.

The intercom buzzed and Phil picked up the line. "Have him come in," he said, after a moment. He hung up and turned to Emma. "Want to meet your new boss?"

She nodded, and stood. Her stomach tightened. She couldn't help it. This man would have a big impact on her life from now on. She hoped against hope that she'd like him. Of course, he couldn't be another Phil, but maybe he'd be nice in his own way.

The door opened as she turned. At first, all she saw was Ellen. Then he walked in.

And her heart nearly leapt out of her chest.

6

EMMA GRIPPED the back of the chair. She couldn't believe what her eyes were telling her. He was here! He'd come for her! She hadn't known how badly she'd wanted this until she'd turned to see Michael standing at the door.

She started toward him, her heart fairly bursting with happiness. "How did you...?" Something made her step falter. Her question died on her lips. It was his eyes.

They weren't happy or excited. They were cool, guarded. Embarrassed.

She looked from Michael to Phil. Then she got it. A thick lump cramped her stomach and it was all she could do not to fall.

Michael wasn't here to sweep her off to a magic castle. Michael was here because he was the new owner of Transco Oil.

Everything had been a lie. He'd tricked her, seduced her, made love to her, and it was all a lie.

The reality came crashing in around her like a load of bricks.

She'd betrayed the company, sold out her friends, stabbed everyone she cared for in the back. Her stomach clenched again and for a moment, she felt dizzy.

She'd been wrong about him looking guilty. Not a hair was out of place, not a worry line to be seen on his face. Oh, sure, he looked concerned, but she knew what kind of an actor he was. This role should get him an Academy Award. Of course, having a vulnerable stooge like her must have made his job pretty simple.

She couldn't look at him. Not when everything was so raw and real. Not when she could remember so clearly everything he'd done to her, and she'd done to him. She headed for the door, wishing he'd just move so she didn't even have to brush his shoulder.

Instead, he took hold of her arm, stopping her just before she hit the door.

"Wait, please, Emma."

"You two know each other?"

Emma heard Phil speak, but she didn't look back. Jerking herself out of Michael's grasp, she met his gaze. It was a dreadful mistake. For one second she almost believed he felt badly about what he'd done. But what did she know? She'd believed him when he'd said she was beautiful.

She felt hot tears in her eyes and made a run for it. Thankfully, Michael didn't try to stop her again. As quickly as she could, she headed for the ladies' room. Thank goodness it was empty, and she locked herself into a stall and sat down.

The tears came immediately. They burned her eyes, seared her cheeks. The humiliation filled her chest and her heart and she wondered if she was going to throw up. That passed, but it was no kindness. Now she was free to concentrate on what she'd done.

It was her information, she felt sure, that had enabled Michael to make the kind of offer Phil couldn't turn down. She racked her brains, trying to think what it was that had tipped the scales. Talking about how Phil wanted to go to Africa? The emphasis on global protection the company held? Or perhaps it was something less obvious. Something a woman who didn't have stars in her eyes would have seen immediately.

Why? Why had she listened? Why hadn't she trusted her first instincts and told him she wanted to dine alone? And why, dear God, why had she decided to go to bed with him? Her once-in-a-lifetime adventure had turned into a never-to-be-forgotten nightmare. Other women slept around with lots of men. She'd done it once. And this was her punishment.

"Emma?"

Emma heard the door swing closed as Margaret walked into the rest room. She willed her friend to go away, or for the earth to simply open up and swallow her whole. How could she tell Margaret, or Jane or Christie what she'd done? They'd hate her. She already hated herself, why not make it a quartet?

"Hon? What's going on? Ellen just called me. She

said you knew the man who bought the company. That you ran out of Phil's office like you were on fire."

Emma sniffled. She couldn't speak, not yet.

"Em? Are you crying?"

Emma nodded. "Please, Margaret. I can't talk yet."

There was a long stretch of silence. Then Emma heard the door open again.

"What's going on?" Christie asked.

"Is she okay?"

So Jane was here, too. Great.

"She's crying," Margaret whispered, as if Emma weren't three feet away.

"You're kidding? What happened?" Christie knocked on the stall door. "You okay? Want me to get you some water or something? Call a doctor?"

"No," Emma said. "I just want to sit here and cry for a while, is that okay?"

"No, it most certainly is not," Margaret said, adding her fists to the banging on the door. "You come out here right this second and tell us what in blazes is going on. Who is that man?"

Emma dabbed her eyes with toilet paper, and stood up. It was no use. They wouldn't leave her be. She'd have to tell them sometime, so it might as well be now. She opened the door slowly, and saw the three of them standing, waiting, all of them looking concerned.

Once they heard what she had to say, that concern would turn to disbelief. Then to anger. Then worse.

"Come on, Em. Spill." Christie tried to smile at her, but it was a feeble attempt.

Emma steeled herself. Whatever their reaction, she deserved it. She deserved it all. "The man who bought the company is the man I was with this weekend," she said, amazed that her voice didn't crack, and that she didn't fall into a million pieces on the floor. "I'm responsible for the company being sold. I talked. A lot. About Phil, about Transco. I'm sure something I said made the difference."

Margaret, Jane and Christie exchanged confused looks.

"He's the guy you...?"

Emma nodded at Christie's polite query.

"Holy cow."

Margaret walked over to Emma and put her arm around her shoulder. Emma almost shook her off. She wasn't entitled to the comfort. "Now, listen. No matter what you said, you aren't responsible for the company being sold. Phil is the only one who could do that. He's the guy that owns the place, not you."

"But I gave Michael the ammunition, don't you see? If I hadn't shot my big mouth off, he wouldn't have been able to carry this off."

"How do you know?" Jane asked. "This might all just be some coincidence. Maybe he did just see you there, by accident."

Emma laughed. "If you knew Michael, you'd

know that couldn't be true. He planned it all. He..."
She lost it for a moment, and it was Margaret's firm
hold that kept her upright. "He lied to me. But I believed him. I believed every little word. Oh, God, I
slept with him. Do you understand? I went to bed
with him! Me! The nun of Transco."

"Honey, you quit worrying about that. You followed your heart, just like always. There was no way
you could have known he would end up here."

"Oh, Margaret, that's not it. You can't put the
blame elsewhere. I walked into his arms with my
eyes wide open. I threw myself at him, for heaven's
sake."

"So, was he good?"

Everyone stopped and looked at Jane. Then Christie laughed. Margaret's arm shook Emma until she,
too, couldn't hold back. She laughed, and for that she
was grateful.

"Well?"

"He was unbelievable. And the worst part is that
he made me feel...I don't know. He made me feel
beautiful. I thought...just for a minute there, that
someone like him could really..." She couldn't go on.
Her throat clenched up tight and she blinked furiously, trying to hold back fresh tears. It didn't work.

"Well, I think he's an out-and-out bastard," Christie said. "How dare he take advantage of you?"

"He didn't have to work very hard at it," Emma
said, after she'd wrestled back some control. She
looked at her cohorts, each one such a dear friend it

made her ache all over again. "I'm going to miss you guys."

"Where are you going?" Margaret took her arm away, but only so she could meet Emma's gaze.

"I'm resigning, of course."

"Don't be a jerk."

"Thanks, Margaret. That makes me feel all better."

"I mean it. There's no reason for you to quit. You're the best thing about this company. You can bet the bastard knows it, too. Hell, he probably decided to buy the company because he'd get you in the bargain."

"Yeah, right. And you expect me to just carry on as if none of this happened?"

Margaret shook her head. "Honey, I expect you to get even."

"What do you mean?"

"She means," Christie said, nodding, "that you have to stay here. And you have to pay that SOB back."

"How am I supposed to do that?"

"I know," Jane said.

They all looked at her as she leaned oh so casually against the long sink.

"You're going to bring him to his knees, that's how. Make him fall head over heels in love with you, and then you get to dump him straight on his rosy behind."

"Me and what supermodel? Have you guys seen him? Have you seen me?"

All three women gave her a dirty look.

"He's so out of my league, I can't even sit in the cheap seats. I could never get him to fall in love with me. I couldn't even begin."

"Want to bet?"

It was Christie's turn to look smug.

"I don't like that tone of voice," Emma said. "It always leads to trouble."

"Trouble is just what we're looking for, darlin'. You just put yourself in my hands. And watch out Michael. He won't know what hit him."

"You guys are insane, you know that?"

All three women nodded. Despite her absolute knowledge that whatever they were planning wouldn't work, she felt a little sorry for Michael. When the Three Musketeers wanted revenge, they got revenge.

MICHAEL TRIED to concentrate on what Phil Bailey was saying. It was about important, bottom-line figures. But all he could think of was Emma.

The look on her face when she'd seen him was pure devastation. He'd known it was going to be bad, but he hadn't known how bad. And he certainly hadn't realized he was going to feel so guilty. Guilt was a commodity he didn't trade in. It was for suckers and wimps, and he'd exorcised the emotion long ago. Until Emma. Now it was back in spades, and he didn't like it one bit.

He needed to talk to her. But what was he going to

say? A lie formed, ready and available. He could tell
her it was all a coincidence, that he'd already made
the offer to Transco before they'd met. No, she'd see
through it. She was clever and intuitive, which was a
large part of the problem.

Especially since he'd decided that he wanted to
see Emma again socially. More than socially. Intimately. Something had happened to him over the
weekend that he couldn't explain. All he knew was
that Emma hadn't left his thoughts. He kept remembering things about her, like the way her skin felt,
how she smelled like flowers, the abandon in her
voice when they were in bed.

The odds of a repeat performance didn't look
good, though. Not after he'd seen her face. But long
odds had never stopped him before. With time and
patience, he could have her back. All he had to do
was figure out how.

"Michael?"

He looked up at Phil. "Yes?"

"Do you need a pen?"

Michael shook his head. "I've got one," he said,
and he took his Mont Blanc pen out of his coat
pocket. He always signed his deals with this baby. So
what if it was a silly superstition. It hadn't done him
wrong yet.

He bent to the paper and did a quick scan for any
changes in the letter of intent. There were none,
which was as it should be. His attorneys and Phil's
attorneys had been working nonstop to put this deal

together in record time. He would have known this morning if something had gone awry. He wrote his name—only halfway through his signature, the ink in his pen stopped. He tried pressing it harder, but it was no use. It was dry.

Phil handed him his pen, and Michael finished signing, even though a small voice in the back of his head sent warning signals. It was just a pen, just some ink, but what a time to quit on him. Just when he needed all the luck he could muster.

Phil stood and held out his hand the second Michael looked up. "I meant it about the people, Craig," he said. "I've gathered some of the best in the business. It would be foolish not to take advantage of that."

Michael took the man's hand and shook it. "I'm well aware of the caliber of employees here. That's one of the reasons I came to you."

"Good. Then we understand one another."

Michael nodded. "I'd like to walk around a little, get the lay of the land."

"I'll take you."

"No, that's okay. I'm sure you have plenty to do. I'll find what I'm looking for." He took his copies of the contract and put them in his briefcase. "I'll leave this here for now, if I may?"

Phil nodded. "Be my guest."

Michael turned to the door. Just as he walked out, Phil said, "It's down the hall, to the right, then room 114."

Michael didn't stop, didn't acknowledge the words. But now he knew how to get to Emma's office.

EMMA COULDN'T CONCENTRATE. Not when she kept hearing what her friends were up to. Christie was on the phone with the beauty shop. That makeover they'd tried to talk her into was now being scheduled for tomorrow. For once, Emma was going to miss a day at work. A whole day. Maybe, Jane had threatened, two. Because after she was finished with the beauty salon, she was going to see a personal shopper at Dillard's. Although she couldn't afford a whole new wardrobe, she had set aside some money for clothes. Actually, that money had been sitting there for over a year.

She heard Jane talking to the shopper, and the words *sexy*, *hot* and *tight* kept coming up. It was ridiculous, really. Her—sexy, hot and tight? No way. Not with her slender build, B-cup breasts and aversion to high heels.

But the girls had made her promise. What could she have done? There was no choice. She'd betrayed them badly, and all they were asking in return was this flight of nonsense. So she'd agreed.

Margaret wasn't sitting idly by, either. She was on her computer, doing research. Not oil company research. Michael Craig was her target. She was going to find out everything she could about the man.

Knowing Margaret, she'd know his blood type in a matter of hours.

By the time Emma had finished her transformation, Margaret, Christie and Jane would have his dossier finished. There simply were no better researchers in the business, so Emma knew it would be complete. She'd bet a week's pay that they would know not just about his financial status, his car and his house, but about his love life up to and including this past weekend.

They called it ammunition. She didn't know what to call it, except folly. But once they met him, they'd see that for themselves. Then perhaps they could forget about all this and get back to work.

Suddenly, the room grew quiet. Emma looked back over her shoulder and saw that all three women were staring at the door. She followed their gazes. He was there.

"Good morning," he said, his voice cool and firm. "I'm Michael Craig."

Margaret stood up. "What can we do for you, Mr. Craig?" she said, her tone so brittle Emma could practically see the words crackle.

"I wanted to introduce myself, and if I may, have a word with Emma."

He looked at her then, but she couldn't meet his gaze. Her face flushed, and it was too easy to recall the blushes he'd inspired over the weekend. Why didn't he just leave?

"I'm Margaret Castle. This is Christie Perkins and Jane Folley."

Michael walked into the room, and held out his hand to Margaret. She stared at it as if he would give her cooties. Finally, she took it, but just for a second.

He greeted Jane and Christie, too. When that was done, he said, "First, I want you to know that you'll always have a place here. I have no intention of downsizing this department. My people assure me we couldn't do better than you four."

Margaret humphed. But Emma was looking at Christie. She was giving Michael a thorough once-over. Really thorough. Good. By the time he left, everything would be settled.

"Now, I was wondering if I might have a moment?"

Margaret, Christie and Jane all looked at her. She gave a small nod, and the three of them filed out of the room. The looks they gave Michael should have scorched his coat, but he didn't seem to notice. He was too busy looking at her.

They were alone, and Emma's heart thudded in her chest. She still couldn't look at him.

"Emma?"

"What?"

"I want to explain."

Now she did look up. That practiced look of concern, of guilt, was on his face. She wasn't buying it. "What's to explain? Everything seems awfully clear to me."

He approached her, but she scooted farther back in her chair. Taking the hint, he stopped. "It's not what you think."

"No? You didn't purposely introduce yourself to me the other night? You didn't hide the fact that you were trying to buy Transco? You didn't get me to talk about the company so you could put all your ducks in a row?"

He opened his mouth to say something, then closed it again. She saw his chest expand with a deep breath, then he let the air out slowly. "No, that's all true. But that's not all there is."

"I know. I left out the part where I get screwed."

He winced. "You don't understand."

"Sure I do. I may be naive, but I'm not stupid."

"No. I didn't sleep with you because of the deal, Emma."

"Right. You were overcome with lust. I understand."

"Why is that out of the question?"

Her face was still warm, but now more with anger than embarrassment. "Oh, please." She stood up and grabbed her purse from under her desk. "I can see this isn't going to work. I'll have my resignation on your desk first thing tomorrow morning."

When she turned back, he was right next to her. He grabbed her shoulders firmly, and looked her square in the eyes. "Don't. I don't want you to quit. I came in here to tell you I'm giving you a raise. I need you here."

"Oh, that's lovely. A raise? So what does that make me? A company hooker?"

He clenched his teeth and she had to look away. Standing this close to him, she caught his scent. Despite her rage, it softened her insides. His touch burned her, his gaze taunted. There was no way she could work with him, or ever see him again. Not when she felt like this even after she knew the truth.

"You and I had something special, Emma. It had nothing to do with Transco."

"Let me go, please, Mr. Craig."

"No."

"I'm afraid I insist." For a split second, she thought he was going to kiss her. It was absurd, given the circumstances, but there it was. He leaned forward slightly, his lips parted. But that didn't happen. Instead, he let her go. She still felt the imprints of his hands on her flesh.

"I wish you'd reconsider. I know what an asset you are to this company, and I'd like you to stay. I won't bother you. I give you my word on that."

"Your word? Gee, that's comforting."

She walked past him, and didn't stop even when she heard him whisper, "I'm sorry."

7

IT HAD TAKEN THEM until eleven forty-five last night, but Margaret, Christie and Jane had convinced Emma to go along with their plan. As Jane said, "Don't get mad, get even." Frankly, Emma hadn't given in for any such noble concepts. She just figured that two days of shopping and primping would give her time to calm down and think rationally, which she couldn't do at home with her mother looking grave and concerned.

She also had to consider the money. She made a very handsome salary at Transco, and she was pretty sure that she wouldn't be able to meet it if she found a job elsewhere. If it had only been her, she wouldn't have hesitated, but she kept up the house, helped her mother, and of course there was her sister Karen's college tuition.

Although she didn't tell the girls, Emma wasn't going to stay at Transco. She couldn't. It would kill her. But she also wasn't going to be rash. Once she returned to work, she'd start sending out résumés. No sense putting everyone in jeopardy because of her pride. All she could do was pray that she'd find a new position quickly.

Now, as she hung her towel to dry on the shower rod, she took a moment to study herself in the mirror. After today, she wasn't going to look like herself. At least that was her hope. She wished she had time for plastic surgery. She'd like to look different, feel different, *be* different. Anyone but her. Anyone without her memories.

She thought of Michael, and turned from the mirror. Images and snippets of conversation from the weekend had intruded at regular intervals, disturbing in their clarity. But hadn't she set herself up for that? She'd *wanted* to remember everything, hadn't she?

He'd even come to her in her sleep, and that had been the most disturbing thing of all. Because she'd welcomed him. She'd opened her arms and her legs to him. She'd made love with him, and in her dream she had given him everything once more. What did that say about her? Nothing good, she was certain.

She managed to get through her morning rituals, which went quickly as she wasn't supposed to wear any makeup. It felt odd that it was nearly ten and she wasn't at work. Old habits were hard to break. But, according to Jane, she was about to transform from a rather average, kind of skinny, nothing special girl into Mata Hari and Kim Basinger all wrapped up in one. Ha. Not a chance in hell.

MICHAEL HUNG UP the phone and looked at his new office. It was bare now. Phil had taken his African knickknacks and his photos the day before, leaving only the Transco map and the basic furniture. Michael's interior designer was due in a few hours, and she would have it put together in no time. Thank goodness he didn't have to think much about that. Doris had worked for him for the past four years, and she knew his taste, and more importantly, that he didn't want to be bothered about anything but the art.

He reached for his coffee cup, and wondered if it would be too obvious to walk down the hall to Emma's office to see if she'd come in. Although he hadn't received the threatened resignation letter, she hadn't come to work for two days. The women she worked with had clammed up on him, claiming they didn't know a thing. He knew that was garbage. They knew; they just wanted him to suffer.

Women. Why did they insist on rehashing every personal thing about their lives with everyone they knew? He'd have preferred to keep what happened between him and Emma private, but that ship had certainly sailed. Now the research team hated him, and they undoubtedly would spread the word. It wasn't the best of circumstances, but it wasn't insurmountable, either. He'd been involved in plenty of hostile takeovers before. Besides, he wasn't going to be headquartered here for long. Soon Jim Cowling was going to move in and take care of the day-to-day operations.

In the meantime, he wanted to do as much damage repair with Emma as he possibly could. She'd been on his mind more and more. He hated it, but it was the truth. As hard as he tried, he couldn't put the episode aside. She was in him, whether he wanted her there or not.

The most upsetting thing had been his dreams. He rarely remembered them, but for the past several nights he'd awakened to such vivid images he might as well have been looking at a television screen. All the images were of Emma. In bed. Naked, open, willing. Softly pretty, moaning his name.

He stood up and walked out of his office. Grace, his secretary, looked up briefly, then went back to transferring files. He turned left down the hall and walked toward research.

She wasn't there. Margaret and Christie were, though.

"Good morning," he said, after a polite knock that went unacknowledged.

Margaret nodded curtly and Christie just gave him a blank look.

"I was wondering if you'd heard from Emma."

Margaret shook her head. "Nope. Not a word."

"I see."

She turned to her computer and started typing furiously. Michael wanted to ask more questions, but it didn't seem prudent. Even if they had information, they weren't going to give it to him.

"If she does call or come in, please have her get in touch with me," he said.

"Oh, she'll be in touch," Christie said.

Margaret shot her a scathing look, and Christie flushed.

What did it mean? What was Emma planning? It didn't sound good, whatever it was.

"Thank you," he said, as he made his retreat. He took his time walking back to his office, trying to make some sense of that cryptic remark.

"Mr. Craig," Grace said when he got to the reception area. "Someone's in your office."

"Who?"

"Emma Roberts."

His pulse immediately picked up. He had to control himself to walk normally, and not break into a run. He nodded at Grace, then headed toward his closed door. Absurdly, he almost knocked.

Instead, he opened the door. But he was unprepared for what he saw.

It was Emma all right, but not Emma. The woman before him had her features, but what had been done to them made all the difference.

Her long hair was now shoulder length, auburn, silky. Pulled back from a face that he could only describe as strikingly beautiful. Emma had been pretty, but now... His pulse raced heatedly as his gaze moved down; he could actually hear his heart pounding.

The woman was dressed in a suit, but it was a suit that was meant to wield power. Feminine power.

Red. Tight, short skirt. Tailored jacket that empha-
sized her small waist and the curve of her breasts.

Her legs looked long, which was some kind of
trick because he knew she wasn't tall. But those
heels—high, spiked, also red—made her legs go on
forever.

He moved his gaze slowly back up, until once
again he was looking at her face. Even he could see it
was just her makeup that was different. A new hairstyle, some mascara and a tight skirt didn't change
the fundamentals about her, but he couldn't deny
she *had* changed.

There was something in her posture, in her attitude. Something strong, and good Lord, sexy as hell.
It was like being hit by a tidal wave, knocked over by
a roundhouse punch. He was immediately erect,
which did *not* happen to him in a business situation.
Especially not in his own office with a woman he'd
already taken to bed!

Emma's eyebrow rose. The right one. It went up,
and Michael's gaze became transfixed. He found the
move erotic in the extreme. It didn't make sense, but
try telling that to his johnson.

"Mr. Craig," she said.

Was it possible that even her voice had changed?
No. It was his imagination that gave it that smoke.

"You wanted to see me?"

He realized with a start that he'd been staring at
her for an inordinately long time. But he was afraid
to move, afraid that if he shifted his position, she'd

look down and see what she was doing to him. Not that she probably didn't know already. He had a quick image of his face, like a cartoon wolf with eyes boinging out and jaw on the floor.

"I'm glad to see you're—" His voice cracked. Cracked! Like a fifteen-year-old! He coughed. "I'm glad to see you're back," he said, this time normally. But he could feel tiny beads of sweat forming on his forehead.

Jeez, what the hell was happening to him? She'd cast some ungodly spell on him. He'd been preoccupied with her before this...this magic act. Now, he felt consumed. He wanted her. On the desk. Right now.

"Thank you," she said, her tone all business, which just frustrated him more. "What can I do for you?"

"You can tell me if you're planning to stay on here at Transco for starters."

She nodded. Her hair shimmered and moved against her neck. "I'm not planning on leaving. For now."

"I'm glad. I hope I can convince you to stay permanently."

"Nothing's permanent, Mr. Craig."

"It's Michael."

"No. It was Michael. Now it's Mr. Craig."

He nodded, amazed that he was having this conversation at all. He wondered if he should mention the transformation, but then decided against it. He had to remain professional at all costs, even when his blood was boiling.

"Is that all?" she asked coolly. "I have work to do."

He scrambled for something to say. Anything that would make her stay. Lunch, he could ask her to eat with him. No. That wouldn't work. Work. That's it. "I'd like to hear what you're working on now," he said.

"Margaret is finishing up the status report. It will be on your desk by noon. You'll receive one every week."

Dammit. Okay. So she'd won for now. He couldn't think coherently enough to come up with something legitimate to keep her here. "That's fine then. Thank you."

She locked on to his gaze and held it steady. The first trickle of sweat started down his back as time stretched. Was she going to say something? No. What she did was worse. She parted her lips slightly, then moistened the top right corner with the tip of her tongue. He almost groaned aloud.

Emma could hardly believe what was happening. She had him. Really had him. The magic had worked, and damn if she wasn't someone new altogether. This Emma was strong, strong enough to face Michael Craig in his office, to hold her shoulders back, to stand tall and proud and use her sex to her advantage. And what an advantage. She hadn't really believed it until she'd seen his face. But now—

His reaction to the new Emma was painfully obvious. His expensive suit couldn't hide everything. Frankly, she hadn't expected such physical evidence, but she was delighted. It confirmed that what she was feeling inside was showing on the outside.

She also saw that he was sweating. Tiny little beads danced on the edge of his hairline. This was better than she'd ever hoped for. When she'd done the move with her mouth, his gaze had followed every nuance. Just to see what would happen, she moved a little to her left. His gaze moved with her. This was actually getting to be fun. Who would have thought some makeup, a new hairstyle, some flashy clothes could bring about this dramatic a change?

But it wasn't just those things that had made the difference. It was the way she'd felt, still felt, when she'd stepped in front of the mirror at the department store yesterday.

The woman looking back at her had been a stranger. Which was, of course, what made the whole thing possible. Emma couldn't have pulled any of this off. But that woman in the mirror, she could do it. She could do just about anything.

Never in her wildest dreams had she suspected that she could look so...so...sexy. There was no other word. It was as if all her secret longings, her torrid fantasies and wicked thoughts had gone from inside to outside. She was the personification of sex, pure and simple. Oh, she wouldn't cause any traffic accidents on the street, she wasn't that beautiful or anything. But within a certain distance, with a certain kind of man, she could do plenty of damage.

And Michael was that certain kind of man.

It was time to let him go. For now. Later, when she had more time to think about how to wield this new power, she'd hit him again. With each new change over the last two days, she'd found the idea of revenge more and more appealing. After this first foray, she knew she was going to love each and every moment.

Michael Craig was in for some mighty interesting times. She was, as Christie had promised, going to bring him to his knees.

She walked toward him, purposefully in a straight line, as if she planned to walk into him instead of around him. She had to concentrate on not wobbling. The heels were ridiculously high, and she wasn't used to wearing them. But they also made her hips move in a different way, held her shoulders back and her chest thrust out. My God, she felt like a vamp, a seductress. She wanted to laugh out loud!

At the last second, Michael moved. She passed him closely, brushing her shoulder against his. And, what the hell, at the last minute, she stopped by the door and turned. Remembering Lauren Bacall's invitation to Bogie in that old movie, Emma leaned just so, tilted her chin down and said, "If you need anything else, Mr. Craig, just...call."

Then she turned and slunk out of the office. She felt his gaze on her back, well, a little bit lower than her back. It was incredibly hard not to giggle. Wait until the girls got a load of her.

MARGARET DROPPED her coffee cup. The hot liquid splattered all over the gray carpet. Her mouth hung open in what could only be termed slack-jawed amazement.

Christie squealed. So high, it was almost inaudible. Her hands went to her face and she squealed again.

Jane had to sit down. Her words, well, one word, was succinct and heartfelt. Entirely unlike ladylike Jane.

Emma swung the door closed behind her. She turned a little too fast in her high heels and nearly took a header, but caught herself in time. The shoes had to go, but she didn't want to ruin the total effect yet.

"I don't believe it!" Christie said. "You're gorgeous!"

"I suppose that's a compliment," Emma said.

"Yes! I mean, wow! I can't get over it. Turn around. Let's see you from the back."

Emma obeyed, feeling slightly embarrassed, but still flush with the triumph of her scene with Michael.

"Has he seen you yet?" Jane asked.

Emma nodded. "Boy, did he ever."

"Well? Spill."

At the mention of that word, Margaret collected

herself and went to get some paper towels. "I never would have believed it if I hadn't seen it with my own eyes," she said, bringing the roll back with her. "Emma, honey, you are a vision. You've always been a pretty girl, but this is a whole new you."

"I know," Emma said. "Can you stand it? It's like I'm someone else. I *am* someone else. And you know what? It feels great."

"I want the name of that hairdresser," Jane said.

"So, come on. What happened with the bastard?" Christie took the paper towels from Margaret's hand and bent to clean up the mess. Margaret smiled, and sat down.

Emma seated herself on the couch. Her skirt hiked up to the top of her thighs. As she tugged she made a mental note to watch that. She was used to long flowing skirts, not this little tight mini. "He was stunned. I'm not kidding. His eyes nearly popped out of his head."

"I'll bet," Jane said, scooting her chair closer. "I can just imagine."

Emma shook her head. "I don't know, Jane. It was more than I ever expected. He got a... I mean, he..."

Jane's eyes widened. "Honest?"

Emma nodded.

"Holy smoke. Give me the number of the makeup lady, too."

Emma laughed. "The weird thing is, I was good at it. I actually enjoyed making him squirm. It was like being an actress. I was playing this sexy lady, and it felt, I don't know, exciting. I don't know who she is, but she certainly isn't me."

"Whoever she is, she's a knockout." Christie tossed the dirty towels in the trash and sat down next to Emma. "So, what are we going to do with him next?"

"I don't know. I haven't thought past getting through that first meeting."

"I've got some information," Margaret said, turning to her desk. She picked up a file, a thick one. "This, ladies, is Michael Craig. The bastard's whole history. And if I'm not mistaken, we've got all the ammunition we need to lead him quite neatly down the path. Before the month is through, our new boss is going to be begging for Emma's hand. At which time, she'll crush him like a bug."

Emma smiled. She got up and went to her desk, opened the drawer and took out a package she'd brought back from New Orleans. She opened it slowly, and pulled out the voodoo doll. With a careful hand, she wrote one word on the doll's chest. *Michael.*

"Ladies," she said, holding up the effigy. "Let the games begin."

8

MICHAEL RUBBED the sudden pain in the back of his neck as he turned his chair so he could look out the window. The Houston sky looked bluer than it was through the tint, but even so, it was a beautiful day. Wisps of clouds hung over the tops of high buildings and radio antennas. To the east, a jet left a vapor trail.

The pain eased a bit and he sighed. Something had gone terribly wrong here today, and he didn't know what to do about it.

If it had been business, there wouldn't be a problem. Someone out to take one of his companies? No sweat. A company he wanted, that didn't want to be sold? Piece of cake. But Emma?

What was he going to do about Emma?

He still couldn't believe his reaction to her. Nothing like that had ever happened to him before, and frankly, it ticked him off. He'd never been blinded by a woman's skirt, and he had no intention of being blinded now. Emma Roberts had been a pleasant interlude. She was important to the company, and that's why he wanted her to stay. That's it. So why did thinking of her, even now, make him sweat?

The trouble was, aside from Emma, it had been too

long since he'd been with a woman. Simple. He could take care of that with one phone call. He pulled his briefcase over and got his private phone book out. As he flipped through the pages, he eliminated one prospect after the other. Before he knew it, he was on the Zs. Not one of the women appealed.

Damn.

He threw the book in his briefcase and slammed the top down. This was ridiculous. He wouldn't spend another moment wasting his time over this schoolkid infatuation—which was all it could possibly be. Picking up the phone, he got Jim on the line, and started planning for tomorrow's meetings. Come hell or high water, Emma wasn't going to interfere with his day one more time.

THE PORTFOLIO ON Michael was a work of art. Information about his childhood, his school years, his girlfriends, his early business training, were all detailed and meticulous. They didn't call Margaret the terror of the Internet for nothing. She deserved an award.

Emma closed the file, and sat back. She focused for a moment on the way it felt to swing her leg when it was crossed like this. Of course she realized how foolish the thought was. Crossing one's legs was not an event of any importance. But she never had. Not this way, at least. She didn't know why. It must have been the kind of clothes she wore before that made her sit like some prim virgin, knees tight together, ankles delicately crossed.

This was better. A lot better. It gave her that surge of power again, the one she'd discovered this morning. She could imagine sitting in a meeting across from Michael, and swinging her leg like this. He would look, all right. Look to distraction.

She sighed. It was so much easier thinking about tormenting the man than actually dealing with her real problem. She couldn't forget the facts of what she'd done. It wasn't his fault she'd been such easy pickings. He'd just plucked her out, and she'd fallen into his palm like ripe fruit.

No, it was simpler to focus on the revenge. It might not be her finest hour, but when it was over, the deep, overwhelming sense of shame would be gone. Wouldn't it? She prayed it would. And, just as important, she'd be finished obsessing about Michael. Banish him from her thoughts, her dreams. Especially her dreams.

She got her purse and lifted his folder, intending to go over it tonight in a lot more detail. She'd find his Achilles' heel and she'd use it. No mercy. That was her new motto. She'd plan and plot and then when it was all over, she'd be free. She just had to be free.

THE MEETING STARTED precisely at nine. Everyone was there, from Michael, at the head of the table, of course, to Jim Cowling, who was the acting president, to the department heads and support staff. Emma chose her seat carefully. Directly to the right of Michael, close enough to reach out and touch him.

He'd barely looked at her this morning. She was wearing the blue suit, which if anything was more seductive than the red one from yesterday. It was slim and not too tailored, and if she leaned a certain way, the top of her breasts showed under the silky white blouse. She intended to lean a certain way.

But first, she had to get used to the reactions of her co-workers. Jim was no problem as he hadn't met her before, and had nothing to compare with the new look. But the others, my goodness, she felt as though she hadn't merely changed her appearance but her whole personality. It made her wonder what people had thought of her before. Had she really been that much of a Milquetoast? Evidently.

Bob Jamison was practically drooling in his coffee. Ted Williams stuttered twice as much as usual, and his face had yet to get back to its natural color.

The women reacted too, and that wasn't so flattering. Alicia, who had never been a close friend, but always a good companion, had barely said two words to her. Fran Bingle had made a rather cutting comment about the length of her skirt.

Well, it couldn't be helped. She had a job to do, and she was intent on doing it right.

She listened as Michael laid out the agenda. They wouldn't get to her for quite some time, so she was able to plan her strategy. It actually helped that Michael wouldn't look her way.

. . She took her time. No need to blow the deal by being impatient. An hour and fifteen minutes went by, and that's when she decided to make her move.

She leaned forward, resting her arms so that Michael would get a nice little peek, but no one else would be the wiser. But that wasn't the important thing. What she did next was. She scooted a little closer to him, slipped off her right high heel, and inched her stocking-clad foot toward his leg.

He froze when she touched him. Just froze. He'd been in the middle of a sentence, something about shipping prices. His face colored, not the way Ted's had, but enough. Just pink around his cheeks and a light flush on his forehead.

He continued manfully, enunciating quite clearly, as she moved her foot up. She felt his leg beneath his pants, and she made sure to rub his calf with the ball of her foot.

Michael coughed. He still didn't look at her, though. She smiled pleasantly, enjoying this maybe a little too much. She couldn't wait to see what he did when she hit pay dirt.

Moving slowly, she found his knee, but didn't linger there long. No, the knee held no interest. The inner thigh did.

She took a quick check around the table. No one seemed particularly aware of what she was doing, although Fran had a rather puzzled expression on her face. But she was looking at Michael, not her.

Jim began to speak, and she held her position. Emma didn't want to waste any moves. It wouldn't be half as much fun if Michael wasn't center stage. So she let herself play along the edge of his thigh. Using her toes, and the ball of her foot to tease and touch.

What she hadn't counted on was the heat that started in the middle of her stomach and continued to climb. Her breathing felt a bit shallow, and she could tell she was blushing a little. It was the feel of him, that's all. Perfectly understandable under the circumstances. She wasn't being turned on. That wasn't it.

But as her foot moved, slowly, inch by slow inch, toward the juncture of his thighs, her heart started pounding in her chest. She stopped, not sure she could do it. But then, Michael started talking again.

She swallowed as she steeled her nerves. Then she zeroed in. It wasn't easy. If she hadn't been as limber as she was from all those years of dance class, she couldn't have pulled it off. Thank you, Madame Kieslev.

After a tiny bit of maneuvering, she touched him *there* with her big toe. Immediately, he clamped his legs together, although she doubted he achieved the effect he was after. Her foot was now trapped, right where it was most uncomfortable—for him at least.

His face reddened, and she turned her head to the side so the others couldn't see hers do the same. She couldn't quit now. Especially after discovering just what an impact her little dance was having on him.

He cleared his throat. Ted coughed. Someone got up for more coffee.

Finally, he opened his legs, but instead of letting him off the hook, she moved her foot another inch. Holy cow. He was certainly paying attention. She hoped like hell there wouldn't be a fire in the building, because she doubted very much that Michael Craig could have gotten up right then, even to save his own life.

She had him. Just where she wanted him. And it felt *good*. This seductress business had its moments. This was certainly one of them.

"I think that about wraps it up," Michael suddenly said.

Emma almost dropped her foot. The look on Jim Cowling's face was priceless. His eyes looked like saucers and his mouth hung about three degrees open. Everyone else had similar expressions.

Michael pushed his chair back, dislodging her foot. She thought for a moment he was going to stand, but he didn't. He just stared hard at his team, letting them know that despite the fact that only a quarter of the agenda had been covered, that he himself had been in the middle of making an important point, the meeting was, in fact, adjourned.

"Um, when do you want to pick this up again, Mike?" Jim asked.

"I'll let you know."

A long silence stretched while Emma put her shoe back on. She didn't dare look anyone in the face for fear she'd blush. So she busied herself with her notebook as one by one, the management group left.

When she stood, Michael said, "Not you, Ms. Roberts. I'd like you to stay."

Emma swallowed hard and sat back down. She looked at Fran walking out the door, wishing she had the nerve to just get up and bolt. But she couldn't. He was still her boss. In front of his team, he'd asked her to stay. She was stuck.

The sound of the door closing was way too loud, and it made her jump. She had to get it together, and fast. They were going to talk, and she knew what effect his words had on her. She willed herself to become the new Emma. Crossing her leg helped. Letting her shoe dangle from her toe helped a lot.

"Want to tell me what that was all about?"

Taking one last big gulp of air, then letting it out slowly, she raised her head to look at him. The question in his eyes wasn't merely curious, it was burning.

"Well?"

She smiled a little cat smile. "No, I don't think I do want to tell you what it was about. Why don't you guess?"

He stood up then, unabashed about the state of his trousers, which had a sort of tent-thing going. She graciously kept her gaze on the upper quadrant of his body.

"Okay," he said. "I'll bite. I think you're trying to get a rise out of me, Emma."

She looked down, pointedly.

He sighed. "That's not what I meant."

She looked up again, more pleased than she had any right to be. When she was this Emma, she didn't have any compunction about being a smart-ass. Or about playing her cards out to the last ace.

"So why are you going to so much trouble, Emma? If not to rile me?"

"What do you mean?"

"The hair, the makeup. That suit."

"This old thing? It's been in my closet for ages."

"Liar."

"I beg your pardon."

"You've never had an outfit like that in your life. Up until yesterday. And I think I know why you're wearing it now."

"Do tell, Professor."

He moved closer to her, and it took all her courage not to physically back away. She looked down at her shoe again and tried to remember how powerful she'd felt just moments ago. But when he was right next to her, when she could smell his aftershave, and feel the heat from his body, the new Emma took a header, and it was just the old Emma left to fend for herself.

Her cheeks heated, and so did her solar plexus. She got that feeling back, the one from the weekend.

The electrical charge that he sparked in her whenever he was near.

"I think you want me to fall for you, Emma Roberts," he said, his voice a low, exasperating whisper. He leaned down, his mouth just a breath away from her ear. "I think you want me to want you, so you can tell me to go jump in a lake."

She tried to think. It was hard, what with him being so close. Had the air conditioner stopped working? It was stifling, and she could feel tiny beads of sweat on her neck. She opened her mouth, ready to confess all, when a voice in her head—Margaret's voice—shouted, "Stop!"

Remember what he did to you, Emma. He used you to buy the company. He seduced you so you would tell your secrets. He made you think a man like him...

"Don't be ridiculous," she said, the voice of the new Emma strong and proud and putting him in his place. "I was just amusing myself. I'm surprised you didn't recognize that. You're so good at playing games."

"So it *is* revenge."

"Revenge is such an ugly word."

"But an accurate one."

"If that's what you want to call it, fine."

"What would you call it?"

She stood then, and moved so that her chest was touching his. Not her whole chest. Just the parts he would care about. While she was in the area, she moved her knee, too. Not sharply, as she briefly contemplated, but subtly. Just enough to make contact once more with that most independent of his body parts. He was still paying attention.

"I'd say I'm leveling the playing field, Mr. Craig. Remember, I've got the home court advantage here."

He looked down, capturing her gaze. His eyes were still filled with smoky desire, but there was something else there, too. Something that shook her up a bit more than she liked. A connection, based on a memory they both shared. He'd seen her at her most vulnerable. No matter how many times she managed to tweak his interest, he would always have that on her.

Instead of making her weaken, the realization just made her more determined. He was going to be the vulnerable one. No matter what it took. She'd have that from him.

"What happened to the old Emma?" he whispered. "Is she ever coming back?"

"She's in New Orleans," Emma said. "Playing with pirate ships and Cupids."

"I haven't been able to stop thinking about her," he said, as he moved his hand to her cheek.

His gentle caress made her forget herself for a moment. She closed her eyes. The feel of his flesh upon hers conjured memories that swarmed around and inside her. The bed. His arms. Her moans.

When she opened her eyes, he was still staring at her. Unbelievably, she saw her own want echoed in his gaze. But how could that be? He'd gotten what he'd wanted, hadn't he?

Then she remembered that she'd put that new want there on purpose. She'd worn the suit, cut her hair, walked that walk. What had she expected?

Not this.

Not the ache she saw there now. She'd expected lust, and what he was feeling was so much more.

She knew, because she was feeling it too.

She backed away, needing the distance. But he caught her hand, pulling her right back so she was once again pressed against him.

"Feel that, Emma?"

Of course she did. There was no distance between them at all, and his need was clearer now than ever. Only now, it wasn't just a novel way of keeping score.

"That's what you do to me, Emma. Like this, or like you were in New Orleans. But if I were you, I'd be careful with what you do to me."

"Or what?"

"Or you just might find out what I can do to you."

9

EMMA LOST IT. All her courage, all her determination. Touching him, she had no defenses against the heat in his eyes or the power behind his words. She felt suddenly foolish and helpless, a child trying to play a very grown-up game.

"Let me go," she said.

He didn't budge. If anything, he squeezed her tighter. His mouth opened slightly, and she knew he was going to kiss her. If he did, she might as well throw in the towel. There was only one chance that she could get out of this with even a smidgen of victory. But she had to act fast. One more second, and it would all be over. She had to go on the offensive.

Before his head dipped even an inch closer, she screwed up her courage and kissed him.

She held nothing back. She kissed him with all the power of the dreams he had shattered. She kissed him with the memory of her night as Cinderella. She kissed him as if her lips could wake him from a long night's sleep and set him free.

He didn't stand a chance.

Michael had to pull back. He stepped away from her so that there was a healthy distance between them, and still her kiss lingered. Damn her to hell, she'd done it to him again. She'd caught him off guard, tackled him at the knees. That kiss had turned his mind to mush and crumbled his resolve.

He wanted her so much, he couldn't speak. With her lips moist and open, her eyes wide and challenging, she exuded sex and need and he was no match for its power. There was no doubt in his mind that she could have him any way she wanted him. He'd do whatever she asked. Anything. Step in front of a train, stop a bullet. Anything as long as he could take her in his arms and in his bed and be inside her.

He'd laughed at other men and their sexual obsessions. Called them weak and spineless. Now he understood. There was no choice involved. His need for Emma was as real as concrete and just as unchangeable. With a start, he realized that it wasn't just sex that had him ensnared. It went much deeper than that.

He was mesmerized by the two sides of this enigmatic woman. Her soft vulnerability, and this newly revealed streak of calculating eroticism. The combination was more than he'd ever expected to find in one living, breathing woman. And here she stood in front of him. The only problem was, he couldn't have her.

At least, if she had her way.

"I have to get back to work," she said, and he heard a little shake in her voice.

He knew at the heart of her she was no femme fatale. The wide-eyed girl from New Orleans was inside that Jessica Rabbit body. What he didn't know was if she realized just how successful this act was. He had his doubts. If she knew what he was thinking, she'd be laughing in triumph instead of struggling to maintain her composure.

"Fine," he said. "But remember what I told you. Be careful."

Her mouth tightened. "Thanks for the tip. But I'm not the one who needs to watch my step."

He smiled then. As long as he wasn't too close to her, he could still manage to think logically and effectively. "No? Why don't we see about that?"

Her head tilted to the side as she waited for him to continue. He let her cool her heels for another moment. "Come to dinner with me tonight," he said finally, letting his smile linger as a challenge.

"Are you kidding?"

"You're so confident and in control, I'd think a little dinner would be a piece of cake for you."

Her eyes shifted to the right, then back to his gaze, but only for a second. The problem with the new Emma was endurance. She couldn't maintain the pose when things got dicey. That was good to know.

"It would be. If I wanted to go. But I don't."

"You don't want to? Or you're afraid to?"

"I know you're just trying to bait me."

"Really?"

"Yes. You can't hide those eyebrows, you know."

"Huh?"

"The right one goes up when you play your little games." She pointed to his face. "See? Like that."

He laughed. "My eyebrows are not the body parts you should be wary of."

That one got her. She crossed her arms over her chest. Which wasn't all that good, because it made him look at her cleavage. She wasn't any Anna Nicole Smith, but jeez, in that white blouse she certainly made it clear she was all female. It would have been much easier if he'd never felt the softness of her skin. Or tasted the sweetness of her breasts.

"I'm not wary of any of your body parts."

"No?"

Her gaze skittered to his crotch, then back up again, all in a heartbeat. But he'd seen it. Her blush confirmed the sighting.

"As charming as this has been, I really need to get back to work." She turned to go then, and if he hadn't stepped in her path she would have darted out the door.

"My driver will pick you up at eight."

"I'm not going."

"Wear something..." He took a long, slow look down her body. "Oh, hell. You know what to wear."

"I'm not going."

"Yes, you are."

"Why should I?"

He took one more step closer, even though he knew it was dangerous. All she'd have to do was touch him and his bravado would crumble. His whole plan would backfire. "You'll come because you won't be able to stand not knowing."

She swallowed. Her eyes were dilated and he felt as if he could see right into her. Into her fear, her excitement. An excitement that matched his own.

"Not knowing what?" she asked finally.

"Who's going to win."

"I'M NOT GOING."

"You most certainly are."

Emma gave Margaret her dirtiest look. "Nowhere in your little plans was there any mention of seeing him off the premises."

"It's only dinner."

"It's only dinner with *him*. That's a whole different thing."

"Nothing you can't handle."

"Ha."

"Emma. You can do this. Look what you've done already."

"Made a damn fool of myself. I can't even imagine what the gossip is about me after this morning."

"I haven't heard a thing."

"No one's going to tell you, silly."

"I have my sources."

Emma sighed. That was the truth. Margaret was the most connected human being on the planet.

"So, what are you going to wear?"

Emma put the remains of her sandwich back in the brown bag. She was decidedly not hungry. Truth be told, she was a little sick to her stomach. Thinking about going out with Michael was enough to send anyone to the infirmary. It wouldn't surprise her if she broke out in hives, or suddenly developed a whopping nervous tick.

"Well? What are you going to wear?"

She looked at Margaret, who was just finishing her cold spaghetti. "A uniform."

"What?"

"There's an opening at the McDonald's on Fourth. I'm going to take it."

"Cut it out, Em. I think you should wear black. Didn't Christie say you bought a little strapless number?"

"Would you like fries with that?" she said, practicing. She thought she sounded quite convincing.

"Yes, the black strapless will drive him nuts. And the four-inch heels."

"Would you like to supersize those fries?"

"Maybe wear your hair up. With just a few tendrils falling loose around your face. And don't skimp on the eye shadow."

"How many Happy Meals did you want today?"

"Will you stop it?"

Emma sat back sharply at Margaret's bark. "I'm just rehearsing. Frankly, I think I'd do a great job."

"You're just practicing avoidance."

"Why shouldn't I? Look what I need to avoid!"

"You don't need to avoid one single thing. You have a job to do, and honey, you do it well. Remember how he reacted yesterday? This morning? You've got the man just where you want him. You can't let go now."

"Please let me let go. I'm begging."

"Nonsense." Margaret looked at her sternly. "I don't want to rub salt in the wound, but Emma, the man deserves everything you can give him. Just think about it."

She did, and her spirits went tumbling. The excitement and fear that came with her new identity were excellent diversions. While she was nervous and trying to be brave and sexy, there wasn't room to dwell on the details of her humiliation. That was probably the best part of the whole plan. Now that she'd been jolted back to reality though, the awful memories swamped her. Instead of spurring her on, now all they did was make her want to go home and crawl into bed.

"It's the only way, honey," Margaret said kindly.

"There are other ways."

Margaret reached over and took her hand. "No. This is the only way for you to come out whole."

Emma raised her gaze and met her friend's squarely. "It's too late. I'll never be whole again."

"I don't believe that. And you can't afford to, either. Now, what are you going to wear?"

Emma closed her eyes tightly. Immediately, Michael came to her mind's eye. He was bare-chested, sexy, wanting her. She opened her eyes. "The black strapless number and the four-inch heels."

"That's my girl."

Emma looked down at her hands. "Your girl is scared to death."

"I know, hon. But you don't need to be. You're doing great."

"I don't think I know what that means."

"It means you're taking a bad situation and turning it on its ear. You're not tucking your tail between your legs and running away."

She nodded, but none of that seemed very important at the moment.

"But you want to hear the real reason you're doing this?"

She looked up then, into Margaret's dark brown eyes. "Why?"

"Because all your life, there's been an incredibly dynamic woman trying very hard to make herself known. She's been patient, maybe a little too patient, but I think she knew that someday she'd get her chance to shine. She let you wear your long skirts and your shapeless blouses. She watched quietly as you hid your fantastic brains behind that little-girl shyness. But now, she's not going to be silent anymore. Emma, she...you need to know that 'the new Emma,' as you call it, is you. It's always been you. We've known it for a long time."

Emma felt hot tears well up. One part of her wanted to bolt out of the room, but the other part—the real her, according to Margaret—knew she was hearing the truth. "It's very confusing," she said, her voice a hoarse whisper.

"It doesn't have to be. It might be scary, but that's nothing you can't conquer. Sweetie, it's time you took a stand. Way past time. Don't let this son of a bitch leave you feeling used and tattered. He's not worth it. No one's worth that."

Emma wiped her cheek with the back of her hand. "But if he's such a son of a bitch, why do I still feel this ache inside?"

Margaret shrugged. "Who can say why our emotions take us where they do? Just remember that feelings are feelings. You don't have to act on them. You need to lead with your head on this one, girl. Not your heart. Your heart hasn't done you a lot of favors lately."

"That's for sure."

"Now don't look so sad. Think about how you feel in those new duds of yours. The strength you've found using your feminine wiles. That should pick you right up."

"It does, but only for a while. Then I remember it's me behind the makeup, and it all falls apart."

"Sweetie, it's you on the inside and the outside. Don't sell yourself short."

"I'll try."

"You won't try. You'll *do*. Now, let's get Michael's portfolio out, shall we? I want to go over some data I got this morning. You're gonna love this stuff, Emma. Trust me."

MICHAEL PACED the distance from his dining room table to the far window and back again. If he'd been smart, he would have put on his tachometer about an hour ago. He figured he must have walked a couple of miles already. But he couldn't sit still.

He could just call Eddie. The phone would ring in the front seat of the limo. Emma probably wouldn't even notice. If she was there, that is. But if she was, and she saw Eddie on the phone, she'd know it was him calling, and that he was checking to make sure she was actually there. That would give her an unnecessary advantage. He couldn't do that. Tonight, he needed every ace up his sleeve he could get.

She had it all over him in terms of strategic weapons. Her body alone was the equivalent of a nuclear warhead. That, combined with her anger, made her a worthy foe. Certainly a challenge. But nothing he couldn't take.

And take her is what he intended to do. It was the only thing he could do. Going on like this was completely unacceptable. He wasn't paying attention to business. He had cut an important meeting short. He couldn't eat, he couldn't sleep. It was time to nip this in the bud. Tonight.

He looked at the dinner table, set beautifully by his housekeeper. Candles, bone china, flowers. Perfect. The music he'd selected was slow and sexy. Again, perfect. Champagne chilled in the ice bucket, a dinner courtesy of La Griglia warmed in the oven. The stage was set, ready for the key player to arrive.

His plan was a simple one. He was going to have her in his bed one last time. Finish this game once and for all. Let her know that when she played with Michael Craig, she'd better be playing for keeps.

She'd see that he wasn't a man to be trifled with. He'd get over this ridiculous obsession. He felt sure that once the nonsense ended, the two of them could work together. She'd see that what he'd done in New Orleans hadn't been the crime of the century. Making love to her here in Houston would reaffirm that he hadn't slept with her just to get information. She was a smart woman. She'd understand.

He looked at his watch again. Five minutes had passed since the last time. She should be here by now. Traffic couldn't be that bad. He'd call Eddie. Eddie would be discreet.

Michael went to the phone and lifted the receiver. After he'd dialed the first two numbers, the front door opened. Emma walked in.

All his plans and strategies flew out the window. She'd won, and she hadn't even said hello.

10

IT WAS A MISTAKE. Emma knew it the moment she walked into his apartment. She should never have come. A strapless dress was no match for the man in front of her. Not when he was wearing that tuxedo. If she was smart, she'd just throw her hands in the air right now and cry uncle. She was only human, after all.

She stood by the door and took in the scene as well as she could. Her gaze kept slipping back to Michael, even though Christie had repeatedly told her to get the lay of the land first. She was looking for signs of seduction, and boy did she find them. Champagne, candles, dinner for two.

She hadn't even realized she was going to his apartment until they'd arrived at the building. By then, it was too late to tell Eddie to take her home. Well, okay, it wasn't too late. She could have insisted. But Michael was so close, and she was wearing this dress.

Now she realized she should have left, even if she'd had to walk home. The music alone was enough to suck the bravado right out of her. Gato

Barbieri. The music from *Last Tango in Paris*. Jazz, just as Margaret predicted.

"Come in," Michael said.

She jumped a little. His voice had brought her out of her panic-induced haze. Jane's words came to her, thankfully, so she knew what she had to do. Doing it gracefully was another matter, but since she had no alternate plan, she would give it the old college try.

She smiled, hoping that it came out looking seductive instead of just loony. Then she walked, making sure her chest stuck out and her bottom wiggled. She probably looked like a damn fool, but Jane had insisted. Michael's reaction made her relax a little. Sure enough, his gaze locked on her chest.

If he thought about it even for a minute, he'd realize that her very generous cleavage was courtesy of the WonderBra, and that once that was removed, her boobs would drop like lead weights. She'd pointed that fact out to Jane, who'd simply laughed. She said that men, unless they were under thirteen or senile, didn't care one whit how we went about it, if the end result was big hooters. Jane was a wise woman.

Michael didn't look up until she reached the couch. Then he kind of snapped out of it and blinked several times. His smile faltered, but a second later he got it together. At least as far as she could see. Time would tell.

"Champagne?" he asked.

She nodded. Her instructions were to sip, slowly,

one glass of champagne. No more. No wine. She needed her faculties.

When he turned to open the bottle, she flexed her shoulders. Being a sex kitten was really hard on the back muscles. She also took the time to look around his place.

It was gorgeous. Expensive, she'd expected. That it was this beautiful surprised her. The decor was high art deco, which she'd known from his profile. What she hadn't known was how stunning his taste was, or how very extraordinary his artwork would be. A Tiffany lamp stood on one table, an Erté bronze on another. The paintings on the wall were just a few samples of a much larger collection that he loaned out to various museums. Here he had two Cassandres, both lit exquisitely. She glanced at the table to look at his Lalique crystal. It was far more stunning than she'd imagined.

"You like it?"

He moved next to her soundlessly, the thick carpet muffling his steps. The champagne flute he offered her was also Lalique. She was almost afraid to take it.

"I like it very much," she said. "The whole apartment is wonderful. But I think my favorite is the Frankl." She nodded toward the large set of sky-scraper drawers that was the centerpiece of the north wall.

His brows went up. "You know Frankl?"

She nodded, as if she'd known about the designer since birth. "I'm a fan of deco."

"Really? I wouldn't have guessed."

"Oh? Do I look like I get all my furniture from Kmart or something?"

He laughed. "No. Especially not tonight. You look stunning."

She lowered her lashes, as she'd practiced about five hundred times in the last three hours. "Thank you." While keeping her head down, she raised her gaze. Christie had assured her that the move was seductive without being obvious. All Emma felt was foolish.

Michael raised his glass. "To beautiful things," he said.

She slowly lifted her glass to meet his. The clink seemed very loud to her. She watched as he brought his drink to his lips then drank, his Adam's apple moving up and down in his throat. She shivered, although she wasn't sure why.

"You're not drinking," he said.

She sipped the cold champagne and she suddenly understood all the hoopla about bubbly. It was clear she'd never had good champagne before. This was the nectar of the gods. She sipped again, stopping only when she saw that he was watching her as intently as she'd watched him just a moment ago. Self-conscious, she lowered her glass and walked toward the windows. The whole city was on view from here, and the skyline was breathtaking. At least she assured herself that was what had taken her breath away.

She felt him behind her, and saw his reflection in the glass. The way he looked, handsome as sin and twice as elegant, brought back so many memories from their weekend together that she felt dizzy. Her gaze shifted out of self-defense and she studied herself, a stranger to her own eyes.

Who was she trying to kid? The man had stolen her heart. There, she'd admitted it. It had only been a weekend, but it had been enough. She'd fallen in love with a strange, dark prince, and no matter what she wore or how she did her makeup, she was still just plain Emma in love with a man she couldn't hope to have.

The realization sobered her, but it also made her angry. Why had he done this to her? Made her think, even for a minute, that she could have it all? He had no right to mess up her life like this. She'd been perfectly content until she'd met Michael Craig. Dammit, the man deserved everything she had to give him, and more.

She turned, facing him head-on. "So, you called this meeting. What's on the agenda?"

He looked a little startled. She hoped he was. Keeping him off balance was a primary objective.

"I thought we'd talk."

"I'm listening."

"About that move you made on me this morning."

She laughed. Threw her head back so her hair, which they'd decided two-to-one should be down and flowing, would get all tousled. "That was just to get your attention," she said, still smiling as if feeling him up with her foot was as common as a knock-knock joke.

"It worked."

"And?"

"What do you mean, 'and'? That's what I'm asking you."

She shrugged. "I don't have an and."

"You just wanted to get my attention. In the middle of a meeting. With the whole development team there. Half of whom I'd never met before."

Her grin broadened. "Yep." She sipped her champagne. Twice.

"So, you have it."

"What?"

"My attention. Now, what are you going to do with it?"

She eyed him carefully. "I haven't decided yet."

"Oh?"

She shook her head. "Nope. There are several options. I figure that if nothing else, tonight will show me which one I'm going to take."

"What are these options?"

"Uh-uh-uh. That would be telling."

He opened his mouth, then shut it again. "Have it your own way."

"I intend to."

He reached his hand out and moved a tendril of hair from her cheek. He lingered there, caressing the side of her face. "The games are fine, Emma. For a while. But eventually, you and I need to come to an understanding."

"Really?" She moved her head back, away from the feel of his fingers. She couldn't deal with the distractions. Not now. "And what am I supposed to understand?"

"That when I made love to you, it was personal. Not business."

"Oh, right. I do understand that. Completely."

"I don't think so."

"Why is that?"

"Because you're still angry."

"So if I really understood your motivation, I wouldn't be, is that it?"

He ran a hand through his hair, clearly frustrated. Good. She was doing what she was supposed to.

"No, you'd still have every right. But you wouldn't be angry for the same reasons."

"You amaze me. You honestly think there's any justification for what you did?"

"As I recall, it was totally consensual."

She stiffened. Funny, but it wasn't hard being the new Emma anymore. "It might have been consensual with the man I thought I'd met. But he wasn't going to be my new boss."

"Okay. Fair enough. I was a heel. A louse. I took advantage of the situation. I apologize."

"Oh, honey. If ever a word was too little too late, that has got to be it."

"What do you want, then?"

"Want? I want to go back and live the weekend over. Only this time you'd tell me the truth. This time, I wouldn't be such a trusting fool."

He moved closer to her, so close that she could feel the heat from his body. He touched her face again, but with his palm, cupping her cheek. Before she could stop him, he leaned over and kissed her.

It was a gentle kiss, as sweet and tender as that first night. This was the kiss they'd shared under the pirate ship.

When he pulled back, he held her gaze. "This time, would you come to my bed, Emma? Knowing who I am? What I do? Would you call my name like you did? Would you drive me insane again, Emma?"

No. She wouldn't tell him the truth. She couldn't. If she did, he would know all of this was just an act. A facade to help her stop feeling so ashamed. Because she *would* go to his bed again. She'd go right now if only...

"No," she said. "I wouldn't."

"I don't believe you."

"That's up to you."

"Why won't you admit it?"

"Admit what?"

"That you enjoyed it as much as I did. That we connected."

She sighed and looked at the table, not really seeing, but not looking at him, either. "Fine. I enjoyed it. It was great. An eleven on a scale of ten."

"Come on, Emma. Don't do this."

Her gaze came back to him sharply. "Don't do this? You bastard. You lied to me, you used me to betray my company and my friends, and you tell me not to do this?" She was blowing it, and she knew it. If she didn't stop now, change gears, get her anger under control, everything would be lost.

It took all her resolve, but she did it. She took a deep breath, straightened her back, calmed herself down. The games were just beginning for Mr. Craig. She didn't want her emotions to botch that up. She thought of Margaret's words. Feelings are just feelings.

After one more sip of champagne, she smiled. It felt right. Not forced. "But that's all water under the bridge, isn't it? We have to work together now."

"Right," he said, his eyes narrowed with suspicion. "How come I don't think that's going to be so easy?"

"Maybe because you feel guilty. But don't bother. I've said what I needed to say. As far as I'm concerned, it's over. We don't ever have to bring it up again."

He didn't say anything. He just studied her carefully. The sweet thing was that she wasn't worried about that. He wouldn't see anything to be alarmed about because she felt perfectly calm. More than calm. She was in the zone.

"Now, I thought I was here for dinner," she said.

"Of course," he said, stepping back a little awkwardly. She could tell she'd confused the hell out of him. Good.

"Have a seat," he said, walking over to the table and pulling out a chair for her. "Everything's ready. I just have to get it from the oven."

Her first thought was to offer to help, but she kept her mouth shut. Femme fatales didn't serve dinner. They got served.

She sat down, making sure her skirt rode up her legs just enough to show him that she was wearing thigh-high stockings. That touch was courtesy of Christie, the devil.

When he didn't move for a long moment, she knew he'd seen what she meant for him to see. This was all going according to plan, and unless she blew it again by letting her emotions get the better of her, he would be a puddle of Jell-O by the end of the night.

He coughed softly, then headed quickly to the kitchen. She pulled her chair in, and thought about what she was supposed to do over dinner. First thing was to play with her wineglass.

She took her middle finger and let it glide over the rim. Around and around. Just lightly touching the glass. This was intended to make him aware of her hands. Of her long red nails. According to Jane, this would make him think of other things she could do with her fingers. More personal things.

He came back with two plates, both for her. One a

salad, the other ravioli with a rich cream sauce. It looked and smelled delicious.

She continued doing her thing to the glass. When she looked up, Michael was staring. His eyes had a dreamy look about them, and Emma couldn't help but smile. The girls were too damn good. They ought to write a book.

She stilled her finger and about five seconds later, he blinked. Then he turned and went back to the kitchen, but not before she heard his sigh. She almost felt sorry for him. Almost.

He came back with his salad and pasta. After he put the plates down, he poured them each a glass of deep red wine. Then he looked at her, smiling. "Can I get you anything else?"

She shook her head. "No, this looks wonderful."

"Thanks. I didn't cook it."

"Oh?"

He sat down across from her. "Sorry. Cooking isn't one of my specialties. But I order it well."

"At least you know your shortcomings."

"That I do."

The food portion was next, and Emma tried to remember what it was she had to accomplish. For the life of her, all she could think of was the glass maneuver. She held her left hand down, out of his line of sight, and glanced at it. She'd written a few reminders there, on her palm, just in case. The word *sensual* jarred her memory.

She turned back to Michael. He had his fork in his

hand, but he hadn't started eating yet. He was too busy watching her. He wanted something to look at? She'd be happy to oblige.

Lifting her fork, she brought it to her plate and speared a small piece of pasta. Slowly, very slowly, she lifted it to her mouth as she leaned forward. Michael would have a clear shot of her cleavage, while at the same time he could see her exaggerated movements as she ate the morsel.

It felt awkward as all get-out, but she made sure to pull the ravioli off with her lips, drawing it out as long as possible.

She was able to gauge Michael's reaction immediately. His gaze went from her bust to her mouth and back again. It was almost too easy, really. Like taking candy from a baby. The guy might be a business tycoon and ruthless as hell, but at the core of him he was still a man. God bless testosterone.

She continued eating in just that way, taking her time, occasionally sipping wine or dabbing the corners of her mouth with her napkin. Michael barely touched his food. He didn't speak, and neither did she, but there was so much going on, he didn't seem to notice.

When she was finished, she put her fork down, put both elbows on the table, and leaned even farther down.

Michael put his wineglass down on his spoon and it tipped over. The mess wasn't bad; there had only been a smidgen left, but he jumped up anyway.

To quote Christie, Michael was thoroughly discombobulated. On to step two.

"I'll just wipe this up," Michael said, as he headed for the door.

"It was a lovely meal, Michael. Thank you."

"You're welcome. I've got dessert," he called as he disappeared into the kitchen.

"That's okay. I really couldn't eat another thing." She stood up and waited a few seconds, then she bent down and ran her hands up her right leg, pulling her stocking up. She'd timed it perfectly. He came back just as she passed her knee. She didn't look at him. She just concentrated on her position, on giving him the view she wanted him to have. And she didn't stop until she'd pulled the stocking all the way up her thigh, taking the hem of her dress with her.

When she straightened up, she looked surprised, as if she hadn't realized he was there. Damn, but it was fun. His face was pale, his mouth open, the sponge forgotten in his hand.

"I like the music," she said casually, grateful beyond measure she recognized the piece. "I saw Bolling in concert with Rampal."

"You like jazz?" he asked as he started blotting up the wine.

"Of course. Especially the older stuff by Parker and Bessie Smith."

He stopped cleaning for a second to look at her. "They're my favorites."

"Really?"

He shook his head. "How do you like that?" he said, more to himself than her.

"I also like basketball but not baseball. Hockey on occasion." She laughed a little as she walked toward the windows, making sure each step counted. "I hate Hemingway, love Steinbeck and Faulkner. Don't care for chocolate ice cream, but love Hershey Kisses. And I think *The Godfather* was the best film ever made." She turned to him and smiled. "Anything else you'd like to know?"

He tossed the sponge on the table and walked toward her. "It's amazing," he said. "You and I could be twins."

"Not identical."

"No, definitely not." He reached her, moving in past that safe distance that would keep them from touching. Which he did. In one of the slickest moves since Houdini's escape from the straitjacket, he had her in his arms. Pulling her close, he whispered, "I sure do like your taste."

Then he kissed her. And she melted.

11

ROCK HARD AND READY, Michael pressed his body against Emma's, making sure she knew exactly what he had in mind. It wasn't as if he could hide it. The woman had aroused him the moment she'd walked into his apartment. As the evening had worn on, his situation had steadily worsened. It was a peculiar type of torment, one he didn't particularly care for. Not that he didn't like being aroused. He just didn't like being totally unable to control it.

Kissing her wasn't making things better. But he couldn't stop. Not if there'd been a gun pointed to his head. He had to taste her, to touch her. She was a drug and he was completely, irrevocably addicted.

Their tongues danced, their lips meshed, their taste mingled in such a way that it would be forever branded in his mind. Kissing had always been pleasant, but this... This changed kissing forever. It was a new kind of erotic, blending pleasure and pain in a way he'd never felt before. Pleasure from the kiss itself, pain from the reaction it was causing.

He moved his hand to the top of her dress, just to the curve of her pale, silky breast. He moaned as he made contact, teased beyond endurance by the feel of her skin.

She pushed herself slightly forward so his palm cupped her completely. Even though her dress covered most of her, the swell, the curve, the promise of what lay beneath was enough to send him reeling.

Then, oh damn, then she brought her hand to his erection. He struggled not to embarrass himself. He couldn't hold on for long, though. Her fingers played a delicate pattern over the length of him, and even with his clothes lessening the effect, it was just too much. He broke the kiss.

She looked up at him with her smoky eyes, her mouth still moist and swollen from their kiss.

"Come with me now, Emma," he said, barely recognizing his own voice.

She shook her head in slow motion.

"Don't tease me like this. You can see what you do to me."

"I want to," she said breathlessly. "But..."

"But what?" He moved his lower body against her hand. She pressed him firmly, then the hand was gone.

Emma stepped back. She had to. If she touched him once more, she'd give in, and that would spoil everything.

But, holy cow, this was tougher than she'd expected it to be. Tougher than it had any reason to be. Why—if she knew who he was and what he'd done—did she want to make love with him so terribly much? He was a ruthless bastard. He'd hurt her like no one else in her life. And yet she was drawn to him in a way that defied logic, defied reason. He intoxicated her far more than any champagne ever could.

"But what, Emma? Tell me."

"I can't," she said, struggling to remember Margaret's voice. Christie's warnings. Jane's sage counsel.

"I know you want it as much as I do," he said, taking a step toward her.

She backed away. There was a danger zone with Michael. Anything closer than arm's length. Even though the girls had told her to make him suffer, she couldn't. Not any more. Because he wasn't the only one in pain.

She wanted him with her body, but more than that, she wanted him with her heart. This was a job for someone stronger than her. Someone who wasn't a sentimental fool.

"Talk to me, Emma. Don't just leave me like this."

She took a deep breath. She had to carry on. Her pride depended on it. How could she face the team if she caved in now? "I'm sorry, Michael. I'd appreciate it if you called your driver. I want to go home."

The look on his face made her ache. Disappointment, hurt, betrayal and anger were all there, clearly defined in his mouth, and most especially in his eyes. She recognized each emotion. They'd been hers since Monday.

"I thought you said we'd let the past go. That we'd start from scratch."

"I did. I am."

"Then why?"

"I don't think I need to answer that," she said, purposely making her voice stern, even though she felt weak as a baby.

His mouth tightened and she could see his struggle. Absurdly, she wanted to comfort him. Which was decidedly against the rules.

"You want me to court you, is that it? Flowers? Candy? Dinner and a movie?"

She shook her head. "No, that's not it."

"Then what? For God's sake, Emma. Tell me what you want from me. Tell me what I have to do to bring you back."

"I'm not going to sleep with you, Michael."

"Is it because I'm your boss?"

"No," she said, even though that was part of it. It just wasn't the part that mattered.

"It's not because you don't want to. I can see that in your eyes. You can't kiss a man like that and not reveal something."

"Wanting you has nothing to do with it."

He ran a hand roughly over his face. His cool facade, the one she'd been so impressed with when she'd first arrived, was gone now. Left in its place was a man in torment. She'd gotten what she'd come after, so why didn't she feel better? Why was the ache in her chest so heavy?

"What will it take?" he asked, his voice low, desperate.

"I won't make love with you until..."

He moved quickly then, reaching out with both hands to grasp her arms. "Until what?"

She swallowed hard. This was the most difficult moment of all. Not because she was afraid to say the words, but because once she said them, she wouldn't be able to take them back. And once she said them, she'd see just what she meant to him. The real truth this time. She'd know forever that all he'd wanted her for was sex.

Her resolve evaporated, and she knew she couldn't say it. She just couldn't bear to see his reaction. God help her, she still needed the illusion that she could mean something to him.

"Please call Eddie," she whispered.

"You're not going to answer me, are you?"

She shook her head.

He looked as if he wanted to shake her. But he didn't. He just let her go. When his hands left her arms, she wanted them back again. She'd done every single thing according to plan. But she'd lost anyway.

He walked to the phone, lifted the receiver, and then he turned his back on her. The game was over. No hits, no runs, no errors. Just over.

MICHAEL WATCHED the sun rise. A small part of his brain recognized the beauty of the sky, and resented it. He didn't want to see anything beautiful. Not when he felt like this.

Emma had kept him up all night. She'd left shortly after eleven, and he'd opened a bottle of Scotch and planted himself on the couch. His plan to get stinking drunk had never materialized. The booze just wasn't strong enough. He could have polished off the whole bottle, and he wouldn't have felt better.

He kept remembering that one word. *Unless.* Unless what? Unless he apologized? He'd done that already. Unless he sold the company? If that was it, he was in trouble.

He'd made his bed, to coin an unfortunate phrase, and now he was lying in it. Emma could have been his, if he'd played his cards right. If he hadn't used her. The irony was, he could have gotten the company without her information. It would have been a little more expensive, but nothing that would have hurt him in the long run. So it had all been for nothing.

If only he could forget about her, everything would be back to the way it was, and he'd be fine. But forgetting about Emma was like trying to stop breathing. She was just as necessary now. Why? He'd stopped asking that question at three this morning. What difference did it make? The reason wasn't going to get him out of this mess, so there was no profit in dwelling on it. It was enough for him to recognize that he was well and fully hooked. To a woman who would never forgive him.

If she had, if she'd simply brushed aside his be-havior, he probably wouldn't be feeling this way right now. Again, ironic. With a little bit of humilia-tion thrown in for good measure.

He had to shower. Get ready for work. But he didn't want to. That was another problem. If there was one thing he'd been able to count on, it was his honest pleasure in going to work. Emma had taken that, too.

He leaned forward, elbows on his knees, head in his hands. Blaming Emma was only a temporary ref-uge. She wasn't the villain here. Whatever game she was playing with him, he had no right to complain. But dammit. He'd have to wrap up his work at Transco, and quick, so he could get out of there. Maybe if he didn't see her, or hear her, he'd be able to get her out of his mind. Maybe.

Until he could leave, he'd just have to use some willpower. Stop thinking about her all the time. Get busy, distract himself. There certainly was enough to do at the office. He stood, determined to get through the day without any thoughts of Emma Roberts.

HE BLEW IT the moment he got into the shower. He continued to blow it as he dressed, drank his coffee, drove to work, went over his E-mail, and met with Cowling. She never left him, not even for a short break.

So where did that leave him? Going crazy, that's where. Jim had looked at him as if he was already there. It got so bad, that he'd actually asked Michael if he was feeling okay. The truth was Michael was *not* feeling okay. Michael was feeling like hell. All because of one word.

Unless.

Like a hated song that repeats over and over until you want to scream, the word had invaded his brain, taken over all the higher functions. And still, he couldn't figure out what it meant.

He glanced at his watch. It was nearly three. He hadn't slept in over thirty-two hours. His throat scratched, his muscles ached, and that weird pain he'd been having lately in his neck had bothered him on and off all day. Something had to give. No, someone had to give. And it wasn't going to be him.

He stood, determined to end this garbage here and now. Emma would explain. He'd see to it. He hadn't become one of the wealthiest men in Houston by letting other people call the shots.

He walked quickly out of his office and down the hall, his resolve growing with each step. Emma might have a right to toy with him, but enough was enough. She'd made her point. Now they were either going to get on with it, or let it go. But the games stopped. Period.

Her office door was open. All four researchers were at their desks, working on their computers. Emma looked focused, in control. Well rested. Obviously, she had no trouble keeping thoughts of him at bay.

That hurt. He hadn't known until he'd seen her that he expected her to be feeling as lousy as he did. That turning him down hadn't been an easy choice. Wrong again. Being wrong was becoming a habit with him. At least as far as Emma was concerned.

"Can I help you?"

He turned, jolted out of the mental quicksand by Margaret's curt question.

"No, thanks. I need to speak to Emma."

She didn't look at him. She kept on typing. He waited, none too patiently, until finally she saved her work, then casually turned to face him. Damn her for looking so calm. So beautiful.

"Yes, Mr. Craig?"

"Can I see you for a moment?"

She shrugged. Shrugged! As if it didn't matter one way or the other. Okay, no need to panic. Maybe she was just putting on a good face.

"Margaret, I'll get with you on that Gulf project when I get back."

Margaret looked from Emma to Michael. Her scowl wasn't hard to interpret.

He waited again while Emma took her sweet time getting up. Finally, she was next to him, and then she led him out into the hallway.

He didn't say anything until they'd reached the photocopy room. No need for her cohorts to hear him. He turned to look at her, preparing himself for what he knew was going to be a battle.

"What's on your mind?" she said, as if nothing at all had happened last night.

"I want to talk to you."

"Okay," she said, smiling a little too brightly. "You've got the floor."

He cursed himself for not planning his opening salvo. Knowing how he felt, he should have rehearsed this conversation, made contingency plans for each of her possible responses. "About last night..."

She blushed. Finally, a reaction. He breathed a sigh of relief until he thought about what the blush meant. Was she embarrassed that she'd kissed him? Touched him? Did she regret it? Or was she just pink with the memories of their intimacy?

"I'm sorry," she said, turning her head slightly to the right and looking past him. "I wasn't very fair to you."

That was better. At least she recognized that leaving him with that word dangling like a cartoon bubble over his head was cruel and unusual punishment.

"I left without thanking you for the lovely dinner. I don't know where my manners were."

Michael rocked back on his heels. "What the hell are you talking about?" he said. "I don't give a damn about the dinner."

Her eyes widened and her lips parted in surprise. "My goodness, I was just trying to be polite."

"Screw polite. I want to know what you meant."

"Meant by what?"

"Unless."

"Pardon?"

He felt his anger rise in his stomach like the mercury in a thermometer. "You know what I'm talking about."

"No," she said, far too innocently. "I'm afraid I don't."

"Maybe this will remind you." He stepped up close to her, and took her hand. Making sure she was staring him right in the eyes, he put her hand where it had been last night. Where it was hard, just like it had been last night. Just before she'd said it.

Her blush deepened from pink to crimson. "Michael," she said, only the word came out in a rush of air.

"Yes. Michael. You remember me now, right? You remember what you did. What you said."

She nodded, tugging at her hand. He let her go, shocked himself, now that the flash of madness had passed. "I'm sorry," he said, stepping back from her. "I didn't mean to do that. It was completely inappropriate. I have no business touching you at all." He kept backing away, not sure what he might do next. It was impossible to be near her. He lost his mind around her.

"Wait," she said, reaching out and taking his arm. "Don't go yet."

Now it was his turn to be surprised. He'd have

thought she'd want to be rid of him. As quickly as possible.

"I do know what you mean," she said, looking at him with troubled eyes.

Eyes filled with the kind of pain he recognized all too well. So she had been acting. The realization should have made him feel better, but it didn't. He'd thought he wanted company in his misery. Not so. He wanted to take her pain away, to make her feel better. It wasn't what he expected—a totally new experience. Emma was giving him lots of those. Almost none of them pleasant.

"Michael?"

"Hmm?"

"Why are you looking at me like that?"

"Like what?"

"That. With those eyes?"

He knew what she meant. He just had no explanation. "These are the only eyes I have."

She smiled sardonically. "Touché. I guess I deserved that."

"I didn't say it to be mean."

She looked away. "I know."

"So, will you tell me?"

She didn't turn back for a long time. He breathed deeply, concentrating on the air filling his lungs. It was a relaxation technique he'd learned years ago, but he'd never used it outside of a business context. It helped, but only a little.

When she finally faced him again, the pain and vulnerability were gone. Vanished as if by magic. He

was caught off guard again. Hadn't she just said...
What the hell?

"I'd better get back to work, Mr. Craig. Unless
there's something else?"

He didn't know what to say. His thoughts sput-
tered like a dying engine. Of all the responses in the
world, this was one he would have never guessed.
What had happened in those few moments? What
decision had she made? Clearly it hadn't been in his
favor. He could deal with that. It was this on-off
thing that was driving him batty.

"You're in the wrong line of work," he said, after
he'd regained the power of speech.

"Oh?"

"Yeah. You should work for the FBI. You'd be a
great double agent."

Her shoulders sagged. "Okay. You win. Let's just
stop this now, while we can. I can't do this anymore."

"Stop? Before you've told me?" God, he sounded
so desperate and pathetic.

Emma's struggle was clear on her face. She was
deciding something, again. Something that affected
him deeply, but of course she wasn't going to let him
in on it.

"There's nothing to tell," she said, finally. She
straightened her posture, and he knew that unless he
did something drastic, she was going to keep toying
with him. Well, the hell with that.

"No," Michael said. "I'm not letting you get away
with this."

"I don't think you have a choice."

"I'm not letting you leave until you explain yourself."

She studied him for a moment. "Why is it so important to you?"

"You tell me you won't come to my bed. Unless. And then nothing. You don't think I have a reason to wonder about that?"

Her brows knitted, and she turned her head slightly to the right. The move was familiar now, and that bothered him, too.

"This is more than wondering," she said. "If I didn't know better, I'd think I was more than a means to an end to you."

"You were never that."

"Then what? Why should I go to your bed, Michael?"

He hadn't been prepared for that one, either. He couldn't tell her the truth. That would give her ammunition enough for three world wars. He had to think fast. Use his negotiating skills to put her on the defensive.

He used the only weapon he had. He touched her cheek. Softly. With the back of his hand. "You're so very beautiful," he said.

She closed her eyes and leaned into the caress. Then she stepped back, opening them once more. "No. I won't. I won't let you do that to me. I meant what I said last night. I will not go to your bed. Ever again. Unless..."

And then she turned, and before he could stop her, she ran down the hall and turned the corner.

He ran after her, close on her heels. He almost had her, but she dashed into the ladies' room. He didn't even have to think about it. He just followed her inside.

"This is the ladies' room," Emma said, even though she wasn't surprised that he'd followed her inside. "You can't be in here."

"It's my company. I can do what I want."

"What if someone comes in?"

He went back to the door and turned the metal lock. "Satisfied?"

She shook her head. "I came in here because I wanted to be alone."

"No, you came in here because you wanted to torture me some more."

"Torture you? Don't be absurd."

He walked toward her, and she backed up until her butt hit the long sink counter. The look in his eyes wasn't charitable. In fact, he looked as if he were about to commit murder.

He didn't stop until he'd come so close to her she was forced to lean back a little. He grasped her by the shoulders, and she could feel his anger from his hands through her jacket.

"You," he said, his voice low and dangerous, "are driving me crazy."

She started to say something, but the look he gave her, wild-eyed and warning, made her keep it to herself.

· "I can't sleep. I can't work. I can't do anything but think about you and that damn *unless*. I've apologized, every way I know how. I've called myself every kind of fool. I've tried to ignore you, but you won't let me, will you? It's all part of your plot, isn't it? You want me to go insane, right? Well, I won't. Because you're going to tell me. Right now. Aren't you?"

Emma couldn't have been more shocked. The plan had worked! She had him, just as Margaret and Christie and Jane had promised. He couldn't stop thinking about her! It was more than she'd hoped for. Infinitely more. She finally felt ready to tell him. To say the words that would make everything perfect, if he answered correctly. Oh, there was still the fear that he wouldn't. But for the first time she felt as though there was a chance.

Every bit of research they'd gathered on Michael pointed to a negative response. There was nothing on paper to give her any reason to believe she could change that. But then they'd all thought it would take weeks to get him here.

"Well?"

She said one last little prayer. "I won't go to your bed, Michael," she said carefully, aware of the butterflies in her stomach, the constriction in her chest, "unless..."

"Dammit, unless what?"

She'd run out of excuses. She had to say it now, or never. "Unless I'm your wife."

12

EMMA HELD HER BREATH. His face, especially his eyes, would tell her more than his words. In an instant, she had her answer. She let go of her breath...and her dreams.

It had all been about sex. Not love. That was clear from the stark panic she saw written all over his face. Marriage was the last thing on his mind. At least, marriage to her.

When his hands dropped to his sides, she turned, but then she saw his reflection in the mirror. That was worse, somehow. She'd rendered him speechless. Not with her sexy new haircut, or her new clothes, or even her bitch-on-wheels attitude. All it had taken was the hint of a relationship—a real, committed, lifetime love—and he was struck dumb.

"Wife?" he said, his voice so full of confusion she almost laughed.

"That's right, Mr. Craig. I'm sure you've heard the term before."

"But..."

She turned back, forcing herself to concentrate on the anger that still stewed inside. Not anger at him, but at her own stupidity. How could she have ever thought this would turn out happily? Like oil and water, she and Michael didn't mix. He was a Ferrari, and she was a station wagon. Her crush on him was as realistic as having a crush on Tom Cruise. It wouldn't happen. Not in this lifetime.

"Now that that's settled," she said, "I'd better get back to work." She started for the door, but he stopped her, his hand grasping the exact same spot on her arm as before.

"Wait a minute."

"What for?"

"Because we need to talk."

"No, we don't. There's nothing to say."

He pulled her back, forced her to face him. She couldn't look at him, though. She just couldn't.

"You really want me to marry you?" he asked.

If she hadn't been so busy being humiliated, she would have been insulted. "Not anymore."

"Quit it. I'm serious."

"So am I."

"Now come on, Emma. Give me a minute, will you? I mean, that came out of left field."

She nodded, smiling bitterly. "Right. Sex was in the ballpark, but marriage? Completely unrelated. I understand."

"No, that's not what I meant."

"What did you mean?" She studied him now, no longer afraid to see his reactions, or let him see hers. Let him see the fire in her eyes, and let him believe it was there because of him.

"I meant that I just hadn't been thinking along those lines. That's not what our relationship was about."

"Relationship? You call what we had a relationship?"

He sighed and lifted his hands in surrender. "I can't win, can I?"

"Oh, you've won, all right. You have your company. You had me. What's left?"

"Having you again."

"I don't think so. I'm through with being had."

"I didn't mean it that way, and you know it. You're assuming an awful lot. Jumping to some pretty wild conclusions. Why don't you try just being straight with me? Isn't that what you asked me to do?"

"You're right," she said, folding her arms across her chest. "Here's where I stand. I'm leaving Transco as soon as I get any kind of offer I can live with."

"Why?"

Incredulous, she burst out laughing. "Are you really that obtuse?"

"How did this get so complicated, dammit? We had a great weekend together, and don't you deny it. Something clicked between us, and you can't deny that, either. Now we work together, and we have a chance to have a lot more of them. What's so terrible about that? What's the crime?"

"Aside from the fact that you're a lying, conniving

bastard, nothing. It's a great plan. If all I was interested in was sex."

"You were interested last Saturday night."

She winced. "Boy, you sure do hit below the belt."

"I'm prepared to fight as dirty as I have to, Emma." He moved toward her, slowly, as if he were trying to catch a wild creature.

"Why? What's the point?" she asked, stepping back.

"This." He caught her arms and pulled her to him. His kiss was hard and hot and it reminded her of all the things he could do to her. Make her knees weak, her head spin, her heart thud in her chest. And, God help her, make her wet with wanting him.

He didn't let up. His tongue toyed with her lips, then slipped inside her mouth. When he moved his arms around her, pressing her tighter against him, she wondered if he could feel her excitement through her clothes as she could feel his.

It was crazy. Kissing shouldn't do this to a person. It shouldn't do this to her. She had no business running her fingers through his hair, or moving so that she rubbed the hard parts of his body.

He moaned, and she felt the rumble in his chest. His hand found her blouse, and then her buttons. As smoothly as a magician conjuring a silver dollar, he had her jacket open, and then she felt him touch her breast. It was her turn to moan.

His mouth left hers and she gasped. He nibbled on her earlobe, then her neck. "This is why, Emma," he whispered. "Because you make me need you like this."

Her eyes fluttered open. And what she saw made her gasp.

Margaret, Christie and Jane were watching her. Three heads, all in a row, peaked over the bathroom stall doors. Three pairs of eyes wide with shock. Three mouths hanging open.

Michael lowered his mouth to her bra-clad breast. Emma pushed him back, quickly closing her jacket, embarrassment coursing through her just as heat and want had flowed a moment ago.

"What? What's wrong now?"

She saw her three ex-friends duck. "I just..." What was she going to tell him? She couldn't let on about the girls. But she also couldn't pretend that nothing had happened between them. He'd felt her reaction. Lying about it wasn't going to work.

"I can't deal with this now," she said. "When you touch me, I get all confused."

"Welcome to my world."

She had to smile. She really had put him through the spin cycle this morning. "I think we both need time to think," she said. "And to cool down a bit."

"Yeah," he said, scratching his head. "I guess."

"Go on. Get out of here before someone catches you. We'll talk later."

"Promise?"

She nodded. What else could she do?

"And promise me one more thing?"

She glanced at the bathroom stalls. "What?"

"That you won't quit."

"I can't promise you that."

"At least until we have a chance to talk again. Okay? Just till then."

She looked at his face, so earnest, so confused. "All right. At least until then."

He opened his mouth, then shut it.

"What?"

"No, I'm gonna leave while I'm ahead. At least, I think I'm ahead."

She smiled. Then she walked to the door and turned the lock.

True to his word, he didn't say another thing. He just gave her one last puzzled look, then he walked out the door.

Emma waited for a moment, estimating the time it would take him to round the corner and go down the hall, then she turned to face the bathroom stalls. "All right you Peeping Toms. Get out here. He's gone."

Three bathroom doors opened, and Margaret, Christie and Jane walked out. At least Jane had the decency to look sheepish. Margaret and Christie just looked astonished.

"That kiss!" Christie said. "I just about melted, and I was behind a metal door."

"What were you thinking?" Margaret said. "You almost blew it completely. And you had him, right until you let him kiss you."

"I had no idea," Jane said. "Oh, honey, I don't envy you. How are you supposed to fight that?"

"Thanks for the commentary, but why the hell didn't you let me know you were in here?"

"When were we supposed to do that?"

"When I walked in, that's when."

"Michael came in two seconds after you. How were we supposed to know you were going to have sex right there on the sink."

"Margaret, we did not have sex."

"Technically, no. In every other way, you did so."

"Oh, Margaret," Christie said, putting her arm around the older woman. "You've been single too long."

"Oh, hush. You know what I meant. So, what are we going to do now?"

"We?" Emma said. "I think this group experiment is over, don't you?"

"No," Christie said. "It most certainly is not."

"I played my last card. He trumped it. Or weren't you listening to that part?"

Jane shook her head. "Sorry, I have to agree with Christie. This thing isn't over. Not by a long shot."

"It is for me. I resign."

"You can't!" Margaret took her by the arms. "You're inches from winning."

"Winning what? You heard his reaction when I brought up marriage."

Margaret's frown deepened. "Honey, what did you expect? His reaction was just about what we figured it would be. Remember? We planted the seed, that's all. He'll think about it, toy with it. It'll make him look at you with new eyes. That's all."

"Did you want him to say yes?" Christie asked.

Emma heard the incredulity in Christie's voice. Of course they would be shocked. How could they know that her motives had changed? That she no longer wanted Michael's scalp, she wanted his heart. "No, of course not," she said, trying hard to make the words sound like the truth.

"You're in love with him," Jane said, "aren't you?"

Emma tried to deny it. Instead, she had to concentrate on stopping her tears from flowing.

"Even after what he did to you?"

It was no use. She couldn't carry it off. She closed her eyes and nodded.

"Oh, honey," Jane said, her voice filled with sympathy. Or was it pity?

The tears she'd tried to hold back broke free and she turned away from her friends. She didn't want to see the looks on their faces. The contempt. The censure. She already felt enough of those things for herself.

But as she brought the back of her hand to her face to wipe the tears away, she felt hands on her shoulders, and before she knew it she was in the middle of a group hug.

"Stop it, you guys," she said, her voice muffled. "My makeup is getting destroyed."

"The hell with your makeup," Margaret said. "Why didn't you tell us?"

"I had my suspicions," Christie said. "But the clincher was that kiss."

Emma gave them each a tight squeeze and they broke apart. To her surprise, she saw that Jane and Margaret had been crying, too. She smiled weakly. "You don't have to worry. I'll get over it."

"Of course you will," Margaret said. "I'm just sorry you have to go through any of this."

"We just want you to be happy," Jane said.

"It's not like I'm dying or anything," Emma said, her voice finally growing steady. "So don't everybody start wearing black."

Margaret shook her head. "The more I think about it, the more I realize we're on the right track. As long as we can keep the two of you from kissing, this is all going to work out just fine."

"Margaret, what are you talking about?" Emma could hardly believe her ears. Hadn't she understood? The game was over. She was in love with the target. Nothing was going to change that, except time, and perhaps a long stay at a sanitarium.

"I'm talking about taking your life back, Emma. Believing in yourself."

"It's no use. But hey, at least I got a nifty new haircut, right?" She sighed. "To be honest, the game was over before we started. I fell for him the moment he sat down at my table. It was all over but the credits."

"It's not over. Not at all."

"How do you mean?" Christie said. "What's she supposed to do now?"

"Just what she's been doing. Confusing the hell out of him. Making him crazy wanting her."

"To what end?" Jane asked.

Margaret looked at them all as if they were not understanding on purpose. "To walk away with her pride, for heaven's sake."

"Pride?" Emma said. "How am I supposed to get that back? I'm in love with him, and he doesn't love me."

Margaret put her hands on Emma's shoulders and looked her straight in the eyes. "Do you trust me?"

"I'm not sure. Not when you're looking at me like that."

"I'm serious now."

"Okay, I trust you."

"Then will you believe me when I tell you that the worst thing you could do right now is give up?"

Emma sighed. "I'll try. But it's not easy."

"I never said it was going to be easy. Just promise me you won't throw in the towel. That you won't quit. That you'll carry on with the plan, just as if nothing had changed."

"Margaret, you expect too much of me."

"No, I don't. I know you can do this. You're strong, Emma. Stronger than you know."

Emma wanted to say no. To forget the whole thing. But looking into Margaret's confident brown eyes, she couldn't. She'd already disappointed her friend once. She didn't want to do it again. "All right," she said.

Margaret smiled. "Great. Now, go fix your makeup. You have work to do."

Emma looked at the mirror and laughed. "I'll say. I'm a wreck."

"Christie will bring you your purse. Come on girls. Let's go."

Jane gave Margaret a puzzled look. "I don't get it."

Emma heard Margaret's whispered, "I'll explain later." But when she turned to ask what that was about, the girls had gone. She was alone. Alone with the knowledge that she'd agreed to this farce. That Michael didn't love her, and never would. That no matter what happened, the pain in her heart was going to be there for a long, long time.

13

"MIKE, ARE YOU OKAY?"

Michael looked blankly at Jim Cowling. It took him a second to register the question. He nodded, even though he was most decidedly not okay.

He focused on Jim, who was leaning forward in the wing chair across from Michael's desk.

"Let me ask you something. What do you know about Emma Roberts?"

Jim seemed surprised at the question. "Well, she sure as hell wasn't what I expected."

"What did you expect?"

"I don't know. Not her. She's supposed to be the best geographic researcher there is. According to Randy, she's got brains she hasn't even used yet. He also said she was a little on the shy side, but she didn't seem shy to me."

Michael wondered if Jim had seen Emma's footwork the other day. No. He hadn't looked under the table. Maybe he'd guessed, but Michael doubted it. His comments were based on her looks, and that new attitude. There was nothing shy about that.

"Why do you ask? Think she might leave? You

know, I hear Shell wants her. Pretty badly. They've got the money, too."

Michael didn't like that one bit. "Find out what they're going to offer her, will you?"

"Sure thing. Is that it?"

"Hm? Oh, yeah. You have everything you need?"

Jim frowned. "I'm set. But I wonder if maybe you should see a doctor. You look like hell."

"Thanks."

"Hey, I'm just telling you the truth. You haven't looked right since Monday. Is there something you want to tell me?"

"Yeah," Michael said, smiling. "I'm pregnant."

"Very amusing. Really."

"Get the hell out of here, would you, Jim?"

He stood and picked up his briefcase. "We can't afford to have you laid up, buddy. Do yourself and the company a favor. Don't stick your head in the sand. Get a physical. Take a vacation. Do what you need to, okay?"

Michael stood, too. He walked around his desk and put his hand on his friend's shoulder. "Don't worry. I'm not planning to have a heart attack. At least not today."

Jim gave him one last look, then he left, shaking his head the whole way. Michael stared at the door for a long time. His thoughts, of course, were on Emma.

Marriage.

He hadn't anticipated that. He should have—

Emma was a woman, after all. But he hadn't. Maybe because of how they'd met. Or maybe because the "new" Emma didn't look like his, or anyone's, idea of a wife and mother. But now that she'd brought it up, he found himself thinking about the concept. Frankly, it gave him the willies.

He had no intention of getting married. Not now. Not later. Not to anyone. Michael Craig subscribed to the religion of bachelorhood. He'd never confessed this to anyone in his life, but half the reason he was as driven as he was, was because women were attracted to money and power. The combination had been, and always would be, a female magnet. The formula had worked for him for a long time, and he saw no reason to mess with it now. Not even for Emma.

Just for reassurance, he went to his briefcase and pulled out his black book. Filled with numbers of beautiful women, available women, women who could keep a man awake all night. He flipped through the Cs. Toni Chapel. Perfect example. She was twenty-three, six foot two, and she had a thing for the outdoors, and he didn't mean camping. He hadn't seen her in a long time. Maybe she'd like to do a nature hike this weekend.

Picking up the phone, he dialed the first three numbers, then paused.

Toni was a knockout, all right, but he had to face it. She was no Emma.

He hung up, dejected all over again. Not only had

Emma Roberts turned him into a zombie at work, she'd also ruined his sex life. Great. Wonderful. He might as well shoot himself now.

There was only one solution. He had to get Emma out of his thoughts. Out of his brain. Certainly out of his libido. But how? Leave the country? Good idea, except that he'd just bought this company and there was no way he could be away for any length of time for at least six months. Lobotomy? That sounded reasonable. He wondered if his health insurance covered that procedure.

He sat down hard and leaned back in his leather chair. There was a mountain of work on his desk, all things he'd been putting off. He turned his chair so he could look out at the Houston skyline.

Marriage. He'd always seen it as a sucker's deal. Be with one woman for the rest of his life? That would be like eating chicken for every meal forever. Okay, with Emma it would be like eating caviar, but still. Every meal? Every day?

Except...

Emma wasn't like anyone he'd ever met before. It wasn't that she was sexier, although whatever pheromones she produced clearly had his name on them. No, what made Emma so unique was that she was so damned unpredictable. An enigma. He never knew what she was going to do next. He had the feeling that wouldn't change, even if he knew her a hundred years.

She new Frankl. How many women had he been

out with? He wouldn't hazard an estimate. How many had recognized the Frankl design? One. Guess who?

She liked jazz. Okay, so several other women had liked jazz, but Emma liked Charlie Parker!

She was smart. He'd been out with smart women before. As a matter of fact, it was one of his basic requirements. Vacuous females held no interest. But Emma was smart in a way he could relate to. She understood his line of work. She knew enough about business that their conversations were always stimulating. He remembered how they'd talked in New Orleans; Emma had been particularly insightful. He'd thought at the time that she'd be a valuable asset to the company, and his opinion on that hadn't changed. There was no way he was going to let Shell, or any other company, have her. Transco needed her.

He needed her.

He stood up so fast he nearly knocked the chair over. *No.* He was not going to marry her. He didn't give a damn if she was the most exciting woman in the entire world. She was not going to get him to propose. No way. The woman hadn't been born who could make him change his mind about this. He'd never give in. Never.

EMMA SAW Michael's secretary, Grace Porter, sitting alone in the cafeteria. She looked a little lonely, a little bored. Emma lifted her tray—laden with her salad with fat-free dressing, diet cola and slice of cheesecake—and headed toward the woman's table. She wasn't sure why she wanted to talk to Grace. As a matter of fact, she was a little nervous that Grace had heard something too personal for things to be comfortable. On the other hand, Grace had been with Michael for years.

"Mind if I join you?"

Grace looked up, surprised, but smiled easily as she shook her head.

As Emma took the food off her plate, she gave Grace a surreptitious once-over. Quite attractive, Emma guessed she was in her midforties. Neat, precise, but with laugh lines around her eyes and mouth that offset her almost rigid posture. The suit she wore was expensive, a DKNY, if Emma recalled correctly from her recent foray into the world of designer ready-to-wear. Michael had to pay her well.

As she sat, she caught Grace checking her out. Well, tit for tat. It was only fair.

"I'm glad you came over," Grace said, that easy smile once again making Emma feel welcome. "I haven't had time to meet many people here. And if I know the boss, I'll be leaving just after I make some friends."

Emma's chest tightened. Of course she knew Michael wasn't going to stick around, but the words still bothered her. She inhaled, then blew the air out slowly. "How long have you been working with Michael?"

"Close to ten years now," Grace said, shaking her head. "Boy, I can hardly believe it."

"I know what you mean. Time seems to speed up every year."

"Wait till you hit forty. You'll be stunned."

Emma took a bite of salad, barely tasting it. "It must be interesting, though. Working for him."

"It is. My only complaint is that I don't stick around any place long enough for my taste. But moving from company to company has its advantages. I never get bored."

"I'll bet."

"This move, for example." Grace sipped some soda, then ate a bite of fish. "This has been really different."

"How so?"

"Well, there's always a pattern. Mr. Craig is what you'd call a hands-on man. He likes to be on top of things from the start."

"Hasn't he been?"

Grace shook her head. Emma noticed that her short, dark hair was starting to gray, but that it looked rather nice on her.

"No, this one has been different."

Emma wanted to press her, but didn't know how. Was it different because of what had happened in New Orleans? Or different because he'd been as distracted as she'd been?

"For example, last weekend..."

Emma held her breath.

"He was scheduled to come back from his trip on Saturday. Right after he'd made the offer. But he didn't."

"He made the offer on Saturday?"

Grace nodded. "In the morning. He had the plane ready for that afternoon, but he canceled."

Emma's heart beat a mile a minute. She could hardly believe what she was hearing. Michael had made the offer to Phil Saturday morning! Which meant he'd gotten all the information he needed on Friday. Which meant he was with her on Saturday night because...

"I think," Grace said very quietly, "that he stayed because of you."

Emma gasped.

Grace chuckled. "I am his personal secretary," she said, "privy to all sorts of information."

"But how did you...?"

"After ten years, I know the man pretty well, Emma. Something is going on, and all my instincts say that it's because of you."

Emma wanted to ask a million questions, but only one seemed appropriate. "Why are you telling me this?"

"Because I like him. He's a decent man. Oh, he can be ruthless, but he's fair, too. He doesn't take advantage of anyone's misfortune, even though he'd be deeply upset if he thought anyone knew that. When he takes over a company, he tries really hard to make sure no one gets left out in the cold. He doesn't make arbitrary layoffs. He tries to place people in his other companies, if they don't fit where they are."

"But, what he did to me..." Emma stopped, fearing she'd overstepped her bounds.

"I'm not sure what happened between you two, but I will say one last thing. I've never seen him like this before. Never. And, if I were in your shoes, I'd stick around to see what happens. He's worth it."

Emma felt her face heat. She stared at her cheesecake, her thoughts tumbling around in her head so fast she felt dizzy.

Grace checked her watch, then stood up. "I'm sorry I don't have more time to chat, but I've got to get back to work."

Emma managed a smile. "I'm sorry, too."

"I'd like for us to be friends," the older woman said. "I may not be around for long. But then, who knows? Maybe I will."

"I'd like that," Emma said, meaning it. She had a feeling Grace was a good person to know. Not just because of her relationship to Michael, but because she seemed solid and intuitive, two traits Emma respected very much.

Grace put her hand on Emma's shoulder for a second before she left, and the gesture felt very reassuring. But now that she was alone with her thoughts, Emma didn't feel assured at all. Confusion like this made it impossible to think straight. She wanted to leave, to go someplace quiet and peaceful, away from work and Michael and friends, so she could sort things out.

Did her newfound knowledge make any difference at all? It certainly didn't change the fact that Michael had used her to get the company. Okay, so he hadn't slept with her to get that information, but nonetheless, he'd lied to her, and tricked her and no matter how great Saturday night had been, it didn't excuse the rest.

But it also meant that what he'd said about making love had been true. It had been personal, not business. For the first time since Michael had walked through Phil's door, she was able to think about that night without her humiliation completely overshadowing her logic.

She remembered his face as he'd looked at her. The surprise in his eyes, the passion in the set of his mouth, the need so evident she'd been rocked to her toes. What if none of that had been acting? What if it had been real?

Could that possibly mean that Michael had fallen for her, just as she'd fallen for him?

Emma had never believed in love at first sight. Her practical mind could count off a dozen reasons it couldn't be true. Yet it had happened to her. She'd fallen for him the moment he'd sat down at her table, and the rest of the weekend had just cemented her feelings. It was her misfortune to find love for the first time with a man like Michael, but there wasn't anything she could do about it. Except get over him. If that was possible.

Her biggest allies had been the facts. She'd clung to them every time her emotions got the better of her. Hung on to them for dear life. Now those facts were becoming blurred, and she wasn't happy.

If Michael had fallen for her, wouldn't he have answered her differently when she'd brought up the subject of marriage? Would he have dismissed the idea so vehemently?

How could she know? Every bit of research they'd gathered about him pointed to a man who loved his freedom. He had never had a relationship that lasted longer than six months. Mostly, they were brief affairs, and to her surprise, she'd found many of the women he knew continued to date him periodically, even after not seeing him for months at a time.

As soon as she'd heard that, she'd known she wouldn't be capable of doing that. Michael was an all-or-nothing proposition for her. She'd go insane if she had to wait months, heck even days, for him to call.

But why worry about that? Why couldn't she be as cool and casual on the inside as she looked on the outside? She'd hoped that becoming the new Emma would give her the kind of confidence she saw in other women. Take Grace, for example. There's a woman who'd be steady as a rock no matter what.

Or was that a facade, too? Was anyone what they appeared to be? Was Michael? Was he as confused as she was? As uncertain about what to do?

"Grace said I'd find you here."

Emma heard his voice and looked up sharply. Her question of a second ago was answered. Of course he wasn't uncertain. He looked like nothing could shake his firm hold on what he wanted, and how he wanted it.

Just seeing him in his dark tailored suit, his remarkable jaw set in that determined way of his, she got that tightness in her belly that only he could cause. Before this, she'd had to touch him, or at least have been very, very close to him to have this particular reaction. His danger zone was getting bigger. Pretty soon, she imagined she wouldn't be safe in the same state.

"What can I do for you, Mr. Craig?" she asked, sure he knew exactly what he was doing to her.

"Can you spare a moment? I'd like to talk to you in my office."

She shouldn't go. His office wasn't large enough. She'd be in trouble the moment he closed the door. But she stood, anyway.

"Oh, I interrupted your lunch. This can wait."

She looked down at the table. Even the cheesecake had no appeal. "It's all right." They walked together to the door.

They didn't speak as they went down the hall. Her stomach was busy doing flip-flops while she practiced emergency relaxation techniques. He was too close for even one of them to take effect.

At his reception area, she saw Grace, who smiled kindly. Was that a message? Did Grace know why

Michael had come after her? Was there pity in that smile? Oh, God.

Michael stood by the door so she could enter first. She tried to remember to walk the sexy walk, but with her mind such a jumble, she tripped on the carpet. His hand was there to steady her, and that was that. Any illusion of safety evaporated the moment she felt his touch. She was officially a wreck, incapable of coherent thought or speech.

She looked up at Michael, just in time to see a little look of panic in his eyes. He let her go, coughed, walked quickly over to his desk.

"I, uh, wanted to talk to you," Michael said, walking behind his desk, behind his chair. "I have a proposition for you."

For a wild second, Emma thought he meant to propose. It was the word, of course. She realized that in the next second. But still, her heart kept on hammering. Her thoughts kept tumbling. She made her way to the wing chair, and grabbed on to the top of it, fearing she'd do something ridiculous, like swoon. Did people still swoon?

"I've done some thinking about what you said. About...us."

She couldn't say anything. She just nodded.

"I'm not willing to let this go. Frankly, I'm not sure why. But that's not important. The fact is, I want to be with you, Emma. I don't want you leaving the company. I don't want you leaving me."

"I see," she said, but of course, she didn't. What kind of proposition did he have in mind?

"I think I know what you want. I can't give you that, but I can offer something close."

Her grip tightened on the chair. How could he look so calm? So at ease? Then she glanced down, and saw he had the same death grip on his chair that she had on hers. That made her feel a little better, but not much.

"I want you to be my..." He stopped and frowned. "I'd like to set you up in..." Again, he paused, the troubled look on his face deepening. "The arrangement I had in mind was..."

"Are you asking me to be your mistress, Michael?"

At first, he looked relieved. Then when he saw her face, the worry came back. "Yes," he said. "It's not marriage. But it's the best I can do."

In a startling burst of clarity, Emma understood that he was telling her the absolute truth. It was the best he could do. It was more than she had expected, by far. But could she do it? Could she be satisfied being Michael Craig's mistress? The truth was, she didn't know. Even though her instincts said, no, the part of her that ruled her heart told her to wait, to listen. That it was this, or nothing.

"Emma?"

She opened her mouth to say no. But what came out instead was, "All right."

14

MICHAEL WAS STUNNED. He'd never expected her to say yes. He'd wanted her to, but the odds were so great, he'd resigned himself to a bad ending. Emma had agreed to be his mistress!

"Are you sure?" he said, still unable to believe what he'd heard.

She nodded, but the look on her face was as incredulous as his own had to be. He let go of his grip on the chair and walked over to Emma. She looked so very beautiful in her white suit. The long jacket nearly reached the bottom of her short, snug skirt, and below that, those magic legs went all the way down to her white high heels.

He thought of her as his for a moment. Waiting for him eagerly in the new apartment he'd get for her. How he would like to watch her take off that jacket, that skirt. He wondered if her hose were thigh-high stockings. He hoped so.

His gaze traveled back up to her face. The conflict he saw there made him feel ashamed of his erotic thoughts. This was a major deal for Emma. It wasn't minor for him, either. He'd debated the wisdom of asking her to be his mistress for a long while. Back and forth, yes, no. It was a tiny step from mistress to wife, and he wasn't sure he was willing to get that close. But losing Emma—that wasn't to be contemplated.

"Are you sure?" he asked again, this time taking her lovely face in his hands. He caught her gaze, studied her intently. He could see that although she'd said yes, she'd meant maybe.

"Talk to me," he said, letting his hands drop away. Immediately, he wanted the feel of her again, so he took her hands in his.

"I... You just surprised me," she said, her voice a shy whisper.

"You don't have to make up your mind now. Think about it."

"I want..."

"What, Emma? What do you want?"

She withdrew her hands and took a step back. "I want to think about it."

"Remember," he said, smiling a little, "your first instinct was to say yes. That has to count for something."

She smiled back, although it didn't reach her eyes. "I'll remember."

"Okay. We can talk tomorrow, then?"

She nodded. Then she walked toward the door, and he noticed she didn't have that saucy swing to her derriere, even though she was wearing those heels. He liked this walk, too. It didn't seem to matter what she did, how she acted, what she wore. He was entranced with all the Emmas there were. Now, he had to wait, and hope she would once again say, "All right."

"HE ASKED ME to be his mistress."

"He *what?*" Margaret stood up, jostling a stack of papers on her desk and sending them sliding to the floor. She didn't notice.

"He asked me to be his mistress."

"What did he say when you slapped him?"

Emma looked at her toes. "I said yes."

Margaret sat down again. For a very long time, there was nothing but silence in the room. Then the phone rang, making Emma jump. Margaret didn't answer it. Neither did she.

When it stopped, she dared another look at her friend. She sat staring at her with a very worried expression on her face. Somehow, Emma wasn't surprised.

"Now why did you go and do that?" Margaret said, finally. Her voice was soft, almost kindly. Emma would have preferred it if she'd yelled.

"I'm not sure. Maybe because he didn't expect me to. Or maybe because I didn't expect I would."

"Or maybe because you wanted to?"

Emma went to the couch and sat down, slipping off her high heels and tucking one leg beneath her. "I don't know. Honestly, Margaret, I'm so confused my head is spinning. How did I get into this mess?"

"I don't know, honey. All I can think of is that this

guy must be something awfully special if you're willing to go this far."

"He is special. But that's beside the point. What's really got me worried is that I think, for a few minutes there, I was really contemplating being his mistress. Me. Of all people. He doesn't want to marry me. He just wants me around for...well, you know. That's not right. And it's not what I want."

"So, what are you going to do?"

"That's what I'm asking you!"

Margaret shook her head. "I have a feeling I've meddled too much as it is. From this point on, I'm just an interested friend. A neutral friend. Like Switzerland."

"Oh, no you don't. You can't bail on me now. Not after all I've been through."

"But I haven't helped, have I? You're still in a jam."

"If it hadn't been for you and Christie and Jane, I would have quit days ago. I'd be home crying my eyes out, without an income."

"Is that so much worse than what you're doing now?"

Emma sighed. "At least I have an income."

"Can you explain one thing to me?"

Emma looked up. "I'll try."

"What is it about him?"

"About who?"

Emma turned to the door as Christie and Jane walked in from lunch.

"What's going on?" Jane asked. "Anyone want my brownie? If I keep it, I'll just eat it."

Emma shook her head.

"So?" Christie asked, dumping her purse on her desk and flopping into the big chair. "Why do you look like someone's run over your cat?"

"Michael asked her to be his mistress," Margaret said.

"What?" Christie leaned forward and Jane sat down as they both gave the same startled cry at the same time.

"And she said yes."

"What?" Again, the two spoke in a duet.

"Don't get crazy. I'm not going through with it."

"Why not?" Christie said.

"Of course you're not," Jane said, and then looked daggers at Christie.

"Why not?" Christie said again, this time to Jane. "She's crazy about him, and he's nuts about her. So, she won't have a wedding ring. Big hairy deal."

"The big hairy deal is that we're talking about Emma. She isn't mistress material, for heaven's sake. I don't care if she does look like Kathleen Turner in *Body Heat*, she's still our Emma, and she deserves a wedding ring."

Margaret turned to face her young cohorts. "Are you forgetting what the man did? He slept with her so he could buy this company."

"Actually," Emma said, feeling a little left out, "that's not quite accurate."

All three pairs of eyes turned her way.

"I had lunch with Grace today. His secretary."

"We know who she is," Christie said.

"Right. Well, she told me that Michael made the offer to Phil on Saturday morning."

"So?"

"So that means he could have left then. He had what he wanted. But he didn't. He stayed."

"That doesn't make him Saint Peter," Margaret said. "He still used you."

"I know," Emma said, "but it does make a difference. He was with me Saturday night because he wanted to be. Not because he just wanted information."

"What a bewildering decision for a man to make," Margaret said, her voice dripping with sarcasm. "Here's this beautiful woman who's just supplied him with the keys to buying a new company, who's thrown herself at him. Hm. Go back to Houston and work with the attorneys, or stay another night and try and wake Sleeping Beauty with a kiss. Whatever would he do?"

Emma blushed. "It wasn't like that."

"What was it like?"

She closed her eyes and the images from that night came back in a rush. "It was the best thing that's ever happened to me," she said. "It was magic."

"Which brings me back to my question. What is it about him?"

She looked at Margaret. "He listens to me," she said. "Really listens. He respects what I have to say."

"Go on," Margaret whispered, leaning forward so her elbows rested on her knees.

"He makes me feel beautiful. More than these clothes or this haircut. He makes me feel…"

"Sexy?" Christie offered.

Emma nodded. "But there's more to it than that."

"What?" Jane asked.

Emma looked at her hands. "He makes me whole."

Silence. Then Margaret sniffed. "Then that settles it."

Emma risked a peek. Margaret had leaned back in her chair, and had the damn-the-torpedoes look in her eyes.

"That settles what?"

"You're going to have your Michael Craig. And you're going to have him as your husband."

MICHAEL LOOKED at his watch. Three minutes had passed since the last time he'd looked at his watch. It was almost noon and he hadn't heard from Emma.

He'd left word at her office. At her house. At the front desk. But she hadn't called.

So the answer was no. Okay. He'd figured that she was going to change her mind. Why did he need to hear it? Why couldn't he just chalk it up to a damn shame and move on?

At least he'd gotten some work done. Not a great

deal, but some. He knew he was holding everybody up. Jim Cowling was going to call the men in the white jackets soon if he didn't get on the stick. But he couldn't concentrate. Not with this hanging over his head. At the very least, he needed some closure. Real words from Emma's mouth that he could use to silence the hope.

The hell with waiting. He got up and walked out of his office.

"Mr. Craig."

He stopped at Grace's desk. He saw that she'd finished unpacking, and everything in the outer office looked as neat and professional as he could have hoped for. It occurred to him that it had probably been like this for a while, but that he hadn't noticed. "Everything looks great, Grace."

"Thank you. I don't know if I should be telling you this, but I heard something this morning in the ladies' room."

"Yes?"

"Shell has made an offer to Emma Roberts."

Michael's pulse accelerated. He forced himself not to leap over the desk and take Grace by the shoulders. "Oh?"

"It seems she's accepted."

Michael cursed. By the look on Grace's face, he'd cursed aloud.

"I'm sure she'd be amenable to a counteroffer."

"Yes," he said. "Thank you." He walked away before he made a bigger fool of himself. Straight toward Emma's office. By the time he got there, he'd cooled down a little. Not enough. He wondered where the big-time negotiator, the RB of the briefcase, had gone.

He stepped inside, and saw her. Packing. He coughed, just in case the curses running through his head wanted to come out again.

Four heads turned his way. Margaret hung up the phone. Christie and Jane looked from him to Emma, then back again. Emma herself could barely look at him at all.

"So it's true," he said, surprised to see that Emma was wearing a long, flowing dress instead of one of the tight-fitting suits he'd seen her in all week. She looked like the Emma from New Orleans, and that made everything worse.

"I was going to come see you after I finished here," Emma said.

"I thought I had your word."

"Well, sometimes people don't tell the truth. It happens."

He looked pointedly at Margaret. She was quick on the uptake, and herded her two friends out. All three of them gave Emma reassuring pats or glances, which let him know they were all in favor of her leaving.

Once he and Emma were alone, he closed the door. "I thought we were going to talk."

"We can talk now."

"That's a little like closing the barn door, isn't it?"

She put a picture of her mother and sister into the big cardboard box on her desk. "Yes, I suppose so."

"May I ask why?"

She grew still, then she turned to him. "I'm not a mistress kind of gal, Michael. I think we both know that."

"How do you know? You've never tried."

She shook her head. "It's no good, Michael. It wouldn't work. We wouldn't work."

He moved closer to her. "I don't want you to go."

"I can't stay. It wouldn't be fair."

"You think I couldn't handle it? Seeing you every day? I'd never do anything to compromise you, Emma."

"I wasn't talking about you."

That hadn't occurred to him.

She smiled sadly. "We got caught in a little tornado," she said, her voice so gentle and sweet he nearly moaned from the pain of it. "It tossed us all around, making everything crazy. But it's time to settle down now. To get on with it. I can't do that here."

"Don't leave, Emma. The company needs you." He reached out and touched her cheek with the back of his hand, the feel of her a dangerous thing. "I need you."

"No, you don't. You'll see. Once I'm not around, you'll see."

"Here's an idea," he said, knowing he sounded desperate. "Let's start all over. You take some time off, a week, two weeks. Then when you get back, we can take it slow. Get to know each other all over again. See where it leads us."

"I know where it would lead us. Right here. We want different things from life, Michael. No matter where we start, this is the finish line."

She was right, of course. That didn't make it any easier.

He looked at her for a long time. Studied her face, her eyes. He'd never forget her, even though he'd need to if he was going to survive.

Then she surprised him. She leaned forward and kissed him gently on the mouth. The softness of her lips did make him moan this time, and his arms went around her of their own volition. He held her tight, never intending to let her go. He kissed her with all his regret, all his need. And she kissed him back.

His hands moved over her body—touching her a needful thing—and he felt her hands do the same frenzied dance.

He pulled back, just for a second, just to look at her, but when he saw the trail of tears on her cheeks, he pulled back for keeps.

"I'm sorry," he said.

"Don't be. I'm not going to regret this. I won't. You gave me something magnificent, Michael."

"What?"

Her gaze met his for what he knew was the last time. "Me."

EMMA TRIED very hard to believe. She looked at her friends, Margaret, Christie, Jane and now Grace. Each one of them so hopeful, so certain that everything was going to work out perfectly. She had no such faith.

She remembered how she'd felt in New Orleans, such a short time ago. Like Cinderella. A princess in the making. Sure enough, the prince had come to her door, only the glass slipper hadn't fit. A princess no more, she'd lost her belief in happily every after, despite the best wishes of her fairy godmothers.

"Chin up, Emma. It's going to be fine."

"He's going to find out, Margaret. He's a smart man. He'll check it out."

"No, he won't. Besides, even if he does call Shell, we've got that covered."

"But if he doesn't change his mind, come Monday, I won't have any job."

"Of course you will," Grace said. "Shell really does want you. Although I hope you'll reconsider and stay here."

"If things turn out badly, I won't be able to Grace, but thanks."

Her new cohort smiled. "I know him pretty well, Emma. I don't think you have to worry. The man hasn't done anything but think of you for days. His work is piled sky-high. I tell you, he loves you. It's the only explanation."

"He might love me, but that doesn't mean he wants to marry me."

"You have to remember, he's a guy. Guys are slow on the uptake. He just needs a little push, that's all."

"This is some push."

"Grace is right," Christie said. "Besides, what do you have to lose? You might as well play it out."

"Sure, Em." Jane smiled gamely. "Even I think this is going to turn out right. And you know what a skeptic I am."

"Thank you, guys. Really. I don't know what I would have done without you."

"Go on now, before we all start sniveling," Margaret said, holding out the cardboard box for Emma to take.

She did, grateful for something to do with her arms so she wouldn't be tempted to give them all the big hugs she wanted to. One hug, just one, and she'd fall apart.

Moving quickly, she left the office. The walk to her car was the longest she'd ever taken. She didn't look back. She couldn't. Too much of her heart had been left in that building.

She put the box in the trunk and got behind the wheel. Now what? Home? Her mother would wonder what she was doing there and she'd worry herself sick. She'd want to talk, and Emma wasn't capable of talking right now.

She buckled up, turned the radio on really loud, and headed toward the Cineplex. She was going to lose herself in movies, drown herself in popcorn. Cry herself numb.

MICHAEL GOT THROUGH the entire meeting with Cowling and the department heads. It wasn't easy. Margaret sat on his right, instead of Emma. He kept thinking about the last meeting, when Emma had done that thing with her foot. Despite his best intentions, he found himself growing hard, just remembering.

But he forced his mind—and body—to focus on the meeting, to listen and interact. Margaret kept looking at him strangely, no doubt wondering if he was going to say anything about Emma. He didn't.

When his office was empty once more, he didn't wait, he just dug into his in box, again forcing his concentration to remain steady. Blessedly, three hours passed before Emma came back so strongly he had to put his pen down. At least he wasn't going to lose the company by his inattention. Everything critical had been looked at, if not dealt with.

But now that she was back in his mind, he knew it was useless to go on.

What was he going to do about her? Could he really just let her walk out of his life? Was he prepared to go on as if nothing had happened between them?

The short answer was no. Then what? How could he change the woman's mind? How could he win her back?

He glanced down at his desk, at the prospectus for another company he was in the process of buying.

That's when the idea hit him. Full-blown and tied with a bow.

For the first time in a long while, he smiled. He'd go with his strengths. Use his skills. He'd do what he always did. He'd win.

15

THE LIMO WAS PARKED in front of her house. Of course, she knew it was Michael's. What she didn't know was what she was going to say to him. For a moment, she thought about driving on, finding a motel somewhere and checking in for the night. But that wasn't the plan, was it? Margaret had predicted his arrival, although she'd been wrong on the timeline. He was supposed to show up tomorrow. And she was supposed to have had time to get ready.

It was just after seven, and she'd seen two movies, crying through both of them, even the comedy. She glanced in the rearview mirror, and sighed. She looked as if she'd cried her way through two movies. Puffy, red eyes, blotchy skin, her hair a mess. She'd even managed to spill some soda on her dress. Perfect.

She pressed the button for the automatic garage door and drove in, fervently hoping Michael had waited in the car instead of in the house. Lord knows what her mother and her sister had said to him. Mom had probably dragged out the photo albums. Offered him her terrible coffee. Told him about her arthritis. It was all too dismal to contemplate.

But there was no turning back. She retrieved her purse and stepped out of the car, then went into the house. Her mother was talking in the living room. There was no rest room on her way, so she couldn't stop to repair the damage. Instead, she straightened her back, held her head high, and walked right in.

Only Michael wasn't there. Eddie was.

FOR THE SECOND TIME in a week, she sat in the back seat of Michael's limo, wondering what the night was going to bring. Eddie had opened a bottle of champagne for her, but she didn't pour herself a glass. She wanted to be sober tonight, in control. Not that she wouldn't turn into a quivering wreck the moment she saw Michael, but at least she wouldn't be a drunken wreck.

She looked out the window, not recognizing the street they were on. She supposed Eddie was taking another route to the apartment, but it didn't seem to be a wise choice. They should have arrived about ten minutes ago. Maybe there had been an accident on the freeway, which wasn't at all unusual in Houston.

She shifted on the leather seat, crossing her legs. Once again, she was in the red suit, and she had to pull down the short skirt. There wasn't that same rush of power that she'd gotten when she'd first put on this outfit. If she'd had her druthers, she would have changed into something more comfortable, but she'd decided to stick to the game plan no matter what. That way, when it all fell apart, she wouldn't second-guess herself.

Eddie slowed the limo, and Emma looked outside again. They weren't at Michael's apartment. They'd arrived at a security gate. She tried to find a sign, but Eddie drove on too quickly. Then she got it. It was the planes on the tarmac that gave it away. They were at a small airport.

She leaned forward and tapped on the glass that separated her from Eddie. He pushed the window open. "What can I do for you?"

"Where are we?"

"The Sugar Land Airport."

"Why are we here?"

"So you can have that meeting with Mr. Craig. Like I told you."

"Where is this meeting going to be held?"

"I can't say."

"Can't, or won't?"

"Can't. I just know that I'm supposed to put you on the plane."

"I see. Thank you." She sat back, wondering what she should do. She didn't *have* to get on the plane. She could simply say no. But then what would she have? Unanswered questions, that's what. It didn't matter that she was scared. Hadn't Margaret told her not to let that stop her?

The limo moved up alongside a Learjet, and stopped. A moment later, Eddie opened her door. He held his hand out and she took it, letting him help her. He didn't let go right away, though. "Good luck, Ms. Emma."

"Thank you, Eddie."

He smiled, and walked her to the steps. The closer she got to the door of the jet, the more she felt like Alice about to plunge down the rabbit's hole.

MICHAEL PACED THE FLOOR like a caged tiger. When the hell was she going to get here? It was nearly ten-thirty and if he had to wait much longer, he knew he was going to go crazy.

He'd been calm right up until he'd heard from Eddie that she was on the plane. Since then, he couldn't sit. He couldn't think. All his pep talks about treating this like an unfriendly takeover had flown out the window. Frankly, he was scared to death.

He just knew she wasn't going to change her mind. It didn't matter that they were back in the same suite as the night they'd made love. Or that he'd had the room specially prepared. His speech, which he'd struggled over more than his valedictory address in college, now seemed ludicrous.

Would Emma really care about money? About a fancy apartment? No. She wouldn't. Not Emma. So what was he doing here? It was a mistake. A king-size, gold medal error. She would think he was a fool, or worse.

The thought of losing her all over again chilled him. Dammit, this plan had looked good on paper.

He'd objectively reviewed all the pros and cons, planned for every contingency. Except one. The big one. That Emma wanted it all.

SO SHE WAS GOING BACK to the scene of the crime. New Orleans. She'd finally gotten the information out of the pilot, after she'd reasoned that as soon as she arrived, she'd know where she was. What she hadn't asked was what Michael had been thinking to bring her back there. The pilot wouldn't know. And she wouldn't find out until she was face-to-face with the man in question.

It wasn't fair. But of course, that was the point. Michael knew how she felt about the city. What really bothered her was how those special memories were going to be tarnished. Once tonight had come to its inevitable bad end, she'd have to work hard not to think of New Orleans as the place she'd lost it all.

Didn't he realize she wasn't going to change her mind, no matter the setting? That being his mistress was something she just couldn't live with?

It wasn't as if she hadn't thought it through. My Lord, she'd thought more about this one issue than any other decision she'd ever made. She had pictured herself living in a fabulous apartment, decorated in high deco, of course. She'd seen the gorgeous wardrobe in her closet, imagined her mother and sister taken care of, that burden off her shoulders. Mostly, she imagined Michael coming over. Using his own key. Coming to her bed.

And that's where it got uncomfortable. Where it would always be uncomfortable. She wasn't the kind of woman who could be kept. End of discussion.

"Ms. Roberts, can you please make sure your seat belt is securely fastened? We're starting our descent."

She buckled in tightly. Although the jet was incredibly luxurious, it was small, and that made her nervous. Looking around she realized she hadn't paid enough attention to the jet. She'd been so wrapped up in her own thoughts she hadn't even noticed the outright luxury all around her. The seats alone were noteworthy. Gorgeous tan kid leather, soft and comfortable enough to sleep in, she was forevermore spoiled for coach travel. Everything about the jet was first class. Everything was so very Michael.

Outside, she could see the lights of New Orleans. Her pulse quickened as she tried to spot a landmark. They were still too far away. As they flew lower and lower, she grew more and more certain she wasn't up to this. She would simply tell the pilot to take her back home. That's right. That's exactly what she was going to do.

But she didn't.

When it was time, she got off the plane, just as Michael had known she would.

He surprised her again by not meeting her at the airport. Instead, there was a limousine, navy this time. The driver was a woman. She was young and attractive, and Emma figured she was earning her way through college. Probably doing well, if her service was always this good.

She made sure Emma was comfortable, opened the champagne, poured a glass, turned on the television, adjusted the air-conditioning, then left Emma alone.

It occurred to her that if circumstances were different, she'd have thought of this as a modern-day Cinderella's carriage instead of the car used for funerals.

MICHAEL POURED HIMSELF a glass of champagne, then decided against drinking it. Instead, he called down to room service and ordered up a bottle of Scotch. Why waste time? He'd need to get well and truly drunk tonight, and champagne wouldn't do the trick.

He paced some more, wishing he could take off this damn tuxedo and put on some jeans and a T-shirt. He tugged at the tie, but it didn't loosen. Dammit, he was such a jackass. Maybe he should just get the hell out of here. Leave her a note. Tell her that this was all a gift from him, to say he was sorry. She'd believe that. Why not? He was sorry. Sorry he'd ever dreamed up this wild, stupid scheme.

So what was the alternative? Marry her? Live the rest of his life with Emma by his side? Would that be so terrible?

The short answer was no. It wouldn't be terrible at all. It might even be...

· What was he thinking? Hadn't he sworn that he wouldn't give in? That he'd keep his bachelor status no matter what? Even if it meant he'd be miserable without her?

He laughed aloud. For the first time, he got just how ludicrous he sounded. He sat down hard. Damn, but he needed that Scotch.

EMMA STOOD OUTSIDE the hotel, and looked up. He was waiting, in their suite. It wasn't too late to turn back. She could swing by a bank machine and get enough money to buy a plane ticket home. It was the only sure way. If she went up to the room, there was a fifty-fifty chance she'd change her mind. She knew her limitations, even if her friends didn't.

They'd coached her, of course. Told her to make him suffer. Be tough, sexy, seductive. Make him see what he was giving up.

But all she could think about was her own loss. A life without Michael was a high price to pay for her moral convictions. She laughed aloud. Moral convictions, indeed. It was nothing so noble that kept her from agreeing to Michael's proposition. It was her own desire that motivated her, and she knew it. Halfway would never be enough. Where he was concerned, there was no middle ground. Either she would give herself totally, love him completely, no holds barred, or she wouldn't love him at all.

She turned, ready to hail a taxi. But then she remembered her friends. Margaret, Christie and Jane.

The three Musketeers. They'd been so positive. They'd made her promise. How could she let them down now?

THE KNOCK ON THE DOOR startled him. He dug out his wallet, prepared to give the bellman a hefty tip for bringing him the desperately needed Scotch.

He swung the door open, and stopped in his tracks. It wasn't the bellman. It was Emma.

The moment he saw her, all his doubts evaporated like mist in a breeze. She was the most beautiful thing he'd ever seen. This woman, who had captured his heart when he wasn't looking. He wanted to make her happy. To give her the world on a platter. To wake up with her every day, and go to sleep with her every night.

Emma stared at Michael's face, then at the money he was holding out to her. He looked so surprised, she wondered if he was expecting someone else. "What's that for?" she asked.

His eyebrows came down in confusion, then he followed her gaze to his hand. "I thought you were a bottle of Scotch."

"Ah," she said, not knowing what else to say. When he didn't move, she said, "Would you like me to go get you a bottle?"

His brows were still down, but now his right one arched. "A bottle?"

"Of Scotch?"

He gave a little shake of his head, then stuffed the

bill in his pocket. "No, no. Come on in." He stepped back to let her pass.

When she did, it was her time to do eyebrow tricks. Except she wasn't confused. She was stunned! The whole room was filled with flowers. Vases and vases of roses, lilies, mums, daisies, all colors of the rainbow, all breathtaking. The room itself was infused with their soft aroma. Candles flickered on the table, champagne waited in a crystal ice bucket, soft music played over hidden speakers. It was a fairy-tale room, a suite of unexpected beauty and surprises.

She looked at Michael, and his smile told her she'd responded just as he'd wanted her to. It wasn't hard to remember the last time he'd looked at her like that. It was right here, in this city, in another room full of surprises.

"Grace mentioned you liked flowers."

She laughed. "It's gorgeous, Michael, thank you. But..."

"Don't. Wait. I have something to tell you, but first let me get you some champagne."

She nodded. She was in no particular rush to get to the awful part. Even if it was temporary, she wanted to feel good for a little longer.

He poured two glasses of bubbly, and held hers out. She took it, her fingers grazing his lightly. The spark that had always been between them came back in full force. She was tempted to say it was static electricity, but that would be a lie. It was magic, pure and simple.

He knew it, too. She could tell from how he looked at her, how he shook his head, hardly believing what his eyes had seen, what his body had felt. "How do you do that?" he asked.

"It's not me. It's us."

"Us," he repeated thoughtfully, as if the word had a whole new meaning. Then he touched her flute with his own, the clink audible over the gentle music, and brought the glass to his lips.

She joined him, amazed again at how good the sparkling wine tasted. But that was Michael, wasn't it? Sparing no expense. Bringing her the best.

"You look very beautiful, Emma."

She lowered her lashes. Despite the change, the new look, she still found it hard to accept his compliments. "Thank you." She let her gaze travel up his body, remembering with pleasure the tuxedo and how he'd looked the first time she'd seen him. "So do you."

He smiled. "It's hard not to think about that first night, isn't it?"

She nodded, glad he was sharing the memories with her. "I thought you were a paid escort, remember?"

"Right. And I thought you weren't my type."

"Really? You never told me that."

"I figured out my mistake pretty quickly."

He started to move closer to her, but then he

stopped. He stepped back, purposefully, just far enough away so that they wouldn't touch. When he put his glass on the table, Emma's chest tightened, knowing the brief respite was over. It was time for the final goodbye. Just when she was feeling so happy.

"Emma," he said, "I...we..." He shook his head, and took another step back. "I don't know how you do it, but when I get too close to you, I can't think."

"I know what you mean."

He took a deep breath of air.

Emma couldn't stand it. Her heart was about to burst. "Look, it's no good. All the flowers in the world can't make it good. I can't be your mistress, Michael. I won't."

"I know."

She turned from him, unable to look him in the eyes. "Why did you bring me here, then?" His laughter made her turn to stare at him. "I don't see how you can laugh about it."

He sobered, but not all the way. There was still a glint in his eyes, a small upturn at the corner of his mouth. "I'm sorry. It's just that everything has changed."

Now she was really confused. She stepped closer to him, trying to understand what was going on. "Michael, what are you talking about?"

He took in a big breath of air, and let it out all in a whoosh. "Something...happened."

"What? For God's sake, tell me."

"I brought you here to convince you to change your mind. I had it all worked out. Down to the smallest detail. I even had your apartment picked out. In my building, by the way. One floor down."

"But?"

"But now, I don't want it anymore."

Her heart lurched. This was worse than she'd anticipated. At least his words were worse. She couldn't reconcile his expression, though. He looked so darn happy. How could telling her he didn't want her anymore make him that pleased?

"Don't you want to know why?"

She nodded slowly, not really sure she did.

"Because I love you, and I'd like you to be my wife."

She froze. Every cell in her body stilled, not believing what she'd just heard.

"Did you hear me?"

"I don't think so. You want to run that by me again?"

He took a step closer, but still kept an arm's length away. "I said, I love you. I want to marry you."

She tried to speak. But her throat closed up. All she was able to do was make an odd little squeaking noise.

"Emma? Are you all right?"

She nodded.

"Um, would you like to say something?"

She nodded again, but she still couldn't actually

do it. The only thing she did manage to do was cry. Great big tears cascaded down her cheeks.

He took another tiny step closer. "Are those 'Yes, Michael, I'd love to marry you' tears?"

She nodded, willing herself to move, to talk, to rush into his arms. But she didn't take a step.

"Whew. You had me worried there for a minute."

She smiled. Swallowed. "Can I ask you something?" she said, grateful to have her vocal cords back.

"Uh-huh."

"What happened?"

"I woke up. I don't know any other way to explain it. I just knew that letting you go would be the stupidest thing I could ever do. But it was more than that. I don't want you just to stay around. I want you mine. I want to grow old with you. I want us to have kids. Share the bathroom. Go on crummy vacations."

"Are you sure? I don't want you to wake up tomorrow and regret anything."

"Emma, you make me... Damn, it's hard to find the words."

"I make you what, Michael?" she whispered, barely daring to breathe.

He took one more step toward her. "You make me whole."

She closed her eyes, and let the feeling of pure bliss wash over her. He did love her, just as she loved him. When she opened her eyes, she shook her head. "One last question?"

He smiled.

"Why are you all the way over there?"

"I didn't want you to think I was just trying to get you into bed."

She laughed as she swiped the tears from her cheeks. "I believe you."

Then he was there, and she was in his arms. "You've changed everything, you know," he said. "I'm going to have to get a new briefcase."

"What?" She looked up into his beautiful eyes.

"You've turned a perfectly respectable ruthless bastard into a pussycat."

"I wouldn't go that far."

His smile faded, only to be replaced by a look that told her everything. His love for her, his desire, his certainty. "How far would you go?"

"To the ends of the earth," she said.

Then he kissed her.

And she *was* Cinderella.

* * *

Jo Leigh's next Temptation® Single Sheriff Seeks...
will be available in the summer 1999.

JORDAN! DARCY! MORTIMER! GAGE!

Four best-selling authors brought together for your reading pleasure in the 1998 Stars of Romance Collection!

Penny Jordan's latest blockbuster, *To Love, Honour & Betray* plus nine best loved full-length stories from three world-class authors—**Emma Darcy, Carole Mortimer** & **Elizabeth Gage.**

HUGE SAVINGS! FREE MYSTERY GIFT!

Take advantage of this exclusive offer from the Reader Service™ and **SAVE 25%** off the combined cover prices. Plus, you will also receive a Mystery Gift **absolutely FREE.** Simply complete your details below, including your current club/subscription number and return the entire page to the address below. *You don't even need a stamp!*

✂ YES! Please send me the **1998 Stars of Romance Collection** and my FREE GIFT! I understand that I will receive these books on 14 days no obligation home approval and if I decide to keep them, I will pay just £15.59 saving me over £5.00 off the combined cover prices. Postage and packing is free! The FREE GIFT is mine to keep whatever I decide about the books.

18IESR

Ms/Mrs/Miss/Mr ....Initials ....
BLOCK CAPITALS PLEASE

Surname ....

Address ....

....

....Postcode.............................

Club/
Subscription No. [ ][ ][ ][ ] / [ ][ ][ ][ ][ ][ ][ ]

Send this whole page to:
THE READER SERVICE, FREEPOST CN81, CROYDON, CR9 3WZ

Non Reader Service subscribers please send an SAE for details quoting ref: SR998

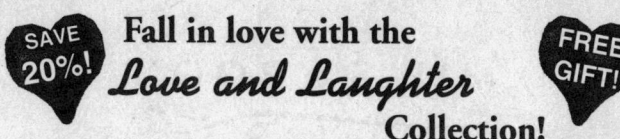

SAVE 20%!

FREE GIFT!

Fall in love with the
Love and Laughter
Collection!

Celebrate with 9 stories that will capture your heart!

***Love and Laughter*—Elise Title, Barbara Bretton & Lass Small.**
Three new titles combine hilarious humour with touching romance!

***A Funny Thing Happened on the way to the Delivery Room*—
Kasey Michaels, Kathleen Eagle & Emilie Richards.**
When three couples go to the delivery room they get a bit more than
their own little bundles of joy—they find the promise of love!

***Fortune Cookie*—Janice Kaiser, M.J. Rodgers & Margaret St. George.**
When it comes to predicting their romantic future, our heroines all
come to learn one thing—always expect the unexpected!

HUGE SAVINGS! FREE MYSTERY GIFT!

Take advantage of this exclusive offer from the Reader Service™ and
SAVE 20% off the combined cover prices. Plus, you will also receive a
Mystery Gift **absolutely FREE**. Simply complete your details below,
including your current Club/Subscription Number and return the entire
page to the address below. *You don't even need a stamp!*

YES! Please send me the Love and Laughter Collection and my FREE
GIFT! I understand that I will receive these books on 14 days no
obligation home approval and if I decide to keep them, I will pay just £12.59
saving me £3.00 off the combined cover prices. Postage and packing is free!
The FREE GIFT is mine to keep whatever I decide about the books.

18IELL

Ms/Mrs/Miss/Mr...................................Initials ....
BLOCK CAPITALS PLEASE

Surname ....

Address ....

....

....Postcode.............................

Club/
Subscription No. ⬚⬚⬚⬚ / ⬚⬚⬚⬚⬚⬚⬚⬚

Send this whole page to:
THE READER SERVICE, FREEPOST CN81, CROYDON, CR9 3WZ

Non Reader Service subscribers please send an SAE for details quoting ref: LL998

mps
MAILING PREFERENCE SERVICE

We reserve the right to refuse an application and applicants must be aged 18 years or over. Only one application per
household. Offer open while stocks last. As a result of this application, you may receive further offers
from Harlequin Mills & Boon and other carefully selected companies. If you would prefer not
to share in this opportunity please write to The Data Manager at the above address.

MILLS & BOON®

Reader Service™

The best romantic fiction direct to your door

Our guarantee to you...

The Reader Service involves you in no obligation to purchase, and is truly a service to you!

Your books are delivered hot off the press, at least one month before they are available in the shops.

Your books are sent on 14 days no obligation home approval.

We offer free postage and packing for subscribers in the UK—we guarantee you won't find any hidden extras.

Plus, we have a dedicated Customer Care team on hand to answer all your queries on
(UK) 0181 288 2888
(Ireland) 01 278 2062.

There is also a 24 hour message facility on this number.